After mass crime

A Project of the Center for International Studies and Research (CERI – Sciences Po/CNRS), the International Peace Academy, swisspeace and the United Nations University

After mass crime: Rebuilding states and communities

Edited by Béatrice Pouligny, Simon Chesterman and Albrecht Schnabel

United Nations University Press

TOKYO · NEW YORK · PARIS

United Nations University Press
United Nations University, 53-70, Jingumae 5-chome,
Shibuya-ku, Tokyo 150-8925, Japan
Tel: +81-3-3499-2811   Fax: +81-3-3406-7345
E-mail: sales@hq.unu.edu
General enquiries: press@hq.unu.edu
http://www.unu.edu

United Nations University Office at the United Nations, New York
2 United Nations Plaza, Room DC2-2062, New York, NY 10017, USA
Tel: +1-212-963-6387   Fax: +1-212-371-9454
E-mail: unuona@ony.unu.edu

United Nations University Press is the publishing division of the United Nations University.

Cover design by Sese-Paul Design

Cover photograph of Gihembe Refugee Camp, Rwanda reproduced by kind permission of Kresta King Cutcher (Copyright 2006)

Printed in the United States of America

ISBN 978-92-808-1138-4

Library of Congress Cataloging-in-Publication Data

After mass crime : rebuilding states and communities / edited by
Béatrice Pouligny, Simon Chesterman and Albrecht Schnabel.
    p.   cm.
  Includes bibliographical references and index.
  ISBN 978-9280811384 (pbk.)
  1. Nation-building. 2. Peace-building. 3. Political atrocities.
4. Postwar reconstruction. I. Pouligny, Béatrice. II. Chesterman, Simon.
III. Schnabel, Albrecht.
JZ6300.A48   2007
341.5′84—dc22   2006039809

Contents

List of tables

List of contributors

Dr Natalija BAŠIĆ has been a research fellow at the Institute for East European Studies at the Free University of Berlin since 2002, and is Research Director South Eastern Europe (Serbia/Croatia) for the research group "Traditions of Historical Consciousness", funded by the Volkswagen Foundation. Her main interests include historical consciousness, identity processes and cultures of violence as well as several specific aspects of Yugoslav and post-socialistic historical, political and military problems.

Dr Roberto BENEDUCE, an ethnopsychiatrist, is Associate Professor of Cultural Anthropology on the Faculty of Psychology and Associate Professor of Psychological Anthropology on the Faculty of Letters, University of Turin. Between 1988 and 1993 he conducted research on Dogon systems for the healing of mental disorders in Mali. In Albania (1999),

Eritrea (1994–1997), Ethiopia (1997), and Mozambique (2000–2001) he has worked as a consultant for UN Agencies (UNICEF, UNOPS) and the World Health Organization, analysing social and psychological consequences of war, atrocities and violence. More recently he conducted research in South Cameroon (among the Bulu, 2001–2003) on symbolic structure and changes in so-called "traditional medicine", as well as on the impact of HIV/AIDS and the role of independent African churches on healing behaviours. In 1996 he founded the Frantz Fanon Centre (Centre of Psychotherapy for Migrants, Refugees, and Victims of Torture) at Turin, and is coordinator of training activities in the EU Project on Rehabilitation of Victims of Torture in Italy.

Dr Simon CHESTERMAN is Global Professor and Director of the New York University School of Law

Singapore Program. Educated in Melbourne, Beijing, Amsterdam and Oxford, he has written widely on international institutions, international criminal law, human rights and the use of force and post-conflict reconstruction. Dr Chesterman is the author of *You, the People: The United Nations, Transitional Administration, and State-Building* and *Just War or Just Peace? Humanitarian Intervention and International Law*. He is the editor of *Civilians in War*.

Dr Roberta Anne CULBERTSON is Director of Research and Education at the Virginia Foundation for the Humanities. She earned her PhD in Anthropology from the University of Virginia and her BA from Sweet Briar College. She worked in public service on refugee mental health, mental health and health promotion, and criminal justice for twelve years before joining the VFH in 1989. As Director of Research and Education, Dr Culbertson conceived and created the Institute on Violence and Survival and raised the funds for its development. She has received grants from the National Endowment for the Humanities, the Rockefeller Foundation, the Dart Foundation, and the Wardlaw Foundation for her work on violence.

Dr Bernard DORAY, a psychiatrist, works as a therapist and researcher at the Centre de recherches et d'actions sur les traumatismes et l'exclusion (CEDRATE) at the Maison des Sciences de l'Homme (Paris).

Dr Leslie DWYER is Visiting Assistant Professor of Anthropology and Coordinator of the Peace and Conflict Studies program at Haverford College in Pennsylvania. After receiving her PhD from Princeton University in 2001, she was awarded postdoctoral fellowships from the MacArthur Foundation and the H. F. Guggenheim Foundation and UCLA's Center for Southeast Asian Studies before joining Haverford. She has conducted research in Indonesia since 1993, most recently on the cultural and political implications of the violence of 1965/66. She is currently completing a book, *"When the World Turned to Chaos": Violence and Its Aftermath in Bali*, in collaboration with Degung Santikarma. Her next project is an ethnography of the social and political life of discourses of "trauma" and PTSD in Indonesia, and their emergence within contexts of clinical practice, humanitarian intervention, democratization and the "war on terror".

Dr Maurice EISENBRUCH is Vice-Chancellor's Advisor on Diversity; foundation Director, Institute for Health and Diversity; and Professor of Culture and Health at Victoria University (Melbourne, Australia). He is also Professor of Multicultural Health and Director of the Centre for Culture and Health at the University of New South Wales. He graduated in Medicine from the University of Melbourne and has postgraduate qualifications in child psychiatry, medical anthropology, psychology and education. During the 1980s, Dr Eisenbruch worked with Southeast Asian refugees while based at the Department of Social

Anthropology at the University of Cambridge and at the Department of Social Medicine and Health Policy at Harvard Medical School. He developed the concept of "cultural bereavement". During the 1990s, Eisenbruch taught at the University of Paris and was Director of Studies (Associé) at the School of Advanced Studies in Social Sciences in Paris. He was Head of a research operation at CNRS (National Centre for Scientific Research), examining the power of healing, and he led various projects in medical anthropology concerning mental health, maternal and child health and HIV/AIDS in Cambodia. He serves on the WHO-EU Task Force on Migrant-Friendly Hospitals and Cultural Competence. He was UNESCO consultant on Cultural Mapping and Cultural Diversity Programming Lens to Safeguard Tangible and Intangible Cultural Expressions and Protect Cultural Diversity. He contributed to the UNESCO Expert Consultation "Promoting Standards for Socio-Cultural Research on the Issues of HIV/AIDS and Trafficking". He was UNESCO/UNFPA consultant on cultural issues in HIV/AIDS and WHO/EU consultant on cultural issues in malaria. He is chief investigator with the Buddhist Institute in an ARC-funded project on post-conflict healing. He was Professor of Clinical Psychology and Anthropology at Royal Phnom Penh University.

Dr Louis KRIESBERG is Maxwell Professor Emeritus of Social Conflict Studies, Professor Emeritus of Sociology and founding director of the Program on the Analysis and Resolution of Conflicts at Syracuse University. His most recent writings include the second edition of *Constructive Conflicts: From Escalation to Resolution* and *International Conflict Resolution: The U.S.–USSR and Middle East Cases.* He has authored more than 100 articles and book chapters related to conflict resolution and peace studies and co-edited *Intractable Conflicts and Their Transformation* and *Timing the De-Escalation of International Conflicts.* He also lectures and consults about matters relating to coexistence, constructive conflict resolution, reconciliation and peacemaking in the Middle East and other regions. He is currently doing comparative research on reconciliation and changing accommodations between ethnic, religious and other communal groups.

Dr René LEMARCHAND is professor emeritus of Political Science at the University of Florida, Gainesville. Shortly after receiving his PhD from UCLA, Dr Lemarchand came to Gainesville in 1962, where he became one of the founding members and an early director of the University of Florida's Center for African Studies. While he has broad interests in African politics, Dr Lemarchand has earned a reputation as one of the world's leading experts on the politics of Rwanda and Burundi. In the course of his career, he has published more than ten books on African politics, including his Herskovits award-winning *Rwanda and Burundi, Political Awakening in the Belgian Congo, Green and the Black: Qadhifi's Policies in Africa,*

LIST OF CONTRIBUTORS xi

Selective Genocide in Burundi, American Policy in Southern Africa, Political Clientelism in Patronage and Development, Burundi: Ethnocide as Discourse and Practice, and *Burundi: Ethnic Conflict and Genocide.* He has worked as a consultant for the United Nations, the World Bank, USAID and others.

Dr Jean-Clément MARTIN is a historian, professor at the Université Paris I and the Director of the Institut d'Histoire de la Révolution Française. He is a specialist on the history of the French Revolution. He has studied the war of Vendee in relation to the French revolution, and published *La Vendée et la France* and *La Vendée de la Mémoire, 1800–1980.* In this context he has also worked on war massacres and the analysis of the history of massacres.

Maurice NIWESE is a PhD candidate at the University of Louvain, Belgium. He is the author of *Le peuple rwandais un pied dans la tombe* and *Celui qui sut vaincre.*

Dr Béatrice POULIGNY is a political scientist and a senior researcher at the Centre for International Studies and Research (CERI – Sciences Po), Paris. She has field experience as a practitioner with the UN as well as with local and international NGOs in different parts of the world. In 2002/03, she was a Fulbright New Century Scholar. She is the author of *Ils nous avaient promis la paix: Opérations de paix de l'ONU et populations locales/Peace Operations Seen from Below: UN Missions and Local People.* She developed and coordinated the research-action

project: "Re-Imagining Peace After Massacres: A Trans-Disciplinary and Comparative Effort Towards the Prevention of Failed States and the Rebuilding of Functioning Societies" with Guatemala, Kivus/Ituri (East Congo), Bosnia-Herzegovina and Cambodia as pilot countries. Several contributors to this volume actively participate in that project's field research.

Degung SANTIKARMA is an anthropologist, journalist and human rights activist. He has been the recipient of grants from the John D. and Catherine T. MacArthur Foundation and the H. F. Guggenheim Foundation for research on the massacres of 1965/66. In 2001, he founded *Latitudes,* a monthly magazine on Indonesian culture and politics. He has published widely on issues of violence, identity politics and reconciliation in Indonesia, and is currently completing a book, *"When the World Turned to Chaos": Violence and Its Aftermath in Bali,* in collaboration with Leslie Dwyer.

Dr Albrecht SCHNABEL is a Senior Research Fellow at swisspeace – Swiss Peace Foundation, Bern, Switzerland. He works in the early warning programme FAST International and directs the research programme on human security (HUSEC). He is also a Lecturer in International Organizations and Conflict Management at the Institute of Political Science, University of Bern. He received his PhD in 1995 from Queen's University, Canada. Most recently, he served in the Peace and

Governance Programme of the United Nations University, Tokyo, Japan (1998–2003). He has taught at Queen's University (1994), the American University in Bulgaria (1995/96), the Central European University (1996–1998), and Aoyama Gakuin University (2002/03). He has published widely on ethnic conflict, conflict prevention and management, peacekeeping, peace-building and humanitarian intervention, and is currently leading an international four-year project on "Operationalizing Human Security" within the Swiss National Centre of Competence in Research (NCCR) North–South. His most recent publications include the following co-edited books: *Human Rights and Societies in Transition* (with Shale Horowitz), two volumes on *Conflict Prevention: From Rhetoric to Reality* (with David Carment), and *Security Sector Reform and Post-Conflict Peacebuilding* (with Hans-Georg Ehrhart).

Dr Thomas SHERLOCK is an Associate Professor of Political Science at the United States Military Academy, West Point. He received his PhD in Political Science from Columbia University in 1993. He has previously worked as an Instructor at Columbia University (1989), as a research analyst at Radio Liberty in Munich (1989), as a research fellow at the Kennan Institute for Advanced Russian Studies in Washington D.C. (1990) and as an adjunct lecturer at Hunter College (1993). His research and publications focus on history, politics, myth and memory in the Soviet and post-Soviet space.

Dr Scott STRAUS is an Assistant Professor in the Department of Political Science at the University of Wisconsin–Madison. He received his PhD in 2004 from the University of California–Berkeley. Straus works on violence, human rights and African politics. His book on the Rwandan genocide, *The Order of Genocide: Race, Power, and War in Rwanda*, is under contract with Cornell University Press. Straus also co-authored, with David Leonard, *Africa's Stalled Development: International Causes and Cures* and, with Robert Lyons, *Intimate Enemy: Images and Voices of the Rwandan Genocide*. Straus has published articles in *Foreign Affairs*, the *Journal of Genocide Research* and *Patterns of Prejudice*; he translated *The Great Lakes of Africa: Two Thousand Years of History*; and he has received fellowships from the National Science Foundation, the Social Science Research Council and the United States Institute of Peace. Prior to his academic career, Straus was a freelance journalist in Africa.

Dr Kimberly THEIDON is an Assistant Professor in the Department of Anthropology at Harvard University. She received her PhD in Medical Anthropology in 2002 from the University of California at Berkeley. Her research focuses on psychosocial trauma, transitional justice and the politics of reparations, with a regional specialization on Latin America. Most recently she directed a research project on community mental health, reparations and the micropolitics of reconciliation with the Ayacuchan office of the Peruvian Truth and Reconciliation

Commission. A book-length manuscript based upon this research, *Entre Prójimos: La política de la reconciliación en el Perú*, was published in 2004 by the Instituto de Estudios Peruanos. Dr Theidon is currently conducting research in Colombia and Ecuador on two interrelated themes. The first focuses on the causes and consequences of populations in displacement, refuge and return, with a particular interest in the role of humanitarian organizations in zones of armed conflict. The second topic is local-level peace initiatives in Colombia. She is the director of Praxis – An Institute for Social Justice.

Acknowledgements

The research presented in this volume builds on the work undertaken by a trans-disciplinary research group created at the Center for International Studies and Research (CERI – Sciences Po/CNRS) in Paris, in February 2001, by Béatrice Pouligny and Jacques Sémelin. During the initial brainstorming phase (2001/02), the group offered a space in which political scientists, sociologists, historians, anthropologists, lawyers and psychiatrists reflected together upon the issues faced in such situations in different countries on the basis of concrete experiences. Furthermore, the group's sessions were open to practitioners and actors on the ground, from particular humanitarian associations or those involved in post-conflict reconstruction. Twenty-three papers were presented and discussed during eight sessions.

On the basis of these first findings, the International Peace Academy (New York) and the United Nations University (Tokyo) joined CERI to launch an international call for contributions in order to enlarge the exchanges. After a selective process, a meeting was organized in New York in June 2003, dealing with different aspects of how best to approach rehabilitation of post-mass-crime societies. The meeting examined the impact on individuals, society at large and the organizations involved in providing assistance in the post-conflict phase. The intention was to bring together political scientists, sociologists, historians, anthropologists, lawyers and psychiatrists in an effort to offer a trans-disciplinary examination of how mass crime is, and should be, addressed in post conflict peace- and society-building. Since 2003 swisspeace (Bern) has joined the effort, and the project team has further discussed, commented, improved and completed their respective contributions to the present book. Most of the contributors are experienced scholars as well as practitioners. The aim is to bring together the various disciplines that address mass crime in a manner that mirrors the multifaceted experiences of those affected by mass crimes.

A key question for the project is how to identify and build on capacities for peace that exist within a post-conflict society. This depends on an understanding of the rules of social and political life in a given society and how disparate actors may be encouraged to participate without recourse to violent confrontation. This volume reflects the current state of our collective reflection, with a combination of case studies and transversal reflections based on different field experiences. It also provides the basis for moving to the fieldwork-based phase of the project, which aims to understand the multiple ways collective frames of reference (shaped by perceptions as well as institutional and social processes, at both local and international levels, at the crossroads of individual and collective histories) have been transformed by mass violence, and to develop tools in order to help identify and support local resources to build peace and prevent the re-emergence of conflict. International as well as local interdisciplinary teams in Guatemala, the Kivus/Ituri (East Congo), Bosnia-Herzegovina and Cambodia engaged in a multi-year project called Re-Imagining Peace, for which CERI was joined by the Virginia Foundation for the Humanities, whose Director of Research and Education, Dr Roberta Culbertson, has been very inspiring for the entire project and deserves specific thanks. We also thank Sebastian von Einsiedel for his invaluable assistance in organizing the June 2003 authors meeting at the International Peace Academy, and Yoshie Sawada of UNU's Peace and Governance Programme for taking excellent care of the administrative aspects of this book project.

The editors gratefully acknowledge the financial support of the Centre for International Studies and Research/Fondation Nationale des Sciences Politiques (France), the Fondation Charles Léopold Mayer pour le Progrès de l'Homme (FPH), the United Kingdom Department for International Development, the United States Institute of Peace (USIP), IPA's Conflict Prevention Program, the Government of Japan and the United Nations University, without which this project would not have been possible.

Paris, New York, Bern
September 2006

Introduction: Picking up the pieces

Béatrice Pouligny, Simon Chesterman and Albrecht Schnabel

Interventions in the aftermath of mass violence tend to focus on war-crimes trials today, elections and institution building tomorrow. The frame of reference is macro, at the level of the state, although the experience of mass crime by a population is also micro, at the level of the community. When selective interventions take place at this level, they are generally premised on Western health models, infrastructures and institutions. In application, these programs have ranged too often from the ineffective to the actively unhelpful. A key reason for this is that insufficient attention has been paid to the radical transformations in belief systems and codes of conduct of the individuals and communities who experience mass crime. Such transformations define a host of reconstruction issues: questions of communal and national identity; justice and reconciliation; the redistribution of property, land and wealth; the writing of history; the rebuilding of trust; and the capacity to build a new political system.

This volume aims to fill this gap in the literature by offering a transdisciplinary analysis of the impact of mass crime on the project of rebuilding of social and political relations. This conceptual foundation is then used to formulate recommendations on the most appropriate practical interventions that can help re-establish functioning societies in such circumstances.

"Mass crime" is a term intended to embrace widespread killings and related atrocities such as mutilation, rapes, destruction of villages and deportations – frequently, but not always, perpetrated by a state actor.

After mass crime: Rebuilding states and communities, Pouligny, Chesterman and Schnabel (eds), United Nations University Press, 2007, ISBN 978-92-808-1138-4

As a concept, it is intended to emphasize that analysis and intervention in these contexts must take into account the totality of such acts and their consequences, beyond the actual massacres. If one wishes to help "build peace" following acts that call into question the very existence of a society, it is first necessary to understand how a population allows – or actively encourages – such acts to take place. This approach rejects the notion of simplistic explanations, be they ideological or cultural, such as seeing a given population as inherently belligerent or violent. Mass crime points instead to a profound crisis of the various institutions that regulate social and political interaction. In addition to perceptions, it is these institutions – understood in their anthropological sense[1] – that hold the key to understanding why a society has turned on itself, and what might be done from within and without to save it.

Re-reading mass crime

In addition to an expanding literature on transitional justice and post-conflict reconstruction, there is already a significant literature on selected historical cases of mass crime as such, notably the Holocaust and, to a lesser extent, the Armenian genocide. The studies presented here draw on more recent cases, including Peru, Rwanda, Burundi, Bosnia-Herzegovina, Croatia, Kosovo, Russia and the former Soviet Union, the Baltic Republics, Ukraine, Chechnya, Indonesia and Cambodia. The practice of massacre throughout the twentieth century has characterized the strategies of a number of actors, particularly in the context of war. Indeed, the annihilation of civilian populations may in fact be central to their logic of action and have an important impact on post-war situations. Yet the specific challenges posed by these situations have been largely neglected in peace studies. The usual disconnection between fields of expertise partly explains this reality: Whereas everybody understands why mass crime is traumatic to the individuals involved, the collective consequences of such trauma remain largely unexamined. In addition, empirical and micro-level analyses have been missing, explaining why most discussions on mass-crime situations are general and speculative. The presentation here of the results of empirical research undertaken in very different contexts aims to remedy this and suggest a more rigorous methodology for future research.

Methodology and ethics

It is not possible to respond to the different needs of the victims and survivors of mass crime if one does not understand the local forms and logic of social ties, their transformations and the manner in which local actors have tried to survive and understand mass violence: their cultural strategies of dealing with death, mourning and suffering. In other words, we need to understand "how people make and unmake lethal violence", as one of the authors puts it.[2] The individuals who endure mass crime are often those who are the most invisible. This is not to suggest that such people are not seen; rather it is that they are seen first and foremost as passive victims. It is necessary, therefore, to find ways to recognize their transformation into survivors and begin, once again, to see them as *actors*. More than an abstract concern, this way of seeing is directly linked to the identification and utilization of local resources. An example is the success of certain traditional healers dealing with children traumatized by war and with those children who fought as soldiers.

Two methodological consequences derive from this. First, ethnographic micro-level research is necessary to help understand the capacity of victims and perpetrators to reconstruct new forms of social ties. The research presented in this volume illustrates the importance of this emphasis on the local both for the understanding of why and how mass crime occurs, as well as the identification and assessment of the capacity to build peace. Atrocities and violence characterizing recent conflicts and wars reveal an internal logic, a specific kind of "rationality", as well as "techniques" that ask for specific investigation. However, only a proper analysis of contexts, actors and historical frameworks helps to avoid the risk of essentializing universal, hidden structures that could underlie all events and that fall under the labels of "atrocity", "mass crime", "mass violence", "genocide" or "dirty war". It is necessary to consider the variety of experiences, histories and dynamics of massacres and disaggregate global categories generally used to refer to such events.

The second methodological implication is that, in addition to standard medical and psychological variables, work in post-mass-crime settings requires an examination of the meaning and significance that individuals and groups assign to these events. These cultural factors require attention to the symbolic and social worlds within which people in post-mass-crime settings operate. It is commonplace to hear that culture and context "matter", and that any intervention – peace-building or otherwise – must be "culturally sensitive". This has been truer of rhetoric than reality. The chapters by Roberto Beneduce, Maurice Eisenbruch, Kimberly Theidon and Scott Straus in particular show the importance of context, as well as of avoiding essentializing or romanticizing culture. As a "system of meanings commonly shared by the individual members of a single collectivity" – to follow Clifford Geertz[3] – culture is characterized by a high level of heterogeneity. It consists of ensembles that, although allowing actors to conceive of themselves and of their actions, are not necessarily entirely coherent. Moreover, in times of war, this system of meaning may undergo profound changes. That means that a caveat must be lodged against idealizing a more peaceful "traditional" past; or traditions that no longer exist or have been used, misused and transformed by entrepreneurs of violence. In other words, we must avoid both naive and normative approaches to such matters, as well as a tendency to see post-conflict societies as passive environments or as political and social vacuums. This is not only mistaken – war is transformative, as well as destructive – but it also ignores the very foundation of any lasting post-conflict solution. Identifying the norms and values but also the individuals who, within a social group, may play a critical role as intermediaries is to locate that which changes and continuously reinvents itself within a three-fold dialectic: the insider–outsider dialectic, that of emotion and rationality, and the dialectic of tradition and innovation. In other words, one must attempt to understand that which takes place within the group itself and in its exchange with outsiders, the emotional, the spiritual and the apparently rational, and that which relates to the past or looks to the future.

This requires a trans-disciplinary and holistic approach. Each perspective, on its own, is insufficient for capturing these multiple links, while, from the point of view of the trauma, the links between the fields of psychiatry, politics, sociology, anthropology and law (from a historical perspective) are made naturally. One of the main innovative aspects of this project is the effort to re-articulate the relationship between what happens at the level of individuals and communities, and what happens at the level of social and political processes (both at national and international levels). Most research focuses on one perspective or the other, in part because they are studied by different disciplines that do not conceptualize and focus their investigations in the same way. For example, neither genocide studies nor anthropology have developed significant ties with the emerging fields of peace-building and state-building. In the latter fields, the impact of mass crime in post-war situations has been considered primarily as questions of justice and "reconciliation". But very little has been documented as to the relation between legal or paralegal processes (e.g., international tribunals, truth and reconciliation commissions) and social or psychological processes.[4] Indeed, peace studies is itself almost completely disconnected from mental health studies, which in turn bifurcates along individual and collective perspectives, as well as between the camps that endorse and reject post-traumatic stress disorder (PTSD) approaches.

The contributions presented in this volume offer concrete examples of re-establishing these different connections in our understanding of post-mass-crime situations. The authors sometimes use different methodologies; some are more empirical than others, some more interdisciplinary in their own right. As such this diversity reflects the importance of this conversation between different disciplines and approaches.

The volume is organized in four parts. Part 1 (which comprises two chapters) examines the main ethical and methodological issues that both academics and practitioners face when dealing with mass crime and post-mass-crime situations. The first chapter is written by a political scientist (Béatrice Pouligny), a psychiatrist (Bernard Doray) and a historian (Jean-Clément Martin). The authors analyse the main difficulties they face in their respective disciplines, continually traversing the boundaries between them and interweaving their perspectives, underlining the interconnectedness of methodological and ethical issues. This dynamic is explored first in relation to how the commentator situates him- or herself in relation to "evil" (mass crime). The second section explains the method used by the authors to develop a comprehensive approach to violent situations. The third and final section of the chapter explores the responsibility of any outsider (particularly a researcher) in the process of writing history and constructing a narrative of massacres. This offers a first exploration of the interrelations between different memories of massacres, a topic also analysed in some case studies in the third part of the volume.

Chapter 2 follows this line by offering a medico-anthropological approach of post-mass-crime situations. Roberto Beneduce, both an academic and a practitioner, has a dual background as psychiatrist and anthropologist. The basis for effective analysis or action lies in the ability to rethink concepts otherwise taken for granted. To avoid engaging with an idealized Western vision of mass crime, it is necessary to stress the continuum of local/social dynamics and global/economic dynamics in the processes of mass crime; at the same time it is necessary to recognize the interaction between individual and collective rehabilitation, and therefore the limits of psychiatric methods alone. On the first aspect, Beneduce questions the historiography of mass crime. He emphasizes the need for an accurate analysis of local forms of violence and its reproduction, of its historical roots, as well as of the ways in which it has been embodied in ritual strategies and the social imaginary. In these cases, violence can become an everyday way of life, without any "uncanny" or "extraordinary" character. In some African countries, mass crime is not an exception, an anomaly in the course of history. On the contrary, structural violence is inscribed in continuity with the colonial state. Other chapters in this volume, dealing with Peru and Rwanda in particular, refer to the way that a "state of war" may shape identities and contribute to the "militarization" of the mind. Beneduce argues, among other things, that humanitarian strategies may prove useless if deep roots of violence are ignored or underestimated. Specific examples demonstrate the relevance of this issue within peace-building intervention and, more generally, in social and community rehabilitation in times of war and post-war.

Another aspect that receives specific attention is the degree of adequacy of Western psychiatric categories such as "trauma" or PTSD in non-Western countries. Although taken for granted in many peace-building operations, these terms are contested even within the Western canon. Research carried out by the author, as well as reflected by a vast medico-anthropological literature, suggests that these categories are unable to encompass all the cultural and psychological meanings of trauma-related experiences in such environments; in particular they may omit the moral dimensions of suffering. Beneduce defines "the question of memory and trauma" as a "moral rather than medical or psychiatric issue". His research also indicates that local healing strategies and cultural conceptions of death or mourning represent both a useful ("therapeutic") tool for individuals or communities affected by traumatic experiences, as well as a potential resource to mimic when dealing with fear, uncertainty and concerns about "pollution", which characterize both war and post-war time in many non-Western countries. This reality is confirmed by later chapters discussing Cambodia, Peru and Rwanda. Unfortunately, international teams of experts have sometimes ignored or underestimated these kinds of local resources. They are usually put under the disputable label of "harmful traditional practices": in this way they reproduce the dominance of Western psychiatry both as an academic discipline and a medical practice, but confront great difficulty in matching individual grieving/healing to social grieving/healing. Community-based rehabilitation should take into consideration these resources for the additional reason that the language and the ideology of local healers or other social actors, apart from controversial uses sometimes described in the literature, are largely shared by the population and therefore can participate to reconstitute a common perspective in post-war contexts. Indeed, in post-mass-crime situations, the community needs to be re-invented as well as rehabilitated.

These first two chapters map the conceptual terrain within which further research and intervention should be undertaken on the subject. Although they are not meant to establish fixed boundaries within which subsequent chapters are to confine themselves, they provide reflective and critical practitioners concrete avenues to re-conceive their approach to post-mass-crime situations.

Individuals and communities

In addition to analysis of the Holocaust, genocide studies has developed in recent years as a significant sub-discipline in its own right. At the intersection of political science and history, offering a mixture of case studies and broad comparative analysis, genocide studies has shown how the perpetration of large massacres may be located at the political level within the processes of state-building, the seizing of power, riches and territory, as well as collective mobilization. It is well known that the extent to which political manipulation, aimed at exacerbating the mutual fear between communities, can bear heavy consequences in the eruption of violence. From an analytical perspective, however, the choice between the perspective of "a war of all against all" and "the pure manipulation of peaceful populations" is a false analytical dichotomy. The two always coexist: both capable of building up violence and deliberate political manipulation. The political level, albeit significant, is never the only important factor. It contributes, in particular, to the construction of new social identities. In this regard, the forms taken by ethnic divisions in society are generally no more than one element of a wider problem, as they belong to other conflicts such as those between the generations, between men and women, between social groups and between urban and rural dwellers. When the large-scale movements of people reconfigure the boundaries of ethnic identity, when social networks are torn and acts of terror remain unfathomable, uncertainty can go beyond ordinary limits and precipitate general violence.

The negation of humanity that holds the potential for mass crime within it, the negation of what binds human beings together, this "otherworldly" expulsion, as evoked by Hannah Arendt, deeply affects each individual as such and in their relationships with others.[5] Indeed, it is the possibility of social life that is under attack. In contemporary wars, a large percentage of crime is committed in the immediate domestic or communal environment; perpetrators frequently come from the same areas as those they assassinate or mutilate. In the region of Ayacucho, in Peru, during the war, the enemy might be a son-in-law, a godfather, an old schoolmate or the community just across the valley. Kimberly Theidon's chapter quotes survivors who recall that their neighbours wore masks during raids: "If they had taken off those masks, we would have recognized them." Similar incidents have been reported in other cases, such as in the African Great Lakes area. Disguise is supposed to help both the perpetrators and their victims to deal with their identity and intimacy. Research presented in this volume recalls that there are specific ways of "constructing the enemy", something that obliges us to revisit the cliché that a population typically "dehumanizes the enemy" during times of war. So-called "intimate" crime leaves particularly deep marks, both individually and collectively, weakening the regulatory foundations of society. The chapters in this volume analysing post-massacre situations in Peru, Rwanda, Bosnia-Herzegovina, Croatia, Cambodia

and Indonesia offer strong illustrations of that pattern and its consequences in the aftermath of wars.

Violence also deeply affects the cultures and structures that shape this
immediate environment. This is notably illustrated by drastic evolutions
in the family sphere, in the relationships between men and women, fathers and mothers, parents and children – partially explaining the drastic
increase in domestic violence in the aftermath of massacres, as exemplified by the chapter on Cambodia. These evolutions have much to do with
the institutionalization of violence, but also with the questioning of the
codes of conduct and values jeopardized by the killing process. The chapters dealing with the individual trajectories of former combatants and militia members in the former Yugoslavia and Rwanda offer complementary elements of this key aspect.

The four chapters of part 2 present the main results of field studies in
Cambodia, Peru, Rwanda and the Balkans. Each explores the way mass
crime has been understood by both individuals and local communities,
and how they are coping with the consequences, including when these
are leading to new violence. They show that the behaviour of the majority of people enters into what the writer Primo Levi called the "grey
zone" that generally envelops the majority of the members of a society
in times of conflict.[6] There can only be partial, ambiguous answers to
the key question of "When, why and how does the acceptance of, and respect for the Other, become transformed into the demonization of the
Other?"[7] In this sense, the role played by communal solidarity is extremely revealing, as are the trajectories of individuals who, in such
circumstances, may become perpetrators of mass violence. These case
studies also show that mass crime comes to profoundly disturb and re-
shape all the moral categories and frames of reference that make social
life possible. Therefore, understanding the conditions in which peace
may be built in such a context is to attempt to render intelligible these
numerous transformations. The studies presented in this volume illustrate the importance of constantly articulating their individual and collective dimensions. Analyses of the genealogy and the reproduction of
violence call for a methodological approach that is able to combine systematically social and political analysis, local history and a global perspective. In the absence of this interweaving, interpretations remain fragmented, leaving key aspects in the shadows. The experiences of these
past years have shown that, from Central America to the Balkans and
the Horn of Africa, problems and contradictions in the processes of
peace are much more conspicuous.

This is especially the case when it is presumed that these processes can
be guided by a simple "desire for reconciliation". Beliefs and belief systems after violence are not only cultural products but products of a

myriad of individual traumas interacting with one another, causing new traumatic incidents and leaving in place structures of thought that may themselves be a barrier to sustainable peace. Many of these structures of thought are neurologically supported: after violence, many survivors tend to suffer measurably increased rates of general nervous arousal, sleeplessness, anxiety, paranoia, depression and grief – all of which affect the ways in which they interact with cultural symbols, with each other, and with their remaining family members. Less discussed, but made evident in the research presented in this volume, survivors also report extremely expanded or extremely contracted perceptions during trauma, producing experiences – of miracles, transcendent horror or the disappearance of all normal perception – that may not fit in with more everyday views of the world. If "evil" has been felt as a concrete presence, for example, simply seeking to forget or recast it as injustice may not address issues that will emerge later in problems of distrust and retribution, affecting the way individuals depict themselves as human beings and citizens. Therefore, variables of what might be termed "soft power" need to be considered as crucial factors underlying conflicts and reconciliation, as well as holding the keys to the reconstruction of community and society.

In chapter 3, Maurice Eisenbruch examines the impact of mass crime on the rebuilding of social, cultural and spiritual relations in post-conflict Cambodia. The focus is through participant observation with 1,164 healers carried out over 14 years, to reveal how traditional culture and healing provide a meaning for the consequences of mass crime. The healers were observed in the course of their day-to-day work with local communities in hundreds of villages all over the countryside, as well as in the towns where most of the international aid programs are based. The healers and their patients were tracked, sometimes for a decade or more, allowing an examination of changes that spanned the years during and following the conflict.

Three challenges for cultural competence in peace-building are identified. The first is the spiritual consequences of mass crime, noted since the early 1990s and summarized by the Western cipher PTSD, yet classified differently by the local population. The Pol Pot doctrine of purging foreign elements echoed the belief that the enemy is within, in the form of spirits in the community or ethnic minorities within the nation, and that these must be ritually ejected. The second challenge is to understand the upsurge of contagious diseases such as HIV/AIDS noted since the late 1990s, and seen by the population as reflecting their post-war vulnerability, as the enemy germ or as a Trojan horse brought by foreigners who came to bring the peace. Third, the return of conflict in the late 1990s is often stereotyped as "a social modelling and identification with the violence of the Khmer Rouge". Yet, they reflect a loss of group identity with the coming of age of youth born in the wake of the Khmer Rouge, further weakened by the avalanche of Western values and unprotected by cultural codes and religious codes of conduct. The time-proven ways by which ordinary people and their healers seek to resolve community disharmony, such as treating "ancestral spirit disorder", for example, may be evolving into pernicious new incarnations of trauma as parents traffic daughters, children shoot parents, brothers gang rape sisters and lovers hurl acid. These are culturally malignant ways to resolve conflict for which the prescribed healing rituals on their own can no longer work.

In such a context, Cambodian monks and healers dispel a number of stereotypes. The first is that Cambodia's peaceful past was set upon by Pol Pot's mass crime – yet the Khmer Rouge designed their revolution upon their mastery and manipulation of that culture. The second is that Cambodia's post-conflict woes (PTSD, AIDS and social violence) stem from the Khmer Rouge regime, although it is of no use to blame the Khmer Rouge alone. The healers draw upon Buddhist doctrine (such as reincarnation) expressed as local folk stories (such as the legend of Angulimala) to help people come to terms with why good as well as bad people may do bad things to good people.

The Cambodian experience illustrates how much capacity-building for peace needs to take into account the transformative effects of war. In that perspective, Eisenbruch's chapter offers an important echo and complement to Beneduce's. Humanitarian aid can feed a cargo cult, the people embracing culturally foreign aid that may further undermine local capacity for healing. Eisenbruch argues that Buddhist monks and traditional healers can assist Cambodian authorities and the international humanitarian organizations in the identification of resilience factors within the local society, support rather than be engulfed by international humanitarian efforts and point the compass toward cultural competence in post-conflict peace-building.

Such "cultural competence" is also strongly advocated by Kimberly Theidon, in chapter 4. She explores how *campesinos* in the highlands of Ayacucho constructed lethal violence in the context of Peru's fratricidal war, and how the concepts and practices of communal justice have permitted them to develop a micro-politics of reconciliation at the communal and inter-communal levels. From 1980 to 2000, an internal war raged between the guerrilla group Sendero Luminoso, the *rondas campesinas* (armed peasant patrols) and the Peruvian armed forces. Three out of every four people killed during the war were rural, Quechua-speaking *campesinos*; the department of Ayacucho alone accounts for 40 per cent of all the dead and disappeared. Theidon shows how much war was interpreted but even more experienced concretely as an attack against cultural practices and the very meaning of what it means to live as a human being in these villages. As communal life has been severely distorted, moral reasoning and concepts of justice have undergone drastic changes. Nevertheless, this has not prevented citizens from attempting to re-build the social and communal ties attacked by mass violence.

This argument resonates with chapters 5 and 6, which present the results of micro-level research dealing with the trajectories of individuals who took part in the atrocities in Rwanda and the former Yugoslavia. In both situations, there was also significant regional and local variation in the perpetration of the horror. In chapter 5, Scott Straus emphasizes that detailed micro-level research on the causes of mass crime has implications not just for understanding the origins of those crimes, but also policy decisions after atrocities have been committed. The accepted historical narrative of the Rwandan genocide masks a more complex empirical picture of how the violence started and the manner in which it spread. National elites promoted genocidal violence from the centre, for example, but that call was met with varied responses, ranging from support to resistance. Straus argues that a disaggregation of the event and a closer inspection of why the dynamics of violence take hold and, thus, why individuals kill can yield insights into the crime's origins that in turn affect how the future is imagined. Such research is difficult to conduct and does not yield conclusions easily, but it may be the most effective way of designing post-mass-crime reconstruction projects that are both responsive to local concerns and build upon societal strengths; surprisingly, perhaps, Straus' chapter concludes that this research suggests some reasons for optimism about Rwanda's future.

One of the clear and important lessons drawn from the Rwanda case study is the importance of disaggregating the category of "perpetrators". Similarly, in chapter 6, Natalija Bašić shows that war experiences of "victims, perpetrators and bystanders" in the former Yugoslavia and its successor states were very heterogeneous. Her research focuses on the experiences of former combat soldiers in the wars in the former Yugoslavia, between 1991 and 1995. Its aim is to analyse from a trans-disciplinary perspective the formation of violence – the readiness to fight and kill – in anthropological, political and cultural terms. Bašić collected biographical stories of former combatants, all of them relatively young, and then analysed the way the interviewees depicted their war experiences in connection with the creation of new identifications and the change of older collective ones. She highlights the importance of defending or protecting one's own, be it one's house, family, country, nation or a better world. She also shows how fighting and dying in the group – in a group of men that could convey a substitute feeling for family – may appear as more normal than suffering post-traumatic effects in a civil environment. Even if the interviews conducted by Bašić did not allow her to assess the extent to which interviewees were actually involved in acts of violence and the reasons for their involvement, they gave crucial elements about the interpretations perpetrators of violence attributed to their actions in retrospect.

Interestingly, Bašić concludes that, on the basis of her research, it appears that former combat soldiers, despite ethnic or national differences, may have more in common with each other than with their fellow citizens. Such a diagnosis might indicate a brighter future for the country than its recent history suggests. This diagnosis directly echoes Straus's on Rwanda. In this case also, micro-level research indicates that the prospects for post-genocide confidence and trust among social groups might be greater than many Rwandan and outside observers believe. In both cases, the challenge ahead is to deal with the different memories and representations built around mass violence and imagine different modalities to re-build positive ties between the different components of the community.

Memories and representations of mass crime

Particularly crucial in such a process are the public and private rituals and narratives that sustain collective and individual memories of the history, causes and course of mass crime, and allow the re-interpretation and re-assertion of the belief systems. This is a complex and ambiguous process in which the symbolic world and the imaginary play a decisive role in the transformation of the meanings of history and of belonging. Therefore, research has to be concerned with the entangling of individual and collective memories, in the way in which they come to rewrite more distant memory. This should ultimately lead to the question: who writes history and for whom? The chapters in part 3 dealing with history and the politics of "reconciliation" address the use and abuse of memories of mass violence in the construction of a national history.

As such, they offer different views of the connections and disconnections between the local dimensions of rebuilding processes – more specifically dealt with in previous chapters – and national ones. The examination here focuses on "non-narratives", impossible or confiscated narratives (what Paul Ricoeur has called "hindered memory", "manipulated memory" and "obliged memory")[8] and in the authorized public narratives of the past that either give sense to individual memories or mutilate them. Such a process of constructing a narrative is all the more complicated by the historical courses of events in which mass crime and the paradoxical workings of memory are most often situated.[9] In many instances, this aspect has to take into account the memories of massacres committed in history. The roles of state and political actors are key in these processes.

Chapter 7, by René Lemarchand and Maurice Niwese returns to the case of Rwanda, viewing it though a different lens. Where Straus approached it through micro-level research, Lemarchand and Niwese situate it in the larger historical context of a cycle of interethnic violence that has periodically engulfed Rwanda and its neighbour Burundi. Their account is primarily a challenge to the view that the 1994 genocide can be viewed in isolation – epitomized by the temporal jurisdiction of the international criminal tribunal established to deal with the genocide, but with a mandate only to examine acts committed between 1 January and 31 December 1994. They argue that the dominant discourse of Hutu killers and Tutsi victims is itself a barrier to reconciliation, a discourse that should be complicated by historians to reflect the complexity of relations between Hutu and Tutsi – and their joint colonial past – if new, post-genocide identities are to be constructed.

In chapter 8, Leslie Dwyer and Degung Santikarma reflect on the way survivors of violence themselves try to deal with their memories and manage them in relation to the official discourses. Their analysis is based on a collaborative ethnographic fieldwork project they have been engaged in with survivors of Indonesia's 1965/66 state-sponsored anti-communist violence. Their work has focused on the island of Bali, which experienced some of the most intense violence, with some 80,000 to 100,000 suspected leftists (approximately 5 to 8 per cent of the island's population) killed by military and paramilitary forces. For the past four decades, Balinese have struggled with a legacy of oppression and violence – reinforced by ambivalence about articulating memories of terror. Although supported by a social, political and economic context that suppresses or denies these memories, the contradiction between this veneer and the lived experiences of the population is occasionally revealed. The authors show how ambiguous and ambivalent remembering and forgetting may be in their collective and symbolic effects, stressing the importance of not presuming that these processes are linear.

Historical discourses may promote both conflict *and* peace-building, just as memories do. This core ambivalence is examined by Thomas Sherlock in chapter 9, assessing the reinterpretations of Baltic, Ukrainian and Chechen history in the Soviet and post-Soviet periods. The chapter first addresses the Baltic case and then turns to Ukraine and Chechnya. The essential precondition for historical reinterpretation in the post-Soviet space was the desacralization by counter-elites of the central myths that legitimized the Soviet empire and its rule over the Baltic, Ukrainian and Chechen nationalities. This process of public delegitimation of Soviet myths emerged during *perestroika* in the late 1980s and shocked Soviet society with a flood of negative revelations about the past, including severe criticism of the actions of Stalin and even Lenin. The entire official Soviet narrative was called into question, forcing political and academic authorities on the defensive. Emblematic of the crumbling ideological edifice of the Soviet system was the official decision in 1988 to cancel secondary school exams and discard existing history textbooks as virtually useless. This struggle over how to interpret the Soviet past seriously weakened the normative support of the Soviet state, contributing to its collapse in 1991. For each case, the chapter charts post-Soviet change and continuity in Russian interpretations of Baltic, Ukrainian and Chechen history, using new history textbooks and other materials as guideposts. Although some of the new Russian textbooks are little better than their Soviet predecessors in terms of substance and style, other Russian textbooks represent significant advances over the Soviet period, and often compare favourably to American textbooks on Soviet history. For example, a respected, widely used American university textbook argues – erroneously – that the Western democracies in 1939 "ardently" sought an alliance with the Soviet Union to stop Nazi aggression.[10] By contrast, some of the Russian textbooks under review offer a more balanced and accurate account of this controversial historical period.

Peace-building strategies and the insider–outsider dynamic

In chapter 10, Louis Kriesberg focuses more specifically on the role of international actors who seek to intervene after atrocity and discusses the main challenges these situations pose to them. He first refers to the nature of destructive conflicts and how they are transformed, before turning to the examination of the ways international governmental organizations and international nongovernmental organizations affect the durability of peace following the commission of mass crime. Kriesberg offers a series of recommendations to render outsiders' contributions more useful.

Reflection on what the role of an outsider should be in such contexts remains very complex. Further on-the-ground research is needed in order to understand the processes sketched out in this volume – as well as their limits. The possibility of building peace depends on an understanding of the rules of social and political life in a given society, and how disparate actors may be encouraged to participate without recourse to violent confrontation. Such understanding also helps to identify appropriate roles for outsiders. An obvious but important aspect of this is assessing the manner in which external assistance programs are considered and evaluated by a target population.

Perhaps an easier starting point is simply calling for greater understanding. Field personnel must be conscious of what happens in periods following mass crime – beyond surface appearances of disorder and chaos, or physical and mental survival. Our volume offers some important keys in that perspective. Importantly, outsiders should never forget that, whoever they are, they represent an outside world that may be seen as having abandoned or neglected local populations while they were under attack.

"Peace must be re-imagined, even re-invented after mass crime." To a large extent, this is an important lesson emphasized by the different contributions in this book. In the final chapter, Roberta Culbertson and Béatrice Pouligny offer an integrative analysis, reflecting both on the main theoretical principles and on the practical lessons that can be drawn from the volume. They focus on three main components. First, they stress the need for understanding the nature of the transformations effected by war and mass violence. This means, among other things, understanding that there cannot be a mere return to the past and that the prospects of such a return should not be romanticized. Second, they insist on the importance of moving between different levels of organization on the ground, and understanding the multiple connections and disconnections between micro- and macro-dimensions of violence and post-violence. Third, they focus on some key elements regarding the work of re-insertion in survivor communities. One main lesson from their analysis is that the matter of insider and outsider knowledge must become a dialog-ical exchange in the hands of the local communities.

Conclusion: Mapping mass crime

Peace-building is not a linear process. The roads to peace are less like highways than bumpy and potholed roads – sometimes barely marked; sometimes not marked at all. It is these roads that outsiders who wish to contribute to peace-building must take, both physically and symboli-cally.[11] The analyses offered in this book may provide some useful directions but they are not a road map.

Any external scholar or practitioner comes from a particular culture, a fact that need not be disempowering but must be acknowledged when interacting with other cultures. Such issues should be included in specific training before deployment in the field. Whatever the political pressures on international organizations to send people quickly, pre-briefings should never be neglected. It is crucial that field staff understand the local context in which they will have to work, and receive specific preparation in order to face and manage what may be a traumatic experience for them also.

More than in any other post-conflict situation, post-mass-crime peace-building requires a fundamental transformation of the way in which both analysts and practitioners envisage their role. Their efforts must permit the understanding of what was at stake during the mass crime for society (the groups and individuals of which it is composed), and what is fundamentally changed in the political, social and communal fabric of the population in question. Through such an analysis it may be possible to identify that which – even involuntarily, even in the apparent "chaos" – can be salvaged by a community and used as the basis upon which it and it alone can build peace.

Notes

1. The institution is understood as a mode of organisation of the mechanisms of exchange between the individual and the social group, which may relate to so-called "primary" institutions such as the family or community.
2. See the chapter in this volume by Kimberly Theidon.
3. This system allows the actors to situate themselves in the social game and give a particular meaning to the action and the social institutions in the collectivity concerned. The culture so defined does not create permanent identities but organizes the behaviour of the different actors (including those who take power). See Clifford Geertz, "The politics of meanings", *The Interpretation of Cultures*, New York: Basic Books, 1973, p. 89.
4. An exception is the United States Institute of Peace Special Report *Trauma and Transitional Justice in Divided Societies*, following a conference organized in March 2004, Washington, DC: USIP, Special Report 135, April 2005.
5. On the subject of the experience of totalitarian violence, Hannah Arendt referred to "the experience of not belonging to the world at all, which is among the most radical and desperate experiences of man". Hannah Arendt, *The Origins of Totalitarianism*, 6th ed., New York and London: Harcourt Brace Jovanovich, 1979, p. 475.
6. Primo Levi evoked this "grey zone" to explore the spectrum of behaviour of the victims of the concentration camps. He also suggested that this zone included the killers, without nonetheless considering there to be a symmetrical relationship between perpetrators and victims. Primo Levi, *Naufragés et rescapés*, Paris: Gallimard, 1989.
7. Denis-Constant Martin, "Identity, culture, pride and conflict", in Simon Bekker and Rachel Prinsloo, eds, *Identity? Theory, Politics, History*, Pretoria: Human Sciences Research Council, 1999, p. 197.
8. Paul Ricoeur, *La mémoire, l'histoire, l'oubli*, Paris: Seuil, 2000. See also his previous work more specifically dealing with the link between memory and history, Paul Ricoeur, *Temps et récit*, vol. 3, Paris: Seuil, 1983–1985.
9. Tzvetan Todorov, *Les Abus de la Mémoire*. Paris: Arléa, 1993.
10. Donald Treadgold, *Twentieth Century Russia*, Chicago: Rand McNally, 1977, p. 336.
11. Béatrice Pouligny, *Peace Operations Seen from Below: UN Missions and Local People*, London: Hurst/Bloomfield, Conn.: Kumarian Press, 2006, p. 269.

Part I

Methodology and ethics

1

Methodological and ethical problems: A trans-disciplinary approach

Béatrice Pouligny, Bernard Doray and Jean-Clément Martin

This chapter examines the ethical and methodological issues raised by social science research conducted in situations where mass crimes have been committed. Our analysis is based on our respective experiences as researchers and practitioners in different historical and contemporary settings. Many of the problems that we address are the standard fare of any social science researcher, given the particular nature of the "object" of such research. These issues are, however, exacerbated when working in unique situations of extreme violence, where the analyst is faced with the practical difficulties of implementing a code of ethics, something that is often easier to define than to apply. The mere fact that we decided to write this chapter from a cross-disciplinary perspective embodies our approach to these complex and painful situations. Indeed, both scholars and practitioners run the risk of "simplifying" situations that are too complex to understand, explain or describe in any other way. Saying that we know the answers when, in reality, we have everything to learn, or thinking that the other person's reality can be reduced to what we can comprehend, are temptations against which we must be on guard. Our shared belief is that, in order to address the most desperate and wretched situations, the greatest wealth of expertise is required. This should be a basic moral principle. By continually traversing the boundaries between disciplines and by interweaving various perspectives, one can hope to build interpretive frameworks and to develop investigatory methods that will assist in integrating individual and collective dimensions of extreme violence.

After mass crime: Rebuilding states and communities, Pouligny, Chesterman and Schnabel (eds), United Nations University Press, 2007, ISBN 978-92-808-1138-4

This integration of individual and collective levels of experience is highly desirable in the wake of a collective tragedy because these events cannot be simply boiled down to a collection of individual tragedies. In such circumstances, it is the culture itself, the possibility of social life, which is under attack. In light of this fact, mass-crime situations require the formulation of both individual therapies and collective initiatives. Because individual therapy takes place under emergency conditions, it is only rarely offered and its effectiveness is controversial. By "collective initiatives" we mean not only those methods used for rebuilding self-esteem, such as psychodrama, but also other therapeutic techniques that benefit from the dimension of group work. Community healing is first and foremost a matter of mobilizing cultural resources aimed at restoring collective memory, encouraging personal narratives and accounts, re-integrating child soldiers into their community or re-establishing links to the dead whose bodies were not treated with the dignity and the rituals worthy of a human being (as occurred in Rwanda and in Bosnia-Herzegovina). All of these efforts contribute significantly to rebuilding human relationships after the experience of a mass crime.

This close interplay between the individual and collective levels is necessary, as individuals cannot be considered in isolation from the culture to which they belong. When people have been affected by mass crimes, the proximity between these levels can be observed in the interconnectedness between the gravity of symbolic attacks (such as the loss of media for transmitting traditions or the repeated transgression of taboos), as in the cases of Cambodia or Guatemala, and the risk of unintentional symbolic violence displayed, for example, in humanitarian intervention operations. This connection is the basis for a common ethics between specialists of psychology and those in the social sciences when they intervene in peace-building processes. While people are part of their culture, they cannot be reduced to its simple expression. One frequently hears discourse in which social entities are personalized and nations characterized just as individuals are. Such personification may be used to justify amalgams such as that between a criminal state apparatus and a criminal nation.

Our common ethics imply that we share the same respect for human beings, alive and dead, who are the direct subjects of our work. This common ground has allowed us to collaborate across different disciplines (political science, psychiatry and history). We began our exchange during brainstorming meetings organized at the Center for International Studies and Research in 2001/02, attempting to encourage the cross-fertilization of our questioning in an effort to delve more deeply into the complexity of post-mass-crime scenarios. In our view, this process has confirmed the fact that ethics and research methods are inseparable. This chapter offers some avenues of thought in this direction by first examining the question of situating oneself in relation to "evil". The second section of our contribution explains the method we use to develop a comprehensive approach to violent situations. The third and final section explores the responsibility of any outsider (particularly a researcher) in the process of writing history and constructing a narrative of massacres.

Situating oneself in relation to "evil"

For scholars concerned with the field of international relations as well as with collective violence, situating oneself (both as a researcher and as a human being) in relation to a situation of mass crime means re-examining a number of preconceptions that have in fact shaped studies on international security for over a decade. Conflicts have all too often been characterized as irrational, as a result of that regrettable habit of qualifying as irrational anything that our framework of analysis cannot (or can no longer) explain as non-existent or inexplicable. In that vein, the theme of "barbarity" has resurfaced with a vengeance, particularly in relation to situations of mass and extreme violence. The label "barbarous" generally serves not to denote that which is present in everyone, but rather to describe the behaviour of another person or another people. It is most often, albeit unconsciously, linked to a desire to distance oneself – as if for reassurance that the labeller, at least, is not like that.

This denial may be easily understood from the perspective of psychiatry. From that viewpoint, one of the fundamental laws of the human world can be summed up in a simple equation: The prohibition of familial endogamy (incest) results in the benefit of social exogamy (relations of alliance and cooperation, recognition of other human beings as like oneself and deserving of interaction within human society). Even experiences that one perceives to be widely shared, however, manifest the local conception of "human society" as generally excluding what the ancient Romans called the *limes*, a part of the human world expressly relegated to a more or less radical estrangement or "otherness". War, the theatre of all cruelties and transgressions of human laws, by nature solidifies and permanently fixes the rejection of the other in a state of estrangement. One is then confronted with barbarism, that is, face to face with someone else who is not considered human. For the analyst of this situation, it is evidently important not to let oneself be overcome by facile binary thinking ("good" vs "evil", "black" vs "white"). Indeed, it is essential to reintroduce complexity when observing and intervening in such situations. It should be noted that a sense of complexity does not mean one of indifference, nor does it entail the attitude that would lead to considering massacres as part of the natural state of things, an intrinsic manifestation of the human order and therefore something one should simply deal with in the best way possible. We believe, on the contrary, that mass crimes are more legible when they are placed in the context of basic human laws (cooperation of exchange or the taboo against murder, for example) than when they are confusingly represented as both an expression of those laws and a transgression of them.

An overarching, moralizing and binary view that involves merely the struggle between "good" and "evil" seems to us to lead to an impasse in reasoning. For each of us in our respective disciplines, proposing an alternative procedure in terms of the ethical construction of a method first and foremost corresponds to a deontology both professional and personal: that of relating to those who resemble ourselves. For therapists working with victims of extreme violence, the challenge involved in such an approach is particularly acute. Even if the victim is unable to recognize the humanity of those who have caused him or her immense suffering, it is necessary for the therapist to visualize the humanity of the perpetrator. If it is not possible to humanize the image of the perpetrator, the victim too is dehumanized and the traumatic fragment of the victim's story is removed from human intercourse. In that process, the divide that has already been created by the psyche in the representation of the trauma is widened. This challenge naturally presents itself differently for the researcher, since he or she does not adopt a therapeutic approach, but it is nevertheless comparable. While the mind seeks to reassure itself by constantly attempting to determine the boundaries of good and evil, the analyst has to be able to transcend such limitations and envisage the situations in their full complexity, far removed from preconceived categories, which, though comforting, are of little help in advancing knowledge and discussion.

The role of the historian is a peculiar one here. At first glance, things may seem much more straightforward. Clearly, one can accomplish prescribed tasks scrupulously by elucidating the conditions in which an act was committed, drawing up a list of the victims and assessing the responsibilities of the violent actors. In this way, the historian fulfils the ordinary expectations of society and conforms to the deontological demands of the field. Yet a large-scale massacre, even when it took place in the distant past, has certain implications that lead the historian to a methodological and ethical reflection in order to avoid the postulation of "inhumanity" as accounting for the atrocities committed by long-gone populations. The study of mass crimes is constantly altered and shifted by the development of political and judicial processes (the creation of an International Criminal Court being one of the most recent). The historian thus cannot ignore the fact that he or she is also an agent of history and contributes to the formation of the collective judgment of the society in which he or she lives. With this in mind, the analysis applied to the society under study must be turned with equal measure to the work of introspection.

When these truths are laid out, the implication is that the historian must create a "patchwork" with his research, in Claude Lévi-Strauss's sense of inventing a new procedure by piecing together elements of disciplines and methods that are no longer adequate on their own. Mass crimes encompass all aspects of the humanities and social sciences. Charisma, submission and the conformity of "ordinary men" manifest many of the features of both individual and collective psychology, which are of great importance in these kinds of crimes. As Christopher Browning pointed out, the Holocaust was ultimately possible because, at the most basic level, individual human beings put other human beings to death in large numbers and over an extended period of time.[1] This observation concerning the capabilities of ordinary men carries with it the implication that the methodological approach to history must be conditioned by ethical concerns that become tangible to the writer's audience in the choice of style and point of view. The history of a massacre must move away from the use of qualifiers, particularly of adjectives that describe the features of the victims (such as "pregnant women" and "very young children"), as well as from the presentation of the historical narrative as a deposition of killings or as a certified or reconstituted description of cruelty. The use of the word "enemy", for instance, is a purely affective designation that evokes reflexive and instinctive judgments. One's usage of terms must therefore be thoroughly precise. The idea of "irrationality" obscures not only the organization and deliberate method, which are always at work in these kinds of practices, but also overshadows the banality of the actors, who are, after all, ordinary humans. Instead of resorting to such all-encompassing notions, one should be attentive to the oft-present mechanisms (political, social and psychological) that allow analogous events to emerge under different circumstances.

Finally, the place of the historian within the context of his own time is relevant insofar as it influences his approach. It is notable that while the idea of violent death is currently taboo and subject to a universal impulse to expel it from the social world, it nonetheless remains omnipresent in one's consciousness. As an illustration of the potential diversity of historical interpretation (and revisionism), we can look for comparison to the massacres committed during the French Revolution. Those transgressions could be interpreted as the vengeance of a society in the process of shattering the religious order, as the turmoil accompanying the eruption of the people onto the political scene or even as a foreshadowing of totalitarianism. In any case, these massacres seem to constitute a significant chapter in a story of universal significance. Beyond the categories of "good" and "evil", however, are more complex approaches to analysing such events, involving the search for social, psychic and political mechanisms necessary to understand mass crimes. Placing the individual at the heart of the process is the first and most crucial step in doing so.

In other words, this alternative approach to critical analysis recognizes the importance of understanding the human condition in all its complexity. It means that we should at times put down our pens, look up from our papers and computer screens, transport ourselves back to the world of the living and ask ourselves: Do things happen like this in "real life"? Is this how my fellows breathe, think, relate, love, hate, clash and sometimes kill each other? Too many academic, diplomatic and bureaucratic discussions take place as though working with "objects" outside the speakers' own world (where human life is valued), as if the people in question are not also men and women. Each of those situations nevertheless causes one to consider the value that one places on one's own humanity and consequently on that of others. It is by scrutinizing this need for distance that we as researchers have examined the way we have personally dealt with situations of violence and, more specifically, with the people in these situations. The exercise we delineate in this chapter is a methodological process of developing a "comprehensive" perspective (in the sense of *verstehend*)[2] and of shifting the focus of the research from "object" to "subject". It requires building linkages between the worlds of peace and war that the human impulse to reject death wishes to drive further apart.

Towards a comprehensive sociology

The negation of humanity inherent in mass crime, the denial of that which binds human beings together, that "other-worldly" experience,[3] affects the innermost part of the individual. To reach it requires us to adopt the approach of someone trying to "understand", in the primary and fullest sense of the term. A comprehensive sociology is developed from the perspective of meaning. It seeks to enter the other person's subjectivity through a decentring process in order to try to "understand the other" from within, as one is invited to do by the philosopher Paul Ricoeur. Such an approach is necessarily delicate and complex. It calls for a certain – and sometimes uneasy – empathy. Nevertheless, understanding the rationale of extreme violence and the nature of the interactions it brings into play does not mean either trivializing or excusing such acts. To understand is neither to absolve nor to eliminate all responsibility through the kind of reasoning that postulates that men inevitably become violent when placed in a particular socio-historical context. Also, taking interest in individuals who participated in the massacre of their fellow beings, including of their former neighbours or family members, is not to forgive but rather to acknowledge the fact that, in the descent into violence, the perpetrators are rarely "insane". The debate that has surrounded Hannah Arendt's use of the term "banal" in reference to Adolf Eichmann,[4] echoes the criticisms that can be levelled at social science researchers when they suggest going beyond the opposition between "civilian" and "soldier", "victim" and "perpetrator" or "resistance" and "collaboration". In fact, attempting to "understand" rather than to "explain" means emphasizing the limits of any exercise in theorizing and categorizing where often only partial, ambiguous and makeshift answers exist to account for processes that are reconstructed in hindsight through the filter of analysis. A comprehensive sociology will attempt, in Ricoeur's words, to perceive the subject as historical consciousness.[5]

For the political or social scientist, this may mean that he or she tries to get as close as possible to the viewpoint of the local people. In other words, the aim is to try to take seriously the way in which the individuals and groups concerned have understood and explained the events subjectively and empirically. This means that they are no longer simply an "object", but become the "subject" of the research. This is not a straightforward operation. First, the approach adopted by a researcher seeking to "understand" is demanding and often painful from a psychological as well as an ethical viewpoint. It entails critical analysis of the scholar's underlying perceptions of those situations and constant examination of the imagery that works on one's own conceptions of "peace", "war" and "violence" and, to an even greater extent, the "unthinkable". At first glance, things may appear "simpler" to the analyst than to the practitioner because the confrontation with violence is, barring exceptions, less immediate. Such psychological hurdles do, however, exist and need to be acknowledged so that they may be overcome and the persons interviewed during investigations can be "heard". This is a perpetually incomplete process. In each investigation, a scholar's outlook traverses a series of stages. Scholars must sometimes force themselves to "take risks", which are often less physical than mental: They risk a severe blow to that which makes them human, gives them faith in humanity and sustains. This effort is complicated by the usual operational and corroborative methods of research. There is always a strong temptation to look for details in the field that will corroborate existing theories, neat typologies and other intellectual constructs that are fostered by one's profession, leaving aside (albeit unconsciously) anything that would contradict them. From such an approach, if reality does not fit the scholar's image of it, it is highly likely that reality is ultimately judged wrong.

This fallacy stems from the fact that frameworks of intervention and analysis are greatly influenced by the catchall, undifferentiated image of the victim as civilian and passive. As a result, a genuine effort has to be made to perceive other people as capable of being something other than victims, capable of asserting themselves as actual participants and of re-evaluating their situation and commenting upon it. Common methods of intervention sometimes give rise to a process of dehumanization that reduces the other person to a symptom rather than a story. In the fall of 1996, the refugees in the Congolese province of North Kivu were no more than dots on satellite pictures to the diplomats in New York discussing the advisability of undertaking a humanitarian operation. For a number of humanitarian agencies that intervene in post-massacre situations, the act of describing the trauma experienced by the populations they assist externalizes and objectifies it, rather than taking it as it is: beyond words, gestures or impossible narratives. In our field investigations, we found that a recurrent theme in many of the interviews was that no one had ever taken the time to listen to people tell their stories (an activity Hannah Arendt considered to be specifically human).[6] Listening to others putting their stories into words is to restore those who have suffered trauma to what makes them human and unique.

The interviewing exercise in itself is rather complicated. In this process, both patience and prudence are essential to the analysis. The role and status as an "outsider" immediately places the researcher in a position of power. When interacting with the researcher, local people have very different capacities and resources that enable them to give voice to their perspective. With this in mind, the researcher must assess the context of the interview very cautiously and try to reach an understanding with the people who agree to tell their precious and sensitive stories. One must also attempt to create an atmosphere of security. With an objective of forming such an environment, participatory methods take on an importance not only for the information they can yield but also because they allow the forging of trusting relationships. Jean-Claude Métraux, a psychiatrist who developed a methodology for collective mourning, has identified different elements that may help construct group identity. He has also stressed the importance of recognizing that the group acquires an inviolable "sacred" element, or areas of silence that outsiders have to respect. In the collective interviewing process, this space should be symbolized and ritualized at the beginning of each session. Those working with children and child soldiers in a context of war are aware that the researcher's relationship with the children falls outside even the social codes governing relationships with adults (who are in and of themselves outsiders), such that it may be important to simply play with the children or encourage them to draw. Interviewers may need to meet people on several occasions before starting to gather details of direct interest to their research; they should never consider irrelevant the time spent in markets, on public transport, around a fire preparing a meal or at evening gatherings, or times spent just being there, sharing simple, everyday tasks, waiting and listening, even in times of silence. In the context of creating trust relationships, the degree of consent on the part of those interviewed is a particularly delicate matter. It involves, *inter alia*, explaining in understandable terms who the researcher is, what the purposes of the research are, the possible uses of the research findings and any other contextual details (such as the interviewees' willingness to be personally quoted or even identified). The level of transparency that the researcher can adopt depends on the context, the security conditions under which he or she is working, and the position of the person to whom he or she is speaking. As a general rule, the weaker the interviewee's position, the greater the researcher's concern for transparency should be in order to mitigate, at least partially, the basic inequality of the interaction. Finally, it is of utmost importance to adhere consistently to the terms that have been established in the relationship.

Whether or not one needs to use an interpreter or other intermediary can also be a determining factor in the relationship. Regardless of the research subject, it means dealing with the intercultural dimensions of the investigative process. Researchers, approaching the subject from the perspective of their own culture and language, will refer to political concepts that have different connotations or alternative meanings for the participants. This issue is particularly relevant when reference is made to concepts that do not have direct equivalents in the language of the host country. Matters can become even more complicated when one is confronting issues of war and peace, life and death, and the integrity of human beings. One often tends to reduce such questions to the dialectics of the universal and the particular. Such a dichotomy not only leads to a theoretical and practical impasse but also distorts the real challenge that all human interchange poses: Are we capable of fully understanding what our interlocutor says to us, and what is important in his eyes and not in ours? Like the humanitarian worker who must agree to put aside the plan he had brought, choosing rather to listen and formulate a scheme to be undertaken jointly, researchers must be prepared to alter their investigation programs.

A comprehensive sociology aims at defusing the symbolic violence that weighs upon the relationship between the one who holds knowledge and the one who is the "object" or "subject" of that knowledge, the one who contemplates events as a distant observer and the one who lives them in the flesh, in a traumatic way. But it also rightfully attempts to bring greater knowledge and understanding than an objectivist approach.

While having a particular perspective on reality can no doubt be a significant advantage in interpreting it, one should be careful to take the methodological precaution of allowing "the space for different points of view"[7] that is essential to the sociological approach to reality. This approach is very similar to the therapeutic practice that privileges the subject and the meaning he ascribes to his acts and narratives. In the domain of psychology, this perspective is akin to the path Jerome Bruner,[8] one of the founding fathers of cognitive psychology, intuitively pursued before cognitive psychology lost its substance by prioritizing information over meaning. Advancing the idea of popular psychology, he pointed to the psychic resiliency in experiences that have shown that by "telling it like it is", people are also implicitly saying how things should be. In other words, they provide both the design and the background image upon which their narrative is silhouetted. This is important because when the subject recounts the unfolding of an event on the backdrop of what he considers to be the normal order of things, it means that he relates what makes up a psychic event or a trauma. Bruner also emphasized the use of rhetorical figures. Far from being useless ornaments, figurative speech describes the scope of the latent possibilities the narrator could employ to describe the context that, in turn, makes the event readable.

Moreover, listening to the subjective dimension of the account tells us what actually made it an event for the speaker. Only then can the researcher come to grips with the entire complexity of subjective events. Indeed, we cannot conceive of a kind of narrative that is unconcerned with subjective events since these so powerfully reveal the collective motivations of social actors. Finally, even if they are not explicitly set as "therapeutic" objectives, it is certain that the compilations of testimony re-establishing the truth of great massacres and acts of multiple, organized cruelties have a powerful effect on survivors. Survivors can feel dispossessed or, conversely, they can benefit from the recognition, which can result in major liberation from personal trauma and re-symbolization (reinserting subjects back into their culture and the history of their communities). In this sense, the description of these events, if indeed there is an attempt to seek the most exact and precise account, cannot claim to be neutral, especially when it ultimately becomes a question of selecting the form in which this individual and collective story is to be made public.

Contrary to appearances, historians do not find themselves in a much more comfortable position, given that (as is the case with all the other analysts) they are placed in a position where certain intentions will be attributed to them, or they will be asked to choose sides. Their role is essential because it is their responsibility to sort through the sources that are used, which are of a varied nature: contemporary official documents detailing the facts (laws, decrees, government reports), judicial records, papers written by professionals after the fact, the participants' memoirs or witness testimony gathered long after the massacre or even transmitted through an oral history of protest. In any case, studies of this type of massacre reveal the fact that official documents are frequently silent regarding what has occurred, most often using euphemisms to describe the incidents or even suppressing what has transpired. Trials initiated against the perpetrators of violence have generally taken place several years after the fact and in contexts where these actors have lost all political credibility, with the consequence that the judicial decisions as well as the testimony gathered on such occasions are not exempt from critical suspicion, and rendering the documents issuing from these procedures difficult to exploit. When speaking about their work, the investigators of the Offices of the Prosecutors of the International Criminal Tribunals for the former Yugoslavia and for Rwanda offer numerous illustrations of the complexity of such processes. Paradoxically, personal memories – even those transmitted in literary form – have sometimes shown themselves to be the most relevant sources, despite their intrinsic weaknesses. Indeed, such memories offer hints of the obstacles impeding all attempts to reconstruct the events; while the truth they elucidate remains incomplete, they nevertheless ensure that silence does not prevail. Furthermore, given the nature of personal memories as a source, the presence of suffering bodies often looms larger there than it does in the archives, obliging the historian to accord significant attention to witness accounts.

Moreover, writing the history of a massacre entails the obligation of recording the number of victims, establishing the conditions of death, identifying those responsible and clarifying the command structure involved. This phase is at once an indispensable and an ambiguous one, as it runs the risk of confounding the task of the historian with that of the memorialist. The historian's work is, by definition, circumscribed in a critical perspective and has the goal of offering conclusions that are subject to revision; the memorialist, on the other hand, aims to authenticate his conclusions, to record the recognized facts, and has as a mission to preserve the list of victims from oblivion. From there tensions are born. First of all, it is often necessary to contradict the tenets of ordinary memories, which can be constructed from the point of view of the "executioners" when they were the victors (as in the case of the Armenian Massacre). The massacre must also be set within the logical framework that gave rise to it, while at the same time the interpretation lent to it by the victims has to be questioned in some cases. The massacre is integrated into a network of reactions placed in a historical context that should be established in all its complexity. First of all, verifying the stories of the victims raises questions about their character and their role in the descent towards violence: some of them could have been themselves perpetrators before being put to death or implicated in the conflict that unleashed the violence, while others were caught up in the genuine hazard of the massacre. The situation is even more complex when the path taken by those responsible for the violence is the subject of examination: Were these "ordinary men" who were drawn into the act, organizers of political violence, authentic wielders of violence or pathological cases taking advantage of an exceptional and transitory situation? For the historian required to make a determination while taking these stories into account, there is not always a clear dividing line between the path of the "executioners" and that of the "victims" but there are rather entwined destinies in the sense that the massacre becomes a singular event, resulting from a particular conjunction of circumstances that precludes any specific meaning. Thus, it is clear that the use of historical methodology can doom the practitioners of social science and the victims of massacres to a clash of expectations and mutual misunderstanding.

Engaging in a "narrative-building" process

In all the forementioned activities, the analyst – whether a social or political scientist, a psychiatrist or a historian – will, in his or her own way, construct a narrative. The accuracy of the analysis will depend largely on the attention paid to the complexity of the situation, the historical knowledge of the groups concerned, and the researcher's capacity for listening to the interviewees and for understanding beyond the words and the silence. Any outsider needs to understand that, when confronted with differing organized narratives, his personal response will be to propose his own alternative interpretation. That dual process warrants particular attention.

Any process of constructing a narrative has to be viewed as occurring at the intersections of collective history and psychic history, individual histories and group relations, and group linkages and the workings of culture.[9] Such an activity is doubly complicated by the historical course of events in which mass crimes and the paradoxical functioning of memory are most often situated. Emphasizing the "narrative" element within the social science researcher's work raises the dual question: Who is making history, and for whom? These questions clearly implicate the work of the historian, who can help to render memory dispassionate, but others are also involved. Any analysis contributes to sustaining this historical creation process within a given society. It is particularly complex when it comes from an individual outside the group (which is the case of most academic work on situations of post–mass crime), since it seems as if it represented the view of a world from which one was "expelled" at the time of the tragedy. Furthermore, there are different systems of "creating meaning" within which the analyst must situate himself. Three systems can generally be distinguished. First, there is the establishment (or historical "clarification") of facts that could serve as a basis for a public recognition of the gravity of what has happened. The second option is the subjective, and theological or philosophical, elaboration at both the individual and collective levels of a method for organizing memories and lending sense to them. The final system is composed of the realms of fantasy and of the arts, which keep what has occurred from passing into oblivion, and, to an even greater extent, help to ask continually the key question: How and why could such a thing have happened?

Although these different registers and methodological viewpoints do not generally coincide, they coexist, intermingle and sometimes enrich each other. This association can generate contradictions, which must be recognized as such, as they can transcend well-constructed discourse sanctifying a "consensual" vision that is often nothing more than the imposition of one version of history upon the others. On the contrary, symbolization must allow for the opening and forging of a pathway between the different systems of truth so that they may share in mutual recognition, move closer together and finally meet, even if this process is difficult and even painful. In this way, one perceives that research work is first and foremost one point of view among others. To the extent that social science research proceeds from a certain interpretation of reality, it belongs to the vast domain of the practice of "creating meaning". Scientific investigation is able to construct creative linkages within the three aforementioned systems without becoming tainted because it possesses certain particular characteristics. That which makes scholarly inquiry unique is not only its duty to formulate hypotheses and constantly submit them to criticism, but is also its duty to remain vigilant to the danger of being instrumentalized by those in power. We wish to take concrete cases and lived experience as our point of departure before returning to their implications for research and analysis.

The act of establishing the facts flows from investigative work of a scientific character, but its results generally spill over into the domain of pure knowledge. The analytic process must permit the identification of those responsible for crimes committed as well as allow for the beginning of rehabilitation for the victims as survivors, in such a way that they can overcome their feelings of guilt. Indeed, guilt feelings not only constitute an important psychological dimension of the relation between the executioner and his victim but they also form a part of the strategy of repression. In Guatemala, even though there is an *arqueologia foranea* that is dedicated to excavating clandestine cemeteries in order to identify and re-bury the bodies, part of the army and those who support it (who can be found among the political class as well as the rest of society) still claim that the majority of the 200,000 dead in the war were guerrillas or those who supported them, and even that the Mayan *indigenos* massacred each other. The process of establishing the facts, which is happening in this case through a long and painful procedure of exhuming mass graves, must also permit the dignity of the deceased to be restored.

Public acknowledgement of the events should allow the survivors and victims' relatives to engage in a mourning process. In Haiti after the September 1991 coup d'etat, when no trace of those who were killed could be found – neither their bodies nor a list of names were produced (while those concerned generally had no civil status at all) – those who would deny suffrage to the poor carried out their intentions in the most hideous manner. They distributed leaflets claiming that the poor – who were explicitly targeted by the campaign of terror and violence – were worth nothing, not more than cockroaches among the refuse of the miserable quarters where they lived. This kind of official discourse intends to eradicate completely events from both individual stories and the collective memory, as if they never existed, and thus leaves them no space to take hold so that they may be retold or reflected upon.[10]

The trans-generational transmission process is in this way particularly impeded. Children, including those who were only babies at the time of the events, have a need to be able to give sense to the scars they carry even though they do not retain any clear memories of what happened. A particularly striking example can be found in Cameroon among those who survived a massacre of some 400,000 Bamilekes in 1961.[11] Several emigrants from Cameroon, who were undergoing psychotherapy for different reasons in their adult emotional lives, separately came to the realization that aspects of their neuroses, or simply of their difficulties in life, were linked to the events of the massacre. They were far from their homeland at the time, however, and knew nothing of those events. The official history in Cameroon and France alike had imposed a leaden silence upon that period.

It is quite common to observe that members of the generation immediately succeeding the one that endured periods of extreme violence have trouble making sense of entire segments of their lived experience or even of their own identity as a result of the silence maintained by their parents and, more generally, by the adults of the community. In Cambodia, particularly among those younger than thirty years of age, who compose the majority of the Cambodian population, the memory of genocide is completely devoid of reference points, as if swallowed by a collective amnesia that has caused a number of analysts to remark that Cambodians "want to forget". However, if visitors take the time to listen to their interlocutors, to meet them several times over a sufficiently long period such that a relationship of mutual trust can develop, and if they interest themselves in the writings and different forms of expression employed by these youths, they will discover the extent to which this history is omnipresent for them. Their encounter with history is thus conveyed precisely because it is impossible for them to retell the story that was transmitted to them nonverbally, through silences and other strategies that their parents employed in order to survive with such a past. The public narrations of the past, those that are authorized or official, such as celebrations, commemorations and monuments, can lend meaning to individual memories and give to the new generation the possibility of facing the "unthinkable": the attempt to make a whole society disappear. But official memories can, conversely, mutilate personal memories.[12]

The articulation that originates in a research project then becomes a production of culture and finally a collective work of memory. It does not come in and of itself, especially because it entails a real effort to ascertain that each individual can be heard, not only as a "victim", but also as a person capable of reflection on his situation and commenting upon it. Listening to another put his story into words is to re-introduce him in his full humanity and restore him to the possession of his individuality. Concrete experiences show us that this work is not accomplished of its own accord, in particular because the investigative process or legal proceedings do not always demand that the tortuous path of the individual narrative's insuperable sufferings be followed. The testimony of a young woman before the International Criminal Tribunal for Rwanda tragically highlights this rift between the individual's story and bureaucratic procedures. During the genocide, she had been raped several times by members of the Hutu militia. In the course of the hearing, the defence attorney asked of her: "There was no water during the genocide, to such an extent that you must have smelled quite unpleasant; explain to me how, despite that, these men could have raped you a number of times." The young woman's response was without appeal: "Sir, I understand that you are not so different from the Hutus." Here we have a very current example of the discrepancy between two different registers of truth. People working for the defence of human rights regularly hear investigators complaining of the divergent accounts and ever-changing testimony they receive: "Why don't we ever get the same version of what happened?" Staying with the example of Rwanda, one might ask: Why did the woman who had at first declared that her mother was killed in a church later claim that the murder took place in the swamps? Had she "lied"? Or rather was it simply that it was less painful to her to portray her mother as having been assassinated in a respectable place and not in the middle of nowhere, hunted down like an animal? Reflection on the process of constructing a narrative should in itself be an object of interdisciplinary research.

The difficulty for someone directly confronted with such situations lies in accepting that the work of reconstruction, like the work of history, involves an impossible exercise, not in objectivity but in objectification. As if the horror were not enough, the analyst is confronted by contradictory memories and accounts that are unspeakable or even impossible to reconstruct. Conflicting depictions and imageries will form around acts of violence. Different myths will be conjured up, offering varying interpretations of the event, including the most "delusional" (in the psychoanalytical meaning of the term). These memories are constructed in the interweaving of individual memories and collective memories, which rewrite more distant memory that includes even long-term history, as in the cases of the Balkans or the Great Lakes region of Central Africa. Celebrations and commemorations play a major role in this respect. The same is true of "places of memory". In the case of the Rwandan genocide, such places can be found in Rwanda itself, as well as in the larger Great Lakes region, Europe and the United States. Narratives from the outside recounted by original members of the group (particularly refugees) become linked to those of "survivors" who remained or returned to the country after the event. One interesting example of the analysis of such constructions can be found in anthropologist Liisa Malkki's work on Hutu refugees.[13] The anthropologist and psychiatrist Maurice Eisenbruch carried out a comparable study in Cambodia,[14] and Janine Altounian's reflections on Armenia are also worthy of mention.[15]

In the historian's case, the authentic, scientific establishment of the circumstances of a massacre that is destined for a wide audience can become a component of a work of "justice". The issue at stake is participating in the verification of indispensable truths so that the community can begin to rebuild. The critical dimension of history can be threatened to the extent that the historian attempts to establish certainty in his work, especially with statistics, in spite of the widely recognized fact that, by definition, the conclusions of all historical studies are likely to be questioned by subsequent work. The debate surrounding the exact numbers of the Nazi genocide of the Jews is a well-known example of this. At times the search for irrefutable evidence can also generate demonstrations of evidence that rely upon material proof, such as the construction of the crematory ovens. In this way, historical researchers provide an illustration of how historical demonstration participates in the construction of collective memory.[16] Historians, however, must content themselves with "vulnerability", in Bruno Bettelheim's expression, in the formulation of their conclusions, as they are not unassailable vis-à-vis the perspective of the witnesses and their descendents. Faced with these social realities, the writing of history is a delicate task because it must not only account for the initial facts and place them in context, but it must also acknowledge the confrontation between conflicting memories. Furthermore, it must reveal the processes of instrumentalization and mythification, while avoiding engaging in a senseless diatribe against the state or other power-group.

At the same time that they are negotiating access to the object of their research, historians are confronted with a history of memory in and of itself. After the population's initial traumatism, silence reigns, owing to the absence of verbalization on the part of the survivors, the desire of those responsible to minimize what they have done, and most of all to the will of the state authorities to close the door on a period of conflict.[17] Far from working on a dead issue, however, the historian is faced with the "second life" of his object. History lives on in the subjectivity of the descendants; thus the historian must deal with the expectations of the victims or their descendants, who make a well-known and legitimate demand – the acknowledgement of their suffering. In this "competition of victims"[18] phenomenon, historians can find themselves drawn, against their will, into the struggle over memory. Consequently, the critical writing of history stumbles upon an obstacle that is difficult to obviate. The massacre is in itself an absolute, a finality and an extreme, after the experience of which the routine of daily life is profoundly shaken. How can one admit that "history continues"? How can one even begin to comprehend the fact that the violence has created new social connections, notably between the groups that supported the perpetrators? For the survivors and the descendants of the victims, the massacre is a rupture in the historical thread that must now be mended, in all its complexity and contradictions, in order to restore the continuation of history. The historian's narrative must not aspire to serve as a substitute for the voices of the witnesses, nor even for the narratives of the descendants of the "victims" or the "executioners", given that it operates on a different level and aims, by its very nature, to prevent individual and collective life from becoming caught in the cycle of vengeance. Nevertheless, the narrative, grounded in scientific method, must be offered to the community with deliberate acknowledgement of its limitations and of its debt to both the witnesses and present-day criticism.

In this manner, historians mingle their work with that of culture and the individuals composing it. They must, however, assume their own position. The ultimate objective of history is to give meaning to past events and to inscribe them in the passage of time, doing so with the hope of preventing or limiting the chances that tragedies will recur, or at least raising the population's awareness of the risks. This is a constitutional element of history in the scientific sense: It aims to transform that narrative into a moment of comprehension and social intervention, so that it becomes the occasion to participate in that development essential to all societies, that of putting the past behind us.

All these considerations are particularly important to keep in mind for researchers and practitioners who work on contemporary history. Indeed, those who are used to conflict and post-conflict situations know that in such circumstances, most critical information concerning the conflict is difficult to obtain or has been manipulated. Statistics on refugee flows, for example, are subject to negotiations and adjustments between local authorities, warring parties, humanitarian organizations, Western governments and so on. The way in which a conflict is defined and portrayed at the international level has more to do with diplomatic struggles (for example, the debates in the United Nations Security Council) than with the conflict itself. In the field, there are generally as many explanations and views of a conflict as there are people involved. Several contributors to this book will emphasize the difficulty of identifying what counts as "evidence" of a mass crime. This is a particularly tricky issue in such circumstances. As a consequence, researchers have to be mindful of their potential reactions. Because they do not know what they are "witnessing", even after the event, they might tend to (re-)present an undifferentiated round of suffering or a carnival of horror that ignores the political and social dimensions of the drama. Scholars may also be tempted, as in the case of humanitarian workers or journalists, to "rework" the account in order to overlay their own "authentic" version of the facts or, quite simply, to construct their own narrative. Since trauma is overwhelming, there is a risk that this narrative could take the place of the unbearable silence and replace the impossible words.

This last aspect is particularly important from an ethical point of view. In fact, listening and recording the words of the other is not sufficient, as the example of Guatemala shows. In that country, exceptional work was done by the Proyecto de Recuperación de la Memoria Histórica (the Project on the Recuperation of Historical Memory published a report, *Guatamala: Nunca Más*, by the archbishop of Guatemala City) and the Comisión para el Esclarecimiento Histórico (Historical Clarification Commission). A large space was reserved for the testimony of witnesses and survivors. Nonetheless, the people concerned have felt frustrated because nothing was done to return their narrative to them. A multilingual version of the testimony for a general audience is in the process of being prepared, although it is coming quite late in the eyes of the victims. As a general rule, one must question the role played by reconstructed narratives in a national or international legal framework, as in the case of truth and reconciliation commissions and, to an even greater extent, in the cases of the International Criminal Tribunals for the former Yugoslavia and Rwanda, insofar as they attempt to offer a certain representation of what has occurred. The work of Mark Osiel shows how these judicial mechanisms shape collective memory and reveals the many contradictions in that process.[19] For example, the recollection of events, reduced to a few "symbolic" cases and to a narrative that is disconnected from the victims and their families, can work against a genuine "effort of memory". For these people, their point of view has not been understood – the deaths or disappearances of their children and loved ones are qualified as being of negligible importance, and there is an attempt to make them believe that all of it never really happened. Reproaches of this kind are often heard in countries where truth and reconciliation commissions have been set up, even in those where the process is deliberately presented to the outside world as an undeniable success, after the example of South Africa. In Bosnia-Herzegovina, officials in the Office of the Prosecutor at the International Criminal Tribunal for the former Yugoslavia admit that many of the accounts received over the years have not been transmitted to the Hague because the massacres that they shed light upon are not "important" enough according to criteria based on the number or identity of those responsible, measures that are difficult for those affected to understand. Those voluminous files that the prosecutor decides not to pursue because the Tribunal does not have the time or the means to address them, those dozens of witnesses that the judges refuse to hear – such decisions are the result of material and human limitations that can be understood rationally. But what about the pain of the victims and their families? The words of suffering, frustration, anger and also bitterness that are evoked serve to remind us that the work of memory cannot neglect this subjective dimension.

Several reasons can be given to explain the importance of including these subjective dimensions in the work of memory on both the individual and the collective levels. First of all, the experience of traumatic events may differ greatly from region to region and among different people or groups of people; moreover, dates and places, which are considered particularly important and even representative of the violence, can vary significantly. In this light, the reconstruction of local histories of violence becomes essential. Second, the religious, cultural and symbolic dimensions of the trauma can be as important as the more "objective" ones, since they are both factual and immediate, such as with the disappearance or death of a loved one, or the experience of torture. Furthermore, in Guatemala and Cambodia alike, the genocidal project had the declared intention of destroying a culture and a history. In the narratives of victims and survivors, these aspects form an integral part of the violation of their rights and their emotional experience. Third, the representations and the imaginaries that are built around the experience of violence allude to myths that provide varying interpretations of the events. The borders between what one knows and of what one is unaware, and between what one has seen and has imagined are often considerably blurred, particularly in times when rumours are legion and feeding the fires of fear. In such circumstances, the historical constructions of threats and the enemy must be examined, and must not be reduced to simplistic manifestations of paranoia and extremism. In her work on Hutu refugees, Liisa Malkki shows how the circumstances of exile can transform the meaning of history and of belonging, and how a particular refugee camp became a site where experiences, memory, nightmares and rumours of violence converged to shape and re-shape the moral categories of good and evil.[20] As a result, forgetfulness and manipulation can predominate even if the community has a good knowledge of history, to the point where it no longer seems necessary to mention well-known facts. Working with imaginaries implies that one can never think that enough has been said, nor can one allow silence to reign in a space where various forms of revisionism could materialize. This is an even greater imperative given that the fields of the imaginary and of the unexpressed word are long afterwards burdened by the scars of violence, leaving them even more vulnerable to manipulation on the part of the perpetrators of violence.

Conclusion

Understanding how and why people commit mass crimes is essential to prevent future catastrophes and to mitigate their destructive consequences. Yet researching or working in this kind of situation is particularly difficult. The usual questioning of social scientists and practitioners is intensified in all respects. In addition to the unique moral and psychological issues involved in the act of a massacre, the subjective nature of the events as well as the difficulty of obtaining, classifying and analysing information oblige us to re-evaluate constantly our personal ethics while simultaneously keeping open all potential avenues of thought and research. There is no easy explanation for the tragedy of mass crimes; there is no single or definitive answer to all the questions they raise. This is the reason why a multi-disciplinary approach seems particularly important in such contexts. Fully aware of the highly subjective nature of any analysis that may be put forward, researchers also have to bear responsibility for it with respect to their audience. Moreover, fulfilling one's personal responsibility as a researcher or practitioner also means considering the issue of one's commitment to the people who are the subject of one's investigations. Thus the question of the status of the researcher's work is raised. To whom is it directed? It appears to us that this kind of questioning should also consider the direct or indirect consequences that research could (or should) have for the people concerned. This reflection must include an exploration of the potential policy implications of the work and of the methodological choices. Of course, one should not ignore how social scientists and other intellectuals (including psychiatrists) have contributed to the commission of mass crimes. The histories, interpretations and ideologies that some of them have helped elaborate have greatly contributed to terrible and destructive violence in the past. More often, however, analyses produced by scholars and practitioners may have an effect not only on international decisions and portrayals communicated to the wider public, but also on the specific direction taken in humanitarian agendas and aid programs. Much remains to be done in order to increase our current level of accountability in these matters.

Notes

1. Christopher Browning, *Ordinary Men: Reserve Police Battalion 101 and the Final Solution in Poland*, New York: Harper Collins Publishers, 1992, p. 9.
2. The term *"sociologie compréhensive"* (henceforth without quotation marks) in French is meant to be not all-embracing. It means that it is developed from the perspective of meaning: It seeks to enter the other person's subjectivity and perceive it as *historical consciousness.*
3. On the subject of the experience of totalitarian violence, Hannah Arendt referred to "the experience of not belonging to the world at all, which is among the most radical and desperate experiences of man" Hannah Arendt, *The Origins of Totalitarianism*, 6th ed., New York and London: Harcourt Brace Jovanovich, 1979, p. 475.
4. *Eichmann in Jerusalem: A Report on the Banality of Evil*, first published 1961.
5. See Paul Ricoeur, *La mémoire, l'histoire, l'oubli*, Paris: Seuil, 2000; *Temps et récit*, Paris: Seuil, 3 vols, 1983–1985; Jean Greisch, *Paul Ricoeur: L'itinéraire du sens*, Grenoble: Million, 2001.
6. Hannah Arendt, *The Human Condition*, Chicago: University of Chicago Press, first published 1958, p. 110.
7. Pierre Bourdieu, *La misère du monde*, Paris: Seuil, 1993, pp. 9–11.
8. See Jerome Bruner, *Car la culture donne forme à l'esprit: De la révolution cognitive à la psychologie culturelle*, Paris: Eshel, 1991.
9. See René Kaës, *Violence d'Etat et psychanalyse*, Paris: Dunod, 1989.
10. Ibid.
11. This figure represents 10 per cent of the total population of Cameroon at the time and more than 70 per cent of the Bamileke population.
12. See Maurice Halbwachs, *La mémoire collective*, Paris: Albin Michel, 1997; Marie-Claire Lavabre, "Usages et mésusages de la notion de mémoire", *Critique Internationale*, no. 7, April 2000, pp. 48–57.
13. See Liisa Malkki, *Purity and Exile: Violence, Memory, and National Cosmology among Hutu Refugees in Tanzania*, Chicago: University of Chicago Press, 1995.

14. See Maurice Eisenbruch, "Mental Health and the Cambodian Traditional Healer for Refugees Who Resettled, Were Repatriated or Internally Displaced, and for Those Who Stayed at Home", *Collegium Antropologicum* 18, no. 2, 1994, pp. 219–230; see also his contribution in this volume.
15. See Janine Altounian, *La survivance: Traduire le trauma collectif*, Paris: Dunod, Coll. "Inconscient et culture", 2000.
16. See Daniel Pressac, *Les crématoires d'Auschwitz*, Paris: CNRS, 1993.
17. In the case of French history, see for instance Jean-Clément Martin, *La Vendée de la Mémoire*, Paris: Seuil, 1989; Henry Rousso, *Le Syndrome de Vichy*, Paris: Seuil, 1990.
18. Jean-Michel Chaumont, *La concurrence des victimes*, Paris: Découverte, 1997.
19. See Mark Osiel, *Mass Atrocity, Collective Memory and the Law*, New Brunswick, NJ: Transaction, 1997.
20. See Malkki, *Purity and Exile*.

2

Contested memories: Peace-building and community rehabilitation after violence and mass crimes – A medico-anthropological approach

Roberto Beneduce

There is no amnesic society[1]

As an anthropologist and a psychiatrist, I have worked in different war and post-conflict contexts since 1994.[2] My involvement in rehabilitation and training programs first of all focused on the evaluation of war trauma effects on populations and the psychosocial needs of specific vulnerable groups – orphan children, female-headed families and so on. At the same time, I have been involved in training social and health workers. The issues I have addressed during seminars and informal meetings concerned trauma, post-traumatic stress disorder (PTSD) and cultural responses to bereavement and suffering. In some cases, such as when I was in Mozambique, I had the possibility of working with traditional healers, whose activities were strategic in the community and in the individual treatment of trauma and violence. In all of these cases, I came to understand the importance of a historically rooted outlook and the value of a culturally sensitive approach, given that dealing with traumatic experiences and painful memories – symbolic as well as material wounds – does not permit univocal strategies.

A large literature has critiqued the abuse of PTSD in non-Western societies and has emphasized community approaches in rehabilitation strategies. On the other hand, in contexts where ethnic conflict, enduring war and "structural violence" destroy the basis of social cooperation, it is the term "community" itself that has to be rethought. Past experiences demonstrate that the success of rehabilitation and peace-building strategies

After mass crime: Rebuilding states and communities, Pouligny, Chesterman and Schnabel (eds), United Nations University Press, 2007, ISBN 978-92-808-1138-4

closely depends on a deep understanding of the cultural, historic and economic roots of conflicts and the mechanisms of their reproduction, as well as the deep social transformations caused by wartime. Given these presuppositions, this chapter focuses on the following aspects:

First, how can "the past" contribute to the perception of and solutions to current conflicts? Is history a resource or a curse, sustaining an apparently never-ending cycle of hate, suspicion and vendettas? To what extent do embodied memories contribute to the reproduction of violent behaviours? How many forms of "historical conscience" or memory does one have to take into consideration when working on reconciliation strategies in post-conflict contexts?

Second, atrocities and violence characterizing recent conflicts and wars reveal an internal logic, a specific kind of "rationality", and thus call for specific forms of research. Only a proper analysis of contexts, including global and local forces, can avoid the risk of essentializing universal, hidden structures that would underlie all events falling under the "atrocity", "mass crime" or "dirty war" labels. As Donald Crummey stated, "The real challenge is to see violence within its social setting, to appreciate its roots in social conflict, and to understand why and how people turn to it."[3]

Third, rehabilitation strategies need to be based upon accurate analysis of forms of violence and their reproduction, the social roots of particular violence and the ways by which it has been embodied in rituals, habits and the social imagination over time. In many cases violence becomes an everyday form of life, without any "mysterious" or "extraordinary" character. Colonial rule and organized forms of violence in post-colonial states have often played a direct role in the genealogy of some cases of mass crimes as well as in their macabre expression. Specific examples help when considering the relevance of this issue within peace-building intervention and, more generally, in social and community rehabilitation in war and post-war periods. Humanitarian strategies could become useless if the deep roots of violence are forgotten or underestimated.

Fourth, this chapter briefly considers how new forms of "occult economies"[4] and "emerging power complexes"[5] intersect with local or regional economic interests, thus contributing to the reproduction of war and its organizational impact (e.g., land access and gold, diamond and mineral exploitation are at the heart of the current conflict in the Democratic Republic of the Congo). Koen Vlassenroot and Timothy Raeymakers have emphasized how a double shift in authority takes place: "from patrimonial to military (and non-territorial) networks of control, and from 'traditional' to armed rulers".[6] These shifts have to be analysed in order to explain to what extent "armed conflict changed relations between power and powerlessness, and to what extent these changing strategies and relations should be seen as a 'side-effect' of war or, on the contrary, a reflection of an enduring social transformation" able to produce an alternative system of power and profit.[7] These aspects are particularly relevant in my research about violent identity formation among young people and self-representation in contemporary Africa.

Fifth, the last aspect that receives specific attention is the question of how adequate are psychiatric categories such as "trauma", "mourning" or "post-traumatic stress disorder" in non-Western countries. My experience, in addition to a vast medico-anthropological literature, suggests a) that these categories are not able to cope with all the cultural and psychological meanings of trauma-related experiences in these societies, and b) that local healing strategies and cultural conceptions of death or mourning can represent a useful ("therapeutic") tool for individuals or communities affected by traumatic experiences. Unfortunately, international teams of experts sometimes ignore or underestimate these kinds of local resources, putting them under the disputable label of "harmful traditional practices". Nevertheless, the so-called "traditional healers" constitute a potential resource to cope with fear, uncertainty and "pollution" concerns that mark people's experiences during and after war in many African or Asian countries. This chapter stresses that community-based rehabilitation should take into consideration these spontaneous resources for another reason as well: The language and the ideology of local healers or other social actors, apart from controversial uses sometimes described in literature, are often largely shared by the population and can therefore assist in reconstituting a common perspective and re-establishing pre-war forms of authority.

The purpose of these considerations is to contribute to the historical, cultural and psychosocial logic sustaining the reproduction of violence as well as reconciliation and rehabilitation process after violent conflicts. The success of peacekeeping interventions largely depends, as stated by John Borneman, on the ability to promote agreement about the present (not a consensus or an idealized harmony) based on understanding, and "a departure into new relations of affinity marked not by cyclical violence but by trust and care".[8]

The past as an ambiguous resource, or How to "unlock the past"

There is no one way of relating to the past and the future and therefore of being in history.[9]

Analysis of the genealogy and the reproduction of violence calls for a methodological approach that is able systematically to combine social and political analysis, local history and a global perspective. In the absence of this interweaving, interpretations remain fragmented, leaving in the shadows key aspects, amongst which are the economic interests that are often at the root of recent conflicts. The experiences of these past years have shown that, from Central America to the Balkans and the Horn of Africa, problems and contradictions in the processes of peace have proven to be much more complex than some peace building interventions imagined. From Somalia to Bosnia-Herzegovina, the "desire for reconciliation" of the groups involved has not been enough to ensure stability and avoid prolonging conflict and punishment. The panorama in Africa is particularly confused and the solutions to be adopted are made extremely difficult by the complex evolution of the post-colonial state. Nevertheless, an accurate analysis of the context and the uniqueness of each conflict rarely precedes peace-building interventions and community-rehabilitation strategies. For these reasons, these efforts have encountered many difficulties in attaining any degree of success. It is easy to understand why the reconstruction of a new social fabric and productive bargaining between groups and interests often remains only a project.[10] In addition, when a preliminary analysis of the economic, ethnographic and social horizon does not define the strategies of intervention, "violence", "atrocities" and the "barbarian" character of wars and people risk being the main categories shaping the debate. This leads to the reproduction of old stereotypes. Africa has long been represented in the Western imagination as a place of nightmares (from cannibalism and witchcraft to a type of sexuality described as "distinct" and unregulated), and this dark and worrying image continues to be evoked.[11] Achille Mbembe's reflections regarding these risks are particularly pertinent: "Distance has to be equally taken with regards to a series of clichés and fantasies that view politics in Africa as only a pathology."[12] These clichés (the so called New Barbarism argument) are at the heart of Irving Kaplan's thesis on Sierra Leone's recent conflict that was so strongly criticized by Paul Richards.[13]

Whatever view is adopted, the role that history has played in the genealogy of violence and current conflicts is uncontested. John Lonsdale emphasizes that Africa's past, in spite of its burden of violence and pain, could come to the "rescue of its future".[14] The seemingly obvious invitation, to reclaim historical and anthropological depth when thinking about strategies of peace building and community rehabilitation, however, poses as many problems as it resolves. History's "subversive"[15] contribution to the resolution of contemporary problems and the construction of a new balance remains controversial. Some researchers underline that history is sometimes a "scarce resource",[16] whose interpretations and rewritings remain subject to distinct obstacles.[17]

Concerning the pervasive language of victimization and the freezing of the past in a nativist and Afro-radical discourse, Mbembe has stressed more recently that "The encounter between Africa and the West resulted in a deep wound: a wound that cannot heal until the ex-colonized rediscover their own being and their own past." Nevertheless, "the past is imagined as not only the home of the truth of the self but also the site of its falsification through the violence committed by the other. To summon the future, one must first unlock the past, or more precisely, break the chains that link that past to a demonic lie: the supposed existence of a *hole* at the very heart of the African being."[18] This of course becomes highly problematic when the past is perceived as humiliated, tortured or negated. In some cases, history becomes a resource, which, figuratively speaking, is absent or cannot be appropriated. It is so for those who have not known anything but conflict and humiliation. This is the case for the Betsileo in Madagascar: "For the descendants of the slaves ... it was not the pressure of history and memory that was felt as a kind of violence, but the very lack of it."[19]

Even though the adoption of a historically deterministic model cannot, alone, offer explanations of violence and the mechanisms that lead to its reproduction[20] or provide useful insights for the prevention and management of future conflicts, exploration of the distinct ways in which different social groups or societies conceive "history" and understand the various strategies for creating, reproducing or erasing specific "habitus" (to use Pierre Bourdieu's term) remains a priority.[21] The necessity of this reflection, for this questioning of history and society, becomes clear in all its intensity in those cases in which collective memory seems to have come up against a real collapse of reason created by violence and atrocities experienced during conflicts. This violence is often impossible to place, seeming to have occurred simply *out of history*. As Inge Brinkman recounts, the dominant theme in the accounts of Angolan refugees in Namibia was the absurd character of much that had happened, and much less attention was placed on any attempt to analyse the scope of the macabre violence perpetrated against them.[22] This sensation of oppressive senselessness is felt even more where violence seems to arise without direct connections to other events or strategies, without conceivable political ends: as if it were created by a separate logic or, as has been suggested, autonomously. Looking at the cases of the Renamo (the Mozambican National Resistance Party), the Revolutionary United Front in Sierra Leone or the National Patriotic Front of Liberia provides clear examples of guerrilla movements that have spread terror and that do not have any political program worthy of the name.

When violence and fear become a way of life, against a background of repeated insecure conditions and a general experience of terror, everyday life seems to become a real cultural and social apocalypse. The psychological defence against this sort of experience manifests itself often in a type of indifference, a stunned and generalized apathy or, depending on the case, participation in acts of violence, banditry and rebellion.[23] This aspect deserves particular attention when rehabilitation interventions are planned or carried out, from the moment that this complex combination of individual (psychological) and social metamorphoses possibly becomes a serious obstacle to the strategies that are normally used in conflict contexts. The recent move from an emphasis on issues of health and social justice to a central role for human rights constitutes another issue, not without its consequences. The shift of attention on the part of donors, non-governmental organizations (NGOs) and the mass media from structural problems and long term interventions, which were oriented towards assuring better living conditions (e.g., social justice, bettering scholastic and health institutions, better access to resources, increase in family income), to only emergency cases, has begun to pose problems in international law.[24]

When looking at more concrete strategies of peace keeping and community rehabilitation, one must deal with another dilemma: How to respond to the psychological needs of the victims of these atrocities and violence if one does not know the local forms and logic of social ties, their transformations and above all the cultural strategies of dealing with death, mourning and suffering?[25] How can interventions be made without an initial analysis of local conceptions of illness and healing? Is a universal, medically founded notion of "trauma" sufficient to intervene in an appropriate manner? What role can religious leaders, traditional doctors and local associations (e.g., women's groups, youth groups) have in the reconstruction of the social fabric and a "minimum standard" of community and sharing? What contributions can and do local agents make to the healing of individual and collective suffering? Barely mentioned in the many available reports and manuals, this resource has been, with few exceptions, more than often simply ignored. The difficulties encountered by models of rehabilitation and peace-building plans proposed for times of war or post-conflict periods are due not only to the complexity of the situations, but also to their chosen methodological approaches, which overlook cultural and social specificity. As will be stressed in a following paragraph, attitudes underlying experts' intervention strategies and some concepts such as "PTSD", "rehabilitation" and "humanitarian emergency" can even be counterproductive and contribute to the reproduction of scenarios dominated by confusion and passivity.

The world falls apart: Uncertainties and atrocities

The globalization era is characterized by the increasing weakening of nation-states, economic deregulation, new forms of pauperization and criminalization, occult economies, new forms of "alien-nation" and most importantly a large social as well as epistemological uncertainty.[26] Against some predictions, globalization is making the conundrum of cultural difference even more complex. These uncertainties are well expressed by new figures of modernity (such as foreigners, consumers, vagabonds and *Sapeurs*[27]) and, above all, by illegal migrants and refugees, people without a state, who are directly produced, according to the well-known analysis of Hannah Arendt, by the crisis of nation-states. It is not without reason that the Arab term to define an illegal migrant in Morocco is *"harraga*, 'the burner', pointing to a literal 'incineration' of identity, a reduction of the self to an unclassifiable being that defies categorization – a beyond of all citizenship".[28] Nor does uncertainty only concern identity and appearances. Adam Ashforth underlines how in post-apartheid South Africa spiritual insecurity pervades personal relations, family and close relationships. According to Stephen Ellis, "There is a broad agreement among Liberian religious thinkers that the occurrence of war is prima facie evidence of grave spiritual disorder."[29]

The relationship between globalization, uncertainty and violence are worth closer examination. For example, Jon Abbink has brought into focus an explicit connection between new forms of violence that articulate the lives of ethnic groups such as the Chai in Ethiopia and the spread of new languages and images diffused by "video-culture". The excess of violence seen in recent years expresses among other things a struggle to monopolize the instruments, idiom and exertion of violence itself.[30] The entrance of the state into local society has therefore not necessarily eradicated or diminished, as one might have hoped according to Norbert Elias's well-known model, the recourse to violence;[31] in many cases, it has simply changed its nature and scope. This prospective theory has also been assumed by Bogumil Jewsiewicki, who states that the autonomy of the actual conflicts reveals a search, on the part of the actors involved, for strategies and resources that allow them to transform the post-colonial state into local and regional political institutions. In addition to these processes, other dynamics beg consideration, in particular those derived from those big bazaars that are globalization and modernity.

At the moment when multinationals began to bend the laws of nation-states, recombining at their own will forms of production, mechanisms of distribution and circulation of goods, the sovereignty of states saw a rapid and definitive decline. This contributed to the drawing of what Arjun Appadurai defines as a new order of uncertainty.[32] The forms of this uncertainty vary, but it is usually accompanied by the growth of an intolerable level of anxiety with regards to relations between groups and individuals and the definitions of the boundaries of the social body and corporate groups. When large-scale movements of peoples put into discussion the boundaries of ethnic identity, when social networks are torn and acts of terror are no longer unfathomable, uncertainty can go beyond ordinary limits and precipitate general violence. The devices of violence and massacre, of the mutilation of bodies and of torture, then become strategies aimed at creating "a macabre form of certainty".[33] The devastation of bodies paradoxically becomes a device for creating certainty in the face of difference, assuming the character of a "brutal technique (or folk-discovery procedure) about 'them' and, therefore, about 'us'".[34] Sexual violence expresses a particular aspect of these dynamics: "The penis in ethnocidal rape is simultaneously an instrument of degradation, of purification, and of a grotesque form of intimacy with the ethnic other."[35] Liisa Malkki's analysis can be used to document the relationship between uncertainty and ethnic violence. Appadurai begins from the moment that the questions generated by this type of uncertainty about the ways of identifying the ethnic body became one of the premises for the explosion of violence in Burundi. Today this theory offers a privileged reading for the analysis of this kind of crisis.

The colonial attempt to list the physical signs that would have allowed for the identification of differences between the ethnic groups of Hutu and Tutsi (with sufficient certainty to allow one to kill the "other", the enemy) failed. The instability of these necrographic maps successively determines the death strategies put into action: The ethnic body turned out to be itself unstable and "deceptive". Ken Wilson pointed out that in Mozambique the cultic and ritualized manner in which acts of violence were perpetrated had its symbolic and material reasons: to render women's bodies infertile, and to block or render hemorrhagic the vital flows by insertion, impalement or, alternatively, severance.[36] The preoccupation with intervening on certain parts of the body via terrifying acts reveals an attempt to fix and stabilize once and for all the body of the ethnic "other". These acts would eliminate the uncertainty produced by individual physical variations and by the "contamination" produced by exchanges, contacts and marriages.[37] Only the death of the "other", the dismemberment of its body or, alternatively, the inscribing of permanent marks (scars) seem to produce a certainty about boundaries between groups. The body becomes at the same time a source and a target of violence, and, when people survive mutilations and violence, a specific horrific form of embodied history is also produced: an unspeakable history. Furthermore, many of these atrocities committed in ritualized forms make ritual burial impossible.[38] What has been called in the literature the "standardization of the techniques of violence and death" is not uncommon in these phenomena, "routinized symbolic schemes of nightmarish cruelty".[39]

In the fluidity of the positions and the roles generated by these acts, it is possible to include those actors who were the holders of specific powers in the past (that of, for example, killing, of making invulnerable, of witchcraft, of metamorphosis). This becomes possible in new ways, as was the case with traditional healers in Mozambique or in Zimbabwe. This assumes that the terror remains in or falls back into some sense of cultural boundaries, in which the actions of such cultural agents make at least minimal sense. However, to be efficient, a culture of terror has to be able to challenge all of the rules of logic. It affirms through its acts another order of experience. The traumatic successes of terror operations derive largely from the impossibility, for the victims, of giving the acts any kind of meaning. The extraordinary nature of this violence is due in large part to its partial or total disconnection from a shared social order. The production of a "culture of terror", whose incomprehensible or gratuitous nature seems often to negate any possibility of historical analysis, in this way constitutes the peculiar effect of generalized, ritualized and spectacular violence, which appears to be out of space and time. The victims of terror, in their efforts to resist, can do nothing other than emphasize its absurd character. Nevertheless, they feel a necessity in some way to elaborate upon their own human existence, beyond absurdity. In his widely acclaimed research on the war in Sierra Leone and the meaning of terror and violence, Paul Richards emphasized another issue to take into account, which is that terror is also engaged in not only for the purpose of creating or easing a sense of randomness and ennui in its victims; it may well have very concrete and rational objectives:

> Terror is supposed to unsettle its victims. The confused accounts of terrorized victims of violence do not constitute evidence of the irrationality of violence.... Take for instance, a spate of incidents in villages between Bo and Moyamba in September–October 1995 in which rebels cut off the hands of village women. What clearer instance could there be of a reversion to primitive barbarity? ... But behind the savage series of incidents lay, in fact, a set of simple strategic calculations. The insurgent movement spreads by capturing young people. Short of food in the pre-harvest period, some captives, irrespective of the risks, sought to defy the movement and return to their villages where the early harvests was about to commence. How could the rebels prevent such defection? By stopping the harvest. When the news of rebel amputations spread in central Sierra Leone (the rice granary of the war-affected region) few women were prepared to venture out into the fields. The harvest ceased.[40]

The desire to eliminate the "other" or to impose authority creates perverse behaviour. Even though this analysis demonstrates the "rationality" of violence and its varied purposes, it does not diminish its unbearable character: The amputated hands remain irrevocable marks on (into) the body of those women and in collective memory, living signs of death and power. In all these cases, the decomposition of the post-colonial state, the failure of systems of norms and sanctions, seem to be reflected directly in the dismemberment of bodies. During the deterritorialization of identity and social ties, decomposition is added to decomposition, and only the body is left to "create meaning".[41] This is well expressed in the Democratic Republic of the Congo (DRC) or Sierra Leone, for example, by the ritual preparation that often precedes the atrocity and in the care taken by the fighters who participate in these actions in putting on war paint.[42]

Post-colonial subjectivities, wartime and identity formation

Strategies of violence have received more and more attention from anthropologists and psychiatrists, especially in cases that deal with the relation between the dimension of incomprehensibility and the victims' capacity to reconstruct social ties during or after violence; it is also of particular importance to construct new forms of social ties. In addition, it is of particular interest to consider victims' ability to process the experience of terror and violence inflicted by the "other". Speaking about "a state of war", as Achille Mbembe suggests, is extremely legitimate in order to describe the profound impact of this peculiar social logic of violence, suspicion and hate. It perhaps illuminates one of the most complex aspects to keep in mind during strategies of peace building: "The state of war in contemporary Africa should be thought of as an institutionalized imaginary, as a general cultural experience that fashions identities, along the same lines as the family, school, and other social systems."[43] Mbembe's analysis echoes the "habitus of war" concept proposed by Rosalind Shaw,[44] and it is particularly important to this discussion where he defines war in many African countries as an ordinary condition, a sort of permanent mental state: "By war, the African individual changes his/her own subjectivity and produces ... something radically new."[45] In the forms of violence in times of war, the "state of war" in fact becomes the premise for a generalized right to exercise power to kill individually as much as collectively.[46] Apart from this, it is important to remember a further aspect: Terror, death and violence produce a deep psychic change in social actors, the transformation of daily experience, and represent a "high powered tool for domination and a principal medium of political practice".[47]

Youths are attracted to the possibilities offered by these strategies of assertion of the self by, in many cases, voluntarily participating in the activities of war.[48] Bogumil Jewsiewicki argues, "The frame of the subject who lives in Africa is ... mastered by indiscipline. The latter term is the space dominated by tactics: ... cut out his or her past, the subject is removed from his or her own place.... In Africa, where societies have been marked by the slave trade and by colonization, indiscipline offers the subject its sole tactical recourse – a negative one, to boot. Indiscipline makes it possible to resist, to remove oneself from the actions of the Other."[49]

The interest in these problems and inquiries is obvious for rehabilitative psychosocial intervention and the social reintegration of ex-fighters and child soldiers, and for researchers interested in measuring the degree of resilience of individuals and groups in extreme conditions. These issues are also essential to the success of peace-building operations. If, as Mbembe maintains, war transforms subjectivity and inscribes itself almost entirely in the modern "African practices of self",[50] how can one imagine interventions that are able to re-affiliate and re-think identities, subjectivities and ties produced by the logic of war and violence inside the process of peace?

Mass atrocities and wartime violence represent the central issues in these reflections. Nevertheless one must remind oneself of the massive nature of violence in Africa, and that violence plays a role in a widespread machinery of death, often assuming a "structural" character,[51] reflected in class divisions, urban and rural distinctions, the nature of poverty and so on, and in the practice of politics, which becomes increasingly violent. As Jon Abbink observed, the state in Africa has created a new structural opportunity for violence as an instrument for political ends. The structural dimension of violence goes back to its governance: those ways of governing that increase violence and produce disorder and chaos, without contributing to its productive character (this can be said of some East Asian countries).

At the same time, this has rendered the state particularly vulnerable to violent overthrows (the case of the DRC is particularly eloquent).[52] In a context characterized by persistent insecurity, electoral fraud, intimidation and repression, both the blind strength and the weakness of the state are brought to light. In the end, the ethnicization of politics brings these problems to a dead end, where in fact any possibility of change is neutralized *a priori*. It is not by chance that potential criticism of and individual insubordination against the state often becomes, *ipso facto*, mere "criminality", social deviance and a reason for violence exercised against those who cannot put up any resistance.[53]

The notion of *débrouillardise*, largely diffused in French-speaking Africa, is a euphemism or, if one prefers, the dark and ambiguous side of a struggle for survival in which no holds are barred. In the process of increasing production and distribution of violence, "ordinary" becomes strange, bodies are continuously reshaped, dismembered and sacrificed and their borders disrupted. The abdication of any social sense takes place side by side with cannibalistic or "incestuous" logic: "These practices and discourse are first and foremost significant on the level of a collective imaginary, desire and discourse which reflects the deeply felt angst experienced by the subaltern in a social reality that escapes or crushes him, and no longer seems to make sense."[54]

The analysis mentioned above helps to better explain how the attempt to exercise violence or other forms of coercion on the part of groups or individuals expresses also the desire, as mentioned earlier, to exercise a form of power. The evolution of the funeral ceremony in Kinshasa is exemplary of these dynamics: To the official collection traditionally organized by family members to help pay for the funeral costs, a collection on the part of youths has now been added. They build a roadblock and demand a fee from those who pass. To those who refuse, a substance composed of ashes from burnt tires and urine is applied to their arms and face, as a form of sanction. In short, if the moral crisis and poverty described by Guy-Marin Kamandji gives a background to this perversion and trivialization of death, one can also add that death's commemoration according to unexpected and uncontrollable principles also becomes an occasion for contesting and at the same time producing power.[55]

The current expressions of death, violence, war and torture require new conceptualizations from the moment that these practices intertwine with particular expressions of subjectivity. They represent, much more than could be anticipated using traditional anthropological models of ritual, strategies through which global and local orders of exchange and production are articulated. New accusations of witchcraft, eloquent expressions of the many forms of modernity that have proliferated throughout our time, reveal the hidden side of contemporary conflicts. They demonstrate new morals of desire and contradictory forms of assertion and identity formation.[56] Scholars also stress the particular forms by which social insecurity and violence can meet the logic of market and witchcraft. In a climate created by new, growing inequality, characterized by jealousy and envy and made even more unpromising by unemployment, witchcraft remains "a vibrant concomitant of everyday life",[57] which destroys the basis of the judicial system of "modern" states. Accusations of witchcraft consistently reported in the literature are not superfluous in a discussion that analyses the economy of death and violence, strategies of peace building or the possible forms of social ties in post-conflict contexts. Adam Ashforth, in the study previously cited, reminds that it is the suspects of witchcraft who contribute to the erosion of the actual social landscape in post-apartheid South Africa. Arjun Appadurai makes reference to the "brutality" of the theatre of witchcraft, magic and prophecy in order to investigate the gruesome acts in which the body is dismembered and violated in what has been defined by Allen Feldman as a form of "premortem autopsy".[58] Finally, it is once again the language of witchcraft that scrutinizes the relationships between generations and critiques economic and political power, as well as contemporary forms of accumulation.[59]

Between trauma, violence and war economies: Young people as "emerging subjects" in Africa

Switching from theory to action is not easy. The questions raised here bring to light some of the historical and social ties of the form and logic of violence in the post-colonial African context, as well as their reproduction. These questions familiarize an outlook on life in which recourse to violence does not have the "productive" dimension that political analysis in the last decade has insisted upon, where coercion is no longer monopolized by the state, and war or generalized violence represent practices of existence or sustainable livelihoods. These practices could also be considered strategies of formation and assertion of individual and collective identity and of diffused and profoundly internalized relational models. This perspective helps to avoid a double risk: the assumption that the breakdown of social order, mass atrocities and ghastly violence that distinguishes them constitute an "anomaly", an exception, a circumscribed time of chaos or, alternatively, a regression to barbarism.

Situating the dynamics and conflicts through which mass atrocities take shape in a historical and social continuum, one can more or less reduce the deviant, "exceptional" character often attributed to these types of events and that often forms the basis for the strategies of intervention that are based upon a logic of emergency. The hypothesis of a continuum between the state, economic and social crisis in post-colonial Africa, and globalization processes, between this kind of fragmentation and the ordinary atrocities characterizing political life in African countries, allows one to rethink the strategies of psychosocial rehabilitation aimed at helping societies in their entirety or individual groups (e.g., ex-fighters, child soldiers).

In fact, such a devastating fragmentation of social ties and individual conscience represents an additional problem to consider since it contributes to the paralysis of social rehabilitation and reconciliation strategies as well as of peace-building intervention. In other words, it obstructs the reconstruction of a possible everyday life in communities that have lived through a long siege of violence and poverty. And the moment arrives, whatever the role of the personnel in these contexts, to reflect on the "politics of memory"[60] and rhetoric of trauma that are the basis of Western intervention strategies and that direct their actions.

Psychiatrists seem on their part almost seduced by these problems. It is as if, in the dramas of war and in the notion of "post-traumatic stress disorders", they have found a new Klondike that has given them the quickest way to advance the hegemonic culture of their own categories and classifications, and of their epistemological (and moral) assumptions. Some aspects of the structural inadequacies revealed by this psychiatric vocabulary in non-Western post-conflict contexts will be examined here.

To speak of "trauma" today means almost inevitably to speak of PTSD. However, the scenes of war today have radically changed. The percentage of civilian victims has risen from 5 per cent in the First World War to 80 per cent in the Viet Nam War. Estimates are that between 1980 and 1988, 330,000 children and adolescents died in Angola and 440,000 died in Mozambique.[61] Social infrastructure and cultural symbols (e.g., schools, hospitals, churches) represent the current main target of military action in many "low-intensity wars".[62] The growing technicalization of military practice proceeds in parallel with a rationalization of horror and a conscious use of communications media.[63] It also allows for the inclusion of children, who have traditionally been excluded from this scenario: The recruitment of children today is becoming easier than ever. An AK-47, capable of firing thirty bullets with a pull of the trigger, costs less than a goat in many areas of Africa, and it is so light it can easily be shouldered by children of 8 to 10 years of age.[64] Nevertheless, it is rarely admitted that child soldiers can have many diverse reasons for enrolling. They have the chance to join a group within which considerable power can be gained, especially given their age; they are fed and nurtured in circumstances where previously they were not able to count on anyone; and they are armed and therefore feel immeasurably powerful. All this makes children in many cases into aware subjects, rational participants, and therefore no longer merely victims. In Sierra Leone, for example, some of the child soldiers interviewed admitted that they were not forced to enlist. Although the largest group was undoubtedly made up of children who were indeed forced to take part in actions of war, it is perhaps those who were not constrained by menaces to enlist who have the greatest difficulties in the programs of social rehabilitation and in demobilization. Krijn Peters and Paul Richards offer two main reasons to explain child participation in war. Apart from that technological reason (the availability of light and cheap arms), there is a sociological reason: "With their own families scattered by war, children are often intensely loyal to their fighting group, the company of comrades-in-arms serving in some measure as a family substitute."[65] The work of Alcinda Honwana comes from a similar perspective, and makes appropriate use of the dialectic between tactics and strategy as formulated by Michel de Certeau. Honwana maintains that the child soldiers during the period of civil war in Mozambique, innocent and guilty at the same time, and not necessarily passive, were exercising a tactical agency. Theirs was a "specific type of action conceived to confront the actual and immediate conditions of their lives, with the aim of maximizing the opportunities created by a violent and militarized environment", while they remained, in fact, in an extremely weak position.[66] This world bristles with contradictions and tensions: Young people and children are both marginalized and demonized, such as the children accused of witchcraft in Kinshasa. They may be expelled by families and condemned to living as "street children", but they are at the same time objects for involvement in war action and economic subjects able to create new forms of economy.[67]

A further aspect merits some attention: The direct participation of children and adolescents in conflicts does not always and necessarily imply psycho-pathological effects or damage to the development of the personality. When affirmed by constant motivations for the struggle, adult support and a clear ideologization of both conflict and context, research does not always reveal the development of distorted attitudes or the criminal activity associated with drug-taking. This was the case with much of the research surrounding the South African apartheid.[68] Moreover, as emphasized by other research, the long civil war in Northern Ireland has not led to an exponential increase in the number of cases of mental disorders.[69] Finally, Dinka children involved in the Sudanese civil war "managed remarkably well ... drawing on culture-specific coping skills.... Fewer than 5 percent reported their experiences of war and violence as reasons to be unhappy, although nostalgia and a longing for missing family and friends were common."[70] Given these findings, it makes little sense to speak of violence or of trauma in the psychiatric sense, outside precise social contexts. All this requires a deep rethinking of the conditions governing both children's and adolescents' psychological development and role in wartime, a rethinking that can help in recognizing how these "age groups" constitute real social forces today.

Placing the dead: Socio-cultural rehabilitation strategies vs dehistoricization of suffering

History has shown that social reform is the best medicine; it seems imperative that social justice and human rights perspectives should be at the heart of any work with war-affected populations.[71]

If war changes the way of life of its participants and its victims, if it forces the rethinking of the notion of "war trauma", this is also because it produces effects and experiences that often go well beyond psychological categories or psychiatric diagnoses. When violence and the kinds of experiences and effects such as those registered in the course of modern conflicts are brought back into the language of the medical-psychiatric sciences, they become less worrying, they end up being in some measure naturalized. This always happens in any act of medicalization: "Whilst a mass audience may find modern warfare, waged against ordinary civilians, almost unimaginable in its scale and brutality, when that experience is translated into the everyday language of stress, anxiety and trauma, *its character changes and it becomes less challenging.*"[72] One must also consider the vast difference between the psychiatric categories and the local idiom, between Western psychosocial intervention and cultural strategies employed to deal with experiences of violence, death and mourning, as well as symbolic and social change caused by long-term conflict itself.

In Uganda, war and violent transformation have weakened the power and authority of the elderly. As a result, ancient symbols and religious practices have continued to diminish in relevance. The value once attributed to the world of the ancestors is becoming more and more opaque in the common consciousness. The interruption of dialogue and ceremonial traditions honouring the dead has deeply affected emotional well-being in present day lives. Many people today present symptoms of psychological distress or mental disorders. These disorders are often expressed in the form of being possessed by the relatives who have died during the conflict when it was impossible to bury them according to traditional rituals.[73] This is not surprising considering that in a good part of Africa particular representations of the dead are active and that specific ideologies of death regulate their mourning and burial. Similar phenomena are found, for instance, in Mozambique amongst the survivors of the atrocious brutalities inflicted by the military forces of Renamo in the 1980s.

Because so many aspects are systematically excluded from the diagnostic categories and ignored in psychiatric manuals, many authors point out the limits of the notion of PTSD and the questionable universality of its relevance, and critique the idea of a common development starting from radically diverse traumatic experiences. More specifically, critiques have indicated how any presumed advantages deriving from the use of the diagnoses of PTSD (e.g., early recognition of symptoms, easily identified even by non-professionals; a sense of solace deriving from being supported by care groups; the reduction of the feelings of guilt and inadequacy) are far outweighed by the disadvantages.[74] The criticism of perspectives that claim the universal value of Western psychiatry certainly does not mean that the so-called "traditional" therapies and healing strategies rooted in a "culture" are always and necessarily effective in re-solving the problems that are discussed here. Nor is the role of clinics and psychological approaches discounted. Such an affirmation would certainly sound ingenuous, especially when one takes into consideration a popula-tion lacerated by conflicts, its networks of solidarity and social connec-tions destroyed, a culture whose memories have been obliterated and whose symbols have been eroded.[75]

A specific example of the inability of traditional strategies to help vic-tims is represented by the case of rape and violence against women. As my research in Goma District (eastern DRC) demonstrated, in some cases both community and clinical approaches were revealed to be weak or ineffective.[76] In my study the victim, a young woman who became pregnant after being raped, was the object of rejection and a trivializing attitude on the part of her neighbours, while no psychological treatment was made available for her. Only the women of a local NGO involved in human rights took into consideration her suffering and her solitude. Moreover, ritualized violence often gives a sort of paradoxical justifica-tion to perpetrators: Acting in a ritual way exonerates the rapist from di-rect and personal responsibility.

Given these difficulties, community rehabilitation often means actively re-inventing community and re-imagining affiliation. It means admitting that the dimensions of trauma are individual as much as collective, and therefore the politics of memory which one intends to pursue should con-cern both these poles of suffering. But the distance maintained by the technical interventions means that one also needs to know and recognize the existing resources, promoting recourse to these, where they are rec-ognized by the local participants as pertinent, instead of opting for gener-alized exportations of models, interpretations and therapeutic practices.

In spite of some contradictions concerning the role of traditional med-icine, the actions undertaken with traditional healers for children trauma-tized by war and from being child soldiers bear witness to the success of strategies deeply rooted in the social and cultural context.[77] It is neces-sary not to overlook the fact that different strategies, different systems of healing, remembering and forgetting exist. These differences are im-portant where suffering, memory of dramatic experiences and the negoti-ation or ritual ways of dealing with death do not concern only "symp-toms" or "disturbances caused by stress", but rather a political and moral register. Some strategies are about deleting or reformulating col-lective traumatic experiences in particularly efficient ways (through, e.g., rituals, religious ceremonies); at the same time, local (pre-war) forms of authority can be useful in producing new social ties, listening opportuni-ties and affiliations.

The act of forgetting sometimes forms an essential part of the everyday construction and creation of identities, and contributes to solving conflicts and dealing with the experience of collective estrangement that dominates in times of war. The redefinition of individual or collective identities and connections can contribute to the interruption of the cycle of violence and death. However, if forgetting and reinventing identity and ties can represent survival strategies, they are not reliable prescriptions for political action or for strategies of resistance against oppression and domination. The delicate balance between forgetting and remembering cannot be imagined as the simple product of individual choice. This balance is affected by a number of factors: cultural strategies, moral questions, ways in which memories are constructed, narrative landscapes and the particular ways in which communities define their relationship to the past. It is certainly not possible to suggest general solutions. However, based on case material, one can affirm the usefulness of experimenting with strategies of rehabilitation based on the local resources of resilience.

Finally, there is this consideration that helps to avoid any essentialization or reification, both of the suffering and of the experience such as the participation in the conflicts. For many societies, for many minorities, the notion of "trauma" itself, of an event (dramatic but singular), does not fit well with the collective experience of regular, chronic condition of violence, death, exploitation, uncertainty and poverty in which individuals and groups are forced to survive. In an analogous perspective, Liisa Malkki stresses the difference between humanitarian and political perspectives concerning the risk of universalizing and dehistoricizing refugees.[78]

One can conclude that it is possible to conceive of strategies that neither medicalize nor universalize, and approaches that avoid the reification of suffering; however, it is important to invoke a psychology capable of generating new solutions and models, and not simply sustaining the adaptation of individuals to their context (the two perspectives have been put forward by the Iranian psychologist Fathali Moghaddam). It is necessary to anchor peace-building as well as rehabilitation strategies to resilience factors and local social actors in order to avoid the abuse and the trivialization of a medical category such as PTSD. After all, the increasing success of PTSD can also be interpreted as a symptom of changes in the relation between individual personhood and modern life in Western societies.[79] In the background of a medical-psychiatric category (PTSD), in its abuse and in the risk of reification often reported in other categories (such as "child soldiers" or "street children"), can now be recognized more easily the risks and the conflict between diverse uses and rhetoric of the memory and trauma. The experiences of the Balkans and of Kosovo have shown how deleterious the proliferation of psychosocial interventions and the medicalization of the entire population (practically all of whom were diagnosed as having been affected by PTSD and requiring treatment) can be. This circulation represented the expression *par excellence* of the hegemonic will of psychiatry and of Western medicine. Experiences in different socio-cultural contexts do not only underline the limitations – and in many cases the uselessness – of some strategies but cause one to rethink especially the presuppositions on which they are founded and their presumed capacity for adaptation to any and every context. The medical-anthropological approach summarily traced here should be held in mind when exploring solutions and interventions for populations and groups affected by the violent consequences of war. It is also important to bear in mind, however, that these populations and groups belong to historical-cultural worlds different from the Western experience, and that there are different ways to be in history.

Conclusion

The medical-anthropological reflections for this chapter have explored some of the profiles of violence and mass atrocities, as well as possible connections with other social problems (e.g., the crisis of the post-colonial state in Africa, privatization of violence, globalization, new orders of uncertainty), in order to offer alternative critical questions for peace-building and rehabilitation strategies. "Understanding the architecture of a society is valuable not only in its own right – as a work of anthropology – but also a blueprint for change."[80] While examining the limits of medicalizing approaches, which are rarely concerned with finding cultural resources and local actors (such as institutions, associations or religious and traditional leaders: civil society), I wanted to underline the importance of community approaches because the suffering and wars from which they are derived are individual as well as collective experiences. Working on peace processes that concern collective subjects contributes to forms of sharing, to social moments and to that minimum of alliance upon which a social fabric can be reconstructed. Recovery, in circumstances where trauma is collective, can only be social.

The communal management of material and symbolic resources constitutes a strategy whose utility has already been demonstrated in refugee camps as well as in social rehabilitation activities. The question of memory and trauma, which is a moral rather than a medical or psychiatric issue, takes a critical role in these strategies because it is around the strategies of remembering and politics of memory, from the discourses on trauma (and social pain), that the major obstacles to reconciliation projects are often created. The right to speak about history, to give testimony of the events of which one has been a protagonist or victim, differs from

simple "remembering" and "elaboration of traumas" that have been suffered. It is important not only because it allows for a rethinking of history, but also permits its questioning. This process could allow for the
creation of strategies, which even through "silence" about past dramatic
events create the possibility for the construction of specific forms of historical consciousness.[81] These strategies, these more or less shared ways
of remembering or conceiving the past, are important to recognize because they are rehabilitation resources: given that individuals, groups
and minorities *use* them and *within* them they *feel* that it is possible to re-
act once more in the future. This feeling is the presupposition for social
change.

A balanced articulation between local actors and external actors, between cultural strategies and intervention rooted in other types of knowledge, can constitute the best strategy for managing complex interactions
and the different profiles of suffering. However, no generalizations can be
allowed. Most of all, no proposal can forget the power relations and domination that often make the strategies mentioned above impracticable.
The reality of the Ituri and Kivu conflicts in the DRC, with the uncertainty about the area's political future, its still large number of child and
adolescent participants in war and the presence of uncontrolled militias,
or the condition of fear and generalized diffidence in countries such as
Sudan and Sierra Leone certainly represent a challenging testing ground
for the strategies mentioned in this chapter. Individuals who suffer, perhaps those who suffer the most, are often those who are the most invisible. Opportune places and occasions in which to treat individuals and
communities in their fragility must be found, but the individuals must be
recognized once more as people, not only as victims.

In conclusion, support for research on the events of war and mass
atrocities should promote a particular commitment at the local level. Reflection on the profound and often hidden roots of these types of events
and historical analysis are often risky because they present a clash between memory and counter-memory, truth and counter-truth, that en-
snares any attempt to overcome, to negotiate, to trust. Nevertheless, the
political and moral dimensions, as much from suffering itself as from the
events that determined them, make it impossible to escape these aspects.
Desire for vendetta can surely be an obstacle or make it difficult to carry
out these interventions: expressing these feelings does not mean having a
mental illness, as many studies would suggest. What one person considers
a vendetta could signify an act of social justice for another. Social memory plays an important role in the process of psychosocial rehabilitation,
in as much as silence (which does not mean forgetting) does: "With 90%
of recent wars being civil, negotiations between ordinary people about
their feeling of mistrust or revenge and about issues of responsibility, cul-

pability, and restitution must be typically pragmatic.... Recovery [from the catastrophe of war] is not a discrete process.... It is practical and unspectacular, and it is grounded in the resumption of the ordinary rhythms of everyday life."[82]

The right to speak must be given back to people who are in search of redemption of their present, to people who need to establish a connection (a correct distance) with those who are dead. External actors, individuals or groups who show their alliance with those who are suffering or who have suffered, indeed play a fundamental role. At the same time, peace-builders and experts should avoid any type of alliance with groups that participated in the logic of terror (an error that happens more often than one would think). The possibility of overcoming the sense of loss, humiliation and death without resorting to anger or to revenge is perhaps the most difficult task in the processes of peace-building and psychosocial rehabilitation.[83] This stake requires an interdisciplinary and critical approach, which guides each intervention, and has people as its central focus.

Notes

1. Valentin Y. Mudimbe, "Where is the Real Thing? Psychoanalysis and African Mythical Narrative", *Cahiers d'études africaines* 27, no. 107/108, 1987, pp. 311–327.
2. The following notes are an attempt to synthesize experience and reflections that have accrued over different times and places, in Eritrea, Ethiopia, Bosnia-Herzegovina, Albania, Mozambique, Palestine and the Democratic Republic of the Congo between 1994 and 2004. I acknowledge Roberto Bertolino, psychologist, and Luca Jourdan, anthropologist, for their comments and suggestions on DRC, as well as Enrique Querol, psychologist, for his comments concerning Mozambique.
3. Donald Crummey, "Introduction", in D. Crummey, ed., *Banditry, Rebellion and Social Protest in Africa*, London: James Currey & Heinemann, 1996, p. 1.
4. Jean and John Comaroff, "Occult Economies and the Violence of Abstraction: Notes from the South African Postcolony", *American Ethnologist* 26, no. 2, 1999, pp. 279–303.
5. Mark Duffield, "Global Governance and the New Wars: The Merging of Development and Security", unpublished PhD thesis, 2004; Christopher Parker, "Transformation without Transition: Electoral Politics, Network Ties, and the Persistence of the Shadow State in Jordan", in I. Hamdy, ed., *Election in the Middle East: What Do They Mean*, Cairo: Cairo Papers in Social Science, 2004.
6. Koen Vlassenroot and Timothy Raeymaekers, *Conflict and Social Transformation in Eastern DR Congo*, Gent: Academia Press Scientific Publishers, 2004, pp. 42–43.
7. Ibid., p. 53.
8. John Borneman, "Reconciliation after Ethnic Cleansing: Listening, Retribution, Affiliation", *Public Culture* 14, no. 2, 2002, pp. 281–304, 282.
9. Maurice Bloch, "Internal and External Memory: Different Ways of Being in History", in Paul Antze and Michael Lambek, eds, *Tense Past: Cultural Essays in Trauma and Memory*, London: Routledge & Kegan, 1996, pp. 215–234, 229.
10. Roberto Beneduce, *Bambini fra guerra e pace: Il caso di Eritrea ed Etiopia. Uno studio*

su bambini che hanno bisogno di particolari misure di protezione – Rapporto di missione, Firenze: UNICEF – ICDC, 1999, pp. 1–52; Roberto Beneduce, "WHO Mission to Albania on Mental Health of Refugees from Kosovo", unpublished report for WHO Copenhagen, 1999, pp. 1–28; Kisangani N. F. Emizet, "The massacre of refugees in Congo: A case of UN peacekeeping failure and international law", *Journal of Modern African Studies* 38, no. 2, 2000, pp. 163–202.

11. Valentin Y. Mudimbe, *The Invention of Africa: Gnosis, Philosophy, and the Order of Knowledge*, Bloomington and Indianapolis: Indiana University Press, 1988.

12. Achille Mbembe, "Pouvoir, violence et accumulation", *Politique africaine* 39, 1990, pp. 7–24, 12. See on these issues Jean-François Bayart, Achille Mbembe and Comi Toulabor, *Le politique par le bas en Afrique noire: Contribution à une problématique de la démocratie*, Paris: Karthala, 1992.

13. "Lacking any Cold War roots, or evident religious or ethnic dimensions, but possessing a high quotient of apparently bizarre and random acts of violence, many perpetrated by children, this conflict is cited by Kaplan as a prime instance of the New Barbarism.... According to Kaplan, the war was a product of social breakdown caused by population pressure and environmental collapse, but although the local history of resource acquisition is relevant to understanding the war there is no run-away environmental crisis in Sierra Leone.... The data on population trends and land resources confirm the essential soundness of this point of view." Paul Richards, *Fighting for the Rain Forest: War, Youth and Resources in Sierra Leone*, Oxford: James Currey, 1996.

14. John Lonsdale, "Le passé de l'Afrique au secours de son avenir", *Politique africaine*, no. 39, September 1990, pp. 135–149.

15. "Why is history subversive? ... It is therefore just because History is a result of struggle and a reflection of change, that it is seen as a threat to all dominant social groups in all systems of exploitation and oppression." See Ngugi wa Thiongo, cited in John Lonsdale, "Le passé de l'Afrique au secours de son avenir", *Politique africaine*, no. 39, September 1990, p. 135.

16. Arjun Appadurai, "The Past as Scarce Resource", *Man* 16, no. 2, 1981, pp. 201–219.

17. Kay B. Warren, "Mayan Multiculturalism and the Violence of Memories", in Veena Das, Arthur Kleinman, Mamphela Ramphele and Pamela Reynolds, eds, *Violence and Subjectivity*, Berkeley: University of California Press, 2000, pp. 296–314. With regards to the Hutu–Tutsi conflict and the contrasting ways of remembering the past "through different ethnic lenses", see the chapter by Lemarchand and Niwese in the present volume.

18. Achille Mbembe, "On the Power of the False", *Public Culture* 14, no. 3, 2002, pp. 629–41, 634.

19. David Graeber, "Painful Memories", *Journal of Religion in Africa* 27, no. 4, 1997, pp. 374–400, 377. Therefore, it is no surprise that in the Betsileo language the word for "history", *tantara*, can also mean "privilege".

20. On the "rendering of the past in the present", see Michael Taussig, "History as Sorcery", *Representations* 7, Summer 1984, pp. 87–109.

21. On different expressions of memory and ways of remembering, see Paul Connerton, *How Societies Remember*, Cambridge: Cambridge University Press, 1989.

22. Inge Brinkman, "Ways of Death: Accounts of Terror from Angolan Refugees in Namibia", *Africa* 70, no. 1, 2000, pp. 1–24.

23. Frank Van Acker and Koen Vlassenroot, "Les 'Maï-maï' et les fonctions de la violence milicienne dans l'est du Congo", *Politique africaine* 84, 2001, pp. 103–116; William J. Dewey, "AK-47s for the Ancestors", *Journal of Religion in Africa* 24, no. 4, 1994, pp. 358–374.

24. "In the name of human rights, political malaise requires the same quick, superficial and temporary cure as biological illnesses.... The concept of being obliged to intervene and

having access to the victims ... becomes by default the right to interfere." See Bernard Hours, *L'idéologie humanitaire, ou le spectacle de l'humanité perdue*, Paris: L'Harmattan, 1999. In the same line, Chrétien's analysis: "Since there is a century, the temptation is great to deal with this phenomenon in philanthropic terms, social assistance (healthcare) as 'the right to interfere'." See Jean-Pierre Chrétien, "Les racines de la violence contemporaine en Afrique", *Politique africaine* 42, 1991, pp. xv–xvi.

25. About the notion of "cultural bereavement", see Maurice Eisenbruch, "From Post-Traumatic Stress Disorder to Cultural Bereavement: Diagnosis of Southeast Asian Refugees", *Social Science & Medicine* 33, no. 6, 1991, pp. 673–680. See also Christina Zarowsky, "Writing trauma: Emotions, ethnography, and the politics of suffering among Somali returnees in Ethiopia", *Culture, Medicine and Psychiatry* 28, 2004, pp. 189–209.

26. Adam Ashforth, "Witchcraft, Violence and Democracy in the New South Africa", *Cahiers d'études africaines* 38, no. 150–152, 1998, pp. 505–532; Arjun Appadurai, "Dead Certainty: Ethnic Violence in the Era of Globalization", *Public Culture* 10, no. 2, 1998, pp. 225–247; Jean and John Comaroff, "Réfléxions sur la jeunesse: Du passé à la post-colonie," *Politique africaine* 80, 2000, pp. 90–110.

27. This term is derived from SAPE: Société des Ambianceurs et des Personnes Élégantes. See René Devisch, "La violence à Kinshasa, ou L'institution en négatif", *Cahiers d'études africaines* 38, no. 150–152, 1998, pp. 441–469. On "unruly modernity, establishing itself with the help of subversive practices" in DRC, see Tshikala K. Biaya, "Parallel Society in the Democratic Republic of Congo", in Simon Bekker, Martine Dodds and Mashack M. Khosa, eds, *Shifting African Identities*, Pretoria: Human Sciences Research Council, 2001, pp. 43–60.

28. Stefania Pandolfo, personal communication.

29. Stephen Ellis, *The Mask of Anarchy*, London: Hurst & Company, 1999, p. 269.

30. Jon Abbink, "Ritual and Political Forms of Violent Practice among the Suri of Southern Ethiopia", *Cahiers d'études africaines* 38, no. 150–152, 1998, pp. 271–295.

31. An analogous process happened in Europe and ex-Yugoslavia, where the state's hegemony has been pursued by democratizing violence, in its various expressions (e.g., ethnic, legal), through the support of paramilitary terrorism. On these issues, see for example Allen Feldman, "On Cultural Anesthesia: From Desert Storm to Rodney King", *American Ethnologist* 21, no. 2, 2002, pp. 404–418.

32. Appadurai, "Dead Certainty".

33. Ibid., p. 229.

34. Ibid.

35. Ibid., p. 234.

36. K. B. Wilson, "Cults of Violence and Counter-Violence in Mozambique", *Journal of Southern African Studies* 18, no. 3, 1992, pp. 527–582. See also Christopher C. Taylor, "The Cultural Face of Terror in the Rwandan Genocide of 1994", in Alexander L. Hinton, ed., *Annihilating Difference: The Anthropology of Genocide*, Berkeley & Los Angeles: University of California Press, 2002, pp. 137–178.

37. Appadurai suggests that structural analogies exist between this type of preoccupation and those that characterized the "desperate" attempt, on the part of Nazism, to individuate the characteristics of the "real" Jews. See Hinton, *Annihilating Difference*; and Alexander L. Hinton, ed., *Genocide: An Anthropological Reader*, Malden, Mass.: Blackwell, 2002, on the controversial use of the term "genocide". Use of the genocide concept in the African conflicts is more controversial than in other contexts because of the specificity of the state formation in Africa and the legacy of "ethnicity" notion.

38. Sometimes, making ritual burial impossible was a specific psycho-cultural military "technique". It has been used by irregular militias as well as by regular armies (as was the case with US Army in Viet Nam).

39. Liisa H. Malkki, *Purity and Exile: Violence, Memory, and National Cosmology among Hutu Refugees in Tanzania*, Chicago: University of Chicago Press, 1995, p. 92. The demonization and the scorn of the "other" is imperceptibly woven together with "the enchantment of numbers", as was the case with the conflict in the Great Lakes region, where numbers that reduce or multiply the number of victims contribute to the autonomy of the violence-spectacle. See Chrétien, "Les raciness", p. 24.

40. Richards, *Fighting for the Rainforest*, pp. xviii–xx.

41. Michel Galy, "Liberia, machine perverse: Anthropologie politique du conflit libérien", *Cahiers d'études africaines* 38, no. 150–152, 1998, pp. 533–553.

42. The use of tattoos and masks in Liberia, Sierra Leone or DRC war conflicts, or references to secret societies, are indications of these changes, which, through "traditional" signs and languages, in some ways seem to celebrate and reaffirm difference and belonging, authority and power rhetoric.

43. Achille Mbembe, "À propos des écritures africaines de soi", *Politique africaine* 77, 2000, pp. 16–43, 39.

44. Rosalind Shaw, "'Tok Af, Lef Af': A Political Economy of Temne Techniques of Secrecy and Self", in I. Karp and D. A. Masolo, eds, *African Philosophy as Cultural Inquiry*, Bloomington: Indiana University Press, 2000, pp. 50–65.

45. Achille Mbembe, "À propos des écritures africaines de soi", p. 39.

46. Filip De Boeck, "Le 'deuxième monde' et les 'enfants-sorciers' en République Démocratique du Congo", *Politique africaine* 80, 2000, pp. 32–57. Mbembe writes recently regarding the necessity of asking about the reasons for which "In Africa, the struggle for human sovereignty and the satisfaction of biological needs almost always seem to go together with orgiastic participation in different forms of human destruction." See Mbembe, "On the Power of the False", p. 636.

47. Michael Taussig, "Culture of Terror – Face of Death: Roger Casement's Putumayo Report and Explanation of Torture", *Comparative Studies in Society and History* 26, no. 1, 1984, pp. 467–497, 495.

48. Krijn Peters and Paul Richards, "'Why We Fight': Voices of Youth Combatants in Sierra Leone", *Africa* 68, no. 2, 1998, pp. 183–210; Vlassenroot and Raeymaekers, *Conflict and Social Transformation*. See also Richards, *Fighting for the Rain Forest*; and van Acker and Vlassenroot, "Les 'Maï-maï'".

49. Bogumil Jewsiewicki, "The Subject in Africa: In Foucault's Footsteps", *Public Culture* 14, no. 3, 2002, pp. 593–598, 595.

50. Achille Mbembe, "À propos des écritures africaines de soi".

51. On relations between violence and health, and on the concept of "structural violence", see Anthony Zwi and Antonio Ugalde, "Towards an epidemiology of political violence in the third world", *Social Science & Medicine* 28, no. 7, 1989, pp. 633–642; and Paul Farmer, *Infections and Inequalities: The Modern Plagues*, Berkeley: University of California Press, 2001.

52. Jon Abbink, "Violence and state (re)formation in the African context: The general and the particular", paper presented at the War and Society Seminar, Session: Warfare, Violence and Social Structure, Aarhus University, Denmark, 28 April 2000. According to Gérard Prunier, the colonial impact on continental Africa produced, among other things, the creation of states without nations and, what is particularly important for our discussion, the *profitability* of violence. See Prunier, "Violence et historie en Afrique", *Politique africaine* 42, 1991, pp. 9–14. See also Yves-André Fauré, "Les constitutions et l'exercise du pouvoir en Afrique noire: Pour une lecture defférente des Textes," *Politique africaine* 1, 1981, pp. 34–52.

53. Patrick Chabal, "Pouvoir et violence en Afrique postcoloniale," *Politique africaine* 42, 1991, pp. 51–64.

54. Filip De Boeck, "Beyond the Grave: History, Memory and Death in Postcolonial Congo/Zaïre", in Richard Werbner, ed., *Memory and the Postcolony: African Anthropology and the Critique of Power*, London: Zed Books, 1998, pp. 21–58, 47. On *débrouillardise*, see Gauthier de Villers, Bogumil Jewsiewicki and Laurent Monnier, "Manières de vivre: Économies de la 'débrouille' dans les villes du Congo/Zaïre", *Cahiers africains/Afrika Studies*, special issue, no. 49–50 (edition of 2001), 2002.

55. Guy-Marin Kamandji, "Rites mortuaires à Kinshasa: Traditions et innovations", *Cahiers africains/Afrika Studies*, special issue edited by J.-L. Grootaers, no. 31–32, 1998, pp. 63–87, and, in the same issue, Tshikala K. Biaya, "La 'Mort' et ses métaphores au Congo/Zaïre, 1990–1995", pp. 89–127. Mbembe stresses the role of private indirect government in these contexts: "To grasp the scale of the various forms of *privatization of sovereignty*, it is important to recall that the struggle for the concentration and private control of the means of coercion has taken place in a context marked both by the world-wide deregulation of markets and money movements.... Put differently, functions supposed to be public, and obligations that flow from sovereignty, are increasingly performed by private operators for private ends." See Achille Mbembe, *On the Postcolony*, Berkeley: University of California Press, 2001, p. 80. On "generalized despotism", see Mahmood Mamdani, *Citizen and Subject: Contemporary Africa and the Legacy of Late Colonialism*, Princeton, NJ: Princeton University Press, 1996, pp. 37–62. On routinization of terror, silence as a survival strategy and "militarization of mind" in Guatemala, see Linda Green, "Fear as a Way of Life", in Alexander L. Hinton, ed., *Genocide: An Anthropological Reader*, Malden, Mass.: Blackwell, 2002, pp. 307–333.

56. See Jean and John Comaroff, eds, *Modernity and Its Malcontents: Ritual and Power in Postcolonial Africa*, Chicago: University of Chicago Press, 1993, on witchcraft and modernity. On religion in Africa, see also Jean-François Bayart, *Religion et modernité politique en Afrique noire: Dieu pour tous et chacun pour soi*, Paris: Karthala, 1993.

57. Ashforth, "Witchcraft, Violence, and Democracy", p. 506. See also Alain Marie, "La violence faite à l'individu: La communauté au révélateur de la sorcellerie", *Politique africaine* 91, 2003, pp. 13–32.

58. Quoted in Appadurai, "Dead Certainty".

59. David Ciekway and Peter Geschiere, "Containing Witchcraft: Conflicting Scenarios in Postcolonial Africa", *African Studies Review* 41, no. 3, 1998, pp. 1–14; Peter Geschiere, *Sorcellerie et politique en Afrique: La viande des autres*, Paris: Karthala, 1995; Peter Geschiere and Francis B. Nyamnjoh, "Witchcraft as an Issue in Tembehe 'Politics of Belonging': Democratization and Urban Migrants' Involvement with the Home Village," *African Studies Review* 41, no. 3, 1998, pp. 69–91.

60. Ian Hacking, *Rewriting the Soul: Multiple Personality and the Sciences of Memory*, Princeton, NJ: Princeton University Press, 1995. See also Ian Hacking, "Memory Sciences, Memory Politics", in Paul Antze and Michael Lambek, eds, *Tense Past: Cultural Essays in Trauma and Memory*, London: Routledge & Kegan, 1996, pp. 67–88.

61. Beneduce, *Bambini fra guerra e pace*.

62. Derek Summerfield, *The Impact of War and Atrocity on Civilian Populations: Basic Principles for NGO Interventions and a Critique of Psychosocial Trauma Projects*, London: RRN-ODI, 1996.

63. On "cultural anaesthesia", see Feldman, "On Cultural Anesthesia".

64. Graça Machel, *The Impact of War on Children*, London: Hurst & Company, 2001.

65. Peters and Richards, "Why We Fight," p. 76. In addition, Vlassenroot and Raeymaekers (*Conflict and Social Transformation*, p. 21) remember that in most rural areas of Eastern DRC "rural militias (Mayi-Mayi, FDLR, etc.) have replaced customary chiefs as the main local power reference".

66. Alcinda Honwana, "Negotiating post war identities: Child soldiers in Mozambique and

Angola," *Bulletin du Codesria*, no. 1–2, 1999, pp. 4–13, 9; and "Innocents et coupables: Les enfants-soldats comme acteurs tactiques," *Politique africaine* 80, 2000, pp. 58–74.

67. De Boeck, "Le 'deuxième monde'". Janet Roitman speaks of *bush economies* in reference to the illegal traffic in arms and drugs on the border between Cameroon and Chad, which involves young protagonists in considerable financial transactions. At the same time, Ibrahim Abdullah speaks of *lumpen youth culture* to underline how youths and the exploited classes represented variables closely parallel to the processes of ethnicization and radicalization (both of these works are quoted in Jean and John Comaroff, "Réfléxions sur la jeunesse"). The informal character of most African economies makes the distinction between illegal and legal, illicit and licit completely irrelevant for some authors. See amongst others Gérard Prunier, "Le magendo: Essai sur quelques aspects marginaux des échanges commerciaux en Afrique orientale", *Politique africaine* 9, 1983, pp. 53–62; Stephen Jackson, "Nos richesses sont pillées! Économies de guerre et rumeurs de guerre au Kivu", *Politique africaine* 84, 2001, pp. 117–135; and Vlassenroot and Raeymaekers, *Conflict and Social Transformation*, on criminalization of informal economy in war contexts. In addition, see the entire monograph "Enfants, jeunes et politique" in *Politique africaine* 80, 2000. On youth as emerging issue in Sub-Saharan Africa see also Nicolas Argenti, "Air Youth: Performance, violence and the state in Cameroon," *Journal* of the *Royal Anthropological Institute* 4, 1998, pp. 753–781; and Nicolas Argenti, "Kesum-Body and the places of the Gods: The politics of children's masking and second-world realities in Oku (Cameroon)", *Journal of the Royal Anthropological Institute* 7, 2001, pp. 67–94. See also Carol B. Thompson, "Beyond Civil Society: Child Soldiers as Citizens in Mozambique", *Review of African Political Economy* 26, no. 80, 1999, pp. 190–206.

68. Naomi Richman, "Annotation: Children in Situations of Political Violence", *Journal of Child Psychology and Psychiatry* 34, no. 8, 1993, pp. 1286–1302. The protagonist role and the (often surprising) consciousness of the children and adolescents, their capacity to make choices and to act, have hardly ever been considered relevant aspects in the interventions of social rehabilitation by the humanitarian organizations and in the images they continue to produce of childhood and adolescence. On psychological consequences of violence in occupied territories, see Jan Peteet, "Male Gender and Rituals of Resistance in the Palestinian Intifada: A Cultural Politics of Violence," *American Ethnologist* 21, no. 1, 1994, pp. 31–49.

69. Summerfield, *The Impact of War*.

70. Olle Jeppsson, quoted in Derek Summerfield, "War and mental health: A brief overview," *British Medical Journal*, no. 321, 2000, pp. 232–235. See Comaroff and Comaroff, "Réfléxions sur la jeunesse" for a wider exploration of these issues and contradictions.

71. Summerfield, *The Impact of War*, p. 33.

72. Patrick J. Bracken and Celia Petty, eds, *Rethinking the Trauma of War*, New York: Free Associations Books, 1998, p. 1.

73. Tim Allen, quoted in Summerfield, *The Impact of War*.

74. The following list summarizes some of the limitations of the notions of PTSD: a) The category of PTSD creates a medicalization of suffering, a parcelling up and a reification of grief; b) Signs and symptoms, recognized and treated until recently as autonomous or connected to other forms of suffering, have been reclassified and combined within an arbitrary whole (PTSD) in whose centre the notion of stress and that of trauma play the role of unifying terms; moreover, PTSD lacks any specificity; c) Such an operation presupposes a universalistic conception of trauma, that seeks legitimization in the biology of stress, in other terms: in a common substratum for its common definition in all cultures and populations; d) the abuse of the category of PTSD therefore brings about a cancellation of the social and cultural dimensions of bereavement and suffering, and

avoids the consideration of the collective character of the trauma and the fact that very often one is not dealing with "extraordinary" events as the revised edition of the Diagnostic and Statistical Manual IV states, but of continuous processes, articulated in strategies of domination and manipulation, of symbolic and material violence and deprivation; e) PTSD speaks of trauma but it does not consider the different roles of the participants, the historical roots of violence and war, thereby virtually abolishing every difference between victims and perpetrators, between natural events and violence produced by the human hand; f) "trauma" and "stress" become unambiguous experiences, whose expressions seem measurable, and whose diverse social, ethical, symbolic, juridical meanings disappear into statistics; g) the proliferation of the biomedical and behavioural models in the psychosocial and rehabilitative strategies produces inevitably an inhibition of the local resources of treatment, but also of the spontaneous strategies of resistance, collective as much as individual, contributing to a passivization and a victimization of the individuals and the groups. See *Transcultural Psychiatry* 37, special issue no. 3, 2000. Other interventions challenge from an even closer stance a critical medico-anthropological approach to trauma, pain and suffering. This is the case of emerging technologies such as EMDR (the initialization for "Eye Movement Desensitization and Reprocessing"), which claims to be effective at all latitudes because it is not transmitted by cultural specifics such as language, words or verbal associations but rather by the common neurophysiological substrata. On PTSD, see Allan Young, *The Harmony of Illusions: Inventing Post Traumatic Stress Disorder*, Princeton, NJ: Princeton University Press, 1995. A critique about the pseudoscientific language of EMDR is recently made by Debra Stein, Cécile Rousseau and Louise Lacroix, "Between Innovation and Tradition: The Paradoxical Relationship Between Eye Movement Desensitization and Reprocessing and Altered States of Consciousness", *Transcultural Psychiatry* 41, no. 1, 2004, pp. 5–30.
75. Alexandra Argenti-Pillen, "The Discourse on Trauma in Non-Western Cultural Contexts: Contributions of an Ethnographic Method", in Arieh Shalev, Rachel Yehuda and Alexander C. MacFarlane, eds, *International Handbook of Human Response to Truama*, Amsterdam: Kluwer Academic/Plenum, 2000, pp. 87–102.
76. Roberto Beneduce, Luca Jourdan, Timothy Raeymakers and Koen van Vlassenrot, "Violence with a purpose: Exploring the functions and meaning of violence in the Democratic Republic of Congo", *Intervention: International Journal of Mental Health, Psychosocial Work and Counselling in Areas of Armed Conflict* 4, no. 1, 2006, pp. 32–46.
77. Alcinda Honwana, *As instituções tradicionais e a reintegração social dos grupos vulneráveis*, Maputo: u.p., 1993, and "Negotiating post war identities: Child soldiers in Mozambique and Angola", *Bulletin du Codesria*, no. 1–2, pp. 4–13, 1999; David Lan, *Guns and rain: Guerrillas and spirit mediums in Zimbabwe: A comparative study*, Harare: Zimbabwe Publishing House, 1985; Enrique Querol and Nicolas Ofice, "Pràticas tradicionaìs de assistencia as crianças afectadas pela guerra ne provincia de Manica", Cruz Vermelha–Chimoio (unpublished); Pamela Reynolds, "Children of Tribulation: The Need to Heal and the Means to Heal War Trauma," *Africa* 60, no. 1, 1990, pp. 1–38, and *Traditional Healers and Childhood in Zimbabwe*, Athens: Ohio University Press, 1996; Fernanda Varela and Enrique Querol, "Trauma, tratamento e intregação social das craianças afectads pela guerra no contexto africano", Conferençia Reconstruindo Esperancia, Maputo, 28–31 October 2000; see Patricia Lawrence, *Violence, Suffering, Amman: The Work of Oracles in Sri Lanka's Eastern War Zone*, in Veena Das, Arthur Kleinman, Mamphela Ramphele and Pamela Reynolds, eds, *Violence and Subjectivity*, Berkeley: University of California Press, 2000, on oracles' healing work in Sri Lanka. See Eisenbruch too (in this book), regarding the ambiguous attitude that the Cambodian government adopted with regard to traditional healers.

78. Liisa H. Malkki, "Speechless Emissaries: Refugees, Humanitarianism, and Dehistoricization", in Alexander L. Hinton, ed., *Genocide: An Anthropological Reader*, Malden, Mass.: Blackwell, 2002, pp. 344–367.

79. Derek Summerfield, "The invention of post-traumatic stress disorder and the social usefulness of a psychiatric category", *British Medical Journal* 9, 2001, pp. 61–64.

80. Kenneth Roth, "Foreword", in Alexander L. Hinton, ed., *Annihilating Difference: The Anthropology of Genocide*, Berkeley & Los Angeles, University of California Press, 2002, pp. ix–xi.

81. Michael Lambek, "Taboo as Cultural Practice Among Malagasy Speakers", *Journal of the Royal Anthropological Institute* 27, no. 2, 1992, pp. 245–266; Karen Middleton, "Circumcision, Death, and Strangers", *Journal of Religion in Africa* 27, no. 4, 1997, pp. 340–373.

82. Derek Summerfield, "Effects of war: Moral knowledge, revenge, reconciliation, and medicalized concepts of 'recovery'", *British Medical Journal* 325, 2002, pp. 1105–1107.

83. This issue is also the measure of the moral dimensions of these processes: "Reconciliation is, ultimately, about restoring sociality, about re-establishing the trust necessary not just to tolerate but to cooperate in partnerships that can survive even the threat of failure." See Murray Last, "Reconciliation and Memory in Postwar Nigeria", in Veena Das, Arthur Kleinman, Mamphela Ramphele and Pamela Reynolds, eds, *Violence and Subjectivity*, Berkeley: University of California Press, 2000, pp. 315–332. See, on this issue, also Borneman's more "pragmatic" view: "*Reconciliation* I define not in terms of permanent peace or harmony but as a project of departure from violence" (Borneman, "Reconciliation after Ethnic Cleansing", p. 282).

Part II

Individuals and communities

3

The uses and abuses of culture: Cultural competence in post-mass-crime peace-building in Cambodia

Maurice Eisenbruch

This chapter examines the impact of mass crimes on social, cultural and spiritual connectedness in post-conflict Cambodia and suggests some ways to assist peace-building efforts to be culturally responsive. I want to set the scene for comparison with other settings of violent conflict, such as Rwanda, Guatemala and Somalia, and the transformation of social capital, such as post-conflict peace-building and nation-building. I suggest that Cambodia's rich religious and cultural traditions are at the same time victims of the war and offer some solutions to the consequences of war. I look at the ways in which the Khmer Rouge turned their insights into language and culture to more sinister ends. I ask whether traditional healers, with their "insider" view into the cause and cure of post-conflict illness and suffering, are being heeded and given a chance to assist in post-war rehabilitation. Traditional healers could perhaps function as human rights workers in post-conflict situations – helping to alleviate pain and restore moral order and, as keen students of culture and mind, giving meaning to trauma and thus attending to both community and individual healing as Cambodia's situation demands.

The chapters in this book show how an understanding of the local forms of cultural logic are needed in order to respond to the needs of survivors of mass crimes. This chapter respond to this need by suggesting a framework to ensure that post-conflict programs are culturally competent and a new field is opening up to provide the necessary evidence base, namely "cultural competence in international health". It echoes a message put forward by Roberto Beneduce, with his dual background as

After mass crime: Rebuilding states and communities, Pouligny, Chesterman and Schnabel (eds), United Nations University Press, 2007, ISBN 978-92-808-1138-4

psychiatrist and medical anthropologist, in chapter 2, in which he challenges the hegemony of Western medical diagnoses such as "trauma" and post-traumatic stress disorder commonly applied by mental health workers in post-conflict settings. Some governments already support pre-departure intercultural effectiveness training that hints at cultural competence for their development advisors, but in resource-poor countries themselves the concept of cultural competence in health care is generally unrecognized.

The chapter begins with an overview of the events in Cambodia to do with cultural genocide during the Khmer Rouge regime, marked by the disconnection and destruction of many elements of traditional culture. By drawing upon the examples of their transformation of traditional language and the way they labelled people, I argue that the Khmer Rouge leadership used their mastery and understanding of the culture to manipulate and use it against itself. The chapter continues the story by describing fresh onslaughts on Cambodian culture brought during the post-Khmer Rouge 1980s and continued during the 1990s with the outbreak of peace and the ravages of the Cambodian epidemic of HIV/AIDS as well as an upsurge in seemingly new forms of violence in domestic life. The chapter continues with an analysis of reconnection and reconstruction, through the eyes of the traditional healers and Buddhist monks as they draw upon Buddhist and folk legends and traditional rituals in efforts to seek both to explain the suffering and violence and to offer a solution to it.

Method

The work reported in this chapter comes from clinical ethnography and arises from a conclusion in this book that ethnographic micro-level research is needed to deal with making sense of the past in order to move on and rebuild the future. In chapter 1, Beatrice Pouligny et al. argue for the integration of individual and collective levels of experience. In my research approach I am documenting the multiple experiences from individual, family, monk, traditional healer, medium and other gatekeepers in the collective orbit. My method aims to the manner in which the "collective therapies" advocated by Pouligny et al. for community healing in fact may (or may not) take place in daily living as long as people are free to engage in them. My fieldwork method also is informed by Pouligny et al.'s dictum that the engagement in a narrative-building process has to be regarded as occurring at the intersection of collective history and psychic history, as it would appear that in the Cambodian case these levels cannot be considered independently.

The editors of this book note that while the suffering of individuals who have survived trauma is well understood, the collective consequences remain largely unconsidered. In my fieldwork I set out to document the collective consequences through the experiences of the traditional healers, arguably the most informed key informants in the community in their "professional" knowledge of the impact of trauma on families and extended kin as a whole. The limitation of this method is that micro-level analysis, though rich in its access to the symbolic and ritual data, remains relatively poor in linking with the role of the state.

The method also gives voice to another theme of this book, that a trans-disciplinary and holistic approach is needed in order to capture the many dimensions of the lives of the survivors of mass crime. The editors highlight the need to find ways to stop seeing the individuals who endure mass crimes as "victims" but as people. The method reported in this chapter captures the voices of people through the traditional healer as he or she charts their endurance of extraordinary stress in their day-to-day lives. I have also sought in the fieldwork to capture the Khmer Rouge internal logic that underlines the contemporary violence in the civil society. I have avoided generalizations or essentializations – not only did each person have their own biography during the mass crime, but people also had their own pre-crime histories. Some of the contemporary violence might have existed, it seems, no matter what the earlier experiences of the survivors. The data gathered in this chapter put to rest any idea that the pre-1975 era was an Elysium of peace and health.

The editors note the importance of examining the cultural meaning and significance assigned to the post–mass crime events, and the chapter shows these contextual layers painted by the joined hands of the traditional healers with their patients. One layer has to do with the deep historical roots for understanding violence – in this case, through the legend of Angulimala.

Moreover, I discuss the role of traditional healers in community-based post–mass crime rehabilitation. Not all healers – like not all psychiatrists – are equally capable of offering effective assistance. In 1989 I was the first psychiatrist invited to visit Cambodia after the fall of the Khmer Rouge regime. I apprenticed myself to a traditional healer and became exposed to the general vocabulary of traditional healing, its pharmacopoeia and its codes of conduct. I started to meet a range of other healers. I observed the match, or mismatch, between what people believed caused domestic and community conflict, violence and suffering, and what they did about it – who they blamed within or outside their family, neighbourhood and world of spirits; who they sought in the local network for help; and what was the outcome of the various solutions offered. I traced the terminologies and taxonomies of illness. I documented the methods used by monks, for example, as they focused on advice, calming anxieties and encouraging acceptance. I detailed the ritual diagnostic and treatment methods of the *kruu*, the trained "vocational" healers, as they provided medication and magical rituals to help rid people of spells and spirits and, through the public performance of the ritual, to reintegrate the person into the local community. I sometimes participated in the ceremonies as mediums, mostly women, interceded with ancestors and in this way acted as remoralizing counsellors for the women who could not face their future. I documented examples of structural violence, both the current manifestations and also some of the deeper cultural roots. And I listened as the traditional birth attendants helped families through the difficulties around childbirth and the puerperium, which were compounded by the post-war poverty. In the 16 years up to 2005, 1,211 healers and their communities were documented.

The chapters in this book exemplify the fact that culture is not static, not to be romanticized as an idyllic world to be restored post-conflict. A keystone to the method reported in this chapter is that the work is idiographic, with repeated observations over a decade and a half spanning the key political, psychological and cultural transformations of the society in the civil war and then emerging from it. Over the years I have continued to visit, witnessing the social and political constraints on the practice of traditional healing under the Khmer Rouge at first hand in one of their final strongholds at O Bai Tap. On subsequent visits during the 1990s, I saw the attempts of traditional healers to adapt their explanatory models of disease, vocabulary and rituals to the "strange" new scourge of AIDS and to the new and dramatic incarnations of social violence. In various complementary institutional roles in Cambodia (academic, government advisor, consultant to international organizations, co-designer of the Cambodian mental health program of the Transcultural Psychosocial Organization and director of a research project at the Buddhist Institute), I have heard concerns expressed about the inadequacies of the helping professions to handle the new social disorders among the young, but also noted Buddhism's capacity to adapt to new social contexts and witnessed the success of culturally competent community health projects. A brief history of events follows to show what individuals and communities in Cambodia are struggling to comprehend.

Overview of events

R. J. Rummel has estimated that 169 million people have been killed by their own governments during the twentieth century.[1] Witness Cambodia. Its history unfolds as a mosaic of picturesque peasant life and colourful ceremony and horrendous civil conflict and violence played out against cycles of international good intention and neglect. The most recent round of conflict began towards the end of the 1960s when the Viet Nam War and internal power abuse drove the country into a civil war that produced heavy casualties and dislocation, but it was during the subsequent rule of the infamous Khmer Rouge from 1975–1979 that violence took on the unprecedented dimensions termed by some the "Cambodian holocaust". Of those who died, 40 per cent were executed and 36 per cent starved to death. Very few casualties occurred on the battlefield. A third of the executed were city dwellers, the "new people" whose ways were earmarked for eradication by the Khmer Rouge in a radical social engineering experiment aimed at restoring the country to a largely imaginary bygone pastoral ideal.

In what Henri Locard has termed a cultural ethnocide, the Khmer Rouge were at war with the attitude of the citizens rather than their race or nationality.[2] They attempted a complete remould of Cambodian society, disrupting every aspect of daily life. Monks were defrocked, cities emptied and villages renamed. Ritual life was halted, Buddhism outlawed and family life remodelled. The city dwellers were driven into the countryside and forced to share every aspect of life with the rural peasants. No escape was possible. Although Khmer Rouge executioners drew upon certain traditional codes of honour, many customary practices such as those associated with healing were banned. Traditional healers (they include the vocational *kruu*, Buddhist monks, mediums and traditional birth attendants) stood in the way of fundamentalist Stalinist and Maoist communism. They lost access to their important palm leaf manuscripts, which were burned if discovered. The one aspect of traditional healing retained was herbal medicine, such as tree bark for treatment of malaria. This was consistent with Khmer Rouge doctrine – no Western medicine, no superstitious magic, just use of natural resources such as plants for treatment.

After three years, eight months and twenty days of Khmer Rouge rule – all Cambodians can quote these figures – the traditionally reviled Vietnamese "liberated" Cambodia. The surviving population remained scattered over the countryside and in refugee camps and re-education centres and forced conscription continued as low intensity warfare smouldered on even after the brokered peace of 1991. Villages had "two faces", with government control by day and Khmer Rouge insurgence by night. The end of the Khmer Rouge regime had not put an end to the terror.

In 1992 the United Nations peace operations arrived to prepare the way for democratic elections. One and a half million Cambodians were repatriated after long exile in the Thai border camps and elections did eventuate. However, "normal" Khmer life continued to elude and the

United Nations came to be seen by some as just another corrupting foreign presence. Notions of what constituted "Khmerness" were changing as Cambodians, struggling to heal, re-identified themselves using traditional forms in new ways. Into this post-war state of flux marched the Voice of Prophesy Bible Correspondence School, the new scourge of AIDS, further rounds of conflict as Khmer Rouge strongholds persisted and the elected coalition government blew apart and a new and devastating outbreak of social violence. The latter has continued into the new millennium despite the period of relative political calm and reconstruction efforts since Pol Pot's death in 1998. Against the sheer economic hardship that sees one third of Cambodians still under the basic poverty line, three major scourges hinder peace-building: the mental and spiritual consequences of the Khmer Rouge cultural ethnocide and subsequent further threats to tradition; the epidemic of infectious diseases, most notably AIDS; and the new incarnations of social upheaval that have marked the coming of age of youth born in the wake of the Khmer Rouge.

Disconnection and destruction

Perverting the culture with the Khmer Rouge – The late 1970s

With the fall of the Pol Pot regime in 1979, the surviving three-quarters of the population were scattered around the countryside or taking refuge in camps along the Thai border where they remained until repatriation by the United Nations task force in the early 1990s. Some idea of the kinds of the trauma they had experienced began to emerge from relief workers based in the refugee camps and later through Western-trained physicians dispatched to Cambodia to re-establish basic mental health services. What was described amounted to what Alexander Hinton succinctly describes as the "Cambodian semiotics of violence".[3]

Perhaps more insidious than if they had broken cleanly with tradition, Khmer Rouge cadres selectively leaned on tradition in their attempts to get their political ideology to "stick". Part of this manipulation was a reconstruction of Cambodian explanatory models of illness and healer language to reflect fundamentalist ideas. For example, purges by execution echoed the ritual ejection of harmful elements that formed part of many traditional healing rites. Healers had traditionally distinguished between threats coming from outside and those from within. For the Khmer Rouge the external threat was foreign influence and modernity, and the internal one was the corrupted mentality of the Cambodians themselves who had been rendered indolent by Buddhism and immoral by exposure to Western influence. In order to eliminate this corruption, the Khmer Rouge set out to reconstruct the Cambodian mentality. Cadres would address an individual or a commune meeting with the phrase: "To be out of words to reconstruct [brainwash] you, to knock you off with the back of the axe head." This translated as "Words have failed to do the job of reconstructing you so it is time to reconstruct you another way – by death." The last phrase was a macabre play on words, the syllables being a rearrangement of words for "the back of the axe."

Another example of Khmer Rouge manipulation that borrowed from traditional healing was the sinister diagnosis of a psychological condition described in the old manuals as "thinking-too-much madness". It was a term used to describe stress, loss, bereavement, social and economic deprivation and family disruption, all of which were believed to provoke mental hyperactivity resulting in slow destruction of the mind. For the Khmer Rouge the tag became an excuse to sentence workers to death. Those who were slacking at their toil, ill with malaria, hunger or feelings of loss, were said to have thinking-too-much madness and, in being so labelled, had taken their first step to execution. As a result of how the term was used to sentence workers to death, many Cambodians now avoid it or deny that it existed before Pol Pot, but the healers point to their ancient manuscripts where its diagnosis and treatment are fully detailed.

Thinking-too-much madness is interesting from the psychiatric point of view. Relief workers familiar with Cambodian refugees in the 1980s were so accustomed to hearing of the complaint called "thinking too much" that they were moved to label it "the Cambodian sickness". "Thinking too much" has been interpreted as an idiom of post-traumatic stress disorder and an expression of "cultural bereavement". The syndrome continued to be found among former refugees for years after their resettlement, and was linked not only to the trauma of the Khmer Rouge regime, but also to their recollection (perhaps an example of "false memory") of golden pre-revolutionary years. A similar condition to thinking too much, called "brain fag" syndrome or "overworking the head", has been described among Ethiopian refugees in Israel.

Yet another example of manipulation of traditional healer language is found in the Khmer Rouge adaptation of the Pali term *selathoa*. It was originally used for the one hour a week of morality instruction in primary schools. The Khmer Rouge added the prefix "wrong" to create the phrase "wrong morality" (*khooc selathoa*) and used it specifically to accuse the "new people", meaning the bourgeois city dwellers, of having sex outside marriage. Use of the term came full circle when one young healer I spoke to after the fall of Pol Pot blamed a condition, traditionally called ancestral madness, on moral misbehaviour in families (*pañhaa selathoa*). As a young teenager, he had worked in the Khmer Rouge Mobile Teams and incorporated their vocabulary.

Khmer Rouge mind games associated with traditional healing were the ones to which I was most exposed because of my ethnographic work with healers and my role in establishing community health programs, but they were by no means limited to this field. One can witness their habit of replacing the old place names of districts and streets in an attempt to sever people's association with their place of origin. Henri Locard notes that Communist exhortations were wrapped up in ancient Hindu myths and brutal Maoist-inspired formulas paraded as inverted Buddhist aphorisms in the revolutionary slogans that poured out of the Khmer Rouge propaganda machine. My informants described the use of the old Buddhist term *"pa?decca?sa?mopbaat"* when an official wanted to convey to the ordinary people that the regime had its "high" reasons for doing what it did, all the time in fact explaining nothing. *Pa?decca?sa?mopbaat* is a Pali-derived term for an inevitable result arising from an antecedent cause; the chain of causation is a well-known Buddhist formula that sums up, with tragic irony in the case of Khmer Rouge usage, the causes of suffering.

Thus did the Khmer Rouge create a logic for their killing crafted from their own culture and, in doing so, successfully unhinge a society.

Fresh onslaughts on Cambodian culture – The 1980s and early 1990s

Cambodia had long been a distinctly Theravadin Buddhist society and missionaries had noted the indifference of the people to their message. In the aftermath of the civil war there was a renewed crusade for the hearts and minds of Cambodian survivors. A series of 25 pamphlets was printed in easy-to-read Khmer by the Voice of Prophecy Bible Correspondence School. The pamphlets seemed to offer a more dazzling salvation than Buddhism. The appeal of the message was that a Cambodian survivor's rebirth is a simple matter of cutting loose from the past. The other attraction of this new religion was that Cambodians clutching fresh baptismal certificates were possibly going to please the foreign immigration interviewers and boost their chances of getting away.

One particularly poignant assault on the vulnerable was that of Mike Evans, head of Mike Evans Ministries Inc., a Euless, Texas-based group that organizes Christian crusades in developing countries, and the "God Bless Cambodia" crusade. This group arrived in the Cambodian capital in November 1994, promising that the blind would see and the lame would walk. The poor from all over the country sold all they had to pay for the trip to Phnom Penh. Hoping for a miracle to restore the legs of their amputee relatives, they carried them to the stadium. I witnessed these disabled villagers hobbling up the stadium steps and a little later, when the miracle failed to happen, the dismayed masses.

Western-style health messages have further undermined traditional healing beliefs. Apart from Christian missionary drives, post–Pol Pot traditional healers find themselves competing with government health education campaigns promoting new scientific ways to replace folk practices. During the Heng Samrin regime, World Vision International, with the co-operation of the Cambodian Ministry of Health, produced a series of health education pamphlets in easy-to-read Khmer. One was entitled "Some Traditional Beliefs to be Discarded". This "health education" continued the work of the Khmer Rouge in undercutting the cultural messages of the healers – its aim was to "reconstruct" young mothers by making them ashamed of the traditional code of conduct taught to them by their mothers. Its artfulness lay in its mode of presentation, i.e., it was presented in the old garb and contributed to the women's sense that their past was worthless and that they should not "feed" it to their infants.

Today there are dozens of evangelical groups in Cambodia claiming to represent the one true God and tantalizing the confused masses with the promise of a quick fix, namely immediate rebirth in place of Buddhism's extended cycle of reincarnation. When Khmer villagers hear them, some are tempted to conclude that Buddhism is the cause of their misery. In two weekends in early 2003, nearly 800 people were baptized. However, adopting Christianity does not spare them either for if they misbehave after conversion the missionaries blame their Buddhist backgrounds for their crime – an unwitting echo that feeds into the unconscious memories of similar accusations levelled by the Khmer Rouge. The Ministry of Cult and Religion laments the negative impact of such visitors and finally has banned Christian groups from door-to-door witnessing and handing out tracts.

As for the traditional healers, far from being given the chance to function as human-rights workers, they were abused during the war, persecuted during the Vietnamese occupation and squandered in the wake of post-conflict modernization. During the current post-conflict phase, non-governmental organizations have engaged only a part of the healing sector, mainly the monks, and even they have been used only as counsellors and not given the chance to strengthen the "cultural competence" of peace-building programs. The government line on traditional healers has been one of derision. The healers are blamed for spreading superstition and accused of propagating false beliefs about AIDS and of causing ecological damage as they harvest forest ingredients for traditional medicines.

The new scourge of AIDS – The late 1990s and the new millennium

AIDS was first identified in Cambodia in 1991. AIDS-related diseases have killed about 90,000 people in this country of 12.5 million and a further 160,000 people are currently believed to be infected. Fewer than 500 AIDS patients receive free treatment from the government. News articles over the years depict AIDS as Cambodia's new killing fields, a view echoed by Im Sethy, Secretary of State for Education and by United Nations Population Fund Goodwill Ambassador Chea Samnang.

The metaphor linking AIDS to the Khmer Rouge killing fields picks up on some interesting parallels. For the Khmer Rouge, Cambodians had an enemy in their midst, it came from the outside and corrupted the population, who then needed to be saved from themselves. Popular explanations of AIDS reflect various versions of a very similar scenario, including the explanation offered by Khmer Rouge cadres themselves. Members of a Khmer Rouge breakaway group at O Bai Tap in the north-western regions near Anlong Veng told me when I visited in mid-1998 that they had never seen or heard of AIDS and upon learning of the new scourge felt further justified in their isolation and self-reliance. Khmer Rouge ideology reflected long-held beliefs about foreigners bringing pestilence. Before 1975, health workers called sexually transmitted infections (STI) "illness of sexual desire", from the formal Buddhist term. During the Khmer Rouge period, the cadres forced the use of the politically correct term "illness of the community" in which the word for community implied immorality associated with the corrupt Sihanouk and Lon Nol eras. All health problems tended to be seen by the Khmer Rouge in similar judgmental terms – after all, they had been separated from the world for up to 30 years. But as their strongholds fell there were increased fears of contact with the Khmer mainstream and the STI they assumed the latter would carry from Vietnamese prostitutes. The Vietnamese, and especially their beguiling women, had always been considered a peril to the nation. This thousand-year loathing and fear of contamination was given a new voice by the Khmer Rouge, who now saw the Vietnamese as corrupted seductresses bearing the AIDS chalice. The Khmer Rouge enclaves in the 1990s had maintained the xenophobia that had fuelled the mass crime of the 1970s and applied now to the scourge of AIDS.

It was these beliefs that surfaced yet again across Cambodia in the explanations of the origin of AIDS offered by the healers who had returned to their profession in the post-conflict era. The healers were reflecting the popular view that AIDS had arrived in Cambodia with the United Nations Transitional Authority in Cambodia task force (UNTAC) in 1992.

The following are some healer variations on the foreign contaminant theme.

Some healers believed AIDS had been created when an African man mated with an ape which one healer identified as "King Kong". ("Africa" for village Cambodians signified a land where the unfortunate inhabitants had black skin.) The African spread the disease and eventually it arrived in Cambodia. In another version, a woman was seeking refugee in the Cambodian forest when she was overwhelmed by a group of virile apes and forced to have multiple sex with their chief. One day she managed to escape and, some time later, learned that she had AIDS. She ran to the USA, and through her it spread all over the world. In this account a woman rather than a man is the first human to get AIDS, and the woman exports rather than imports the disease. One female medium believed that it was prostitutes' usage of a female version of Viagra, which they took to fortify themselves for their many clients, which had created AIDS. In this version the medicine was "the foreigner", it being imported from Thailand.

The healers felt that Cambodians, impoverished and malnourished, were particularly vulnerable to AIDS even though some considered the Cambodian strain of the virus less virulent. A female traditional healer expressed it like this: Cambodians were too poor to eat proper meals. In France and the United States people had access to more meat and were stronger so the virus that knocked them down must also be stronger. Her logic was that the medicine they needed had to be stronger too and that the AIDS strain in Cambodia was easier to treat. Few healers acknowledged that pre-revolutionary Cambodia had prostitutes, although any older healer was adept at treating syphilis, which was widely documented in the old palm leaf healing manuscripts. In 1990 a former Khmer Rouge cadre had shown me the houses where pre-UNTAC prostitutes plied their trade. They were, he said, "under control, and submitting to regular health tests".

A few healers showed reluctance to blame UNTAC soldiers for the arrival of AIDS and pointed out that AIDS had affected every country. Some put the blame on Vietnamese and Thai prostitutes for infecting UNTAC soldiers. But more commonly, as referred to above, AIDS explanations revealed a deep-seated Cambodian prejudice against outsiders and a prejudice against those with dark skin. It was not unusual to hear that it was the black UNTAC soldiers who brought AIDS to Cambodia. In another xenophobic allusion, it was suggested that the AIDS germ had first been concentrated in the brains of affected monkeys that ate fruit grown on contaminated soil. Foreigners – Japanese, English, American and Australian – ate the monkey brain and, in this way, the germ crossed to humans and entered their blood stream. The UNTAC soldiers transferred it to Cambodian prostitutes and so it passed to Cambodian men. Such allusions suggest that perhaps the Khmer Rouge mass crime tapped some deep-seated xenophobia, which became turned upon itself. One might suggest a direct connection with the genocide, not just a general desire to blame outside influence.

Chris Lyttleton observes that the Thai HIV/AIDS campaign has practiced similar politics of distancing and stigma as campaigns elsewhere, but in Thailand the feared "other" is very much the prostitute rather than the homosexual community or injecting drug users.[4] I have observed the same in Cambodia where the men depict the Vietnamese prostitutes as eagerly patronized and also reviled as archfiends bearing HIV. (Cambodians traditionally also tend to blame malaria on "others in their midst". "Others" originally referred to the autochthonous hill tribe, the Phnong. With the outbreak of civil war in the 1970s "others" came to mean a foreign substance, such as ammunition fumes.)

None of this is to suggest that AIDS is a second killing field, but strong themes link the two – the people were vulnerable, there was an enemy in their midst, it came from the outside and the people needed to be saved from themselves.

The upsurge of social violence and terror – The late 1990s and the new millennium

One might have thought that the end of the long civil war, the receding memory of the Khmer Rouge nightmare, greater economic stability and the birth of a new generation would bring about a reduction in community violence. Indeed, non-governmental organizations working in Cambodia remarked that this generally appeared to be so until the mid-1990s. Until then the Government wielded strong control, directing foreigners to designated places to sleep, placing prostitutes into re-education, regulating citizen movement and ritualizing public venting of anger against the reign of terror through the institution each 20 May of a National Hate Day. The editors of this book note in their introduction that insufficient attention has been paid to the radical transformation of belief systems and codes of conduct of individuals and communities who experience mass crime. Of the reconstruction issues highlighted by the editors, the creation, then the forgetting, of National Hate Day is a cardinal example of the rewriting, again and again, of history. The National Hate Day promoted during the Vietnamese occupation (1979–1989) was an example of the use and abuse by the state for its own purposes of memories, Paul Ricoeur's "manipulated" or "obliged" memory in the construction of a national history. Just as the Khmer Rouge before them had tapped national identity, the Heng Samrin regime tried to engrave memory on the survivors to justify the continuing national struggle against a resurgence of the Maoist–Pol Potist axis.

The first turning point came in 1992 when politicians, wanting to gain popularity for impending elections, relaxed some of the rules. Then a market economy began to emerge and furthered the explosion of personal freedoms leading to the first concerns that people had forgotten how to behave. National Hate Day was disestablished and high schools reduced their history of the Khmer Rouge era to a mere five lines so that, in the words of Henri Locard: "The younger generations do not know what really happened, and the older know but do not understand."[5] In this way, the youth were born and raised in the absence of an explicit narrative of their country's trauma, a vacuum that more violence seemed destined to fill.

In the early days after the fall of Pol Pot's regime in 1979, some demobilized soldiers took to banditry and the odd motorcycle went missing but, after the "complete" outbreak of peace with the collapse of the final Khmer Rouge resistance in 1998, social violence escalated dramatically. The daily newspapers are now filled with detailed catalogues of the day's violence – domestic violence, gang rapes, incest, robbery and murder. People began to ask why, and the stereotypic response was that "it was the Khmer Rouge". One way to grasp the flavour of this violence, and the way it is generally perceived by the community, is to quote from local newspaper articles. This is not to claim that the reports are balanced or accurate, but simply that they portray the sort of awareness ordinary people have about the social violence around them.

Domestic violence

It is estimated that one in four women in Cambodia is a victim of domestic violence. The Department of Sexual Trafficking and Violence states that during 2000/01, alcohol was the cause of 33 per cent of the cases of domestic violence. Other causes of violence were adultery (33 per cent), gambling (16 per cent) and poverty (18 per cent).[6] According to the *Kampuchea Thmey*,

> A 34-year-old man beat his family. The wife had a younger sister and had told her husband the sister would be going to the Thai border to seek work as a green-bean picker, but the husband told his wife to tell her sister not to leave. The wife became furious and told him to tell her himself. At this, the husband became enraged and beat his wife with a one-metre rod. The sister came to help her, but was beaten as well. Then the wife's father came, and he too was beaten. When he had finished beating them, the man was not yet satisfied and burned the house. The neighbours extinguished the fire, with about a quarter of the house gone. Then the wife called the police who arrested him.[7]

Women hurting women

There are growing reports of spurned women on the offensive against husbands and rivals. According to a report in the *Koh Santepheap Daily*,

> The victim was a Vietnamese sex worker. The perpetrator's husband was in love with the prostitute and rented a house for her. When his wife discovered this, she and her aunt grabbed the victim, and the aunt kept her still while the wife slashed her face with a razor. The screaming of the victim attracted bystanders, who immediately restrained the woman and her aunt and called the police.[8]

Rape

Another report in the *Koh Santepheap Daily* offers the following account:

> The man bound the woman by her neck, hands and feet. This is an action of the kind that Dharani would pull the person into the waters and into Hell, and as if the man had excrement on his hands. Normally people rape very young girls, but now they are raping the elderly as well. This woman was almost blind, crippled, impoverished. Her daughter was a widow, and called another elderly widow aged 73 years to come to her house and take care of her. The murderer broke into the house and said that he wanted to rape the 73-year-old. He grabbed her and she told him she'd rather be killed than raped. He let her go and she ran away and hid behind a cashew tree near the house. She heard the older woman screaming for help. The perpetrator had stuffed his underpants into her mouth to stifle her cries. The woman's legs had been broken and her face bitten. She had been strangled. The killer was a 35-year-old man who lived in the same village as the victim. He had separated from his wife where they used to live in Kampot province. In this district in the last few months, six people had been killed, including one child who had also been raped, and a father murdered by his son.[9]

Paedophilia and sexual abuse

In Erin Nelson and Cathy Zimmerman's study of battered wives, more than half stated that their children also were beaten.[10] In a further survey, 16 per cent of women were battered and a large percentage stated that their husbands hit the children. Given that girls who have endured sexual abuse and family violence, including domestic violence, have been found in Cambodia to be prone to move into prostitution, there are long-term effects over the horizon.

> Three young boys aged from 11 to 14 years were arrested for having raped a 5-year-old girl at noon in Banteay Meanchey district. The 11-year-old is the brother of the victim, and initiated the action by persuading his friends. Their mother said that the three confessed that they had just viewed a sex video. She realized only when she saw the bloodstain on her daughter's skirt and her son

told her the truth. She sued and asked the police to take action according to the law. The 14-year-old boy also told the police that when he had lived in the provincial capital he had persuaded his immediate younger sister, then five years old, to have sex with him, and when his family moved to this village he had sex with another little girl. Altogether he had raped three girls, the police confirmed that the root cause of the problem was that a military official had played sex videos at his house and had allowed a big group of boys to watch, arousing them to rape the girls.[11]

Rape committed by children is increasingly common. Many people blame the Khmer Rouge for having caused so many young people to be raised with impunity. Mu Sochua, the Minister of Women's Affairs, came under attack when she recently commented that the prevalence of gang rape and sexual abuse should not be blamed on the Khmer Rouge. Others point to the easy access to pornographic videos. A monk told us the folk expression for incest: "The younger brother takes the mother, the older brother takes the child."

Murder of a parent

A 35-year-old fisherman took a cleaver to kill his mother. He had demanded $200 eight times from his mother, but she was 69 years old and had no means to meet his demands. One day he brought 8 litres of gasoline and threatened to burn her house down. When the police arrested him, he confessed that he needed money and he believed it was no use threatening to kill someone else because they would report him and he would be thrown into prison, but if he threatened his own mother she wouldn't call the police.[12]

In relation to this type of crime a monk explained that alcohol and drug abuse had damaged the body elements within the brain that formed the basis of the mind and the normal innate abhorrence of incest and violence within the family had been weakened by this abuse. This leads into my next theme, which has to do with suggestions for strengthening the cultural competence of international peace-building initiatives, that I launch with a recommendation that traditional healers be allowed to play a greater role. I begin by expounding on how mass violence is being explained by the traditional healers, who include, as previously indicated, Buddhist monks, vocationally trained healers called *kruu*, mediums and traditional birth attendants.

Reconnection and reconstruction

Jacques Sémelin cites this telling observation by René Lemarchand's comparative study of the cases of Cambodia, Bosnia-Herzegovina and Rwanda:

The ideological factors that may be known as either Marxist-Leninism, nationalism or a perverted vision of democracy ... seldom affect the masses unless their language can be radically transformed and adopted to the local culture. It is therefore the re-interpretation, or even the fabrication of myths about the history of the country that allows for the ideological "transplanting" into local culture. It is for this reason that the study of tales, rumors and memories belonging to a culture, as is proposed by Beatrice Pouligny, is important for comprehending the massacres that have been committed within them.... It is in fact this plunge into the imaginary that gives historical and emotional resonance to the ideological discourse.[13]

Sémelin provides the rationale for the following analysis, in which I show how the traditional healers and monks explain the violence and suffering in Buddhist, Brahmanic and folk idioms.[14] The healers attempt to make sense of the contemporary violence through deeply embedded templates of cause-and-effect and morality maps understood to some extent by many ordinary people.

Healers' perspectives on the causes of the violence and suffering

The nation's religious and traditional healing system has begun to retrieve some of its former influence after being outlawed by the Khmer Rouge. Buddhism is gaining new recruits. For example, there were 50,081 monks in 1998/99, compared with 6,500 to 8,000 in 1985–1989. Several non-governmental organizations are beginning to look to Buddhism to guide approaches to health and psychosocial services, and more Cambodians are sponsoring Buddhist ceremonies to commemorate their relatives killed during the war. Other traditional healers have resumed practice and, although they are competing with Western-influenced government health messages and may not wield the same influence on those who spent long years in the refugee camps exposed to other ways, their therapeutic capacities are sought by many ordinary villagers. What light do the healers throw on how Cambodia is interpreting the mass crime of the past three decades?

The sheer scale of the turmoil, particularly the upsurge of social violence, has precluded traditional healers from arriving at any single certainty about causes and cures. Yet, they have some ideas. A monk in Ang Snuol district cited two causes for domestic violence – the cycle of poverty that leads to a search for escape in alcohol, which in turn breeds drunkenness and wife beating, and the cycle of corruption and greed that leads men into dalliance in bars, creating angry wives whose complaints then also result in wife beating. He referred to the saying "a gourd sinks, the smashed glass floats", which refers to an inversion of the natural and that the bad has come to rule the good (this is in fact the title of a memoir on growing up under the Khmer Rouge). The monk said that in the past a gourd would normally float, but in this era something has changed and gourds will actually sink. Until the present day, the child of good parents became a good person, but now good parents can produce bad children, i.e., children who sink like a gourd now sinks.

Another explanation for violence I heard – and it is a view held not just by healers – is that all the million people who were killed during 1975–1979 have been reborn and are now coming of age. These people are looking for revenge and they have a savage character. So they do to others what was done to them. The healers will cite evidence for this – that when some children are born they have marks on their wrists or upper arms which means they had been bound with hands either in front or behind. Sometimes when a child has a mark on the face, and especially on the back of the neck, people will say it was because it was beaten or executed by the Khmer Rouge in its previous life. On seeing these signs, the new parents may feel pity for the child.

Domestic violence

Healers explain domestic violence in the following terms: In former times, a couple married only after their parents had consulted an astrologer to determine physical and emotional compatibility based on year of birth. Now, couples go ahead without this checking. The parents are fearful but resign themselves to the new mode. Other couples were forced to marry during the Pol Pot times and their relationships have come unstuck because their hearts have been forced. Of those forced to marry, they say fully 80 per cent have separated and the remainder only stay together because of the children.

Women hurting women

The visceral rage that leads to revenge attacks by women upon other women is hard to stem. The monks try to soothe with explanations of cause-and-effect, for example, that attacks are the result of women having affairs perhaps in the past life; some have forgotten that adultery is punished by Hell.

> Today there are some who fear but there are others who are like animals – an animal is hungry, it eats; it is thirsty, it drinks. A dog runs after the rabbit that runs and if the rabbit has no bad karma it will run into the forest and the dog does not reach it, whereas if it has bad karma, it will not seek refuge in the forest and the dog will bite it. In other words, it is not the dog's fault. The dog is simply the instrument for the fate of the rabbit. Our karma, like the dog, will pursue us until it catches us and there is no escape. A child does bad to his father, your child will do bad to you.

The women's karma catches up. The acid burns they suffer at the hands of angry wives represent the flames of Hell that are the traditional fate of adulterers.

The newspaper articles cited earlier pick up on the not-uncommon prejudice that marital trouble stems from the Vietnamese, more specifically Vietnamese prostitutes. At least one healer I spoke to was keen to shift the emphasis away from the ethnicity of the prostitutes and onto the risks the profession itself poses for society. Citing the old Khmer saying "*kam put sralav, kam pradav srey khooc*", that is, "do not try to bend the tree that stands firm", he explained that a prostitute has already done wrong many times over and even if she "goes straight" and marries will never be sexually satisfied. So any man who falls in love with such a woman cannot expect fidelity.

Coming to terms with perpetual widowhood

The monks help us to understand the seeming inability of Cambodian widows to remarry and find a path to economic security for their children. There are always going to be people who did wrong in the previous life and should therefore suffer in this one, and therefore there must be people who are born to commit violence against them. It is a system in balance, as reflected in the Buddhist story about the sparrow husband and wife:

> The male sparrow left his female partner brooding the eggs while he went to the forest to seek food. There he saw a beautiful open lotus but when he landed on it in the heat of the day the lotus closed on him and he could not get out. There was a forest fire, and the female sparrow waited for her husband but he did not return. When eventually the fire died down, the male sparrow was able to escape but when he arrived back at the nest he was covered in the aroma of the lotus. The female sparrow, angered and dismayed, vowed that she would never take up with a male in the next life, and committed suicide. The male sparrow also killed himself, vowing that in his next life he would take up with only one sparrow, namely his spouse.

More work could be done with the monks to flush out other such stories to help heal the widows and encourage them to find alternative paths to security.

Rape and incest

The theory of karma has traditionally helped people to explain violation, even serious offences like rape, and continues to do so. For example, if I had raped another man's daughter in the previous life that father when reborn would rape my daughter in this life. As for incest, some healers explain that if in a man's previous incarnation he was an animal, he may not have had the chance to acquire human morality and he may commit incest because animals do not have an incest taboo.

Murder of a parent

Everyone in Cambodia knows that during the mass crime the children denounced and sometimes put parents to death. With the present upsurge of young people murdering their parents, some monks draw upon well-known stories, such as that of Angulimala (from *anguli*, fingers, and *mie*, enemy). Here is a distillation of the stories told by many Cambodian monks in an effort to explain violence through a Buddhist voice:

Angulimala was born in India during the lifetime of the Buddha, and was called Ahimsaka, "The Harmless One". One day, some envious students set up Ahimsaka, and his teacher decided to punish him by telling them that to complete his training he had one more task: to kill 1,000 people.

Ahimsaka set off into the forest and killed anyone he met. To keep count, whenever he killed, he would cut a finger from the person's hand and string the finger on a cord. People began to call him Angulimala, the one with the string of bloody fingers. Eventually, his count reached 999. Only one more finger was needed.

The king's soldiers were out hunting Angulimala, and his mother was also searching for him to save him. Buddha heard her crying, and she told him she had to save her son, so the Buddha went to look for him. Angulimala was waiting for his next victim, saw the Buddha approaching, and shouted that he should stop as he was about to die, but the Buddha continued. Angulimala ran after the Buddha to kill him, but he could not catch up. Gasping, Angulimala called, "How is it you continue walking slowly, and I, running as fast as I can, can never catch you?" The Buddha said to him, "I have stopped harming people, but you have not."

Upon being called Ahimsaka by the Buddha, he returned to his true self. The Buddha told him he could turn to Ahimsaka, and leave Angulimala behind. "Hold on to your despair and grief. The time will come when all of the evil karma you have created will be resolved."

Children heckled the now-harmless Ahimsaka. Children threw stones at him, daring him to cut off their fingers. Miraculously, every stone that was thrown in the city hit not the intended victim but Ahimsaka. Ahimsaka took upon himself the pain and punishment of all the victims, and the evil karma he had created found its resolution. Near death and in great pain, he was told that all the suffering he had given others is resolved. All the fingers he severed were felt by him.

The monk had echoed the story of Angulimala told by the Shakyamuni Buddha in the eighty-sixth sutra of the *Majjhima Nikaya*. The monk was trying to explain that some monks, like the Buddha, have special means to stop violent people from committing further violence. Such stories, which centre on the resolution of evil karma, are accessible to average rural villagers. Characters from these stories appear in films, on the temple walls and in traditional songs and are readily recognized. Pol Pot, as well, was not averse to manipulating the Buddhist notion of karmic predestiny for his own ends.

If the people who survive mass crime have shaky connections with their cultural heritage, the international governmental and non-governmental organizations also affect the durability of reconciliation. The editors of this book recommend that the cultural position of the external actors be included in specific training before deployment to the field. This chapter on Cambodia shows up some of the elements deemed necessary to be included in a cultural-competence toolkit. With their rituals of purging foreign elements, whether they be spirits or ethnic minorities, post-trauma symptoms or incurable imported viruses, I would argue that healers have a capacity to help people deal with personal loss and cultural bereavement that is unmatched by many of the intervention models used by emergency and humanitarian organizations. The latter are inclined to assume that universal principles and practice apply to matters of health and social justice. They do not.

Mental health programs

The forms that the consequences of trauma assume are dictated by both local history and culture, and an understanding of local idioms of distress unlocks the clinical-symptom profile of psychological and social disorder. Combining local resources such as traditional healers with external relief workers can ameliorate the psychosocial problems of large groups, not just individuals. Cultural and contextual variables should be studied at population and individual levels and both Western quantitative research instruments and culture-sensitive qualitative tools are needed to measure post-traumatic stress disorder. Without them the "category fallacy" is perpetuated, where indigenous diagnoses are overlooked and Western categories imposed where they have no cultural validity.

A growing literature attests to the value of traditional healers as "trauma therapists" in countries recovering from war. Patrick Bracken et al., writing on the Luwero triangle that is Uganda's "killing fields", noted that "Not only were they providing therapies for sick individuals, but they functioned as a link with the past and thus contributed a sense of continuity to the family."[15] It seems to me that traditional healers often provide a more comfortable means for the people to resolve their personal sadness and their community problems than do the methods brought by Westerners. More than that, the traditional methods are themselves a way of combating feelings of cultural loss caused by ongoing modernization and development projects. The latest upsurge in social violence in Cambodia is often stereotyped as a social remodelling reminiscent of the violence of the Khmer Rouge, but in fact it reflects a loss of group identity for the youth born in the wake of the Khmer Rouge and the subsequent avalanche of Western values, who faced this double onslaught unprotected by cultural and religious codes to guide their conduct.

People recovering from war and loss are not in an ideal position to absorb new health beliefs. On the contrary, the conservative impulse often seen as a reaction to crisis causes a search to rediscover, draw upon and sometimes even to reinvent older resources, to resort to explanatory models more familiar and more able to offer comfort. Also, an "outbreak of peace" may bring about new problems such as AIDS and social violence as it has in Cambodia, for which conventional medicine has few answers. Some conflict situations isolate victims from conventional Western-style healthcare over long periods, allowing traditional healers to thrive, in which case international reconstruction teams should think twice about snatching them away.

Outsiders may not detect suffering because it can take hidden forms and remain in the background. In a country like Cambodia where trauma has affected everyone, the suffering is visible but its *cultural meaning* may be invisible to the outsider. We cannot assume that violence can always be made meaningful, but my observations in Cambodia suggest that traditional healers are striving to provide meaning to loss and trauma even if it does not make sense to us, and although they are struggling to keep pace with the changing faces of trauma, their meanings may still offer greater psychological comfort to those they are trying to heal. That communities do try to make sense of war and its aftermath is an aspect of healing that the international community needs to keep in mind.

Containing contagious disease

When it comes to confronting the upsurge of contagious diseases such as AIDS and the continued high levels of malaria in Cambodia, international interventions could be more culturally competent. These epidemics are linked in the minds of the people to their post-war vulnerability and their moral and cultural weakening and to the treachery of foreigners whose soldiers of peace brought a devastating enemy germ. The anti-AIDS and anti-malaria campaigns have been informative about "the facts" of safe sex or combating the mosquito, but they could be made more culturally competent, at least for the rural majority, by harnessing the native logic of the Cambodian people about contagion and taking into account the impact of their post-war self-image upon risk behaviour.

Social justice

Healing is not merely about the treatment of suffering individuals; it is about repairing the social and moral fabric of the community within which these suffering individuals reside. Social justice is culturally con-structed. The dismantling of social justice is best done by those who know the culture, and the Khmer Rouge, as I have shown, were masters at this. They knew about the people's ways of thinking. They knew how to tap linguistics and symbols to forge powerful messages. They knew how to tap the archaic, almost xenophobic, fears of the Cambodian peo-ple, a people who had no tradition of tourism or travel and whose per-ception of foreigners was limited to their experience of rapacious neigh-bouring countries, Viet Nam and Thailand – a crocodile and a tiger ready to pounce on either side. It is now too late to put things back the way they were, but some re-centring of power and trust to where it belongs in the community is needed and the international agencies must be kept on track. I would argue that the traditional healers as master narrators and culture brokers are the best placed to perform such tasks.

Some ask if the new upsurge of social violence in Cambodia is related to the fact that Khmer Rouge leaders have not been brought to justice. Westerners in particular question this culture of political impunity. How can survivors co-exist in their villages alongside their former tormenters? Why are people content with the response "The perpetrators will be pun-ished by their karma in the next incarnation"? In many countries, post-conflict peace-building is laden with terms such as "truth commission", "reconciliation" or "remorse", but these Judeo-Christian notions are anathema to Cambodian culture. As Henri Locard notes, "If you express remorse and repentance, you lose face, you put yourself in a position below the person you admit you have offended or hurt."[16]

Possible healer limitations

It is feasible that the time-proven ways by which ordinary people have sought to resolve community disharmony, namely consulting village healers who for centuries have treated their "thinking-too-much mad-ness", "lovesickness madness" and "ancestral spirit disorder", may no longer be effective. The pernicious new incarnations of trauma as parents traffic daughters, children shoot parents, brothers rape sisters, women hurl acid and youth abuse drugs are culturally malignant ways to resolve conflict and manage violence for which the prescribed healing rituals may be inadequate. In the wake of a cultural revolution initiated by those rival scholars of the mind, the Khmer Rouge, and continued by the forces of globalization, I do not claim there is any guarantee that the healers will successfully recapture the best of ebbing traditions and use them to alleviate Cambodia's suffering.

Monks, too, have been exposed to the secular world. They watch Thai television, surf the Internet, communicate on mobile phones and carry guns. There are reports of alcohol abuse and night visits from sex workers as well. Novices are admitted who until recently would have been deemed ineligible because they are physically or mentally unwell – a sign of progress or standards being compromised? The Buddhist Institute has launched a program to rectify reported aberrations but is considering some hard questions: Are monks being effectively trained for outreach work? If cultural traditions are linked, albeit perversely, with the Khmer Rouge, will attempts to restore them be successful? How are the monks making themselves relevant to the youth? Do lay devotees have some lessons to offer? One such devotee has a very popular radio program proposing remedies for social problems and his personal integrity is seen as exemplary. The National Institute for Traditional Medicine, which is part of the Ministry of Health, also faces challenges. Their focus on assessing the pharmaceutical effectiveness of traditional plants could perhaps usefully be expanded to weighing the potential role of vocational healers as indigenous resources for peace-building.

Conclusion

The Cambodian traditional healers have given voice to a particular cultural interpretation of mass crimes, one that may tap the hearts of the people who survived and of their children. Their message echoes several themes brought forward in this book. The first theme is the individual and collective dimensions of mass-crime situations. The editors of this book note how "intimate crime" leaves deep marks individually and collectively, weakening the regulatory functions of society. The Khmer Rouge, like a virus that commandeers the DNA of its victims, drew on the taproots of the Khmer society as they saw it. Basic trust was lost, and to some extent remained lost. In this way, the damage had been implanted and remained in the civil society long after the demise of the Khmer Rouge. Witness the escalation of family violence and the climate of impunity that continued, as well as the questioning of traditional cultural codes of conduct along with an ambivalent uptake of Western commodification as a futile search for happiness.

Roberto Beneduce warns of the need to analyse local forms of the reproduction of violence and its embodiment in ritual and social imagination; the Cambodian traditional healers have shown how Buddhist and local animist beliefs (and ritual) were both adapted by the perpetrators of mass crime and offer an epistemological meaning for the survivors who are coming to terms with "why". Beneduce also warns of the danger of applying Western psychiatric categories such as PTSD; the Cambodian healers provide the international community with an entire lexicon, taxonomic toolkit, panorama of indigenous explanatory models and ritual practices aimed at shoring up the confidence of troubled survivors.[17]

In chapter 7, René Lemarchand and Maurice Niwese show the cycle of interethnic violence in Rwanda and Burundi, and they argue for the need to disaggregate the perpetrators. In chapter 6, Natalija Bašić shows a similar heterogeneity in former Yugoslavia and the successor states. In the Cambodian case the perpetrators and victims were (with the notable exception of the Chinese and Cham minorities) of similar ethnic, religious and cultural backgrounds. The class enemy was truly in the midst, giving rise to a degree of suspicion about even the most trusted senior cadre and perhaps leading to a contemporary sense that anyone could have been (and could be) a closet enemy.

Another theme in this book is the memories and representations of mass crimes. In chapter 9, Thomas Sherlock considers the reinterpretations of Baltic, Ukrainian and Chechen history in the Soviet and post-Soviet periods, showing how historical discourse promotes both conflict and peace-building. The Cambodian case shows a similar public delegitimization of Khmer Rouge myths ("Chinese communism") and the Warsaw Pact myths of the post–Khmer Rouge decade ("Soviet communism") to have emerged during the current love affair with free markets yet it has not been as clean-cut a break as Sherlock's depiction of the post-Soviet scene.

Although it is not possible to trace a sure cause-and-effect relationship between the mass crimes of the Khmer Rouge era and forms of violence described in this chapter, in the eyes of many ordinary Cambodians, there is no doubt that one exists. By giving voice to the traditional healers as barometers of popular culture, this chapter captures at least one strand of that link. The evidence also shows that Khmer Rouge members are themselves a product as well as a cause of violence.

A third theme of this book is peace-building strategies and the role of outsiders. Louis Kriesberg in chapter 10 discusses the role of international governmental organizations and international non-governmental organizations in affecting the durability of peace. Good post-conflict peace-building rests on an understanding of this popular cultural understanding of the mass violence. Aid workers need to address the problems of groups and not just individuals who suffer in the wake of conflict and, beyond that, to structure a culturally competent response to large-scale human suffering. They need to take the wide-angle view in which experiences from diverse disciplines including public health, social science, mental health care and rural development strategies are combined. Rather than imposing a general model of post-traumatic stress disorder on every trauma situation (as may be done by international non-governmental organizations advancing mental health programs), they need to make room for local exponents of folk culture, such as traditional healers, to make their contribution to peace-building.

Capacity building for peace needs to take into account the transformative meaning and effect of war. Humanitarian aid can feed a cargo cult mentality. Some government officials and those from the upper echelons of society may unwittingly undermine local capacity for healing by unquestioningly privileging foreign public health strategies that are part of the package that arrives with multinational investment and missionaries. Traditional healers could perhaps trace a gentler and more culturally competent path towards the best of what is new. They understand the local rules for conflict resolution and can assist in the identification of resilience factors within the local society. Given support to adapt to post-conflict circumstances, I believe they have the potential to point the compass towards culturally competent peace-building. In chapter 4, Kimberly Theidon shows how *campesinos* in Peru explained lethal violence and how the war was experienced as an attack against cultural practices; the Cambodian healers, in explaining such attacks, also offer key elements for cultural competence in post-conflict peace-building. It is not enough, however, to create detailed compendia of the Guatemalan, Rwandan, Peruvian or Congolese cultures and their reactions to mass violence. Cultural competence, while founded on such understandings, calls for the development of generic skills for staff and program developers, and for research and evaluation.

In this new age of global terrorism, the wheel of xenophobia so skilfully manipulated by the mass crime of the Khmer Rouge has turned full circle. The ethnic Cham community in Cambodia is targeted as a fifth column linked to world terror. This new focus echoes the Khmer Rouge attacks on the Cham. The authorities closed the Om Al-Qura Institute and planned to expel 28 foreign Islamic teachers, who they believed were connected with Osama bin Laden. Hambali was arrested as a Jemaah Islamiah leader. And now, the former Khmer Rouge soldiers are being treated for nightmares. Global contemporary fears, such as of terrorism and SARS, again may fuel dark currents of xenophobia not fully quenched in the survivors of the mass crime.

Notes

1. R. J. Rummel, *Death by Government*, New Brunswick, NJ: Transaction, 1994, p. 4.
2. Henri Locard, *Pol Pot's Little Red Book: The Sayings of Angkar*, Chang Mai, Thailand: Silkworm Books, 2005.
3. A. L. Hinton, "Why did you kill? The Cambodian genocide and the dark side of face and honor", *Journal of Asian Studies* 57, no. 1, 1988, pp. 93–122. For further studies of the Cambodian genocide, see D. P. Chandler, 1991, *The Tragedy of Cambodian History: Politics, War, and Revolution*, New Haven: Yale University Press, 1991; M. M. Ebihara and J. Ledgerwood, "Aftermaths of Genocide: Cambodian Villagers", in A. L. Hinton, ed., *Annihilating Difference: The Anthropology of Genocide*, Berkeley: University of California Press, 2002, pp. 272–291; M. Eisenbruch, "Toward a culturally sensitive DSM: Cultural bereavement in Cambodian refugees and the traditional healer as taxonomist", *Journal of Nervous and Mental Disease* 180, no. 1, 1992, pp. 8–10; M. A. Martin, "Vietnamised Cambodia: A silent ethnocide", *Indochina Report* 7, 1986, pp. 1–31. D. J. Somasundaram, W. A. van de Put, M. Eisenbruch and J. T. de Jong, "Starting mental health services in Cambodia", *Social Science & Medicine* 48, no. 8, 1999, pp. 1029–1046; W. van de Put and M. Eisenbruch, "The Cambodian experience", in J. T. de Jong, ed., *Trauma, War, and Violence: Public Mental Health in Socio-Cultural Context*, New York: Plenum/Kluwer, 2002, pp. 93–16.
4. Chris Lyttleton, "Messages of Distinction: The HIV/AIDS Media Campaign in Thailand", *Medical Anthropology* 16, no. 4, pp. 363–89.
5. Locard, *Pol Pot's Little Red Book*.
6. See Cathy Zimmerman's report on domestic violence in Cambodia, available from http://www.ias.org.uk/theglobe/2001gapabangkok/cambodia.htm.
7. See *Kampuchea Thmey*, April 2003.
8. See *Koh Santepheap Daily*, May 2003.
9. *Koh Santepheap Daily*, May 2003.
10. E. Nelson and C. Zimmerman, *Household survey on domestic violence in Cambodia*, Phnom Penh: Ministry of Women's Affairs and Project Against Domestic Violence, 1996.
11. *Koh Santepheap Daily*, June 2003.
12. *Koh Santepheap Daily*, May 2003.
13. J. Sémelin, "Toward a vocabulary of massacre and genocide", *Journal of Genocide Research* 5, no. 2, 2003, pp. 193–210.
14. Ibid.
15. P. J. Bracken, J. W. Giller and D. Summerfield, "Psychological responses to war and atrocity: The limitations of current concepts", *Social Science & Medicine* 40, no. 8, 1995, pp. 1073–1082.
16. Locard, *Pol Pot's Little Red Book*.
17. Roberto Beneduce, this volume.

4

Intimate enemies: Reconciling the present in post-war communities in Ayacucho, Peru

Kimberly Theidon

> The *Senderistas* attacked at night. We would be asleep. The smell of smoke woke us up – the roofs all in flames. Then the screaming. We would grab our children and run toward the river. It was dark, but they wore masks. If they had taken off those masks, we would have recognized them. They were our neighbors. *Díos Tayta*, we've seen what our neighbors can do.
> – Carhuahurán, community in Ayacucho, Peru, 2000

My intention in this chapter is to explore how *campesinos* in the highlands of Ayacucho constructed lethal violence in the context of Peru's fratricidal war, and how the concepts and practices of communal justice have permitted them to develop a micropolitics of reconciliation at the communal and intercommunal levels. One particularity of internal wars, such as Peru's, is that foreign armies do not wage the attacks: Frequently the enemy is a son-in-law, a godfather, an old schoolmate or the community that lies just across the valley. The armed peasant patrols keep watch along the hilltops bordering the villages, but also within the fragile, conflictive communities themselves. The charged social landscape of the present reflects the lasting damage done by a recent past in which people saw just what their neighbors could do.

Since 1995, I have been conducting research with campesino communities in the department of Ayacucho, the region of the country that bore the greatest loss of life and infrastructure during the war. Guiding my research was the conviction that we cannot respond to the needs of survivors of mass violence if we do not understand the local forms and logics of social relations, their transformation and the cultural expressions of

After mass crime: Rebuilding states and communities, Pouligny, Chesterman and Schnabel (eds), United Nations University Press, 2007, ISBN 978-92-808-1138-4

grief, anguish and loss. I was concerned with exploring the individual and collective consequences of mass violence, and with identifying the local resources that have allowed people to dismantle this lethal violence and work towards the reconstruction of social life and sociability.

It is commonplace to hear that culture and context matter, and that interventions – peace-building and otherwise – must be "culturally sensitive". Reiterating the obvious is not my goal. Rather, I want to take this assertion a step further and demonstrate the difference that a culturally informed analysis makes with respect to the complex process of social reconstruction following war. Among the questions that have guided my research are the following: How do people commit acts of collective violence against individuals with whom they have lived for years? When the war ends, what do people do with the killers in their midst? What do local processes of reconciliation tell us about how people dismantle lethal violence? Finally, what are the possibilities and limitations of communal forms of justice, punishment and reconciliation among "intimate enemies?"[1]

Sasachakuy tiempo: The "difficult years"

From 1980 to 2000, an internal war raged between the guerrilla group Sendero Luminoso, the *rondas campesinas* (armed peasant patrols) and the Peruvian armed forces. The Communist Party of Peru–Shining Path (Sendero Luminoso) began its campaign to overthrow the Peruvian state in 1980 in a calculated attack on the Andean village of Chuschi. Founded by Abimael Gúzman, this band of revolutionaries positioned themselves as the vanguard in a revolution to usher the nation towards an imminent communist utopia.[2] Drawing upon Maoist theories of guerrilla warfare, they planned a top-down revolution in which Sendero Luminoso would mobilize the peasantry, surround the cities and strangle the urbanized coast into submission. However, the relentless march toward the future was doubly interrupted: The initial governmental response was a brutal counter-insurgency war in which "Andean peasant" became conflated with "terrorist", and many peasants in the northern heights of Ayacucho rebelled *against* the revolution.[3]

While some northern communities remained *in situ* and organized into *rondas campesinas* to defend themselves against the Senderistas, many others fled the region in a mass exodus.[4] Indeed, an estimated 600,000 people fled from the sierra, devastating over 400 campesino communities.[5] As the Truth and Reconciliation Commission's final report indicates, approximately 69,280 people were killed or disappeared during Peru's internal armed conflict.[6] The Truth and Reconciliation Commission attributes 54 per cent of these deaths to Sendero Luminoso, and 30 per cent to the armed forces.

However, aggregate statistics obscure the intensity of the political violence in the department of Ayacucho. Three out of every four people killed during the war were rural, Quechua-speaking campesinos, and the department of Ayacucho alone accounts for 40 per cent of all the dead and disappeared. Thus, an epidemiology of political violence in Peru demonstrates that death and disappearance were distributed by class and ethnicity.

In addition to the statistics that bear witness to the impact of the war in Ayacucho, I emphasize the extent to which the war was experienced as a "cultural revolution" – as an attack against cultural practices and the very meaning of what it means to live as a human being in these villages. Under continuous threat of attack by either the Senderistas or the military, communal life was severely distorted: Both family and community celebrations were suspended, villagers sporadically attended their weekly markets due to the danger of traveling on remote roads, and many lament how they were forced to leave their dead loved ones wherever they had fallen, "burying them hurriedly like animals".

I realize the phrase "dehumanizing violence" has been reduced to a cliché in the media; however, attentiveness to the language villagers use indicates just how appropriate the term is. To "live and die like dogs," to insist that *"ya no era vida"* – it was no longer life – underscores the extent to which the political violence surpassed any form of acceptable force. As many campesinos have told me, "The Senderistas killed people in ways we do not even butcher our animals." Other villagers have described how they went out with large burlap bags to collect the body parts of their dead loved ones, trying to reassemble the pieces into something resembling a human form. In contrast to Sendero's use of mutilated bodies as testimony to their power, the armed forces tended to hide their victims, using disappearance as a tool of terror.

However, it would be a simplistic reading indeed that would reduce this to a war between the guerrillas and the armed forces. Indeed, rather than being helplessly caught "between two armies", I emphasize the extent to which this was a war between villagers themselves. In the heights of Huanta, villagers began assessing the changing power equation as the military increased both its presence and pressure. Although initially sympathetic to the revolutionary discourse of Sendero, the authoritarian brutality of the guerrillas ultimately alienated the villagers, who not long before had thrown off the domination of the *hacendado*s (large land owners) following Peru's Agrarian Reform. It was in these villages – frequently described as more "traditional" due to their civil-religious organizational structure – that Sendero met its greatest resistance.

Villagers began forming armed peasant patrols as well as a strategic, conflictive and frequently abusive alliance with the military. In the process of "cleansing their communities" of guerrilla sympathizers, villagers slaughtered one another. This was an internal war fought between intimate enemies: In the words of the villagers, "we learned to kill our brothers". Thus, while these villagers assert the Senderistas "had fallen out of humanity", this moral discourse acknowledges that they too engaged in acts they had never before imagined. Clearly the violence was dehumanizing to all involved – to those who were brutally slaughtered as well as to those who learned to kill.

Looking north

If indeed the revolutionary spark in the communities in northern Ayacucho was lit by external agents, clearly there were Senderista sympathizers in these communities.[7] The Senderistas initially arrived to "*concientizar a la gente*" (consciousness-raise the people), and for many villagers the message of equality resonated. However, various factors changed the equation of power and the communal alliances forged.

The Senderista discourse regarding "equality for all" was tempting as long as this referred to levelling the gap between *mistis* (mestizos) and campesinos, between rural and urban people, between abusive authorities and villagers – between categories that could be glossed as rich and poor. Much less attractive was the idea of equalizing everyone within the communities themselves. I recall a conversation with one communal authority who told me, "These *terrucos* (terrorists, referring to the Senderistas) began talking about the *Ley de Común* (Law of Commons). They said we were all going to live as equals. This was the Ley de Común. We were going to put all of our harvests in one room and share with everyone. Everybody equal." His face indicated how unappealing this proposition was.

Additionally, there was a change in the Senderista's strategy. The guerrillas' "moralization campaigns" were initially well received: In their "popular trials", they punished adulterers, cattle thieves and abusive husbands – in short, the "usual suspects". However, they did not stop with those sectors. The Shining Path cadres began closing the markets, prohibiting the sale of agricultural products and burning the saints and the Catholic churches. Faced by these affronts to the material and moral economy, the communal authorities began to throw the Senderista cadres out of these communities. The subsequent reprisals against "innocent people" were a key factor in alienating the rural population. The Shining Path leadership was reproducing a double standard that is all too familiar to rural peasants: The powerful dictate the forms of justice and for whom.

If indeed there was a growing criticism of the indiscriminate violence of Shining Path, there were also changes in the constellation of power in rural areas. The armed forces entered at the end of 1982 and these were the worst years in terms of deaths, rapes and disappearances. However, this repression was accompanied by a re-evaluation of each armed sector by the campesinos. Although Sendero had assured them they were going to win this war with rocks, knives and slingshots, a strong element of doubt entered. Campesinos – like any other dominated group – are very attentive to changes in relations of power. This attentiveness made very clear which group had more firepower ... and who had slingshots.

Also important in the chronology of the violence were the events in the village of Huaychao, where campesinos killed seven Senderistas in 1983. Former President Belaúnde lauded the campesinos for their "heroism" in defense of the Peruvian state. The surrounding communities in the highlands of Huanta were listening – and a number of people told me they decided to "rescue their image" (*rescatar su imagen*) by taking a stance against Shining Path and forging a conflictive, abusive but strategic alliance with the armed forces.

In the chronology of the war, this phase consisted of "closing the narrative ranks" – of constructing a coercive consensus that their communities were against Shining Path and without *una mancha roja* (a red stain, referring to sympathy with the guerrillas). Constructing consensus would draw upon "cleansing" their communities of the sympathizers in their midst. This cleansing would be fatal.

How we learned to kill our brothers

> We knew the Cayetanos had been giving food to the *terrucos* [Senderistas]. In their house up there on the hill, they let them spend the night. We knew what the soldiers would do if they found out. We knew we had to do something to stop it. So we gathered up the family one night, all but the youngest boy, and we took them below to the river. We hung them all that night and dumped their bodies in the river. That is how we learned to kill our *prójimos* [brothers, fellow creatures].
> – Interviews, a community in the highlands of Huanta, 1998

I begin with this emblematic memory, to borrow a term from the historian Steve Stern.[8] He suggests the concept of emblematic memories to refer to collective memories that condense important cultural themes and assume a certain uniformity as they circulate within a given social group. Additionally, I believe this is a foundational memory, indicating the establishment of a new moral order.

According to my oral and archival sources, killing prior to the war was exceptional. As Carlos Iván Degregori argues, a motif in rural villages was "punish but do not kill".[9] Antonio Peña Jumpa confirms that the most severe punishment was banishment from the community and the loss of *comunero* (villager) status and the rights such status implies.[10] Thus, I want to trace changes in moral reasoning and concepts of justice. Both are forged by practice – from our concrete activities in the world – which shape our ideas of the world and our place within it.

I suggest we adopt Sally Falk Moore's insights on legal systems to an analysis of moral reasoning. In her research on "customary law" among the Chagga in Africa, she emphasizes the temporality of law, rejecting as "patently false ... the illusion from outside that what has been called 'customary law' remains static in practice".[11] From this perspective, the political and economic contexts are not external to the law but rather part of the cultural form to which the law gives a certain expression. I think that moral reasoning operates in a similar manner, and that we must be attentive to both the *langue* as well as the *parole* of law and morality.

According to my interviews, the decision to kill the Senderistas and their alleged sympathizers was discussed at length in Communal Assemblies. As David Apter states, "People do not commit political violence without discourse. They need to talk themselves into it. What may begin as casual conversation may suddenly take a serious turn. Secret meetings add portent. On public platforms it becomes inflammatory. It results in texts, lectures. In short it engages people who suddenly are called upon to use their intelligences in ways out of the ordinary. It takes people out of themselves."[12]

The process of forging consensus via discourse and decisions made in Communal Assemblies was accompanied by violent acts and the construction of a moral binary: "us" versus "them". When villagers began to strengthen the boundaries of their communities, it implied justifying the violent acts they were committing against one another. It would be necessary to construct difference – to construct the Senderistas in their midst as radically, dangerously "other".

Constructing the enemy

It has become a cliché to note that people "dehumanize the enemy" during times of war. The phrase is intoned when people begin to kill one another, as though dehumanization is self-evident and explanatory. It figures in with "tribal warfare" and "ethnic hatred", terms that invoke the image of primordial, lethal aggression waiting for a political opening to manifest. In contrast, I am persuaded by Carolyn Nordstrom and JoAnn Martin, who assert that "Violence starts and stops with the people that constitute a society: it takes place in society and as a social reality; it is a product and a manifestation of culture. Violence is not inherent to power, to politics, or to human nature. The only biological reality is that wounds bleed and people die."[13]

Part of the argument I make throughout this chapter is the need for specificity – for understanding how people make and unmake lethal violence. Understanding the thick of regional histories is crucial to disassembling the structures of violence and working towards peace. Thus I take a processual approach to the construction and deconstruction of "the enemy" in the villages where I worked, arguing that if indeed the end product – dehumanization – is a woefully universal phenomenon in the context of war, one must be attentive to the formulaic regional elements of this process.

I have found that constructions of the "enemy" drew upon psycho-cultural themes, extra-local discourses and both "popular Catholicism" as well as the various strands of Evangelical Christianity that became a major social movement in these rural villages during the war. I want to discuss these constructions: Understanding how the Senderistas were stripped of their human characteristics allows us to understand the processes by which they might regain them.

When narrating the war, people use various terms to refer to the guerrillas. Among the terms used to described the Senderistas are *terrucos*, *malafekuna*, *tuta puriq*, *puriqkuna* and *anticristos*. Each term reflects the condensation of concerns regarding evil and monstrosity, also captured by the many campesinos who insist the Senderistas "had fallen out of humanity".

Terrucos is derived from terrorists, and was borrowed from the military discourse about the Senderistas. The Peruvian Armed Forces conducted a classic counterinsurgency war during the first years of the 1980s, and the notion of communist subversion as a cancer afflicting the national body was common. The Doctrine of National Security – that genocidal product of the Cold War and its bipolar cartography – functioned via a double vision. The "communist threat" arrived from outside, spreading from country to country via the domino theory, but there was also the fear of internal contagion that was utilized to justify the repression of domestic dissent. Campesinos re-elaborated this discourse: the cancerous legions of the left appeared as the *plagakuna* – the people of the plague.

Externality also drew upon state policies and discourse as well. At one stage of the war, President Fernando Belaúnde (1980–1985) insisted that the Senderistas were externally financed, although this claim was subsequently proven to be false.[14] However, the theme of foreign intervention was elaborated by the army as part of its *"acción psicológica"* (psychological warfare). The army distributed leaflets in the rural countryside, warning people there existed an insidious threat of subversion. One leaflet portrays campesinos fleeing, shrinking with fear while they point to an enormous beast with claws flying overhead. Behind the beast appears a soldier, running to rescue them. Below the images are the words: "Ayacuchans! The criminal subversives are foreigners who have come to destroy you – Reject them!"[15]

Malafekuna (the people of bad faith) and the *anticristos* (antichrists) draw upon both the idea of "godless communists" as well as the biblical interpretations elaborated by campesinos in the highlands of Huanta. With *malafekuna*, what is implied is that the Senderistas lack any conscience, being people "who were only born to kill". Additionally, given the centrality of the social covenant in the establishment and reproduction of community – a theme I will return to later in the text – the image of Senderistas as people of bad faith reflects a central concern: How does one negotiate in good faith with people who have none?

Also common in my interviews is the term *tuta puriq* (those who walk at night), which stems from long-standing fears about the condemned (*jarjachas*) who walk this earth, inflicting their revenge upon the living. Jarjachas are human beings who have assumed animal form as part of their divine punishment for having sinned. They walk the *puna*, searching for the unfortunate individual who crosses their path.

The puna – where the wild things are. In the classic studies of the Peruvian Andes, social scientists have suggested the savage puna is constructed in contrast to the domesticated space of the village.[16] It is the domain of the jarjachas, as well as the scene for sexual trysts among young people hoping to escape their parents' watchful eyes. I was repeatedly told the Senderistas attacked from the puna, arriving undetected on the wind.

Another common term is *puriqkuna*, a symbolically rich image. Puriqkuna are people who walk, never remaining in one place – transgressive people who are out of place, not belonging anywhere. This shares a certain logic with the claim that the Senderistas were covered with lice. In addition to illustrating concerns with categorical purity, there is another element referenced by this image.

I remember many sunny afternoons in the villages, when thick black braids were unwound and washed. Family members would sit on sheepskins, picking the lice out of one another's hair. These are intimate moments: Mothers search the hair of their husbands and children, and children invite a little brother or sister to draw near, black hair ceding to busy fingers. The idea that the guerrilla walked endlessly with heads covered in lice suggests something fundamental about their lack of ties with both people and place. Human beings live in families: What must those lice imply about the status of the Senderistas?

Perhaps not imply but rather confirm. In an almost mocking fashion, villagers told me the terrucos forbid the use of family terms; instead, everyone was *compañero* or *compañera*. The attempt to revolutionize the affective sphere of the family became a key site of resistance. In Quechua, *waqcha* means both "orphan" as well as "poor". To live without family is to live in material and affective destitution.

In addition to these terms, campesinos are very consistent in insisting that the Senderistas "were gringos – they came from other countries". Indeed, when I was a recent arrival in these villages, many people were terrified of me. They told me, "The Senderistas were tall, Kimberly, like you. They also had green eyes. They looked just like you."

However, at times even alleged racial differences and "foreignness" were not sufficiently distancing. The Senderistas were also described as otherworldly. Don Jesús was one of the oldest men I knew. He assured me he was 100 years old, and from the hours he spent telling me stories, I was convinced he had accumulated a century's worth of experience regardless of his age. Don Jesús had lived through several Senderista attacks. As he told me, "We killed them and saw their bodies. Some of them were women. They had three bellybuttons and their genitals were in another part of their body. I saw them." Bodies were killed, they were seen, and they were examined.

The rich elaboration of corporeal difference is central to the construction of the moral binaries characteristic of a wartime code of conduct. I emphasize that these villagers are phenotypically homogeneous: certainly there is social stratification, but there are no categorical physical differences. Thus people felt the need to construct them. Via the use of the body, political categories were given somatic force. Shifting political allegiances were grounded in imagined bodily difference.

In addition to these terms and the images they invoke, there is another element that echoed throughout our conversations. I was repeatedly told the Senderistas had a mark on their arms. Mama Justiniana had lived in the village during the war years. She described the attacks she had survived and the cold river that had provided her with refuge when the wind had carried the Senderistas to her village on a moonless night. And she knew something else: "The malafekuna had a mark burned into their flesh, on their arms. They all had the mark."

What could that mark be? These villagers have long practiced what has been called "popular Catholicism", referring to the blend of Catholic theology and pre-conquest cosmologies. This Catholicism shares many characteristics with the "pentacostalized" Evangelical Christianity that was widely adopted during the war. This was a potent blend of revelations, faith healing and the imminent arrival of the Antichrist: "And ye shall know him by his mark."

But the mark invokes more than the beast. The lament "Between brothers we were killing" echoes in the interviews I have conducted. The Bible has been a central semiotic resource in the regional histories elaborated about the war, and the original fratricide resonates.

When Cain and his brother Abel each offered the fruits of their labor to God, Abel's gift was accepted while God rejected Cain's. Ignoring a divine warning about the dangers of sins, Cain killed his brother Abel. When God later asked where Abel was, Cain responded with a question of his own: "Am I my brother's keeper?" When God realized what Cain had done, He condemned him to wander the earth, bearing a mark that would last for seven generations.

The Senderista's mark was their condemnation made visible, evidence they had "fallen out of humanity". Erving Goffman has suggested that the stigmatized person is perceived as not fully human, as disqualified from total social acceptance.[17] He also notes that the visibility of the stigma is a crucial factor, as is the "decoding ability" of the audience. Examining the bodies of the Senderistas was a form of divination – of reading their inner evil on the surface of their bodies.

Additionally, stigma is an idiom of bodily difference, and this difference informs the "moral career" of the person who has been marked.[18] The people of bad faith, transgressive wanderers who were only born to kill, the people of the plague – the mark burned into their flesh permitted a diagnostics of evil, blending juridical and religious methods of moral accusation.

Thus people began to kill one another, and for a time this was a means of constructing "community". Indeed, members of one community told me they had buried many dead guerrillas below their village, on the steep slope that leads down to the river. As they explained, "You know, before the houses here were always sliding down the hill; we kept trying to prop them up, but the cliff is too steep. But once we buried the terrucos down there, the ground stopped sliding and our houses stayed put." Evidently, burying Senderistas down below bolstered the community, figuratively and literally.

A chronology of compassion

Reflecting on the process of the war, I have thought of the shifts in power and justice in terms of a chronology of compassion, underscoring the temporal construction of emotion and morality. If indeed in one phase villagers began to kill each other, in another they began to remember their shared humanity and to act on the basis of those memories. As we shall see, they would mobilize the concepts and practices of communal justice to "convert the Senderistas into people again". I believe that various factors contributed to this chronology of compassion – a dynamic chronology that reflected both the new equations of power as well as long-standing patterns of administering retributive and restorative justice in these villages.

Decisions regarding what to do with the Senderistas reflected the perceived level of threat. During the first years of the war (1980–1984), when danger was great and allegiances in constant flux, communal boundaries were rigidified. As I have mentioned, villagers constructed the difference between "us" and "them" – and one goal was to keep "them" at a distance. This was the height of the killing between villagers; indeed, the people with whom I have worked refer to this phase of the violence as the war between *sallqakuna* – between people of the highlands.

However, the government had installed military bases throughout the region by the end of 1984. Even though civil-military relations were tense and frequently abusive, villagers indicate that the installation of military bases lowered the fear of reprisals for taking a position against the guerrillas. Moreover, campesinos began to form the *rondas campesinas* that patrolled both the puna as well as within the communities themselves.

Thus talk of repenting and pardoning is talk about power. One person who placed power centrally in his genealogy of morals – and mercy – was Friedrich Nietzsche. He wrote:

> As its power increases, a community ceases to take the individual's transgressions so seriously, because they can no longer be considered as dangerous and destructive to the whole as they were formerly: the malefactor is no longer 'set beyond the pale of peace' and thrust out.... As the power and self-confidence of a community increase, the penal law always becomes more moderate; every weakening or imperiling of the former brings with it a restoration of the harsher forms of the latter. It goes without saying that mercy remains the privilege of the most powerful man.[19]

At the height of the danger, the community could not afford to patrol both its perimeters and its interior, and mercy was severely restricted. However, as "community" was reconfigured and strengthened, the longstanding emphasis on rehabilitation rather than execution of the transgressor influenced the response villagers had to those Senderistas who claimed they had been forced to kill. There would be a shift in moral discourse and practice. And there would be rituals to deal with those "liminal people" who wanted to deliver themselves to a human community.

Practicing justice

The first person who spoke openly to me about the *arrepentidos* – literally the "repentant ones", referring to the ex-Senderistas – was Mama Marcelina. She was incredibly candid with me from the first moment we met, which was exceptional and surprised me. As she explained the first time I visited, her dead husband had appeared in her dreams the night before, telling her that a gringa was going to visit. He assured her that even though most gringos are dangerous, this gringa would be affectionate. She smiled and patted my knee a few times as she recounted her dream.

Marcelina had what the campesinos call *"el don de hablar"* – literally the gift of speaking. She did not merely tell her stories, she performed them. Spindles became knives, held to the throat to demonstrate how the Senderistas had threatened her. She wrapped my scarf tightly around my head to show me how the guerrilla had hidden their faces with masks, leaving only their evil, squinting eyes shining out from the depths. *Hacendado*s who had left the zone after the Agrarian Reform of 1968 were resuscitated, screeching *"Indios, indios!"*[20] in an imperious tone. History came alive in her store – and part of that history concerned those who had fallen out of humanity, as well as those who arrived in the village begging for a way back in. "They repented for the suffering they endured there in the mountains," she told me. "Oh how they suffered, day and night, always walking. So they would come down to the villages. There in the puna, they began to think, 'I'll go down and present myself,' they said. 'Surely the villagers (*comuneros*) won't kill me,' they thought."

"And what happened when they arrived here?" I asked. "What did they say?"

"They would arrive saying they had been tricked, forced to kill, always walking. 'Pardon me,' they begged. 'Pardon me,' they would beg the community."

I spent several hours while Marcelina described in detail how they received the arrepentidos:

> "'Are you going to stop being like that?' they asked them. If they were going to, we accepted them. 'But careful, don't let the Senderistas enter here.' We asked them over and over again, 'Are you going to let the Senderistas enter here?' They promised they wouldn't. We asked them if they could forget they had learned to kill. They promised they could. So, questioning and questioning, they accepted them. *Pues, runayaruspanku* [they could be people again]! They were peaceful and they weren't going back to Senderismo. They were watched, they were watched for where they might go, night and day. And when they didn't go back, then they were *común runa igualña* – common people like us."

I wanted to know more. I thought about the *quejas* (legal complaints or cases) I had seen in the villages, which prompted me to ask her, "Did they punish them? Did they beat them when they came to repent?"

Marcelina nodded her head. "Oh yes, the authorities whipped them in public. They were whipped, warning them what would happen to them if they decided to return [to being Senderistas]. Whipping them, they were received here."

I was trying to capture some sense of chronology. It is not an exaggeration to say that no woman I ever spoke with used dates when narrating her life or the war years – no dates entered into their narratives. So I asked Marcelina about the soldiers, knowing their sustained presence in the base began in early 1985. She answered, "The soldiers were ready to kill them. They killed them. That's why the arrepentidos asked the community not to say anything to the soldiers. 'Please, don't say anything to them or they'll kill me.' That's how they pleaded, oh how they pleaded, sobbing. So they didn't tell the soldiers. The soldiers killed them, even the children, the women – they killed them. Below in the gorge, they buried so many of them. To kill them, the soldiers made them dig a hole. Once they killed them, they buried them there. When we heard shots, we would say 'It's over, they killed the poor people.'"

I wanted to follow the decisions made with respect to turning people over to the soldiers. "When did the community kill the arrepentidos and when did they accept them?"

Marcelina explained, "When they repented, then they accepted them. When they didn't repent, they were turned over to the soldiers. When they pleaded, crying, crying, they beat them with *chicotes* [braided leather whips] and the people here understood them. They couldn't kill them. *Común runakuna* [common people] couldn't kill them."

"Mama Marcelina, did they only accept arrepentidos from here or from other villages as well?"

"From other places, *pues*," her *pues* letting me know the answer seemed obvious. "When they repented, they stayed here as though they were from here. *Qinan llaqtayarun* (becoming fellow villagers), they stayed here and didn't go anywhere else. So they stayed and are here now, without going to the jungle, to Huanta, going nowhere. As if they were from here – they remained. So we lived peacefully together. *Runayarunkuña* [becoming human beings again], not Senderistas anymore. They said, 'If I was walking with them, it was because they took me with a knife, with bullets, with threats.' Fearing for their lives, they stayed here. How they had suffered, walking at night, with rain and without rain, eating or not eating. Out of fear they escaped and delivered themselves to this village."

"Mama Marcelina, when they delivered themselves, were they alone?"

She shook her head. "The men delivered themselves with their wives, their children. That's how they lived. They always escaped man–woman. When a man presented himself alone, he would then go back to bring his wife and children. He would talk with the authorities so he could bring his family."

"But, they never escaped alone?" I wondered.

"Yes, but when they came alone the soldiers grabbed them and killed them. Or sometimes they took them to Castro [Castropampa, the military base in Huanta]. But those who arrived with their wives and children, no."

The reasoning was complex and I tried my best to understand. Marcelina repeated herself: "They confessed. They would come, asking if they could bring their families. If they arrived alone, we would turn them over to the soldiers. If they arrived alone, there was more distrust. 'What if they have only come to plan another attack?' we thought. But when they arrived as families, we had more trust. They could be *runakuna* [people] again."

The emphasis on confession and repentance is striking. In his analysis of confession in law and literature, Peter Brooks argues, "The confessional model is so powerful in Western culture, I believe, that even those whose religion or non-religion has no place for Roman Catholic practice of confession are nonetheless deeply influenced by the model. Indeed, it permeates our culture, including our educational practices and our law."[21] Moreover, "Confession of wrongdoing is considered fundamental to morality because it constitutes a verbal act of self-recognition as wrongdoer and hence provides the basis of rehabilitation. It is the precondition of the end to ostracism, reentry into one's desired place in the human community. To refuse confession is to be obdurate, hard of heart, resistant to amendment."[22] In short, to be a "moral monster".

The moral script that one must enact is reminiscent of Paul Connerton's emphasis on the cult enacted, which, as he tells us, draws upon the body. Connerton is writing about commemorative ceremonies, but I think we can extend his argument to the rituals of justice, which in part commemorate the moral community as a social group that must be maintained.

What, then, is being remembered in commemorative ceremonies? Part of the answer is that a community is reminded of its identity as represented and told in a master narrative.... Its master narrative is more than a story told and reflected on; it is a cult enacted. An image of the past, even in the form of a master narrative, is conveyed and sustained by ritual performances.... For if the ceremonies are to work for their participants, if they are persuasive to them, then those participants must be not simply cognitively competent to execute the performance; they must be habituated to those performances. This habituation is to be found ... in the bodily substrate of the performance."[23]

To enact the moral script requires more than memorizing the lines: as villagers told me, "The words must come from the heart and not just from the mouth outward." As Marcelina, and others, made clear, the performative aspects of justice were crucial and the performance itself judged. Confessing, atoning, sobbing, apologizing, begging, promising – sincerity would depend on both words and action.

At times, words and action meld. In his work on the sociology of apologies, Nicholas Tavuchis argues, "An apology is first and foremost a speech act",[24] and that apology is "concerned with the fundamental sociological question of the grounds for membership in a designated moral community".[25] In these particular moral communities, biblical narratives inform public apologies. People did not refer to the Bible to explain what happened – villagers did not speak *about* religion, but rather spoke *with* religion. Biblical narrative conventions reflected and contoured individual and communal histories – and the moral scripts that infuse popular justice. And these moral scripts reflect both strands of Christianity: restoration and retribution.[26]

As my conversations with Marcelina – and my observation of the communal adjudication of many *quejas* (complaints) – reveal, the administration of justice in these villages is highly syncretic, based in part on sacramental principles. When I refer to syncretism, I am not only referring to these sacramental principles but also to the blending of theology, politics, economics and law.

Additionally, there is a focus in how much the arrepentidos suffered and the use of corporal punishment as part of the rituals of re-incorporation. Michel Foucault has made us very aware of the place of physical pain in the production of truth.[27] In these communities, villagers combine the religious tradition of confession – the curing of souls and the reaffirmation of community – with legal confession and the need for a process of judgment and punishment. In these juridico-religious practices, both restorative and retributive justice is administered. There is a place for both Christian charity as well as righteous wrath, and an emphasis on settling accounts between perpetrators and those they have injured.

I reflect upon the debates regarding punishment and deterrence. It may well be that punishment does not deter the criminal contemplating robbery or murder; however, perhaps retribution has a deterrence effect on those who have been wronged. Hannah Arendt suggested that it is retribution and forgiveness that break the cycle of vengeance.[28] The administration of both retributive and restorative justice may be what permits the re-incorporation of those who wandered in the puna, cast out of the community of mankind.

Making people

> Judicial space is, before all else, not a tangible physical space, but rather a psychological construction.[29]

In the process of constructing the enemy, we explored how the Senderistas were stripped of their human characteristics, making them radically "other." As one may imagine, one component of administering communal justice was directed towards allowing the arrepentidos to recover their human status.

For villagers, their assessment of the *terruckuna* depended in part upon the *grado de delito* – the seriousness of the crime. People seeking to come back were referred to as *concientizados, rescatados, arrepentidos* and *engañados* (consciousness-raised, rescued, repentant and tricked or duped). The terms reference the degree of culpability, which involved the question of conscience and the awareness of what one was doing.

A concept fundamental to the assessment of accountability is *uso de razón* – the use of reason. This is a term that cuts across social fields: in the religious sense, it is the age at which a child can commit sin; in the political sense, it is related to accountability as a member of the community; in a legal sense, it refers to the capacity to discern right from wrong. Children are said to acquire the uso de razón around the age of six or seven; this is also the age at which children are said to remember things.

Identity is understood as fluid and mutable. Human status is achieved; thus it can be both lost and regained. Just as the uso de razón makes *criaturas* (infants and small children) more fully human, so does the accumulation of memory. When parents spoke to me about their children, they differentiated between the younger and older children by using *yuyaniyuq* for the older ones. *Yuyay* is Quechua for "remember", and the older children were described as the remembering ones, in contrast to little children who are *sonsos* (witless or senseless). People with *mucha memoria* are considered better people, more intelligent – and they have more *conciencia*.

The question of conscience and culpability figures into national legal standards as well. In the *Diccionario para Juristas*, "uso de razón" is defined as "possession of natural discernment that is acquired passing through early childhood; the time during which discernment is discovered or begins to be recognized in the acts of the child or individual".[30] *Discernimiento* refers to the capacity to judge, to choose, to distinguish.

Thus "uso de razón" implies volition, memory, and the capacity to judge right from wrong. This is a central phase in becoming a moral person and entering communal life as an accountable member of the collective.

Conciencia is both conscience and consciousness, an important conflation of the two concepts. I heard, quite frequently, that although people had gone with the Senderistas, some had not realized what they were doing: *inconcientemente se fueron!* – unconsciously they went, not fully aware of their actions. These people were also the *engañados* – tricked or duped by the guerrillas.

"Engañado" is a term that works both ways; that is, "outsiders" use it disparagingly when referring to campesinos as illiterate, ignorant and prone to believing whatever they are told. Villagers realize the insulting connotation of the word; however, they also use it strategically when it serves their purposes to be the "blameless dupes". It is a way of shifting responsibility, as well as indexing how power imbalances shape their interactions with representatives of the state and *criollo* ("white") Peruvian society.

Concientizados were those people who had been persuaded when the guerrillas came to *concientizar* villagers, but did not willingly participate in combat. For instance, one community president insisted there were no arrepentidos in his village, only people who had been concientizados. As he told me, "Arrepentidos are those who were combatants, or the *masas* [masses] that turned themselves in." Thus many of the people captured in the mountains were people that in one way or another had collaborated but were never, to borrow his term, *defensores conscientes de los terrucos* – conscious defenders of the terrucos. Thus bringing them back was rescuing them (*rescatar*).

If you are a bit confused, that is precisely the point. Ambiguity is what allowed this to work. In contrast with positive law that is based upon categories that are mutually exclusive, these categories were porous and fluid. There is a gray zone in communal jurisprudence that allowed for a great flexibility in judging crimes (*delitos*) and transgressors, taking into consideration the particularities of each case. Ambiguity was a resource: In these villages, "unconsciously they went" – and if not, they could certainly try to maintain that it happened that way. The gray zone of jurisprudence left space for porous categories – and for conversions, moral and otherwise.

Becoming *runakuna* again is a moral conversion that carries with it a "change of heart". The notion of purgation figures prominently: cleansing via confession and repentance are long-standing practices. Many villagers, both Evangelical and Catholic, told me that "You must repent from the heart and not from the mouth outward. When we repent, we have clean hearts." They assured me that "After repenting, we are *mu-*

saq runakuna – new people. We are not who we were before." Identity is highly relational and when social relations change, so does the person.

And thus the *puriqkuna* delivered themselves to the community, begging the villagers not to say anything to the soldiers in the base. The pleading, the questioning, the promises regarding what one would forget and what one would remember: there is a contractual morality established by this call and response. However, "contractual" sounds cold and legalistic: I prefer the term "social covenant" because there is a sacramental aspect to the administration of communal justice. In fact, it is said the terrucos *se entregaron* (delivered themselves) to the community; the same verb is used to speak about those who have delivered themselves to God.

Along with the rituals of confession and repentance, there were other elements that contributed to the rehabilitation of those who returned. One day I was looking over the *Actas Comunales* (written record of communal meetings) of one village, and I opened the book to the first page: "Act of the Assembly carried out this day the 18 of February 1986 in the campesino community of (anonymous) in the jurisdiction of the province of Huanta and the department of Ayacucho." Among the items on the agenda were: "talk about the abandoned lands without owners; give the lands to the *recogiados* and others" (terms I will explain shortly); and the need to apply for a loan from the Ministry of Agriculture to buy fortified seeds. I did not know how to interpret the first two items on the agenda. Fights over land are eternal in rural Latin America; however, here the villagers were giving land to the "*recogiados* and others". Who were they?

Spanish speakers will already have noted that *recogiado* is really not a word. However, we must remember that these villagers are Quechua speakers and at times unknown Spanish words are heard in such a way that people can make sense of them. Prior to the political violence, there were no refugees (*refugiados*) in the highlands. Certainly people moved about, and not always of their own volition. However, the category "refugiado" was a product of the war: the term figured in the state discourse, that of the soldiers and on the radio. "Refugiados" was heard as "recogiados," making sense both of the word as well as its meaning.[31] *Recoger* – to gather up, to take in, to shelter. Precisely what villagers were doing with the arrepentidos. "Recogiados [the gathered up ones, the taken in ones, the sheltered ones] and others" were in fact those who had come from other places seeking refuge; they were also those unnamed people who came in search of redemption.

18 February 1986. The entry begins with a list of the abandoned lands. Some of the owners had been killed, and others had migrated to the cities

for security purposes. When family members remained, the land passed to them. However, some lands were retained for communal use, leaving those parcels that were given to the *personas recogiadas y otros*. They referred to these parcels as *volto arroyo*, meaning they were located along the bank of the river below the village. The river ran the length of the gorge below, where the dead Senderistas were buried. The arrepentidos would be kept close, and those cadavers would remind them that they had escaped a similar fate.

But there is something else behind the distribution of land. On the one hand, working on communal land was a form of atonement. On the other, this involved arrepentidos in reciprocity, in social networks. As Mama Marcelina explained to me, "So that they could work, the community divided up land. So they could build homes they gave them land, and land to work. They are still working, and like us they are eating. They became *runa masinchik* – people we work with, people like us."

Runa masinchik – people with whom we work – reflects the dominant moral ideology. There is a great cultural value placed on reciprocity, and this is expressed in various forms of collective labor.[32] In her study of customary law in Peru, Tamayo Flores noted the importance of communal forms of labor such as *faenas* and *ayni* in the highlands. These forms of communal labor establish interdependence among the villagers who participate in them, and are practiced due to the rugged geography of the region, which makes it virtually impossible to introduce technology. Thus, access to communal labor is a necessity for survival, requiring cooperation between families and communities.

However, to treat labor agreements as strictly material or economic configurations obscures the symbolic dimension of these agreements. *Ayni* – the reciprocal exchange of manual labor – is also an ethical concept: Working together and establishing mutual obligations makes "good people".[33] Reciprocity constructs social networks, although not without a hierarchical dimension.

In addition to involving the arrepentidos in mutual obligations, giving them land illustrates another key component in making *runakuna*. I remind the reader of the terms used to describe the Senderistas, one of which was *puriqkuna* – those who walk or wander. Transgressive vagabonds without ties to a place or to family are suspicious people. One form of "making people" is via "emplacement" strategies; consequently, land was distributed and worked, and there was internal vigilance to make certain that certain people stayed in their place.

Thus concepts and practices of communal justice were mobilized to rehabilitate the arrepentidos. One afternoon I was talking with a group of women when I remembered the mark that identified the Senderistas. I asked the women what happened with the mark – the mark burned into the flesh of their forearms.

"Ah, when they began to act like *runakuna*, the mark disappeared," replied Mama Justiniana.

"Yes," added Mama Izcarceta, "the mark disappeared when they became *runakuna* again.

And so the "moral stain" disappears. However, in his study of stigma, Erving Goffman observed that the repair of stigma means passing from someone with stigma to someone who has corrected a particular stigma.[34] The mark disappears, but not the memory of it. Hence the emphasis in so many conversations on the need to *recordar, pero sin rancor* – to remember but without rancor. The goal is to live with the memories but without the hatred. However, this does not imply equality for those who have "converted back" since villagers live in a world of difference and stratification. Coexistence, not equality, defines the common good.

Administering "The Communal"

> Reconcile: to restore to friendship, compatibility or harmony; to make consistent or congruous; *to cause to submit or to accept.*[35]

I would like to turn now to the question of communal hegemony and the administration of justice in these villages. I do not believe that justice is gendered: Arguments positing a womanly "ethics of care" versus a manly "ethics of rights" are essentializing and do not help us understand how concepts of justice are forged in sensuous engagement with the world.[36] However, although I insist justice is not gendered, its administration most certainly is.

In her article on ethnographic refusal, Sherry Ortner critiques anthropologists for "thinning culture" by sanitizing politics and ignoring internal conflicts among "the subaltern". As she insists, "If we are to recognize that resistors are doing more than simply opposing domination, more than simply producing a virtually mechanical *re*-action, then we must go the whole way. They have their *own* politics – not just between chiefs and commoners or landlords and peasants but within all the local categories of friction and tension: men and women, parents and children, seniors and juniors ... and on and on."[37] By overlooking these internal conflicts, we end up with a romanticized notion of the subaltern and of resistance. We also end up with romanticized visions of "community" as the repository of the best of human values. Raymond Williams offers a lengthy entry on "community" in his book, *Keywords*, and it is quite instructive. Let me draw from that entry:

Community: community of relations or feelings; a sense of common identity or characteristics; can be a warmly persuasive word to describe an existing set of relationships. What is most important, perhaps, is that unlike other terms of social organization (state, nation, society, etc.) it seems never to be used unfavourably, and never to be given any positive opposing or distinguishing term.[38]

A romance with "community" obscures the working of power. In these villages, there are various axes of differentiation, and one of them is gender. It is to those groups marginalized from the adjudication of conflicts that we must look if we are to understand the limitations of mandating reconciliation.

I return to my conversations with Mama Marcelina and the juridical-legal rituals she described. As the reader may recall, when she recounted these events there were two "theys" in her narrative: "they" who came asking for forgiveness, and "they" who determined who would be punished and pardoned. Who was the "they" that made these life or death decisions? Who spoke as the voice of "the community"?

Every village authority in the communities with which I have worked was male. What is practiced in these villages is patriarchal justice, and conflict resolution is frequently addressed to the maintenance of "community" rather than the satisfaction of the individual plaintiffs. There is an interest in resolving a range of conflicts within the village. "City justice" is expensive, highly bureaucratic, and rarely do villagers actually achieve the resolution of their cases.[39] Nor has "city justice" been particularly kind to rural villagers; this history of judicial indifference plus a desire to preserve autonomy leads to much adjudication within the villages themselves. However, as Laura Nader insightfully argues, there is a "harmony ideology" that contours conflict resolution in communities such as these, and harmony may be a coercive way of forging consensus and silencing dissent.[40] Thus, while I argue that these practices are critically important to the reconstruction of social relationships at the local level – and that they have played a determining role in staying the hand of vengeance – I do not want to leave my reader with the impression that equality and democracy are the result.

Indeed, for groups that are not allowed a voice in the administration of justice, how does one quell a desire for retribution? For whom does reconciliation sit as a lump in their stomach and a constant irritant of their heart? The women, particularly the widows. There is a form of "memory specialization" at work in these villages, and women in general – and widows in particular – narrate the suffering of their communities. Veena Das has suggested that "the representation of grief is metonymically experienced as bodily pain and the female body is one that will carry this pain forever."[41] The work of grief is "women's work", and women literally embody the suffering of their communities in this gendered division of emotional labor. Thus it is phenomeno*logical* that they would carry the memories of unaddressed wrongs in their nerves, the lower back, in the nape of their necks. Women told me they have "martyred their bodies" by remembering all that happened in their villages. A thwarted desire for justice becomes a felt grievance.[42]

Kay Warren has suggested that, "High theory aside, class is not a separable domain but rather a multidimensional form of stratification that is in practice often gendered, racialized, and saturated with cultural difference. For instance, as a result of the genocidal civil war in Guatemala, impoverished rural widows became a distinctive political-economic class – the result of Mayan family structure, agrarian sexual division of labor, and the violent repression that killed their husbands and left these women without a subsistence base."[43] Widows are the poorest sector of the villages in which I worked.

Indeed, it was the long conversations with widows that demonstrated to me the need for a political economy of forgiveness and reconciliation. Without economic redistribution, asking people to feel "forgiving" is in itself an immoral act. For the widows, their poverty serves as a constant reminder of all that they lost. I am certainly attentive to the ways in which gender fluctuates across social fields. Indeed, I have argued that widows constitute a third gender and do have access to forms of power that single and married women do not.[44] However, although they may enjoy certain freedoms because there is no man at home, they do not exercise control over communal forms of justice. Consensus-making mechanisms may stifle their voices, but not their rage.

Conclusions

I began this chapter stating that one of my goals was to demonstrate the difference a cultural analysis makes with respect to the construction and deconstruction of lethal violence. I think there is a great deal to be learned in post-war contexts by studying pre-existing conciliatory practices that respond to the needs of daily life and governance. Reconciliation is forged and lived locally, and state policies can either facilitate or hinder these processes.

I find it crucial to distinguish between horizontal and vertical reconciliation.[45] The practices villagers have elaborated have been remarkably successful in stopping lethal violence at the communal level; however, to date the soldiers – the armed representatives of the state – have been neither punished nor pardoned. During a visit to Ayacucho in November 2001, the Peruvian Truth and Reconciliation Commission was preparing to begin. I asked villagers how they felt about the soldiers and what they had done in their communities. People were still afraid to openly discuss the long, conflictive, abusive nature of the "civil–military alliance". However, the few comments offered were illuminating: "So the *doctores* de Lima think they can come and tell us we need to be reconciled? If the soldiers want us to reconcile, then let them come here, apologize and repent just like the Senderistas did." My research leads me to assert that national processes of reconciliation remain largely peripheral to the daily lives of people living in areas most affected by political violence unless these processes articulate with and are informed by local logics and practices.

In his work on conflict resolution, Robert Rubinstein has noted, "A recurrent theme in the anthropological literature is that all social behavior has a symbolic dimension. Although warfare and the construction of peaceful social relationships have much to do with considerations of economics and material forces, they also have symbolic aspects that must be taken into account in order to resolve conflicts, avoid war or maintain an established peace."[46] Thus the practices developed by these villagers to make and unmake violence provide insights into regional notions of justice, accountability and reconciliation. Setting these local level processes into dialogue with national debates about these issues underscores the centrality of wedding political insights with cultural analysis.

I conclude by suggesting that the practices of retributive and restorative justice that influence the lives of campesinos in Peru have their homologues in other post-conflict societies. Thus, these villagers offer something more than a glimpse of political violence in one "corner of the world". Rather, their cultural practices and local initiatives offer an example of the reconstruction of society and sociability, family-by-family and community-by-community.

Notes

1. My research has been funded by the Social Science Research Council, the Wenner Gren Foundation for Anthropological Research, the United States Institute of Peace and the Instituto de Estudios Peruanos. Time for reflection and writing was made possible by the Institute on Violence and Survival at the University of Virginia, the Shaler-Adams Foundation and the Harry Frank Guggenheim Foundation. I am deeply grateful for this generous support and for the collegial relationships I have enjoyed with representatives of each of the above institutions. For keen conversation on the themes addressed in this chapter, I thank José Coronel, Efraín Loayza, Elizabeth Jelin, Billie Jean Isbell and Kathleen Dill, and participants in the workshop "Mass Crimes and Post-Conflict Peace-building", New York, 8–10 June 2003. Most importantly, I thank the members of these *campesino* communities for allowing me to live with and learn from them.

2. See Carlos Iván Degregori, *Ayacucho 1969–1979: El Surgimiento de Sendero Luminoso*, Lima: Instituto de Estudios Peruanos, 1990; and David Scott Palmer, ed., *Shining Path of Peru*, New York: St. Martin's Press, 1992.

3. Orin Starn, "To Revolt against the Revolution: War and Resistance in Peru's Andes", *Cultural Anthropology* 10, no. 4, 1995, pp. 547–580.

4. The term "exodus" reflects the influence of Evangelical Christianity throughout the northern highlands of Ayacucho, where Biblical narrative structures became a dominant form of historicizing the war. See Ponciano Del Pino and Kimberly Theidon, "'Así es Como Vive Gente': Procesos Deslocalizados y Culturas Emergentes", in Carlos Iván Degregori and Gonzalo Portocarrero, eds, *Cultura y Globalización*, Lima: Red para el Desarrollo de las Ciencias Sociales en el Perú, 1999.

5. José Coronel Aguirre, "Recomposición del Tejido Social y el Estado", Foro Nacional Sobre Desplazamiento Interno Forzado, 13–14 July, Lima, Perú, 1995.

6. Truth and Reconciliation Commission, *Final Report*, Lima: Truth and Reconciliation Commission, 2003, vol. 1, p. 69.

7. I use the term "community" in two senses. Campesino communities are rights-bearing entities, recognized as such in the Peruvian Constitution. I also use community to refer to a historically situated, strategic collective identity. I am in no way invoking the image of "community" as the repository of the best of human values or as innately democratic. My fieldwork makes clear that one can "have big hell in a small town".

8. Steve Stern, "De la memoria suelta a la memoria emblemática: Hacia el recordar y el olvidar como proceso histórico", paper presented at the workshop on "Collective Memory of Repression in the Southern Cone in the Context of Democratization Processes," Social Science Research Council, Montevideo, Uruguay, 17–18 November 1998.

9. Degregori, *Ayacucho 1969–1979*.

10. Antonio Peña Jumpa, *Justicia communal en los Andes: El caso de Calahuyo*, Lima: Pontifica Univerisdad la Católica del Perú, 1998.

11. Sally Falk Moore, *Social Facts and Fabrications: "Customary Law" on Kilimanjaro (1880–1980)*, Cambridge: Cambridge University Press, 1986, p. 319.

12. David E. Apter, *The Legitimization of Violence*, New York: New York University Press, 1987, p. 22.

13. Carolyn Nordstrom and JoAnn Martin, eds, *The Paths to Domination, Resistance, and Terror*, Berkeley: University of California Press, 1992, p. 14.

14. Nelson Manrique, "La década de la violencia," *Márgenes* 56, 1989, p. 144.

15. Caretas, no. 7373, 1983.

16. Billie Jean Isbell, *To Defend Ourselves: Ecology and Ritual in an Andean Village*, Prospect Heights, Ill.: Waveland Press, 1985 (1978); Irene Silverblatt, *Moon, Sun and Witches: Gender Ideologies and Class in Inca and Colonial Peru*, Princeton: Princeton University Press, 1987.

17. Erving Goffman, *Stigma: Notes on the Management of Spoiled Identity*, New York: Simon & Schuster, 1963.

18. Ibid.

19. Friedrich Nietzsche, *On the Genealogy of Morals*, Translation by Walter Kaufman, and R. J. Hollingdale, New York: Random House, 1967, pp. 72–73.

20. The hacendados were large landowners (haciendas) who exploited the labour of the Quechua-speaking population. "Indio" ("Indian") is a very insulting term in Peru – no Quechua-speaker would refer to him- or herself this way. Indeed they would insist on the term *runa*, which means people. Marcelina is conveying the ethnic discrimination captured by the word "indios".

21. Peter Brooks, *Troubling Confessions: Speaking Guilt in Law and Literature*, Chicago: University of Chicago Press, 2002, p. 2.

22. Ibid.
23. Paul Connerton, *How Societies Remember*, Cambridge: Cambridge University Press, 1989, pp. 70–71.
24. Nicholas Tavuchis, *Mea Culpa: A Sociology of Apology and Reconciliation*, Stanford: Stanford University Press, 1991, p. 22.
25. Ibid., p. 7.
26. Susan Jacoby, *Wild Justice: The Evolution of Revenge*, New York: Harper & Row, 1988.
27. Michel Foucault, *Discipline and Punish: The Birth of the Prison*, New York: Vintage Books, 1979.
28. Hannah Arendt, *The Human Condition*, Chicago: University of Chicago Press, 1958.
29. Jean Carbonnier, *Sociologie Juridique*, Paris: Presses Universitaires de France, 1994, p. 173.
30. Juan Palomar de Miguel, *Diccionario para Juristas, Tomo 1*, Mexico City: Porrúa, 2001, p. 1597.
31. The correct noun form of *recoger* would be *recogidos*; however, as I have suggested, people interpreted *refugiados* by blending the term with a verb that was familiar to them.
32. Isbell, *To Defend Ourselves*; and Peña Jumpa, *Justicia communal en los Andes*.
33. I thank Chema García for a very informative conversation regarding the concept of *ayni*.
34. Goffman, *Stigma*, p. 9.
35. Webster's Third New International Dictionary entries for the word "reconcile".
36. See Carol Gilligan, *In a Different Voice: Psychological Theory and Women's Development*, Cambridge, Mass.: Harvard University Press, 1982; Sara Ruddick, *Maternal Thinking: Toward a Politics of Peace*, New York: Beacon Press, 1995 (1989); for a critique, see Nancy Scheper-Hughes, *Death without Weeping: The Violence of Everyday Life in Brazil*, Berkeley: University of California Press, 1992.
37. Sherry Ortner, "Resistance and the Problem of Ethnographic Refusal", *Comparative Study of Society and History* 37, 1995, p. 177.
38. Raymond Williams, *Keywords: A Vocabulary of Culture and Society*. New York: Oxford University Press, 1985, p. 75–76.
39. Peña Jumpa. *Justicia communal en los Andes*.
40. Laura Nader, *Harmony Ideology: Justice and Control in a Zapotec Mountain Village*. Stanford: Stanford University Press, 1990.
41. Veena Das, "Language and Body: Transactions in the Construction of Pain", in Arthur Kleinman, Veena Das and Margaret Lock, eds, *Social Suffering*, Berkeley: University of California Press, p. 80.
42. Kimberly Theidon, *Entre Prójimos: El conflicto armado interno y la política de la reconciliación en el Perú*, Lima: Instituto de Estudios Peruanos, 2004.
43. Kay Warren, *Indigenous Movements and Their Critics: Pan-Maya Activism in Guatemala*, Princeton NJ: Princeton University Press, 1998, p. 179–180.
44. Kimberly Theidon, *Traumatic States: Violence and Reconciliation in Peru*, doctoral thesis, Department of Anthropology, University of California, Berkeley, 2002.
45. Theidon, *Entre Prójimos*.
46. Robert Rubinstein, "Anthropology and International Security", in Robert Rubinstein and Mary Foster, eds, *The Social Dynamics of Peace and Conflict*, Boulder, Colo.: Westview Press, 1988, p. 28.

5

Origins and aftermaths: The dynamics of genocide in Rwanda and their post-crime implications

Scott Straus

This chapter focuses attention on the politics of governing a society after a mass crime. The case under discussion is the 1994 genocide in Rwanda. The central argument is that a particular understanding of the genocide's causes has contributed to key political and strategic decisions made by Rwanda's post-genocide government. That view essentially sees the genocide as an outgrowth of interethnic division and racist ideology, and it tends to incriminate an ethnic category, the Hutu, en masse. However, recent fieldwork that I conducted in Rwanda calls that framework into question, and by consequence my findings challenge the foundations of some post-genocide policies.

Overall, the approach in this chapter emphasizes the importance of detailed micro-level research in the aftermath of mass violence. As the editors note in the introduction, macro-level generalizations often are made after large-scale atrocity. This was especially the case in Rwanda, where "the Hutus" were seen to perpetrate the genocide and the ideological statements of a few leaders were seen as reflecting majority sentiment. My principal research aim was to test hypotheses in a rigorous fashion: Did ethnic hatred and ideological indoctrination drive the genocide? Was it widespread poverty? To answer these questions, evidence and a methodology to collect evidence are needed. Current answers to these questions were speculative and based on anecdote, which, as the editors note in the introduction, is typical of post–mass violence situations. My research led to conducting a survey of perpetrators, as well as to conducting a micro-comparative study of genocide in different locations – in ad-

After mass crime: Rebuilding states and communities, Pouligny, Chesterman and Schnabel (eds), United Nations University Press, 2007, ISBN 978-92-808-1138-4

dition to compiling data from as many secondary sources as I could find. The result is a new book that systematically evaluates different hypotheses of the Rwandan genocide and that offers a new interpretation.[1] But I also found that my findings had implications for policy decisions after atrocities have been committed. Post-genocide government and international policy rested on a particular macro-level notion of the genocide's causes. The evidence I collected calls that picture of the genocide into question and thus has implications for post-genocide reconstruction. Those post-genocide implications are this chapter's focus.

Background

The Rwandan genocide was a 100-day extermination campaign organized by key members of Rwanda's ruling military and political elite. Those leaders chose violence in a context of simultaneous threats from a newly legalized, primarily Hutu domestic political opposition and a rebel army, whose leadership and ranks primarily consisted of Tutsi exiles.[2] The event that triggered the genocide was the still unsolved assassination of Rwanda's long-time president, Juvénal Habyarimana. After his death, extremists formed an interim wartime government, and they called for the annihilation of the minority Tutsi population, ardent Hutu political opponents and Hutu who resisted the violence. Some three months later – after the rebels had defeated the genocidal regime and installed a new government – an estimated 500,000 Tutsi civilians and a far smaller number of Hutus had been killed.[3] Even by strict definitions, the episode qualifies as "genocide", and the violence is remarkable not just for its horror and speed, but also for the extent of participation it engendered.[4]

In the years since the genocide, the case has attracted a great deal of scholarly and policy attention. One key area of interest is why powerful international actors ignored early warnings of impending mass violence in Rwanda and why they opted not to intervene to stop genocide once it began.[5] Another area of interest is the genocide's domestic causes.[6] A third area of interest concerns post-genocide Rwanda – questions of justice and reconciliation as well as, more generally, state policies after atrocity. The focus of this chapter is the second and third lines of analysis, and the main objective is to use research on the origins of mass violence to analyze the politics of governing a society after such violence has been committed.

To date, an instrumentalist thesis that emphasizes the history of ethnicity and elite planning dominates scholarship on the genocide's domestic origins. Early commentary claimed that "long-standing tribal hatreds" drove the genocide, but such claims are not empirically tenable. In

Rwanda, Hutu and Tutsi intermarry; they belong to the same clans; they live in the same regions; they speak the same language; and they practice the same religions. Hutu and Tutsi are thus not typical tribes, nor are they typical ethnic groups. Moreover, the categories themselves have been considerably altered over time, and as such the categories are neither natural, nor do they mean today what they meant years ago. In particular, European colonial intervention in the late nineteenth and early twentieth centuries imposed racial categories on Rwandan society, and those categories later became the basis for the region's predominant political ideologies.[7]

Scholars have also focused attention on elite planning and state orchestration of the genocide. The "ancient tribal hatreds" argument tends to view the violence as spontaneous and an outcome of state failure. However, scholars have demonstrated the ways in which the violence was deliberately organized. Militias were trained; propaganda was spread; arms were bought; and "dry-run" massacres were perpetrated. Moreover, senior officials called for the genocide and disseminated their message through virulent radio broadcasts.[8] In short, the genocide was neither the spontaneous overflow of ethnic tension, nor of chaos, but rather of deliberate planning and orchestration by senior officials.

By and large, this approach to the study of the genocide has emphasized macro-historical processes and the actions of national elites. In so doing, the approach has tended to eclipse the dynamics of violence at the local and individual levels. To date, there remains a significant gap in analysis and in evidence about why violence took hold across the country and why ultimately so many Rwandans chose to participate in the genocide. And therein lies the basis for my research and for the substance of this chapter. How these questions are answered bears directly on the issues that the current Rwandan government faces. If the underlying factors that drove the genocide are seen to remain in place, then the regime faces a continuing danger and must respond accordingly. If, however, the factors that drove the mass violence were more situational in nature and no longer persist, then the continuing threat may be less than is commonly assumed.

Rwanda's shibboleths

One version of received wisdom on the genocide, particularly inside Rwanda among some key power holders, is that civilian participation in the genocide was massive and that such participation stemmed primarily from mass indoctrination. Many civilians did in fact participate in the genocide, and such participation does distinguish this genocide from others.[9] The question is how many.[10] Some current Rwandan officials claim that three million Hutus participated in the genocide – a figure that effectively criminalizes the entire adult Hutu population at the time of the genocide.[11] Indeed, some officials openly claim that the entire adult Hutu population took part directly or indirectly in the genocide.[12] In the words of one official, when the rebels took power in 1994 and formed a government, they faced a "criminal population".[13] Although not always openly expressed, this view, which tends to incriminate Hutus en masse, represents one important and influential strand of thinking among key power holders in post-genocide Rwanda.

This view is surprisingly consistent with the instrumentalist consensus described above. Because much commentary has stressed the history of racial ideology in Rwanda, one conclusion is that prior to the genocide Rwandan culture was deeply racist toward Tutsi. During three decades of Hutu rule, the argument goes, anti-Tutsi discrimination and dehumanization became a norm, and ordinary Rwandans became inured to hatred of "the other" – even if ethnic categories were constructed.[14] Similarly, one often hears that the genocide was like a "machine" – once the violence was unleashed from the top and implemented through a hierarchical state, ordinary Rwandans rapidly joined in because they typically obey orders and because they were poor peasants who wanted to loot their neighbors' property.[15]

Taken together, these ideas form the basis of one version of received wisdom on the genocide's causes. Rwandan officials often stress that the genocide stemmed from an "ideology of hatred", "divisionism" and "meticulous planning".[16] Even though the same officials also call for "unity and reconciliation" in post-genocide Rwanda, such claims present an undifferentiated picture of the genocide and bespeak a current of thinking that is similar to that described above. Even if Hutus are not directly or openly equated with genocidaires in these official accounts, the Hutu population is presented in these official accounts as brainwashed in racist ideology, easily manipulated and thus prone to succumbing to genocidal incitement.

By and large, this thinking on the causes of the genocide bodes poorly for post-genocide Rwanda. If adult Hutus are genocidaires or they were indoctrinated in an "ideology of hatred" and thereby can easily become genocidaires, then the threat of genocidal violence remains – all that has changed is the leadership controlling the state. This view both breeds insecurity and establishes a plausible claim for repressive state measures. In other words, a particular understanding of the causes of mass participation in the genocide unwittingly creates a dim outlook for "reconciliation" – however defined – and a case for state repression.

Indeed, post-genocide state policy in Rwanda has been heavy-handed, and outside watchdog organizations often describe it as "authoritarian".[17] In the years since the genocide, the government has maintained tight control over public space and discourse. Severe restrictions exist on political parties. In 2003, in the run-up to national elections, the most powerful opposition group, the MDR (Mouvement Démocratique Républicain), was banned, and many opposition supporters faced harassment, prompting one human rights group to call those elections "stage-managed".[18] Opponents of the regime also were arrested, and some disappeared.[19] In 2004, in the name of combating an "ideology of genocide", the government effectively shut down the country's main independent human rights organization.[20] In the post-genocide period, the Rwandan media also has been subject to state interference, and public speech has been carefully regulated, including a ban on public references to ethnicity.[21]

Most often, these measures are taken in the name of fighting "divisionism", changing the mindsets that are seen to have led to the genocide, and maintaining security. Indeed, security remains a top priority for Rwanda's post-genocide regime. Outside the presidency (which is run by the former rebel leader and current military leader, Paul Kagame), the army remains the most powerful institution in the country. This military emphasis complements the regime's concentration of political power – indeed, the two are closely intertwined and should not be overly distinguished. The point is that, in addition to tight control over political space, civil society and public discourse, the Rwandan state exercises a strong coercive presence, both domestically and internationally. These security measures are taken in the name of fighting a potential outbreak of genocide. Indeed, Rwanda's military intervention in the Democratic Republic of the Congo, which began in 1996, is officially justified as an effort to eliminate genocidal forces that remain there.

The reasons why Rwanda's post-genocide regime wields a heavy hand cannot simply be reduced to a particular interpretation of mass participation in the genocide. There are in fact rump elements of the old genocidal regime fighting in Congo. Moreover, the current regime is commonly perceived to represent Tutsi interests, in particular the interests of former Tutsi exiles. As such, the current leaders may fear they lack political support and favor authoritarianism to stay in power. But judging from official rhetoric and from numerous interviews with officials, I would argue that the Rwandan government's post-genocide approach is also based to an important degree on the particular understanding of causes of the 1994 genocide described above. That view considers the Hutu population genocidal or easily prone to genocide, and as such posits a persistent and serious security threat for governing post-crime Rwanda.

Micro-level field research in Rwanda

Nothing *a priori* discredits an interpretation of the causes of mass participation in the genocide that emphasizes mass anti-Tutsi beliefs: that interpretation is plausible, and it is consistent with the outcome of genocide.
However, to date there has been little systematic effort to evaluate empirically why genocidal dynamics took hold throughout Rwanda at the local level and, thus, why so many individuals participated in the violence.
Did the genocidal regime win broad public compliance because of a
deeply racist culture or widespread indoctrination? Or did other factors
come into play? The existing evidentiary record for answering this question is sparse, and thus a next step for scholarship is to conduct in-depth
research at the local level. Such a research agenda will have implications
for both academic theory and for post-genocide reconstruction, as argued
above.

Generating evidence to evaluate why people participate in mass violence is not a straightforward task – for many reasons. First, after such
violence the level of trauma is high, primarily among survivors and their
families. In addition, after the genocide, upwards of two million Rwandans fled the country and many had additional harrowing experiences as
refugees in neighboring countries. Second, how the crime is narrated is
politicized, and all sides often present interested and stylized accounts.
Third, because the research topic was in fact a crime, the questions that
researchers ask have a legal and often prosecutorial dimension. Fourth,
there is a more general methodological problem: What counts as evidence? What kinds of information can researchers use to evaluate competing hypotheses about participation in mass crimes? Much evidence
that contributed to forming the scholarly consensus described above
comes from macro-level sources – from radio broadcasts, from newspaper publications, from national leaders' speeches and from historical
patterns. How can researchers develop more micro-level evidence to tie
specific hypotheses to specific acts of violence?

Different researchers will answer these questions differently. Because
my primary interest is to understand the processes that led to violence
taking hold in communities and that led individuals to take part in the violence, I decided to focus primarily, although not exclusively, on perpetrators. I designed a field research program that consisted of three main
stages. The first and main phase was a nationwide survey of imprisoned
perpetrators. For the survey, I used a stratified random sampling method,
whereby I selected and interviewed sentenced perpetrators who had
pleaded guilty (see below for the reasons for this). The central research
instrument was a semi-structured questionnaire, which I designed to

evaluate competing hypotheses about the dynamics of violence and participation in it. In 2002, when I did this field research, the Rwandan government held roughly 110,000 detainees in prison on genocide charges; of those some 2,000 had been sentenced and pleaded guilty. In total, using this method, I interviewed 210 prisoners in 15 central prisons across Rwanda.[22]

The second research phase entailed comparing the dynamics of genocidal violence in five different locations. In 1994, when the genocide was committed, Rwanda had 145 communes. A commune is an administrative unit that had 50,000 inhabitants on average. During my first research phase, I discovered that the patterns of mobilization that led to the onset of genocide and that took place once violence had begun varied from commune to commune (more on this below). In addition, there was one commune under government control where genocide did not occur. For the second research phase, I selected four communes that exhibited variation in how the genocide was perpetrated, and the one commune, Giti, where genocide did not take place. I in turn studied the dynamics of violence in each commune in depth, through interviews with perpetrators, survivors, current and former government officials and non-participating Hutus.[23]

The third stage of research entailed return trips to prisons. During the first two research phases, one clear pattern emerged: In most communities, certain individuals were key to how the violence unfolded, either for their attempts to stem the killing or in their active promotion of it. While a few individuals in this category fell into my random sample in the first research phase, most respondents were low-level perpetrators. Thus, for the third research phase, I selected particular individuals to interview. They ranged from top communal authorities to young men who were particularly active killers in the genocide. I interviewed 19 using this method. In addition to this field research, I also looked for as much information as I could about regional patterns of violence – in government reports, for example – and consulted court transcripts to verify the perpetrator testimony.

The three phases of field research took place from January through July 2002. The main hypotheses that I examined came from political science (the discipline in which I was trained), from social psychology, from genocide studies and from existing studies of the Rwandan genocide. In the next section, I will briefly summarize some of the main findings from these three research phases. I will also discuss some of the reliability concerns that are central to interpreting the results. Then I will conclude by discussing what the findings might mean for governing post-crime Rwanda.

Findings

Regional and local variation

One important finding from my research is that there was significant regional and local variation in when and how the violence started in different parts of Rwanda. Immediately after President Habyarimana's assassination, national hardliners seized control of the Rwandan state and called for the killing of all Tutsis and Hutu opponents. However, that call did not translate into actual violence at the same time in all regions. In some areas, genocidal violence started within one or two days after the president's assassination. In other areas, however, violence did not begin until four or five days after his death, while in still others the violence did not begin for two weeks or more after the assassination. In many areas, Hutu leaders and ordinary civilians initially responded negatively to calls from the central government to kill Tutsis. By and large, those areas that initially resisted efforts to start the violence were those areas where the domestic Hutu political opposition had the greatest amount of support. Genocidal violence ultimately started and succeeded in those areas, but not before an important delay and not before a power struggle among Hutus.

In terms of how the violence started, significant variation also existed in different local areas. In some areas, local administration officials clearly started and directed the killing. In other areas, however, the push came from military officers. In still other areas, political party leaders and militia took charge. In some areas, local elites outside the official administrative hierarchies mobilized to assume control. And in many areas some combination of these occurred: soldiers worked with local officials or militia or the rural elite worked with political party officials.

The point to emphasize is that, even though the genocidal outcome was similar across Rwanda, how and when the violence started varied considerably. In other words, not all Hutus responded in the same way to the call to commit genocide. That finding is not consistent with the theory that the decision to take part in the genocide stemmed from widespread racist culture and indoctrination; nor is it consistent with the claim that the genocide was seamlessly orchestrated, with peasants all blindly following orders they received over the radio. To the contrary, the evidence of variation in how the violence started and spread points to the importance of factors besides or in addition to deeply ingrained ethnic attitudes.

In particular, I found that intra-Hutu dynamics played an important role in leading to the onset of genocide. After President Habyarimana was killed on 6 April 1994, hardliners called for violence against Tutsis and dissident Hutus, and at the same time the civil war that had started in 1990 but had nominally ended with a 1993 peace accord resumed – the Tutsi-led rebel organization, the Rwandan Patriotic Front (RPF), launched an offensive to take power. At the local level, the effect of these macro-level changes was to put power up for grabs. What ensued was a competition for control among local Hutu elites, the outcome of which was violence against Tutsi. The reasons for this are complex, and are not my focus here. The point to emphasize is that war-related uncertainty and insecurity at the national and local levels created an opportunity for some Hutus to rally to take control. Sometimes local officials maneuvered to keep their power; at other times, influential members of local communities – political party leaders, teachers and businessmen, for example – stepped in; often, a coalition of these local elite and administration officials, as suggested above, would take charge. Critical for this dynamic to take hold was the sense that power was indeterminately held, both because of spreading violence across the country and because of the president's assassination. In other words, civil war and destabilization contributed significantly to the onset of violence, which points to the importance of non-permanent, situational factors.

Perpetrators

My findings strongly support the view that there was mass participation during the genocide. The attacks that killed Tutsi varied considerably in size, but many attacks entailed hundreds of people at once. However, the evidence also suggests that not all Hutus participated in the genocide. In my interviews with perpetrators, I asked a series of questions about the groups in which they participated. Using the evidence from this section of my interviews, I estimated average group sizes across Rwanda and by extension the average number of perpetrators in different locations across the country. Using this information, I estimated that the total number of perpetrators – with a perpetrator defined as someone who participated in an attack that killed another person, even if the individual did not himself kill – to be between 175,000 and 210,000 persons. This number is an estimate, but one derived from detailed accounts of group dynamics across Rwanda. If the estimate holds up as more evidence becomes available, it detracts from claims that the entire Hutu population is collectively responsible for the genocide. While amounting to an enormous number of perpetrators, the figure represents 7 to 8 per cent of the active adult Hutu population at the time of the genocide.[24]

Moreover, while useful, the category of "perpetrators" elides varying degrees of participation in the genocide. There were perpetrators at different levels with different levels of responsibility. National level actors included military officers, government ministers, national political party leaders, radio broadcasters and newspaper editors. Broadly speaking, these actors were responsible for setting the genocide in motion: They defined the course of action that others were supposed to follow. At the local level, the general pattern was a group of influential elites in control; they in turn worked with aggressive youth, former soldiers, militia and otherwise particularly violent individuals. The latter category of actors – the aggressive thugs – often did a disproportionate amount of killing in their communities. Beneath these hard-core elements was a large group of perpetrators – the outright majority – who killed far less and who often faced intense pressure to participate, as we shall see. In other words, while mass participation is a salient characteristic of the Rwandan genocide, not all participants in the genocide participated to the same degree, and thus it is important to disaggregate the category of perpetrators.

As for perpetrator characteristics, my findings suggest that, taken together, the average perpetrator has a similar profile to the average adult male. In terms of age, occupation, number of children, literacy and years of education, the survey results are quite similar to those for the adult male Hutu population in Rwanda. In other words, on the whole, the perpetrator population was not comparatively younger, more unemployed or worse or better educated. The important finding here is that perpetrators appear to have been a cross-section of adult Hutu males – a finding that is consistent with claims of large-scale intra-Hutu pressure to participate in the genocide (more on this below).

Interethnic relations and ideology

From a distance, Hutu and Tutsi look like deeply divided social groups. Inside Rwanda, however, one finds several other salient cleavages, including region, sub-region, clan, religion and especially social status. These cleavages all crosscut the Hutu and Tutsi categories. Moreover, the Hutu and Tutsi populations are highly integrated. Not only do they speak the same languages and intermarry but Hutu and Tutsi families also live next door to each other throughout the country. In my survey of prisoners, I collected information on these questions and asked perpetrators about their relations with their Tutsi neighbors, if they had them, before the genocide. Almost all those interviewed said that they had a Tutsi neighbor, and an outright majority described relations with their neighbors prior to the genocide in positive or neutral terms. As for intermarriage, of the perpetrator sample, some two-thirds said they had a Tutsi family member. In short, the evidence about interethnic relations strongly detracts from the argument that deep divisions between ethnic groups and cultural distance drove participation in the genocide: Hutu and Tutsi lives in Rwanda were highly intertwined before the genocide.

The evidence about racist culture and ideology was mixed. On the one hand, many respondents spoke in categorical terms about "the Hutu" and "the Tutsi", in particular when referencing the crisis period after President Habyarimana was killed. About two-thirds of the respondents agreed that "Hutu" and "Tutsi" were different "*amoko*", a Kinyarwanda word that means both "ethnic group" and "race". Moreover, many respondents repeated elements of the genocidal regime's propaganda – that the rebels killed Hutu children and disembowelled pregnant women, for example. On the other hand, other elements of the regime's propaganda did not seem to have penetrated to the countryside. The key finding here is that while most respondents said they did not think negatively about their Tutsi neighbors, had deep ties with Tutsi and in general did not express generalized hostility to "the Tutsi", many clearly did think in categorical terms about ethnicity before the genocide. This mattered particularly in reference to fears of the Tutsi-dominant rebel army: here the regime's propaganda successfully instilled fear that "the Tutsi" were a threat to "the Hutu" writ large.

Motivation

During the course of the interviews, I asked respondents both direct and indirect questions about their motivation to participate in the genocide. I asked them how they became integrated in the violence in their communities; I asked them explicitly why they joined attacks; and I asked them to identify what they thought was the most important reason they participated. I also asked them whether they looted property, if the radio motivated them, and a series of other questions. Self-accounts of motivation need to be treated sceptically. Moreover, not all participants in a macroevent like a genocide are likely to have the same motivations, and many individuals may have various, or changing, motivations. With those caveats in mind, I would contend that perpetrator self-accounts about why they killed or joined attacks are valuable. When triangulated with other evidence, these statements can reveal perceptions and processes that contributed to individual decisions to take part in mass violence.

As expected, respondents expressed a range of motivations, from material incentives to loot, to doing what others around them did, to joining attacks to avoid suspicion that they were hiding Tutsi in their homes. However, two main types of motivations emerged from these interviews. The first was some form of intra-Hutu coercion or intimidation. Many respondents said that once the violence started in their communities, they faced strong pressure from others Hutus to participate and that they feared negative consequences for themselves and their families, including death, if they refused. The second most common kind of motivation was war-related. These respondents said that in the aftermath of Habyarimana's death, they feared that the RPF was invading Rwanda and was killing Hutus in the process. These respondents in turn accepted the position that all Tutsis were rebel group supporters, and thus, out of a desire to protect themselves and their families, they said, they joined attacks that killed their Tutsi neighbors, including women, children and men. Some respondents also said that they were angry after Habyarimana's death, which they blamed on the RPF, and sought revenge against Tutsi civilians. On balance, those who expressed a kind of wartime fear or anger were more violent than those who said they joined attacks because of pressure from other Hutus.

I also asked respondents a series of questions about the language they used at the time of the killing. The central images and terms that respondents recalled came from the language of war. The key phrase that appeared again and again in perpetrator narratives was the declaration that "the Tutsi is the enemy" or "the Tutsi is the only enemy". Other respondents said that killing was described as "combating the enemy", "going to the front" and "assuring security". Even for those respondents who said other Hutus pressured them to participate in the violence, the way in which they said they understood what they were doing was to join a war against "the Tutsi enemy". This version of events resembles the propaganda that national hardliners broadcast over the radio, but the key mechanism that respondents described was less hatred and prejudice and more wartime insecurity, where the declared "enemy" was an ethnic category.

This discussion of my findings is truncated, and important reliability concerns remain (see below). That said, if this evidence holds up as more information about the genocide becomes available, it would detract from the common-wisdom understanding of the genocide described above. Clearly, ethnicity was a key background condition that allowed the genocide to occur. If ethnicity were insignificant, then the calls to fight "the Tutsi" would not have resonated. But the evidence does not suggest that perpetrators joined attacks because they were permanently brainwashed into hating Tutsi; nor does it suggest that most Hutu perpetrators were inured to despising the Tutsi "other".

Rather, the evidence points to the importance of a nexus of factors that concern war, destabilization and the nature of power in Rwanda. On the one hand, the genocide was committed in a period of acute disruption: during a civil war, immediately after a president's assassination and after several years of multi-party politics. That disruption bred insecurity and opened the way for intense intra-ethnic and interethnic dynamics to keep or take power. On the other hand, the genocide was committed in a country that has a dense state administration, dense geographic settlement and a long history of institutions geared towards mass participation. Once local-level leaders won control in their areas and in a context where control was contingent on subscribing to the national authorities' call to fight "the Tutsi enemy", those leaders in turn pressured other Hutus to participate. That pressure succeeded in part because of Rwanda's institutional and geographic makeup and in part because of a context of generalized violence. In short, ethnicity mattered, but it mattered especially so in a context of war and destabilization, and it mattered in a context where those with power had the institutional capacity to enforce their position and where their threat of coercion was credible.

Reliability

In the interests of brevity and of maintaining a focus on Rwanda's post-genocide environment, I have here limited both the presentation of evidence and my analysis of the dynamics driving the genocide.[25] Still, before turning to the possible implications of this evidence for post-crime Rwanda, the issue of reliability must be raised. Given that my main respondents are genocide perpetrators in prison, the information they supply must be treated with scepticism. That said, when conducting my field research in Rwanda, I took several measures to account for the reliability problems inherent in interviewing perpetrators. While not foolproof, these measures give reason to have some confidence in the results.

First, my research design called for interviewing perpetrators who had already been sentenced, thereby reducing their incentives to lie. Also, having been sentenced, their cases already had been discussed in a court of law, which meant that the crimes for which they had pled and been found guilty had been documented publicly. Second, I interviewed perpetrators in 15 different prisons, which meant that they could not collaborate to deceive. Similarly, I selected respondents to interview randomly, which meant that respondents could not anticipate being called for an interview. Third, I worked with a Rwandan research assistant who helped me assess the veracity of different perpetrator accounts. The assistant was of mixed Hutu–Tutsi parentage; he had lived in Rwanda before and during the genocide; and attackers had targeted him during the killing. Thus, by his identity and experience, and by his intelligence, he was in a position to provide a first-stage check on perpetrator testimony.

I took other measures, too. As intra-Hutu coercion was a recurring and important theme in perpetrator accounts, I tried to verify this version of events in two main ways. First, in my first and third research phases, when I encountered individuals who acknowledged being local-level leaders of the violence, I asked them if they pressured other Hutus to participate. By and large, these respondents readily acknowledged that if they encountered Hutu men who were not participating, they would require them to join attacks. In the words of one local-level leader, non-participating Hutu were treated as rebel "accomplices", and they could be fined, beaten or killed if they refused to take part in the violence.

By the same token, during my second research phase (the micro-studies of the genocide in five communes), I looked for Hutu men who survivors and local authorities agreed had not participated in the genocide. I asked these non-participating Hutu if they had been pressured to participate, and indeed each had been fined, had had property stolen or had been physically beaten for not participating. I also examined other existing sources recorded in different periods, and again these accounts were consistent with the processes described in the interviews I conducted. In short, while the perpetrator narratives must continue to be treated sceptically, I found enough corroborating evidence to suggest that there was significant wartime intra-Hutu pressure to participate in the genocide. There still remained a choice. Individuals could choose to face the consequences of not participating – no matter what those consequences were – rather than committing violence. But the evidence strongly suggests that intra-Hutu coercion played an important role in leading many, although not all, ordinary Rwandans to become perpetrators of genocide.

Implications for post-genocide Rwanda

If the findings from this field research project hold true as more detailed information becomes available, the results have important implications for post-genocide Rwanda. As argued above, the post-genocide government has favored strong control over public discourse and politics and maintained a strong military emphasis. These policies, I have argued, are based at least in part on a particular interpretation of mass participation in the genocide. That view tends to see the genocide as an undifferentiated event, and it tends to posit the main cause of mass participation as mass beliefs and mass indoctrination in a racist ideology. That interpretation essentially posits a persistent threat, because the Hutu population is considered to be either genocidal or brainwashed and thus prone to becoming genocidal. The logical response to such an ongoing threat is strong coercive control over the potentially dangerous population.

However, the danger in pursuing heavy-handed policies is that they risk increasing insecurity and grievances over the long run. Although designed to keep the peace, such policies may ultimately backfire and create resentment that could contribute to future violence and to radical politics.

Here, the micro-level evidence about the origins of participation in the violence may contribute to breaking this security trap. First, the evidence that I collected in Rwanda does not support collective blame of the Hutu population. Not all Hutus were genocidaires, and not all perpetrators participated to the same degree. Second, the genocide was not perpetrated in a seamless, hierarchical, "machine"-like manner. Rather, the violence was the outcome of local-level struggles for dominance, and many initially resisted or tried to avoid becoming involved in it. Third, the evidence suggests that while ethnic categories were an important background condition for the genocide to occur, neither interpersonal ethnic enmity nor a deeply imbibed racist culture was the wellspring of most individual participation in the violence. Rather, specific conditions in Rwanda triggered the saliency of ethnic categories and facilitated a dynamic of violence to take hold. Thus, when considering how prone Rwanda is to future violence, the stress should fall on those situational factors that sowed the insecurity and destabilization that allowed a dynamic of violence to take hold.

All this indicates that some key conditions that facilitated the genocide in the first place may no longer be present. By extension, the prospects for post-genocide confidence and trust among social groups might be greater than many Rwandan and outside observers fear. Choosing the right concept to describe positive relations after a mass crime is difficult. "Reconciliation" is arguably an unrealistic goal for post-genocide Rwanda. The concept suggests that Rwandans return to a pre-genocide state of good feeling, which implies that the genocide's victims forgive their attackers and dismiss what they have suffered. As such, the burden of reconciliation can fall disproportionately to survivors, and many recoil from being asked to pardon or forget atrocities committed against themselves and their families. Indeed, there is no reason to expect survivors should forgive perpetrators or downplay their losses. "Coexistence" is another concept for describing post-genocide interpersonal relations; "coexistence" avoids the imperative to forgive and as such is a more plausible goal.[26] However, the concept can suggest standoff, distrustful relations – a wary cohabitation.

By contrast, the key issue for post-genocide Rwanda concerns trust and confidence. More than reconciliation, the question is whether Rwandans will mutually fear one another and whether, fearing a new outbreak of violence, the state will maintain a strong coercive presence. The micro-level evidence here suggests that the Hutu population is not genocidal in nature. As such, while the post-genocidal government is rightfully concerned with stability, the strong security measures designed to contain expression, to limit political party activity and to cast a distrustful eye on the adult domestic Hutu population may not be necessary. To the contrary, such measures risk creating resentment and a turn towards violent modes of political protest, which in turn could sow insecurity.

The evidence presented in this chapter also has implications for justice, which is a critical dimension to any government's effort to govern after a mass crime. Criminal trials for the Rwandan genocide have been held both in an international forum and in a domestic one. Internationally, the United Nations Security Council established an ad hoc court called the International Criminal Tribunal for Rwanda. This court is responsible for prosecuting the "big fish": national and regional leaders who are most responsible for the genocide. Domestically, the Rwandan government has prosecuted alleged genocide criminals in regular courts, but by 2001 only about 6,000 detainees of about 110,000 had been sentenced. At that rate, government officials reasoned, the trials would not finish for a generation or more. To compensate for this slow pace of justice, the government introduced in 2002 a second process called *gacaca*, which is based on a traditional, informal method of resolving disputes. In the current version of gacaca, ordinary Rwandans from communities where genocide crimes were committed detail those crimes and determine guilt. The sentences are, in general, lighter than in the standard justice system, and they can include community service. The process is reserved for lower-level perpetrators. The most active killers and local level leaders do not qualify for this process; their cases remain in the standard justice system.

Human rights organizations have raised important concerns about the fairness of gacaca for the accused. However, it is worth recognizing that a mass, plebian process of justice is appropriate for the kind of mass crime committed in Rwanda. No perpetrator should be exonerated for his or her choice to participate in the genocide. At the same time, the national and local leaders most responsible for launching, orchestrating and promoting the genocide clearly aimed for mass participation. The evidence I found in my research suggests that in-group coercion was exercised throughout Rwanda and was a key factor in why many participated. Moreover, national hardliners used wartime scare tactics to mobilize a frightened and confused population. While not negating the crimes, these factors warrant careful appraisal of individual criminal responsibility in this mass crime. They suggest that the Rwandans who used power and coercion to mobilize others bear an especially heavy responsibility in perpetrating this crime. The gacaca process tacitly recognizes this distinction, as does Rwandan law set up to prosecute the genocide.[27]

For the international donor community, which has invested heavily in post-genocide Rwanda, the research findings reemphasize the importance of challenging the state's repressive measures. Post-genocide Rwanda's international military actions as well as the government's snuffing out of political space within Rwanda are justified in the name of preventing another outbreak of genocide. However, my research findings suggest that mass genocidal beliefs did not drive the killing. Not only are the current state's security and repressive measures based on a superficial analysis of the genocide's causes, but such measures risk creating the resentments and fears that could lead to long-term risk and instability in the region.

Conclusion

This chapter has argued that understanding the causes of violence has important implications for thinking about the aftermath of mass crimes. The chapter also has emphasized the need to disaggregate a mass crime's causes. Looked at from a distance, the Rwandan genocide appears to be an undifferentiated event, which in turn supports broad and static generalizations about its origins. However, the larger picture masks a more complex empirical picture of how the violence started and spread in local areas. National elites promoted genocidal violence from the center, but that call was met with varied responses, ranging from support to resistance. A genocidal dynamic ultimately succeeded throughout Rwanda, but for reasons that depended less on widespread interethnic enmity and racist indoctrination than on wartime power struggles in the context of dense state institutions and human settlement.

The implications of this analysis for post-genocide Rwanda are surprisingly positive. The logical response to a "criminal population" is continued insecurity, which in turn justifies tight state security measures and restricted public discourse. By contrast, a view of the violence that stresses situational factors and enforcement mechanisms lessens the immediate danger, as long as those factors are absent. In other words, an understanding of the dynamics of violence may increase post-genocide trust between individuals and social groups. Similarly, a view of the genocide that stresses the actors who used violence and mobilized others suggests that post-genocide prosecutions should focus on those actors, not on the masses of low-level perpetrators. Again, such a policy may increase confidence, as opposed to a policy that may increase resentment.

All this points to the importance of micro-level research in the aftermath of mass crimes. Given the scale of a crime like genocide, the analytical temptation is to treat the event in the aggregate. In that way, the full horror is preserved. But disaggregation permits a closer inspection of why the dynamics of violence take hold and thus why individuals kill. Focusing on these dimensions, while still remembering the big picture, can yield insights into the crime's origins that in turn affect how the future is imagined. For Rwanda, micro-level research indicates that the country's future could be brighter than its recent history suggests.

Acknowledgements

I would like to thank Sara Guyer, Victor Peskin and the participants of a 10–12 June 2003 workshop on mass crimes and post-conflict peace-building for detailed comments on earlier drafts. This chapter draws on the findings and analysis in my forthcoming book *The Order of Genocide: Race, Power, and War in Rwanda* (Ithaca: Cornell University Press, 2006). The research was supported by grants from the United States Institute of Peace, the Social Science Research Council and the National Science Foundation. All views contained in this chapter are my own.

Notes

1. Scott Straus, *The Order of Genocide: Race, Power, and War in Rwanda*, Ithaca, NY: Cornell University Press, 2006.
2. Rwanda's domestic population consists of three main ethnic categories: the Hutu, who, according to the country's 1991 census, comprised some 91.1 per cent of the population; the Tutsi, who, according to the census, comprised 8.4 per cent; and the Twa, who comprised less than 0.4 per cent. See République Rwandaise, *Recensement général de la population et de l'habitat au 15 Aout 1991: Analyse des resultats definitifs*, Kigali: République Rwandaise, April 1994, p. 124.
3. Estimates for the total number killed in the genocide vary from 500,000 to more than a million. In my view, the best estimate is of around 500,000 and is found in Alison Des Forges, *Leave None to Tell the Story: Genocide in Rwanda*, New York: Human Rights Watch, 1999, pp. 15–16.
4. Disagreements about the definition of genocide are endemic to the scholarship on genocide. For overviews on this question, see Helen Fein, "Genocide: A Sociological Perspective", *Current Sociology* 38, no. 1, 1990, pp. 8–31; Frank Chalk and Kurt Jonassohn, *The History and Sociology of Genocide: Analyses and Case Studies*, New Haven, Conn.: Yale University Press, 1990, pp. 3–53; and Scott Straus, "Contested Meanings and Conflicting Imperatives: A Conceptual Analysis of Genocide", *Journal of Genocide Research* 3, no. 3, 2001, pp. 349–375.
5. Key books focused on these questions include Joint Evaluation of Emergency Assistance to Rwanda, *The International Response to Conflict and Genocide: Lessons from the Rwandan Experience*, Odense, Denmark: Steering Committee of the Joint Evaluation of Emergency Assistance to Rwanda, 1996; Bruce Jones, *Peacekeeping in Rwanda: The Dynamics of Failure*, Boulder, Colo.: Lynne Rienner Publishers, 2001; Alan Kuperman, *The Limits of Humanitarian Intervention: Genocide in Rwanda*, Washington, DC: Brookings Institute, 2000; Linda Melvern, *A People Betrayed: The Role of the West in Rwanda's Genocide*, London: Zed Books, 2000; and Samantha Power, *A Problem from Hell: America and the Age of Genocide*, New York: Public Affairs, 2002.

6. An enormous amount of work has been published in French and in English since the genocide in 1994. See, for example, Jean-Pierre Chrétien et al., *Les Médias du génocide*, Paris: Karthala, 1995; Jean-Claude Willame, *Aux Sources de l'Hécatombe Rwandaise*, Brussels: CEDAF, 1995; African Rights, *Death, Despair and Defiance*, rev. ed., London: African Rights, 1995; Article 19, *Broadcasting Genocide: Censorship, Propaganda, & State-Sponsored Violence in Rwanda 1990–1994*, New York: Article 19, 1996; Alison Des Forges, *Leave None to Tell the Story*; Mahmood Mamdani, *When Victims Become Killers: Colonialism, Nativism, and the Genocide in Rwanda*, Princeton: Princeton University Press, 2001; Gérard Prunier, *The Rwanda Crisis: History of a Genocide*, New York: Columbia University Press, 1995; and Peter Uvin, *Aiding Violence: The Development Enterprise in Rwanda*, West Hartford, Conn.: Kumarian Press, 1998.

7. On these points, see, in particular, Jean-Pierre Chrétien, *The Great Lakes of Africa: Two Thousand Years of History*, trans. Scott Straus, New York: Zone Books, 2003; Mahmood Mamdani, *When Victims Become Killers*; and Philip Gourevitch, *We Wish to Inform You that Tomorrow We Will Be Killed with Our Families*, New York: Farrar, Straus, and Giroux, 1998.

8. The key book in this instrumentalist/statist vein is Alison Des Forges, *Leave None to Tell the Story*. See also Article 19, *Broadcasting Genocide*, and Jean-Pierre Chrétien et al., *Les Médias du génocide*. This also is the essential view taken by the prosecution at the International Criminal Tribunal for Rwanda (ICTR). Based in Arusha, Tanzania, the ICTR was established to prosecute the top leaders of the genocide.

9. Jean Paul Kimonyo, *Revue critique des interprétations du conflit rwandais*, Butare: Éditions de l'université nationale du Rwanda, 2000.

10. Some scholars estimate the number of perpetrators to be tens of thousands, but most observers estimate a far greater number. For an example of a low-end estimate, see Alison Des Forges, *Leave None to Tell the Story*, p. 260. For an example of a high-end estimate, see Christian Scherrer, *Genocide and Crisis in Central Africa: Conflict Roots, Mass Violence, and Regional War*, Westport, Conn.: Praeger Publishers, 2002, p. 126.

11. A figure of three million perpetrators often has been cited to me in interviews with senior government officials during different research trips to Rwanda in 2000 and 2002. For an example in print, see Philip Gourevitch, *We Wish to Inform You*, p. 244.

12. I base this assertion on interviews that I have done with senior government officials in Kigali in 2000 and 2002.

13. See Mahmood Mamdani, *When Victims Become Killers*, p. 7. Note that Mamdani quotes this as evidence of mass participation in the genocide.

14. See, for example, Colette Braekmann, *Rwanda: Histoire d'un génocide*, Paris: Fayard, 1994, p. 161; and Christian Scherrer, *Genocide and Crisis in Central Africa*, pp. 119–122. This view also is dominant in Philip Gourevitch, *We Wish to Inform You*.

15. These claims are commonly made in casual conversation in Rwanda. For references in print to where Rwandans' obedience is cited as an explanation, see International Criminal Tribunal for Rwanda, "The Prosecutor Versus Jean-Paul Akayesu, Case No. ICTR-96-4-T: Judgement", Arusha, Tanzania: ICTR, p. 17; Christian Scherrer, *Genocide and Crisis in Central Africa*, p. 113; Gérard Prunier, *The Rwanda Crisis*, pp. 57 and 245. For an example in print of where looting is described as the main motive to participate in the genocide, see Gérard Prunier, *The Rwanda Crisis*, p. 248, and James Waller, *Becoming Evil: How Ordinary People Commit Genocide and Mass Killing*, Oxford: Oxford University Press, 2002, p. 69. For an example of reference to the machine metaphor, see Johan Pottier, *Re-Imagining Rwanda: Conflict, Survival and Disinformation in the Late Twentieth Century*, Cambridge: Cambridge University Press, 2002, p. 31.

16. For examples where an "ideology of hatred" and divisionism are stressed, see the "Genocide" section of the Official Website of the Government of Rwanda, at http://

www.gov.ru/; see also "Dealing with genocide and its effects: The Rwandan case", a speech by Fatuma Ndanziga, Executive Secretary of the National Unity and Reconciliation Commission, available from http://www.gei.de/deutsch/aktuelles/pdf/ndanziga.pdf. Note also that the second article of a new constitution recently adopted in Rwanda highlights the "ideology of genocide" and "divisions", both of which the Constitution pledges to fight.

17. See, for example, International Crisis Group, "Rwanda at the End of the Transition: A Necessary Political Liberalisation", *ICG Africa Report*, no. 53, 12 November 2002, p. 1. Even wire news reports refer to the Rwandan government as "authoritarian". On the latter point, see Matthew Rosenberg, "Concerns Raised about Rwanda's Elections", Associated Press, 21 August 2003.

18. Amnesty International, "Rwanda: Run-Up to Presidential Elections Marred by Threats and Harassment", 22 August 2003.

19. Human Rights Watch, "Preparing for Elections: Tightening Control in the Name of Unity," 8 May 2003; available from http://www.hrw.org/backgrounder/africa/rwanda0503bck.htm.

20. On this, see http://hrw.org/english/docs/2004/07/02/rwanda8996.htm.

21. See International Crisis Group, "Rwanda at the End of the Transition", pp. 12–16 and Reporters sans frontières, "Des pressions discrètes et ciblées: Le président Paul Kagame est un prédateur de la liberté de la presse," 1 November 2001; available from http://www.rsf.org.

22. These interviews were conducted in a private office outside of earshot of other detainees. All but a handful of interviews were conducted in Kinyarwanda and translated into French with the help of a Rwandan research assistant (more below). The interviews lasted anywhere from 45 minutes to 5 hours. For further details on my procedures, see my forthcoming book, *The Order of Genocide*, especially chapter 5.

23. In addition to Giti, the chosen communes were Gafunzo in Cyangugu Prefecture; Kayove in Gisenyi Prefecture; Kanzenze in Kigali Rurale Prefecture; and Musambira in Gitarama Prefecture.

24. These figures are based on the population recorded in the 1991 government census. For an extended discussion of the calculations in this paragraph, see Scott Straus, "How Many Perpetrators Were There in the Rwandan Genocide? An Estimate", *Journal of Genocide Research* 6, no. 1, 2004, pp. 85–98.

25. For a much longer discussion of my evidence and my interpretation of the evidence, please see my forthcoming book, *The Order of Genocide*.

26. Laura McGrew introduced the concept to me. A conference in Rwanda also was organized with this theme in April 2002. For more information on the latter, see "Proceedings of the Workshop on Rethinking Peace, Coexistence and Human Security in the Great Lakes", Kigali: Center for Conflict Management, National University of Rwanda, April 2002.

27. The Rwandan law codifying genocide crimes establishes four levels of crimes. See Official Gazette of the Republic of Rwanda, "Organic Law on the Organization of Prosecutions," Kigali: Republic of Rwanda, p. 15.

6

"You can't run away": Former combat soldiers and the role of social perception in coping with war experience in the Balkans

Natalija Bašić

A key consideration for peace-building and a successful stabilization process following the wars in Croatia and Bosnia-Herzegovina during the 1990s is how to begin the process of building roads to reconciliation. A process of extreme violence took place in the middle of Europe. This case in particular has exemplified which potentials lay in modern societies and how willing its members are to decide in favour of war, violence and mass murder. The violence practiced within the Yugoslavian wars spans a wide spectrum – ranging from sabotage, torture and rape to ethnic cleansing, massacre and mass executions (e.g., in Srebrenica[1]).

The process of mass murder that took place between 1991 and 1995 in the former Yugoslavia became generally well known. As a result of the wars in Croatia and Bosnia, almost 250,000 people died. The majority of those killed were Bosnian Muslims; crimes committed mainly by Serbian troops. However, not only Serbians participated in the murders, Croatians, too, had shown great hostility towards the Muslims.

Moreover, in the literature soldiers who participated in ethnic cleansing tend to be defined as criminals, mercenaries or "paramilitaries", committing war crimes on their own account, for payment (for instance, executioners such as Dražen Erdemović earned five German marks for every Muslim killed) or on the orders of warlords. From my point of view that is an incorrect assumption, as it projects an image that is unfounded: "Normal soldiers" as well as regular troops killed large numbers of people, or at least assisted in the killings.

After mass crime: Rebuilding states and communities, Pouligny, Chesterman and Schnabel (eds), United Nations University Press, 2007, ISBN 978-92-808-1138-4

The subject of war crime is an increasingly complex one, and it is not only a matter for criminologists and tribunals; this experience is also frequently part of the life of normal people.[2] To understand the readiness to kill and the role of social perception in influencing such behaviour, this chapter and the primary research upon which it is based examines the perpetrators' retrospectives. Drawing upon transcripts of interviews that have been conducted with former combat soldiers from Bosnia, Croatia and Serbia, this chapter examines the newly structured realities. It begins by offering some information about the historical background of the discussion and the relevance of perpetrator's perspectives in the context of peace-building and stabilization in the Yugoslavian successor states. Excerpts from interviews with former combatants will illustrate why young men were "resolved to risk all" and participated in the armed conflict in former Yugoslavia.

Background

The mass murder in Rwanda took place outside of Europe and could easily be dismissed as exotic, stigmatized as a result of archaic tribal conflicts.[3] But mass murder took place in Europe as well, by and against people who had been socialized into a mostly modern and Central European way of life. Many of the perpetrators spoke several languages, possessed university degrees and were familiar with Western media and lifestyles. Meanwhile, it is well documented that for large parts of the population of former Yugoslavia (perhaps with the exception of the Kosovars), the 1980s passed by without anxiety and in relative security. This changed, however, with the spread of propaganda of ethnic victimhood and of myths of genocide, generating dynamics of conflict escalation and fear of existential threats as violence grew in June 1991, when the Yugoslav People's Army (JNA) began to oppose violently the separatist efforts of (part of) the Republic of Slovenia. For supporters of the idea of a "Yugoslav" national identity, those with strong interethnic relations through family and in particular for the JNA, long the defender of the socialist party, this was a period of major disruption – in the end a catastrophe. Others, especially nationalists, viewed the dissolution of Yugoslavia as proof of the fact that the idea of the Yugoslavian nation had been based on a concept of state and society that had been doomed to fail. They worked on fostering resentment and antagonism through propaganda and violent acts; in this way the abuse of shared history was still part of the ongoing processes, constructions of traditional enmities and long-standing hatred against the ethnic "other" emerged as a potent explanatory paradigm for the horrible conflicts of the 1990s. While in this context the tales and myths of the Second World War that circulated might have been irrational, the effects were concrete.

However, the public was horrified to see that the Yugoslav armed forces did not care about the opinions of the people. Images of abandoned tanks and fleeing soldiers and of resistance showed that acts of violence against neighbours, friends or family were not taken for granted.[4] But the increasingly complicated structures of political and military action were also reflected in the collective and individual perceptions of those soldiers who were directly involved in the fighting. Finally, the anticipation of war divided the JNA and every draftee was to defend what he began to perceive as one's own group – be it Yugoslav, Slovenian, Croatian, Serbian or Bosnian.[5]

As in other cases examined in this volume, most notably Scott Straus's account of Rwanda, acts of violence and "ethnic cleansing" were carefully organized. The existing administrative structure that became ethnicized consisted of a civilian-military organization that supported escalation. In addition, the Yugoslavian society had established a civic defence system. It was thus not unusual that men especially were armed to be able to defend their homes.[6]

New defence collectives emerged; many "completely ordinary" young men, who had grown up with the so-called "Unity and Brotherhood" of the former Yugoslavia, became "completely ordinary" soldiers and draftees, voluntary and involuntary participants in the ensuing events.

Young male adults carried the main burden for the survival of their family or group; easy access to weapons further allowed a type of self-recruitment and also led to the formation of groups that could lead to the practice of war. Men who had voluntarily joined the government troops or opposing armed forces in order to secure the chance of survival for themselves and their families or nation came from very different regions and circles; in civil life, they were students, bricklayers, unemployed or sociologists with doctorate degrees.

Others had already participated in reserve army training during the beginning of the war; they were young recruits or had come of age for compulsory military service during the war and therefore made up the base for subsequent recruitment. The age-specific differentiation corresponds with the deployment of reorganized territorial troops or national armies that also possess much significance beyond political and nationalistic motives. Not all draftees over 18 years of age were called up to join for the army; in fact, to be drafted could therefore mean that one had displayed a certain obedience or belief in community. Only a small fraction was recruited by force.[7] Some of the interviewees also depicted their entry into the army as a coincidence. For most, it had not been difficult to learn everything in a short time. Especially for men from regions in which conflicts existed, shots were fired from "irregular" opposing troops in the night, destruction mounted, disabilities or casualties occurred and the tendency to use weapons and participate in a regular paramilitary or other armed group was likely. These interviewees therefore describe their entry into the conflict as one of "sliding" into the situation. It was different for those who lived a relatively long distance from the war regions, such as for Serbs from Serbia. They had to make a more conscious decision to join the war effort.

Some young men with little experience, but who were considered to be especially capable, were trained under the direction of professional and especially experienced men to become warriors, professional killers and snipers. Most of the men I interviewed fought in more common groups, but some also operated as members of so-called "special units". Depending upon age and qualification, they entered the war as compulsory service men, reservists or professional soldiers. They shot in close range fighting or from a distance, killed and sometimes looted and plundered on command, whereby independent action could also be required. Barely anyone was forced to participate in the fighting. The possibility to make independent decisions existed. Regarding the real motives, a certain amount of voluntarism seems apparent: these men were prepared to use their arms and were capable of carrying out extreme forms of violence – while others refused to fight.[8]

Competent at different levels, certainly with qualitatively different military equipment and the formation of specialized function areas and types of weapons, a splitting into individual spheres of action and experience occurred, differentiated by time, space and social structures. Depending upon the type of opportunities they had, the challenges they faced, the type of war material they were equipped with and the specific fighting in which they were involved, the interviewees had very different experiences as soldiers in a fragmented war. In this process of war, decisions, however, always have to be made anew. This includes the decision not to volunteer to continue to fight after the end of the military service.

The notion of an "identity of defence" implied the emergence of readiness for defending or protecting the own – one's own house, family, country or nation. But it also shows passion for the professional soldier, if not the rational killer. The identity of defence creates actually another mode and scale of mythologization that transcends national identities but does not deny them. The identity of defence as an empirical fact in the case of former combat soldiers in the wars of the 1990s in former Yugoslavia allows a reflection on military formation as well as on the common values, rights, principles and policies that are the foundation of civil warfare processes.

Realities of violence

Recent research on violence and the perpetrators of violence addresses the inner rationale of the perpetrators, and the reconstruction of the social process through which the perpetrator enters specific political and cultural patterns of perception and signification. It can be illustrated how their interpretation spurs them on to actions that appear significant.[9] The goal of such research on violence and the perpetrators of violence is not to focus so much on historical analyses. Instead, the process-oriented view of research on violence and the perpetrators of violence used in this study illuminates various facets of the perpetrator's perceptions regarding the events leading up to the situation where violence occurred, the situation itself and the likely consequences, and the resulting practice of the perpetrators in which what we call "sense (of killing)" is produced. Therefore, this research perspective allows for less of an analysis of (f)actual suffered or committed violence. From a trans-disciplinary perspective the formation of violence, the readiness to fight and kill – in anthropological, political and cultural terms – offers insights on organized collective violence, on individuals and on the experience of combat soldiers, perpetrators and bystanders. It also reflects the extent to which the identity of defence specifies certain constructions of gender. Special characteristics of male socialization were used as vehicles in these confrontations. But the identity of defence is conceived here not only as a gender issue that stems from the unequal distribution of power in war. The whole issue is really simple, if one realizes that murder and expulsion are neither everyday affairs, nor are they regarded as acts that can be explained with the moral rules of everyday life. Nonetheless, from the perspective of the men interviewed for this study – all of whom had combat experience in Slovenia, Croatia and/or Bosnia-Herzegovina – it is of special interest to examine what it means to situate themselves within a community as a collective of fear, which can survive in the so-called "territorial defence".

The sample

The interviewees were chosen according to the following criteria: They had to be male, have been born between 1960 and 1975 and have participated in at least one of the wars in the former Yugoslavia between 1991 and 1995. Furthermore, they had to be willing to speak about their war experiences. Age, gender and war experience were therefore factors that were always considered before the selection of interviewees.

Those included in the sample were found using the "snowball" system, chosen in various post-war groups. They were expected to provide information on their life histories, as well on their geographical, social and (depending on their self-perceptions) ethnic and religious backgrounds, education in school and the military, family relations and relationships to friends and acquaintances, entry into the war, motives, war experiences and the consequences of these experiences. The analysis of the oral material itself was acquired with the help of documentary interpretation and follows the goal of a "comparative structuring".[10]

The interviews for this study were conducted following the war, in 1997 and 1998.[11] They were neither carried out in the entire area of the former Yugoslavia nor were they bound to a homogenous group or rigid selection of the interviewees that adhered to, for example, a specific ethnic category. In this study, ethnic affiliation does not represent a category of difference of primary order, but is rather the result of a socio-historical process that plays a central role in the analysis.[12]

The interviews especially helped to identify the events and experiences that were of importance to the interviewees, as well as the reconstruction of the meaning given to these experiences. The analysis of the biographical stories was led by the question of how the interviewees depicted their war experiences in connection with the creation of new and the change of older collective identifications. It was hereby considered to what extent political images of the enemy have an integrative function, how stories are told and what information they contain. At the same time, the study allowed an analysis of the meaning of individual fear and collective anxiety. Most of all, it focused on how these anxieties were suggested in connection with the loss or the immediate impact on people close to the perpetrators, as well as in connection with the readiness to commit violence. The difference between anticipated and committed violence, the fusion of organizational knowledge, and the expectations and ideals should be underscored here. Furthermore, it was considered how different starting conditions and places of recruitment or self-armament and different employment duration and locations played out in the stories, fantasies of violence and motives. The goal of the interviews was not only to discover the motives for the perpetrators' use of violence,[13] but also to consider the ways in which former soldiers and fighters spoke about their experience. In this way, more could be discovered about the social functions of violence.

The interview material for this study makes up a total of 25 narrative/ semi-directive interviews with male veterans, former combat soldiers who voluntarily participated in the questioning. This small number of interviews allows a qualitative approach. And it was crucial that the interviewees were children or youth approximately between the years of 1980 and 1990, and that they were of conscription age when they entered the war. Accordingly, the interviewees belonged to a "generation" whose parents were mostly post-war children or young adults during the post-World War II era and who were personally linked with socialism in different ways, for example as professional soldiers, as working people, functionaries or relatives of the so-called "generation of the SKOJ" (from *Savez komunističke omladine Jugoslavije*, the Young Communist League of Yugoslavia) or later of the "rebellious generation".[14]

The majority of the young men I interviewed were still children during the Tito era, grew up, began to study or entered the work force in the political and economical crisis of the 1980s. The general model of the life histories is based, among others, on the influences that determined the "political" culture of children and youth; pioneer parades, recitation of partisan poems and movies, scout experiences, school competitions, international work teams, pre-military instruction.[15] In general, a strong acceptance of military service and a specific gender position belonged to this "political" culture, where male identities have been primarily conceptualized as defenders.

Biographical constructions not only provide examples for the rapid change in the interviewees' affiliations, but also illustrate the conditions that had to be set up for the interviewees so that they could express their exclusion from the Yugoslavian community and the consequences of violence with relative ease.

The interviewees had entered the war as young men, as compulsorily service men, as army or police reservists and as professional soldiers who, during the war, transgressed boundaries, expelled, hurt or killed people as front-line soldiers in a troop or as a fighter. They voluntarily or involuntarily committed acts of violence and partly attempted to fulfil the fiction of ethnic purity through expulsion and killing.

These young, "ordinary" men were generally obliged to serve in the military. The acceptance of military service and participation in war is not at all confined to the group of men interviewed for this study, but should be viewed as a wide-spread phenomenon in Yugoslavian society and in the post-Yugoslavian societies.[16] As well, not all interviewees participated to the same degree in the acts of violence as they did in the processes of ethnic cleansing. Not all interviewees were low-level perpetrators; some of those who directly participated in ethnic cleansing were included.

The interviews lasted between one and two-and-a-half hours. The conversations sometimes began before the recording of the interviews and were sometimes continued after the recording ended. For most of the interviews, extensive protocols had been written and, according to the "grounded theory", in contrast to the recruitment experiences, 12 entirely transcribed interview texts were selected for a thorough hermeneutic analysis.[17]

In order to ensure an adequate interpretation and translation, the processing of the interviews generally adhered to the original language (tape and transcript). Only those passages in the text, which were relevant for the analysis, were translated into English. The selection of interviews for single case analyses was made according to the specific principle of "maximum comparison".[18]

The pressure to legitimize violence

As a subject for research and for conversation, combat experiences differ fundamentally from more routine talk about daily life, even when war itself may become a part of daily life. The subject of combat experiences calls for a reflection on the special situation that arises between interviewer and interviewee. In other words, a conversation with a perpetrator of violence or a victim of extreme acts of violence remains a conversation, but it is conducted under very specific conditions of mistrust and doubts, angry feelings and antipathy. Finally it takes courage and commitment to act in a more forgiving way. It is not at all a sign of pardoning or ignoring an injustice or crime, but it does take strength.

According to Daniel Schacter, combat experience causes posttraumatic stress disorder (PTSD), which in turn causes false memories about the experience.[19] "Traumatic experiences" can easily be illustrated through numerous examples of combat stories. Some of the interviewees seemed seriously mentally hurt. But other interviewees used the clinical and psychological concept of PTSD, which has become more popular through media and public discourse and is now closely linked to a victim's narrative. However, during the interviews, all those involved were aware of the fact that fundamental moral and normative issues would be discussed. Experience is usually presented in a chronological perspective. During biographical interviews, a pressure for self-explicatory statements is often perceived; actions, events and interpretations are recounted within a context to establish a plausible perspective of development.[20] And although I promised anonymity in interviews with former combat soldiers this pressure was increased and was transformed into a need for self-legitimation. From the perspective of the interviewee, these interviews were characterized by the anticipation of such legitimatory pressure, whereas the interviewer's perceptions of the interviewee's narrative were typically subject to pre-existing suspicions. These interviews with perpetrators of acts of violence were characterized by a very special form of communication and very unique expectations. The anticipated legitimatory pressure corresponds to the expectation of non-acceptance; the construction of reality based on suspicion corresponds to the assumption that one's partner in the conversation keeps silent or has something to hide. At the same time, nobody declares himself as a murderer or war criminal. In fact, I never asked if there was a charge against any of them.[21]

The longing for a good social standing – the desire to be respected as someone special in society – appeared, through various attempts to impress others, as a form of gendered "war-talk". What some interviewees understood in retrospect to be an episode in the life of a successful man or patriot generated a phase of basic questioning among others. The fact is that everyone was scared of being a "nobody". Demobilization commonly led to isolation, feelings of insecurity and intense despair. Demobilization proved to be difficult in situations where unfulfilled claims (especially in comparison to the generation of the World Wars that had attained privileges, careers and positions in the military, society or politics) collided without means, with asylum and homelessness, with direct consequences of the war, such as invalidity and sickness, and with alcoholism and drug addiction. Some believed that they had actually become more aggressive from their war experiences; this became apparent either in their partnerships or in public in terms of criminal acts.

Employment plays an important role for demobilized soldiers, as it eases the process of social reintegration. At the same time, employment represents the prerequisite needed to fulfil the traditional male role to marry and found a family. However, former soldiers barely receive social acceptance and suffer from financial instability and feelings of insecurity. The interviewees who found themselves in such a situation sometimes cried during the interviews without inhibitions and told their story of the post-war period according to Erving Goffman's model of the "sad story".[22] Some of the interviewees continually displayed bodily reactions and could not, for example, control their nervous legs. At the same time, they drew attention to their suffering and symptoms in order to relate these to the war experiences. An example of this, although in a symbolically obscene form, is exemplified by a Croatian fighter who listed the bodily damages resulting from the war and in a type of self-caricature purported to have become "a real Serb" through an amputation; the "castrated Serb" is the personified opposite of the virile Croat.[23]

"We were only defending ourselves"

In the following, the experience of violence is a topic that is only accessible in retrospect. A factor emerges that plays a role in every case of reconstruction: From a purely subjective perspective, violence can take on a function that provides sense and order. Violence can give orientation in situations of transition in which various factors such as the economy, the definitions of "friends" and "enemies" and the future appear uncertain. Ultimately this leads to the fact that the life-threatening battlefield can appear as comparatively more secure and structured than being a civilian in times of war.

Despite the variety of details in the interviewees' stories, the concept of behaviour underlying the perceptions of violence is dominated by one purpose: Each interviewee claimed to have protected and/or defended the existential interests of a group or themselves. From the interviewees' perspective, defence means to have killed legitimately. They distanced themselves from crimes, but killing and death are depicted as the essence of war, as anthropology of war. The interviews certainly illustrate dramatic pictures of the conditions in which references to the group identity were transformed. Furthermore, they show how the anxiety of neighbours changed into patriotic and national enthusiasm for defence. The perceived escalation of threat, the perception of an "irrational" or "barbarous" opposite group causes an increased acceptance for committing violence. But in which terms is the enemy different from the good? Darko Crljen, a young volunteer from Split, Croatia, told in an interview in September 1998:

> I entered the fight when it came to the liberation of Dubrovnik. It was a besieged city and the Serbs really had no reason to be there, in Dubrovnik. I think it was actually Montenegrins who besieged the city – what were they thinking? What did they have in their heads? Did they want to plunder or did they mean it seriously? They plundered what they could. What were they planning in this city? To occupy the city? That is of course nonsense! We therefore had to de-blockade Dubrovnik. However, for this, one had to move slightly toward Bosnia [laughter]. One simply had to go in because the Croatian border is so narrow there. You see, I even have to admit here that I was in Bosnia.... I think that it was entirely OK to have taken part down there.

With this, a tactic of inner conflict – upheld through the legends of partisan war – was intensified and, with the newly structured groups, a new social basis was formed. Finally, it is the belief of one's own military inferiority that contributes to the feeling that law and morality are on one's side. In this way, conflicts emerge in the interviews with the ever-present danger of one's barbarity and brutalization in the practice of war. It is remarkable that the stories – after the violence was committed – appear to have no negative effects at all on the cohesion of the group, as if only a harmonious cooperation had existed within the groups. To this, once again, Crljen:

You told yourself that you won't go, but it pulls you in, when you are in you go to the end. If my group had not fallen apart, if it would not have ... each time, this means fifteen days on the battlefield, each time one of us is killed, we sing before we go to the battlefield, on the way back there weren't any songs because each time someone is killed, you understand. Twenty of us sit in a truck, on the way back one of us was missing, a second one, there were also injured. So what, it pulls you in. And in the end it came to that, really, you come back home and you can't take the silence, this silence. You dream at night and realize that you are more normal when you are on the battlefield, that means you first realize how screwed-up you are when you come home, at home you dream of grenades, what do I know, grenades, what do I know, let's say you ride a bus, sleep and someone slams the door and you throw yourself to the floor, that gets you down, oh well, not really everybody, not everybody, but me. And if the group had not fallen apart, I would have gone on until the end.

Darko Crljen discovered the battle against death and loss, which caused serious trauma. This experience of violence is not to be separated from the group experience – a perspective from which the image of war as an idealized symbol of a process of community formation (*Vergemeinschaftung*) can stem. This can even happen to such an extent that being at home becomes an "abnormal" state. Fighting and dying in the group – in a group of men which could convey a substitute feeling for family – feels more normal than suffering post-traumatic effects in a civil environment.

Defence seems always understandable from the perspective of the interviewed soldiers and fighters, and does not just mean resistance and opposition or waiting and boredom. Carefulness and responsibility are important components of defence: houses, villages, territories and infrastructure are defended. The definition of the terrain to be defended is interesting, such as that undertaken by the Slovenian Ivica Kunstek, who lives in Banja Luka, and is a former member of the Bosnian-Serbian army:

I didn't want to risk that my children die. From the very beginning, I thought what happened in Sarajevo was pretty stupid, I saw it on television: "I defend my Sarajevo, no one can take my house away!" But you can't defend your house directly in front of the city boundaries because a grenade flies in at 45 kilometres per hour and lands directly in your house and doesn't ask you if you are a Serb, Muslim or Croat. It doesn't ask about that, but kills! One does not defend one's house directly in front of the city boundaries, you really have to go out 40 kilometres in order to defend it if you want to protect the life of your child, if you want to protect that where you were born. I am a Banja-Lukovian, I was born here. If I stay here I'm here, when someone threatens my child – not me, but my child – that is then completely normal?! I can't allow it – I just can't simply allow it – and where? Of course, far away from here, not here, because if he [the enemy] is already here, you can only give up and resign yourself from everything.

This is the "war in front of the front door". The interviewees depict themselves as "liberators" (for example, of villages and, more abstractly, of territories), as "saviours" (for example, of the "population" or even of "humanity") and, most of all, as "forecasters" who were ahead of the enemy. The "forecaster" among the interviewees belongs more closely to the ideological type of soldier. Besides this, others focus on the fulfilment of duties or on "sole survival", whereby to plunder, pillage and shoot "aimlessly" (probably also to murder and rape) could certainly also be connected with this.

That corresponds to the traditional interrelationship between property, family and violence (since the early history of south-eastern Europe).[24] Furthermore, the warriors' willingness to suffer and sacrifice symbolizes a distinctive heroic aspect of collective identity because one counters each challenge – and these are always new – with terms of the past. However, from the perspective of an interviewee the contradiction appears:

> You can't run away. I love this city, I love my home, I love to sit here, drink and work. That's why you have to put on this uniform, exactly as he does across the street and so forth. That means that only the system determines: It only matters to somehow survive. That you have become crazy from it is less problematic.

The individual who told me that is Džubo Isković, a Muslim from Banja Luka, who participated on the Serbian side during the war. Concepts of the enemy were the results of social and state processes of definition. Feelings of threat fed an increasing willingness for violence or at least an understanding for "fighting"; the "others" were considered to be threatening, even by those who had still not experienced violence themselves. The image of the barbarous and irrational "other" has turned into something functional. In this sequence, the opinion of the "other" changed to the "stranger", and for most to the ethnicized enemy. The parties (not state institutions) demanded the provision of effective help to a public that felt threatened; indeed, parties were able to implement advanced preventive measures.

When one considers these factors, the question arises concerning the extent of the actual threat during a certain time-period and in a certain area. Violence and the committing of violence are also experienced through the media and communication. People do not need to experience violence themselves in order to perceive it as an omnipresent threat. The perception of "distress" or "threat" can also be based on suggestions and feelings that are first instrumentalized through politics and powerful media and then can be answered with violence. Objectively viewed, the interviewees refer to two different experiences. However, the consequences are real in the same way. A general feeling of threat was thus developed: Some of them expected attacks or even elimination from the enemy. Throughout, each "patriot" remained bound to the emotional and normative demands of his group.

In the reconstruction of the self-understanding of former combatants, it is revealed how they themselves interpret and depict the dynamics of violence. From this perspective, not only can valuable information be ascertained on how violence and the willingness to kill is developed by people who – in other circumstances – would never have thought of the idea of killing someone, but light can be shed on the answer to the question of how people themselves can experience killing in a meaningful manner.

> I set off – I was so stupid because I thought that my country [the former Yugoslavia] is falling apart, and because I thought that I must help so that it wouldn't happen. Starting with twenty-eight, only eight of us survived. The group fell apart and you take care of how you get along. Me [as a Muslim], I already belonged to a minority there. You couldn't simply walk around the city when there was war. But principally it doesn't matter to you, it is not important at all, what side you are on. It is completely unimportant. It hurts you one way or another – it hurts you the same whether you kill a Muslim, a Croat or a Serb, they are all living beings, people. Therefore what side you are on is not important. What is decisive is what side you have to be on. And also that you take care of everything you have to do, and in a manner that doesn't turn you into an animal, but rather you resist this and you survive it. That is the decisive factor.

For the same Džubo Isaković, who fought as Muslim in the Bosnian-Serbian army, the war and front line experience has a direct reference to social survival. According to the self-descriptions, the military community formation preceded the process of ethnicization. All interviewees describe the multi-ethnic Yugoslavia of their childhoods in a positive manner. Many inflate the situation before the war to a picture of an ideal society:

> No one asks you who or what you are. I was in Zagreb: no one asked me about it. And one was also accepted in Otočić, while one understood, "I am myself, you are yourself." ... There was a life before then! ... We knew each other, one knew who you were, who I was, but that had absolutely no meaning.... We got along great with each other!

Many young men started the elementary level of military training and, as late as the early 1990s, were dispersed in barracks far away from the republics from where they came; they had no concept that there could be a war. Kruno Letica from Osijek told me in 1998:

Well, it was normal, it was an obligation, in agreement with the constitution and all of the valid laws that I could not avoid because I was, so to say, technically able, meaning healthy, because I was capable. The legal prerequisite was like this; one could not avoid this obligation. I basically had no idea if there would be a war. It was like that, although I also know, I mean, the situation in Yugoslavia then, in former Yugoslavia was tense, the political strife and everything that happened. I mean, why, now it probably doesn't have to be condemned. But what I want to say, another word about that, but I had no idea that it could come to war. There was fighting in Kosovo, unrest in 1980, these non-violent protests that also always ended with violence. I mean, I knew that the situation was like that. If I would have come to Kosovo, I would have had expected some sorts of, lets call them clashes, the squelching of demonstrations or whatever. But in Varaždin, that is, Slovenia, I did not anticipate that something like that would happen there because these were areas in Yugoslavia, at this time, that were not troubled with unrest, like with such social, in the form of political will, intentions, and all the rest.

The continuing ethnicization is described in all cases as a more surprising but inevitable process that stems from "others" and to which one reacts. Dargan Petrović, a young war veteran in eastern Bosnia and a former member of a Serbian military task force, told me how he became a soldier and warrior:

I started military service in '89. I was born in 1969, so it was '88, no '89, nearly '90. Yes, I went in December '89. And then I was called up, after things had already started in Slovenia. During military service there were already critical situations, this fucking business [zajebancija] was already beginning, even then the Serbian issue [sbrstvo] and the question of secession were in the air. Yeah, and I myself was also in a fucking state [zajeban] and didn't spare any punches. It was better to avoid provoking me; the word was out: "Better leave him in peace, if you can't leave him in peace, we won't guarantee for anything." I wasn't that fucking bad, but that must have been the way it seemed.

Special characteristics of male socialization were used as vehicles in these confrontations. This is how Petrović tries to explain his state of mind, as people influenced one another as vulnerable beings. And immediately after making this statement, Petrović proceeds to play it down: this was only the way others perceived him. Actions and reactions begin in a process of reciprocal intensification until one finally decides where one stands and for what one fights:

We defended the city, didn't attack anyone, defended the city. People who had formerly lived here in the city, we had to defend ourselves against them! People who were able to do everything in this city, had their homes here, went to school, had their estates, that is pretty strange, people, who could achieve everything and also achieved, these people bombarded Sarajevo and we defended ourselves against them.

Perceptions of the potential for violence in the neighbourhood emerge as decisive breaches from which collective perceptions of belonging changed and the increased need for security were marked by great pressure for homogenization. The insecurity that arises through perceived violence and its increased probability demands actions. New structures of trust and security have to be created – partly immediately, partly gradually – which should dissolve the built-up tension but which, on the contrary, intensify the conflict. Hence, of interest is the following reconstruction of Darko Crljen. The practice of "ethnic cleansing" has had the aim to establish dominance over the enemy. Whatever they did, whether it was violence against civilians or the rape of women or men, it is rarely mentioned and not admitted. But stories about the enemy often confirm this:

> We invaded villages, but they were deserted. I never experienced such a situation, I had really never experienced it, such as that for example in Srebrenica – back then I worked for the Red Cross as the [Serbs], seven to eight thousand men, 12- to 70-year-olds, selected and killed them.... . That is this logic: he is a Muslim, also if he is ten years old, in ten years he will be a Muslim soldier and will shoot you and kill you, so you better kill him right away.

After all, Crljen has good relations to the ethnic others. But in this context, forgiving is not forgetting. Thus provocations, humiliations and insecurity become visible. Militarization and violence gain decisive importance. If the imagined community is transformed into a community in question that demands solidarity and searching for externals from its members, so militarization and violence play a function in the transition from the community demanded by the people to that of the actually created, existential community. Collective ideas of belonging changed and the need for security was bound to the idea of the "purity" of an ethnically homogeneous group. In regard to the creation of a country, perceptions of legal and security issues are connected with images of the state; but it will not take place without the expulsion and murdering of others. Asked about his propensity for violence, the previously cited Petrović again plays this down by making an ironic generalization: "We're all like that: somebody kills somebody, some their wife, some their neighbour." Petrović's voice and gestures revealed that he intended this remark to be sarcastic. The use of sarcasm creates a kind of detachment after the fact, but Petrovićc still appears to be able to abandon this detached attitude at a moment's notice.

As already mentioned, the experience of violence is – from a historical perspective – a topic that can only become accessible in retrospect. Using examples of biographical self-interpretations, it is not possible to assess the extent to which interviewees were actually involved in acts of violence and the reasons for their involvement. However, one can certainly approach the question of what interpretations perpetrators of violence attributed to their actions in retrospect and how they depicted these interpretations in the interviews.

The "identity of defence" is the common factor that exists in the variety of experiences and constructions of meanings that developed in the violence of war during the 1990s. From the perspective of the interviewees, to act in collective defence is not only a stereotypical pattern of justification, but also an active and contradictory process of adapting. Defence is already the opposite of aggression semantically and determines the pretended action of the actor in advance. The subjective interpretation of the identity of defence depends on the definition of events and series of events that are lived existentially and experienced. The clear distinction of the action of one's own group from that of the "others" also plays a role in this way:

> Fair play! I know that all types of stories are circling and are told throughout the entire world, I also read about them in the newspapers. But I was there everywhere and never experienced, never saw ... I was even directly in battles, I never saw that from our side, from our unit prisoners were taken and murdered, were raped. One guy was captured by us for 15 days because he had stolen a bundle of onions from a garden. He was held for 15 days. I think we were the only unit that adhered to a type of fair play in war. We, of course, sent prisoners in Brčko; 15-, 17-year-olds, home. Such a child is not guilty for the fact that we are in war, such a Muslim child. There were no massacres, no rapes, nothing like that. The game was called fair play, fuck, it was war.

Ivica Kunstek, who was drafted as a Slovenian member of the Bosnian-Serbian army, referred to a common professional ethic (which included such principles as "fair play"). The identity of defence that all interviewees take on creates an intersection between individual experience and cultural order. Next to this, a "defensive" war stands for the most acceptable form of violence. And the "defensive" war makes all sides aware of the group boundaries. This manages to override individual experiences of what he himself wants and should want – something simple obedience can never achieve.

The meaning of such reasoning for violence is illustrated in an astounding manner when a fighter is introduced as a "defender", even when he (individually or in a group) practices direct ("indispensable") attacks. The neighbour is a potential enemy and is expelled or killed so that he is not able to act in a threatening manner.

However, the identity of defence is the translation of collectively legitimized violence in individual practice. The identity of defence implied the emergence of readiness for defending or protecting the own: the own house, family, nation or country.

> For most of us I know, for 90 per cent it really sucked! But there are also people who became animals after that!

The construction of reluctance creates a more distanced approach towards the experience of having killed. But it also shows that there is a tendency to passion for the professional soldier, if not for the rational killer. Consequently, the practice of "ethnic cleansing" is described in a euphemistic way and as a routine ("action"). Combat soldiers even portray this development as a necessity for "our security", where perpetrators had simply "to do their job".[25] At first considered a response to an existential threat, it soon becomes a task that one can do well or poorly. Kruno Letica who fought on the Croatian side, notes:

> That's the way war is, war is something that lasts for some time, war is something of its own progression. Everybody can be brought into a situation where he would fight. Then it comes to "cleanups": in houses, you kill what you find, of course never a civilian, never women, never children, never, certainly never prisoners of war. Really, I've never seen that anything like that has happened.... There is murder and after the killing you don't sit down and light a cigarette, make coffee and reflect on how it was. It lasts for some time, the action continues, there is still killing, still shots on either side, the fingers are still on the trigger and it goes on, only one fragment after the other which means: "Good, that one I killed, so let's go on." It doesn't matter that blood is on the walls, that his skull is smashed, that he has no arm, no leg, that he's missing whatever: it is not important. The way of killing and what happens to him is of least importance. Important is a certain efficiency, a mere, mere, maybe I should put it in other words, it is an absolute empirical matter: "That one I really eliminated, so let's go on" – there's not much of a philosophy about it, also no reflecting on why I killed him, what happened to me there, nothing! Kill and go on with it! If I catch him, I kill one more and in doing so I certainly watch out that I'm not being killed. That the end of it.

Processes of ethnic cleansing are transformed into personalized suffering, such as in the case of Kruno who still interprets his actions as resistance.

The reference to professionalism in this context is not only an elaborated legitimation, it is an important element of military rules that, in a subjective reality, creates a distance to the probably most traumatic events in their lives: "You never look in the face, because you want to kill him."

Against this background another question arises: Was it really easy to kill people? At first, each actor wants to make sure that he creates an account of the killed as an action done according to the rules; and that he has not turned into "an animal". This also means that according to most accounts, in combat situation no alternatives existed: "You see him, he is shooting you!" Or: "Civilians are being warned in time to leave the places, those who stay are enemies who should be killed."

Kruno Letica sees this similarly in his own story: He was part of a mobile unit and brought his job as a sniper to mortal perfection, a "clean mission": "Those who don't wear a banderol [the sign of his unit] are going to be killed." Kruno Letica's rationalization also results from the view that, "Civilians are something else, civilians don't run around during combat!"

Conclusion

While policies tend to focus on disarmament and security sector reform, little attention is paid to the (re)socialization of former combatants. Successful reconciliation of former Yugoslavian citizens will be put to a severe test by the extent to which the process of the former combat soldiers' coping strategies with combat experience has been advanced. We have seen that forgiveness takes place when acts of violence are committed by one's own group but not when committed by someone with whom one is not associated.

Within the social perception of the actors in post-conflict societies all kinds of myths of collective violence exist that are used as legitimations, rationalizations and efforts to distance oneself from activities – so that the waging of war and the killing make more sense: 1) Every story reflected the imagined, "felt" situation of the threat of being killed if one didn't defend oneself or that which one possessed. 2) The collective of a powerful reference point: the threat is perceived to be all the stronger the more similar the potential adversary was, or the less clear the differences between the groups were. In this way violence makes sense as it provides distinctness for the group and can later be perceived in a constructive and structured way. 3) The murder, the ethnic cleansing and the "intimate experience of fighting" are defined as work, a professional job. 4) The old military structures with different objectives serve as vehicles for violence. 5) Peer pressure plays an important role: if everybody kills, it is easier to join in instead of refusing.

The concept of an "identity of defence" as an empirical phenomenon is itself a sign of the on-going process of a myth-building, in which similarities between former combat soldiers represent a new social basis, regardless of ethnic or national differences. Yet this concept is unable to tie together the heterogeneous war experiences of victims, perpetrators and bystanders in the former Yugoslavia and the successor states. In sum, the identity of defence – as morally questionable as it may be – is a concept from the perspective of former combat soldiers through which various elements of mass crime can be envisaged.

Notes

1. "Mladićev monstrum napokon progovorio. Za svakog ubijenog bošnjaka u srebrenici dobijali smo po pet eura", *Slobodna Bosna*, 1 September 2005, pp. 28–33.
2. For more on these *Dutzendmenschen*, see Holm Sundhaussen, "Ethnonationale Gewalt auf dem Balkan im Spiegel der Goldhagen-Debatte", in Wolfgang Höpken and Michael Riekenberg, eds, *Politische und ethnische Gewalt in Südosteuropa und Lateinamerika*, Cologne: Böhlau, 2001, pp. 37–51.
3. For more on the Rwandan genocide, see Scott Straus's contribution to this book.
4. Xavier Bougarel, *Bosnie: Anatomie d'un conflit*, Paris: Découverte, 1996, pp. 81–86; see also Catherine Samary, *Die Zerstörung Jugoslawiens: Ein europäischer Krieg*, Frankfurt: Neuer ISP-Verlag, 1995, pp. 35–36.
5. Božidar Jakšić, "Omladina izmedju mira i rata – slučaj bivše Jugoslavije", in Institut za Filozofiju i društvenu Teoriju, ed., *Filozofija i društvo VI: Teorijske pretpostavke razumevanja raspada Jugoslavije*, Belgrade: CFDT, 1994, pp. 97–106. At the same time, the Western academic viewpoint is that the "typical warrior" in the wars of the former Yugoslavia was driven by irrationalism and barbarism. The motives behind and the development of the readiness to fight and to kill have not been captured by academic research. However, the existing scholarly literature is still focused on the causalities and implications of the "traditional brutality" – whether in the fields of politics, ethnology or cultural studies.
6. Natalija Bašić, "Jeden Tag war 'Allgemeine Volksverteidigung' (ONO): Zur militaristischen Kultur und Gewalterziehung im sozialistischen Jugoslawien (SFRJ) 1945–1990", in *Jahrbücher zur Geschichte und Kultur Südosteuropas*, pp. 7–25; Natalija Basic, *Krieg als Abenteuer: Feindbilder und Gewalt aus der Perspektive ex-jugoslawischer Soldaten 1991–1995*, Giessen: Psychsozial-Verlag, 2004; Natalija Bašić, "Die Akteursperspektive: Soldaten und 'ethnische Säuberungen' in Kroatien und Bosnien-Herzegowina (1991–1995)", in U. Brunnbauer, M. Esch and H. Sundhaussen, eds, *Definitionsmacht, Utopie, Vergeltung: "Ethnische Säuberungen" im östlichen Europa des 20 Jahrhunderts*. Münster: LitVerlag 2006, pp. 144–168. Studies of civil-military relations and their social and political consequences are for the most part lacking in the analysis of the wars of the former Yugoslavia. Opšta narodna odbrana (ONO), the JNA defence doctrine, is rarely taken into account during violent processes such as the wars in the 1990s. Moreover, it can be taken for granted, as is shown in many analyses of the post-Yugoslav wars; far from being a "marginal" structure or "collateral" phenomenon, the socialist doctrine of ONO has more influence on formations of violence in the 1990s than most scholars would like to believe. For a discussion of the development of ONO in peacetime, with a special focus on the role of civil-military relations for violent interactions, their elements of military education and their post-socialist consequences, see Natalija Bašić, "Jeden Tag war Allgemeine Volksverteidigung".

7. Jakšić also shares this viewpoint without being able to name exact numbers; for recruitments by force in Serbia see Ilija Popović, "Naknada od JNA", in Helsinki Committee for Human Rights in Serbia, ed., *Heslinška Povelja*, no. 3, 1998, pp. 30–31.

8. Exactly how many men refused to fight, and their reasons for refusing, is unknown.

9. For a historical comparative perspective, see Natalija Basic and Harald Welzer, "Die Bereitschaft zum Töten. Überlegungen zum Zusammenspiel von Sinn, Mord und Moral", *Zeitschrift für Genozidforschung*, no. 2, 2000, pp. 27–50.

10. Philipp Mayring, *Qualitative Inhaltsanalyse*, Weinheim: UTB, 2000.

11. That a new order would necessarily arise from the Dayton Peace Accords was in no way foreseeable at the time of the interviews; see for example Marie-Janine Calic, "Bosnien-Herzegowina nach Dayton. Chancen und Risiken für den Frieden", *Aussenpolitik* 47, no. 2, 1996, pp. 127–135; and her "Probleme der internationalen Friedenssicherung in Bosnien-Herzegowina", *Südosteuropa-Mitteilungen* 38, no. 3, 1998, pp. 215–231.

12. For further analysis, see also Lutz Niethammer, *Kollektive Identitäten: Heimliche Quelle einer unheimlichen Konjunktur*, Reinbek bei Hamburg: Rowohlt-Verlag, 2000.

13. See Marie-Janine Calic, *Krieg und Frieden in Bosnia-Herzegovina*, expanded first edition, Frankfurt: Suhrkamp, 1996, pp. 141–148.

14. These terms for generations in former Yugoslavia reflect of course the socialist and Marxist perspective used by Edward Kardelj, when he discussed the "avoidability" and the "non-avoidability" of war: *Die Vermeidbarkeit und die Unvermeidbarkeit des Kriege: Die jugoslawische und die chinesische These*, Reinbek bei Hamburg: Rowohlt-Verlag, 1969.

15. Despite the different methods between individual research disciplines, the way one deals with politics was one of the most important components in all studies on childhood and youth in the former Yugoslavia and in the phases of transition in other nations; see for example Jordan Aleksić, "Generacija krize – kriza generacije", Marksistički Centar Medjuopćinske konferencije SKH za Dalmaciju, ed., *Omladina izmedju političke apatije i autonomnog političkog subjektiviteta*, Split: Marksistički Centar, 1988; V. Vujičič, *Politička kultura I politička socijalizacija*, Zagreb: Međuopćinske Konferencije SKH za Dalmaciju, 1993, pp. 13–30.

16. Christopher Browning, *Ganz normale Männer: Das Reserve-Polizei-Bataillon 101 und die "Endlösung" in Polen*, Reinbek bei Hamburg: Rowohlt, 1993; Sundhaussen, "Ethonationale Gewalt auf dem Balkan", p. 42.

17. The interview transcripts are forthcoming from Projekt "Ljudi u ratu" and Dokumentacioni Centar, Belgrade. Also see the foreword to the first book in the series, N. Bašić, D. Gojković and V. Delić, *Ratovanja Knj.* vol. 1, Belgrade: Dokumentacioni Centar, 2003.

18. Barney G. Glaser and Anselm S. Strauss, *Grounded Theorie: Strategien qualitativer Sozialforschung*, Bern: Hans Huber Verlag, 1998.

19. Daniel L. Schacter, *Searching for Memory: The Brain, the Mind, and the Past*, New York: Basic Books, 1996.

20. Robert G. Moeller, "War Stories: The Search for a Usable Past in the Federal Republic of Germany", *American Historical Review* 101, no. 4, 1996, pp. 1008–1048.

21. See in particular Natalija Basic, "Vom Ansprechen und Auf-sich-beruhen-lassen. Biographische Interviews mit ehemaligen Kombattanten der postjugoslawischen Kriege 1991–1995", *Psychsozial* 1, no. 91, 2003, pp. 7–25.

22. Erving E. Goffman, *Über die soziale Situation psychiatrischer Patienten und anderer Insassen*, Frankfurt: Suhrkamp, 1973.

23. On the cultural function and mythological meaning of the motives for amputation and castration, see Ivan Čolović, "Fußball, Hooligans und Krieg", in Thomas Bremer, Nebojša Popov and Hans-Günter Stobbe, eds, *Serbiens Weg in den Krieg: Kollektive Erin-*

nerung, nationale Formierung und ideologische Aufrüstung, pp. 261–276. Generally, one can assume that, in times of transition, national discourses – with conceptions of the pure (people's) body – strongly influence the self-images of the interviewees.

24. See especially Karl Kaser, *Macht und Erbe: Männerherrschaft, Besitz und Familie im östlichen Europa (1500–1900)*, Vienna: Böhlau, 1997.

25. In military life, the meaning of "professional identity" has been discussed since June 1991 when Slovenian and Croatian independence was declared. The position of the militaries towards military professionalism and the reconstruction of the Army as a national institution are rather ambivalent. For example, in the Croatian Army strong political influences are recognized; see Ozren Žunec, "Operacija Bljesak I Oluja", in B. Magaš and I. Žanić, eds, *RAT u Hrvatskoj i Bosni i Hercegovini*, London: Bosnian Institute, 1999, pp. 93–110.

Part III

Memories and representations

7

Mass murder, the politics of memory and post-genocide reconstruction: The cases of Rwanda and Burundi

René Lemarchand and Maurice Niwese

Nowhere else in Africa have mass crimes resulted in more bloodshed than in Rwanda and Burundi, two microstates whose minute size belies the magnitude of the tragedies they have experienced. The first will go down in history as the site of one of the biggest genocides of the last century, causing the extermination of an estimated 800,000 people, mostly Tutsi; the second lives on in the collective memory of many Hutu as a "forgotten genocide". Who today remembers that thirty years ago "there took place in Burundi the systematic killing of as many as a quarter million people"[1] at the hands of a predominantly Tutsi army?

There are compelling reasons for viewing their agonies in a comparative frame. Not only are they remarkably alike in terms of their ethnic profiles, in addition to being geographically contiguous to each other, but their fates have been and remain indissolubly linked. One is the mirror image of the other. Nothing affecting the lives of the citizens of Burundi leaves indifferent their kinsmen in Rwanda and vice versa. That their recent histories should bear countless traces of this perverse interaction is not a matter of coincidence. From the early years of independence (1962) to the present, the ethnic confrontations experienced by one state have never failed to generate a violent backlash in the other. Similarly, whatever post-conflict strategies are implemented by the rulers of one state will have lasting consequences for its neighbour.

In each state efforts are being made to come to terms with the past, yet the past intrudes in radically different ways in the minds of victims and perpetrators. In each state ethnicity submerges the identification of indi-

After mass crime: Rebuilding states and communities, Pouligny, Chesterman and Schnabel (eds), *United Nations University Press, 2007, ISBN 978-92-808-1138-4*

vidual responsibilities. Acknowledging past atrocities thus becomes an exercise in the global condemnation of entire communities. Denying the complex realities of "what really happened" is by no means the monopoly of any single group. Just as there are Hutu from Rwanda who insistently deny that a genocide ever occurred, there are as many Tutsi who contend that all Hutu have blood on their hands, while at the same time turning a blind eye to the crimes committed by the Tutsi army within and outside Rwanda.[2] Again, nothing is more typical of how official memory deliberately sifts out the evidence than the calculated silence maintained by the Burundi authorities on the huge bloodletting of 1972. The parallel with the deliberate efforts of the Suharto regime to erase the 1965/66 bloodbath from the collective memories of the Indonesian public is made painfully clear in the chapter by Leslie Dwyer and Degung Santikarma in this volume.

Not the least of the obstacles in the way of restoring a measure of trust between Hutu and Tutsi is that many of the horrors suffered by each community have yet to be publicly acknowledged. The sheer scale of the Rwanda bloodbath has tended to overshadow in public attention the mass killings of Hutu by Tutsi in Burundi in 1972, in Rwanda in 1994 and in the Congo in 1996 and 1997. In Milan Kundera's phrase, they have been "airbrushed out of history".[3] In both states the past is commemorated, reshaped or rewritten to conform to the exigencies of the present, but in neither state are the victims of history prepared to forget – and rarely to forgive.

Why memory matters

As the editors of this volume remind us at the outset, any attempt to deal with issues of societal reconstruction in the aftermath of mass crimes cannot afford to ignore "the radical transformations in belief systems and codes of conduct of the individuals and communities who suffered such mass crimes". A key dimension of this phenomenon relates to how individual and collective memories – whether "thwarted", "manipulated" or "enforced", to use Paul Ricoeur's terminology[4] – contribute to such radical transformations. Belief systems are in part shaped by history, and history in turn is inextricably bound up with the claims of memory. By focusing on the cases of Rwanda and Burundi we try to show how divergent memories of genocide radically transform the perceptions that ethnic communities have of each other and of their respective historical experiences, and by the same token greatly complicate the healing of emotional wounds.

This chapter picks up where Scott Straus's leaves off. Where his discus-

sion breaks new ground is in his effort to bring out the contradictions between Rwanda's official interpretation of the genocide – which assumes a
"mass participation" of Hutu killers driven by "mass beliefs and mass indoctrination in a racist ideology" – and the far more complex, nuanced
picture he draws of what actually happened on the ground. The implication is that this official version is the main justification for policies that
"may ultimately backfire and create the resentment that could contribute
to future violence and to radical politics". Here we carry the argument a
step further: The imposition by the Kagame regime of an official – or
"enforced" – memory not only helps legitimize this one-sided interpretation, but rules out a recognition of the ambivalence of the notion of guilt.
To put it differently, in Stanley Cohen's phrase, post-genocide Rwanda is
where "collective memory [is] pressed into shape by being repressed".[5]
This, we argue, constitutes a major impediment to the reconstruction of
a civil order where Hutu and Tutsi can live at peace with each other.

Memory is a pre-eminently subjective phenomenon, and its moral implications profoundly ambivalent. It blurs the boundaries between reality
and fiction, between "what actually happened" and remembrance of what
happened. This is true of both collective and individual memories. Blind
spots, ethnic amnesia and denials of historical evidence operate to cordon
off unpalatable truths and magnify others out of all proportion. Nowhere
is this more cruelly evident than where ethnic fault lines coincide with
divided memories, where radically different constructions are placed on
the same historical events, and where past atrocities are manipulated to
impute criminal intent to entire communities.

The cases at hand are prime examples. In neither state is there much
room for a public space where collective memories of past atrocities transcend ethnic divisions. Even when Hutu and Tutsi admit that they have
killed each other by the hundreds of thousands there is little agreement
about why it happened, much less about the responsibility borne by one
group or the other. Critical events, such as the shooting down of the presidential plane in Rwanda, or the assassination of President Melchior
Ndadaye in Burundi, are the objects of intense controversy. The factual
truth of these events is not at issue; the moral and interpretive truth is
what draws each community apart.[6] Social identities are thus intimately
connected to how the past is remembered and interpreted. Just as victimization has become the hallmark of Tutsi identities in Rwanda, many
Hutu in Burundi would claim the same identity marker – irrespective of
the fact that tens of thousands of Hutu were killed by Tutsi in Rwanda,
and possibly as many Tutsi were killed by Hutu in Burundi.

Not only is the past filtered through different ethnic lenses; there
are major differences within each community in the way in which it is
remembered – or forgotten. The dysfunctions of memory caused by trau-

matic experiences have little in common with the deliberate twisting of facts by ideologues. The collective memory of the resident Tutsi community of Rwanda, who bore the brunt of the killings, differs in significant ways from that of the "refugee warriors"[7] led by Paul Kagame. And neither has anything to do with the historical memory of those Tutsi who claim a biblical past in the land of Kush, and identify themselves with the Jewish diaspora.[8] The same applies to those Hutu who risked their lives to save those of their neighbours, and the paramilitary murderers who killed hundreds of thousands.

The implications for reconciliation strategies go beyond the simplistic notion that revealing the truth will bring about peace and harmony. Or that yielding to the exigencies of the "duty to remember" will provide the solution. What is to be remembered, by whom and for what purpose — these are the critical issues that need to be addressed.

Our concern with issues of memory stems from a shared conviction that the time has come to recognize the impediments to trust posed by ethnic amnesia and distorted truths about the past. A major obstacle "when confronted with barbarism", in the words of Béatrice Pouligny, Bernard Doray and Jean-Clément Martin in their contribution to this volume, is the temptation of "facile binary thinking ('good' vs 'evil', 'black' vs 'white')," instead, they suggest, it is imperative "to reintroduce complexity". To recognize the complexity of the issues involved in the restoration of trust is not meant to deny the appalling scale of the atrocities committed by Hutu against Tutsi civilians in Rwanda, but to emphasize the fact that guilt and innocence cannot be defined exclusively in ethnic terms. Not all mass crimes qualify as genocide, and while Rwanda and Burundi have experienced both, in each country crimes have been committed by Hutu and Tutsi. More often than not, however, ethnic memories offer little space for such ambiguities. To quote from the same chapter again, "situating oneself in relation to 'evil'" means first and foremost avoiding the temptation to ethnicize genocidal guilt, and recognize that victims and killers are found on both sides of the ethnic fault line.

Even though the professional trajectories and personal experiences of this chapter's authors could not be more different, their views converge on many fundamental issues. René Lemarchand has observed at close range the dynamics of genocide in Burundi in 1972 and Rwanda in 1994. As much as his life-long interest in the history and politics of the region, his analysis is informed by a continuing dialogue with Hutu and Tutsi from both countries, and his sense of personal tragedy attendant upon the loss of close friends in both communities. Maurice Niwese, a graduate student at the University of Louvain-la-Neuve in Belgium, is a survivor of the ethnic cleansing conducted by the Rwandan army in eastern Congo against Hutu refugees. His life experiences in pre- and post-genocide Rwanda, as well as in eastern Congo, are the subject of his autobiographical account *Le peuple rwandais un pied dans la tombe.*[9] He bears testimony to a sequence of events that has yet to be properly acknowledged.

The false twins

Almost every chapter in this volume reminds us of the centrality of "context" – historical, social, geographical – to an understanding of the roots of mass murder. In the cases under consideration this is all the more important given the complexity of their social structures and histories, and the interconnections between the massacres committed in each state. Further complicating the task of analysis, much of this complexity has been unduly simplified through the prism of ethnic memories. What follows is a brief sketch of their historical trajectories, pointing to divergences and similarities.

No other two societies anywhere in the continent had more in common than Rwanda and Burundi: minute in size, deeply stratified, held together by popular allegiance to monarchical symbols and claiming a common colonial heritage, German (1899–1917) and Belgian (1917–1962), they also share strikingly similar ethnic maps. In each state the socially dominant ethnic minority, the Tutsi, held sway over the Hutu majority, the latter representing about 85 per cent of the total population (estimated at roughly 7 million in 1994).

Their commonalities can easily be overdrawn, however. Of the two kingdoms, Rwanda was the more centralized and rigidly stratified. The king (*mwami*) was seen as omnipotent; the court was the "exemplary centre" from which power radiated to the outlying areas through a hierarchy of appointed chiefs and subchiefs. Burundi, by contrast, was a far more complex society, and the kingship conspicuously weaker. Unlike Rwanda, where power gravitated in the hands of a chiefly aristocracy of Tutsi origins, the real holders of power were a socially and politically distinct category, the princes of the blood, or *ganwa*; the Tutsi were themselves divided into two separate groups, the lowly Tutsi-Hima, concentrated in the south, and the more prestigious and status-conscious Tutsi-Banyaruguru, found predominantly in the north; last and not least, the kingship was never identified with Tutsi overrule to the extent that it was in Rwanda. The twin kingdoms, in short, are better described as false twins, and here lies the key to an understanding of their radically different political trajectories.[10]

Colonial rule contributed in no small way to propel them along divergent paths. In Rwanda the colonial state hardened the fissures inherent in the traditional society to an extent unparalleled in Burundi. The hoary Hamitic myth, inherited from nineteenth century ethnographers,[11] provided the missionaries and colonial administrators with the overarching legitimizing framework for the implementation of a singularly pernicious version of indirect rule, where the Tutsi minority was attributed all the virtues of a superior Hamitic "race" and the Hutu the defects of a lower order of humanity, identified with the Bantu people. In practice this meant that the Tutsi would become the sole recipients of Western education, as well as the privileged partner of the colonial authorities, while the Hutu would bear the full burden of compulsory labour obligations, taxes and chiefly abuses.

With the sudden eruption of a Hutu-led jacquerie in November 1959, the stage was set for a Belgian-sponsored revolution. Thus, by the time the country became independent in 1962 power had effectively been transferred to representatives of the Hutu majority. Although the costs of the Hutu revolution in human lives is impossible to determine, the most reliable estimates suggest as many as 10,000 Tutsi killed, as well as some 80,000 forced into exile in the neighbouring territories.

The contrast with Burundi could not be more dramatic. Just as Hutu violence and Tutsi counterviolence swept across Rwanda, in Burundi the transition to independence was comparatively peaceful. Because of its greater political complexity and diversity of social hierarchies, Burundi was spared the agonies of a Hutu revolution before it acceded to independence. Whereas Rwanda celebrated the advent of self-government as a Hutu republic, Burundi crossed the threshold of independence as a constitutional monarchy, with a government consisting of a mixed assemblage of princely Tutsi and Hutu elements. The importance of this historical fact cannot be over-emphasized. Not only does it explain the radically different contexts of genocidal violence in each state; it also underscores the extreme vulnerability of the Burundi state to the Rwandan revolutionary model, and the desperate efforts made by Tutsi elements in Burundi to thwart the demands of the Hutu majority to gain effective political participation. This is the key to an understanding of the 1972 carnage in Burundi.

Connecting threads

There was no direct causal relationship between the 1972 bloodbath in Burundi and the 1994 genocide in Rwanda. Nonetheless, few informed observers would deny that eruptions of ethnic violence in one state have had a powerful blowback effect in the other. It was not by coincidence that one of the worst anti-Tutsi pogroms in pre-genocide Rwanda occurred in January 1973, shortly after the mass killings of Hutu in Burundi; as many as 200 Tutsi civilians, mostly students, were killed by enraged mobs of Hutu, in turn providing the pretext for the seizure of power by northern elements under the leadership of Juvénal Habyarimana. Given the notoriously anti-Tutsi feelings of the northern Hutu, the events of 1973 in Rwanda are worth bearing in mind in any attempt to put the 1994 genocide in historical perspective.

Ethnic violence is a profoundly contagious phenomenon. How violence in one state reverberates in the other is nowhere more dramatically illustrated than by what happened in the wake of the assassination of Burundi's first popularly elected president, Melchior Ndadaye, on 21 October 1993, by elements of the all-Tutsi army acting in complicity with leading Tutsi politicians.[12] The murder of the most talented and popular Hutu politician to emerge on the Burundi scene since independence was the cataclysmic event behind the country's descent into anarchy in the following decade. In Burundi, Ndadaye's death triggered an orgy of anti-Tutsi killings by Hutu supporters, resulting in the deaths of an estimated 30,000 Tutsi, while the ensuing repression caused probably as many casualties among Hutu. In Rwanda the immediate result was to give added impetus to the extremist forces that coalesced around the emergence of Hutu Power, while the massive flight of refugees into the country helped to further crystallize ethnic hatreds. Little wonder if many of the 350,000 Hutu refugees who fled to Rwanda would in time become active participants in the killing of Tutsi in 1994.

Of the many factors that made the two states so vulnerable to each other's enmities none has had a more profound impact than the seemingly endless refugee flows from Burundi into Rwanda, and vice versa. In both states, refugees played a decisive role in relaying the horrors committed against their kinsmen, in magnifying the psychological impact of the killings through their own eyewitness accounts of what happened, in driving home to their neighbours the story of the personal losses they suffered and in putting their own "mythical" constructions on the roots of the tragedies they witnessed. Liisa Malkki has shown how "mythical histories" born out of despair and suffering in the refugee camps of Tanzania have taken hold of Hutu popular imagination in the years following the Burundi genocide.[13] Borrowed from colonial historiography and recast as an ideological weapon in the service of Hutu extremists, the Hamitic myth – depicting the Tutsi as cruel invaders of Hamitic origins – later became a crucial ingredient of the murderous propaganda distilled through Radio Mille Collines during the Rwanda genocide.

Refugees are not a glob of humanity set adrift by ethnic clashes. They are often the agents of retributive violence. Again, no particular group or country has a monopoly on "refugee warriors". The first to launch armed raids into their country of origins were the Tutsi refugees from Rwanda, the so-called *inyenzi* ("cockroaches" in Kinyarwanda). In the early 1960s, from their bases in the Congo, Uganda and Burundi, they repeatedly tried to fight their way back into Rwanda at enormous cost to the resident Tutsi populations. The most costly of such raids took place in December 1963, when hundreds of armed Tutsi refugees crossed the border from Burundi into Rwanda, and came within striking distance of the capital city before they were annihilated by the Rwandan army and its European officers. In Rwanda the result was a bloodbath. According to the best estimates, corroborated by the World Council of Churches, between 10,000 and 14,000 Tutsi civilians were massacred in retaliation, in what some did not hesitate to call genocide.[14]

The second generation of Tutsi exiles drew important lessons for the repeated setbacks suffered by their predecessors. Better organized, well supplied in arms and vehicles "borrowed" from the Ugandan army, enjoying the full support of the Ugandan president Yoweri Museveni and led by battle-tested officers who had fought alongside Museveni's army against the forces of Milton Obote, the Rwandan Patriotic Front (RPF) succeeded brilliantly where the *inyenzi* had repeatedly failed. As they crossed into Rwanda on 1 October 1990, they were able to hold on to their ground against the counter-attacks mounted by the Rwandan army. On the eve of the genocide they controlled approximately one third of the country.

If the genocides in Rwanda and Burundi can both be described as "retributive", to use Helen Fein's taxonomy[15] (in the sense that they came about in response to perceived threats to the state, and to the ethnic group identified with the state), in each case the outcome has been radically different. Not simply because the victims were Hutu in Burundi and Tutsi in Rwanda, or because the number of victims in Rwanda was three times as high as in Burundi, but because the perpetrators of the Burundi genocide remained in power for some twenty years after the slaughter.

The dynamics of mass murder

Genocides are not isolated cataclysms that suddenly erupt like a bolt out of the blue, wreaking chaos and bloodshed through the land, until things finally return to normal. They are rooted in history, and once the killing stops things never return to normal. If post-genocide reconstruction is ever to yield a modicum of peace and harmony, it is important to grasp not just "what happened" but how perceptions of what happened in the past are likely to shape the future.

Burundi: A forgotten genocide

Compared to the sustained media attention attracted by Rwanda, one cannot fail to notice the minimal coverage accorded the Burundi genocide in the Western press. Today it has fallen into virtual oblivion. Given the arcane quality of Burundi politics, one might conceivably argue that failure to acknowledge simply reflects a lack of knowledge. A more important consideration is that many observers, including some well-known journalists and academics, have tended uncritically to endorse the official version of events conveyed by the Burundi authorities, one in which only Hutu are guilty of the crime of genocide. To this day this revisionist view of Burundi history raises major obstacles to a lasting national reconciliation.[16]

On the eve of the 1972 violence, Burundi was a weak state. Threats to its stability came not only from the Hutu insurgency, but also from the enormous tensions that had been building up within the Tutsi oligarchy, pitting Tutsi-Hima against Tutsi-Banyaruguru. The months preceding the slaughter are best described as a situation of semi-anarchy. Intra-Tutsi factionalism was rife, with the Hima–Banyaruguru strife threatening to get out of hand. The country was awash with rumour of plots and counterplots, leading to the arrest and bogus trials of scores of Banyaruguru politicians, while the ruling clique, consisting mainly of Tutsi-Hima from the Bururi province, saw their legitimacy plummet. Stories were heard of a possible return of the exiled king, with the help of European mercenaries. But when the young king Ntare returned to his homeland in March 1972, after being told that he had no reason to worry for his life, it was as a prisoner of the government, then headed by Captain Michel Micombero. And there was of course the ever-present threat of a Hutu insurrection, made all the more likely by persistent factional struggles among Tutsi.

The Hutu insurrection erupted on 29 April 1972, spreading chaos and violence through several localities in the south. Although no one knows just how many were involved, the insurgents could not have numbered more than two or three thousand at the most (rather than 25,000 as the government subsequently claimed). The number of Tutsi killed is equally uncertain, estimates varying from a few hundred to 5,000. The ensuing repression got under way almost immediately, and lasted well into September. Besides the army and the police, the militias, known as the *Jeunesses Révolutionnaires Rwagasore* (JRR), were actively involved in the killings. So, also, were a number of Tutsi refugees from Rwanda, working hand in hand with the JRR. No region was spared. An estimated 600 Hutu soldiers of the Burundi army were massacred by their commanding officers in the days following the uprising. Bujumbura and other cities were thoroughly cleansed of every literate Hutu. In a matter of weeks all Hutu elites and potential elites, including university and secondary school students, were either dead or in flight. But the hunt continued for months thereafter in the countryside, causing hundreds of thousands of refugees to seek asylum in neighbouring countries. On the same day the uprising broke out, King Ntare was shot and killed by Tutsi officers. Restoring the monarchy was no longer an option.

Behind the slaughter lies a great deal more than the imperative of restoring "peace and order". The underlying objectives were 1) to ensure the long-term stability of the state by the wholesale elimination of all educated Hutu, including civil servants, business elites, teachers and students, to which must be added an untold number of unskilled workers; 2) to transform the instruments of force, the army, the police and the gendarmerie, into a Tutsi monopoly (which is still the case today); 3) to rule out the possibility of a restoration of the monarchy; and 4) to create a new basis of legitimacy for the Hima-dominated state by projecting the image of the state as the benevolent protector of all Burundi against their domestic and external enemies.

Critical to the restoration of state legitimacy was an inversionary discourse aimed at shifting the onus of genocidal guilt to the insurgents. Through a variety of official channels, including the White Paper issued by the government, the point that comes across again and again is that the Hutu insurgents had committed genocide against the Tutsi; in putting down the rebellion the state prevented the carnage from taking an even bigger toll.

Foreshadowing the hand-washing response of the international community to the Rwanda bloodbath, nothing was done by the UN or anybody else to bring the bloodshed to an end. Despite alarming cables sent to Washington by the US Embassy in Bujumbura, the State Department was emphatic in its "desire to avoid any indication of the US taking sides in this current tragic problem".[17] Perhaps the most surreal of all international responses to the slaughter came from the Organization of African Unity (OAU), on 22 May, when its Secretary General, Diallo Telli, informed his audience that his presence in Bujumbura "signified the total solidarity of the OAU Secretariat with the president of Burundi, the government and the fraternal people of Burundi". In 1972 in Burundi, as in 1994 in Rwanda, the killings went unabated while the bystanders looked the other way.

Although the decapitation of the Hutu leadership in 1972 would ensure the stability of the country under Tutsi tutelage for the next sixteen years, the murder of Ndadaye in 1993, after what was widely seen as an exemplary transition to multi-party democracy, made dramatically clear the determination of Tutsi extremists to hang on to power, even if it meant plunging the country into chaos. In trying to reverse the verdict of the polls, they ushered in a situation of protracted anarchy, where power seemed to gravitate increasingly in the hands of armed militias at both ends of the ethnic divide. The price paid for their crime far exceeded the plotter's calculation: An estimated 300,000 Burundi died in ethnic confrontations in the ten years following Ndadaye's assassination. The brightest spot on this otherwise very sombre political horizon came in August 2000, with the signature of the Arusha Accords, also known as the Peace and Reconciliation Accords, and the installation on 1 November 2001 of a broad-based transitional government.

Rwanda: Revolution, genocide, exile and retribution

All genocides are alike in the horror they evoke, the intentionality of the atrocities committed and the targeting of the victims. Yet they each stand as singular events, rooted in the particularities of specific historical situations. So, also, with the cases at hand. Both were retributive genocides occurring in response to specific threats to the state. In Burundi the threat came from a Hutu-led rural insurgency that caused untold casualties among Tutsi civilians; in Rwanda it came from the 1 October 1990 invasion of armed Tutsi refugees from Uganda. Both genocides were targeted against specific communities identified with the source of the threat, Hutu in Burundi, Tutsi in Rwanda; and the weak state syndrome was just as real in the case of Rwanda as it was in Burundi. The multiplicity of intra-Hutu rivalries brought to light by the introduction of multiparty competition in March 1991, the depth of enmities between Hutu extremists and moderates, the inability of the government to restrain the extremists from using violence against civilians: these were crucial factors in the rapidly shrinking legitimacy of the Rwandan state on the eve of the genocide.

Again, the identity of the perpetrators was remarkably similar in each case. The military was a central actor in Burundi as it was in Rwanda; the counterpart to the JRR were the party youth militias, most notably the *interahamwe* ("those who fight [or act] together") identified with the ruling party, the Mouvement Révolutionnaire National pour le Développement (in 1992 renamed Mouvement Républicain National pour le Développement et la Démocratie); and just as the Tutsi refugees from Rwanda played a significant auxiliary role in the Burundi massacres, so did the Hutu refugees from Burundi in Rwanda.

Once this is said, the contrasts are no less significant. Burundi never went through anything comparable to Rwanda's Hutu revolution, which, though officially described as a "social revolution", was first and foremost a political revolution. This fact is central to an understanding of the 1994 genocide. Rwanda offers a perfect illustration of the thesis set forth by Robert Melson in his classic work *Revolution and Genocide*, to the effect that war and revolution are key elements in the dynamics of genocidal violence.[18] Just as revolution helps redefine the boundaries of the post-revolutionary community – and identifies the enemies of the revolution with a specific ethnic or cultural community – war heightens the sense of vulnerability of the new community and lumps together domestic and external enemies. Thus from the day the RPF refugees crossed into Rwanda, on 1 October 1990, the invaders were seen as the embodiment of the counterrevolution, threatening to undo everything that had been accomplished since independence.

What Jacques Sémelin calls "le passage à l'acte"[19] – the tipping point where the will to kill becomes the act of killing – is traceable to an extraordinary event: at 8:30 pm on 6 April, as the presidential plane was about to land in Kigali, two SA-16 missiles fired from near the airport scored direct hits, bringing the plane down in a matter of seconds. Among the victims were President Habyarimana, his Burundi counterpart, Cyprien Ntaryamira, and several high-ranking officials, including General Nsabimana, the army chief of staff. To this day responsibility for the shooting down of the plane has yet to be formally established, but recent leaks to the press of the report of the French investigating magistrate, Jean-Louis Bruguière – along with the recent publication of Abdul Joshua Ruzibiza's chilling expose – leave few doubts about the implication of Paul Kagame in the crime.[20] Early the next morning the exterminating mechanism was set in motion. Day after day, for the next hundred days, Tutsi men, women and children were systematically murdered.

Among the victims were tens of thousands of Hutu from the south, whose only crime was their affiliation to opposition parties. Here lies another critical difference with Burundi. At no time were Tutsi deliberately killed by Tutsi in Burundi, the only exceptions being those whose physical traits wrongly identified them as Hutu. But where the Rwanda situation departs most dramatically from Burundi is in the massive outpouring of Hutu refugees into the Congo, and the subsequent search-and-destroy operations conducted by the Rwandan Patriotic Army (RPA).[21] Approximately half of the one million refugees walked back into Rwanda after the destruction of the camps in November 1996; of the remaining 500,000 one might speculate that about a third died of disease, starvation and sheer exhaustion. How many were killed by the RPA is a matter of intense controversy, yet according to the most reliable estimates at least 75,000 are believed to have been wiped out by RPA units.[22] Acting on the assumption that those refugees who did not return

to Rwanda were either *interahamwe* or elements of the ex-Forces Armées Rwandaises, RPA troops engaged in a systematic cleansing of
Hutu civilians in what must be seen as one of the most tragic examples
of a victimized group morphing into killers. This is fully documented in
the reports of the American non-governmental organization Refugees International (RI).[23] Equally damning is the testimony of Kirkpatrick Day,
Field Representative of RI before the sub-committee on Africa of the
Senate Foreign Relations Committee, on 8 July 1997: "Tutsi from both
Congo and Rwanda are hunting and slaughtering Rwandan Hutu refugees, avenging earlier killings.... Many of the refugees are innocent
men, women and children who have been indiscriminately preyed upon
by Kabila ... [whose] ascent is tainted with the blood of thousands of refugees, which could only perpetuate the cycle of inter-ethnic violence....
The genocidaires and those seeking vengeance are both guilty of crimes
against humanity."[24] In a number of cases refugees were lured out of
their hiding places by the prospects of food distribution from non-
governmental organizations, only to be mowed down by Tutsi troops. In
the Kasese camp alone, near Kisangani, sheltering anywhere between
60,000 and 100,000 refugees, at least 30,000 of them were killed by RPA
units since 22 April 1997.[25] In the huge camp at Tingi-Tingi, thousands
were massacred. So, also, in Shanji, Lubutu, Tebero, Obilo, Ubundu and
Mbandaka.[26] The hunt lasted from November 1996 to the fall of 1997,
with RPA units pursuing their victims as far as Mbandaka in northern
Congo, some two thousand miles from Kigali. The thoroughly inhumane
treatment visited upon Hutu refugees appears to fit Helen Fein's definition of "genocide by attrition". Significantly more embracing in its connotation than the UN Genocide Convention, "genocide by attrition",
she writes, occurs "after a group is singled out for political and civil discrimination. It is separated from the larger society, and its right to life is
threatened through concentration and forced displacement, together with
systematic deprivation of food, water, and sanitary and medical facilities."[27]

What Rony Brauman, Steven Smith and Claudine Vidal refer to as "les
conventions de silence" translates in Kigali into a policy of "systematic
disinformation".[28] That tens of thousands of Hutu were killed by other
Hutu during the genocide is almost never openly acknowledged by
Rwanda's authorities, any more than the hundreds or thousands of Tutsi
whose lives were saved by their Hutu neighbours. Nor is the killing of
some 5,000 Hutu by Tutsi soldiers in the Kibeho refugee camp in
Rwanda on 22 April 1995, one of several camps for internally displaced
persons, publicly acknowledged by the Kigali authorities. As Philip
Gourevitch points out, the official body count of 334 appeared "absurdly
low and suggested a cover-up".[29] Thanks to the painstaking inquest un-

dertaken by Alison Des Forges, we also know that between 25,000 and 45,000 Hutu were killed by units of the RPF between the months of April and August 1994, a fact that has yet to be admitted by the Kagame government.[30] The assumption, in short, is that only Hutu have blood on their hands, and only Tutsi blood. The tendency among some Rwandan officials to hold all Hutu responsible for the killings – even though, as Scott Straus shows, the number of perpetrators involved probably ranges from 175,000 to 210,000 – only creates further bitterness and misunderstandings.

Nothing fuels Hutu resentment and exasperation as much as what many see as a conspiracy of silence on the part of the international community about the crimes of the RPF, and its armed wing, the RPA. A notable exception to this silence came on 15 October 2002, when former US Assistant Secretary of State for Africa, Herman Cohen, in an interview to the news agency Congopolis, flatly stated: "I believe that the RPA massacred as many as 350,000 Hutu refugees [in eastern Congo]."[31] That this figure happens to be wildly exaggerated is perhaps less important than its source – or its timing (only five years after the massacres). Although there was no lack of evidence for the crimes committed by the RPF in Rwanda during the civil war, and then in the Congo, both the UN and the US have consistently resisted pressures to acknowledge such atrocities.[32] The most devastating source of evidence of the killings perpetrated by the RPA in 1994 is found in the so-called Gersony report, penned by the head of the United Nations High Commissioner for Refugees (UNHCR) team sent to investigate conditions in refugee camps. As reported by Alison Des Forges, "When the team and the head of the UNHCR attempted responsibly to bring the information to the attention of the international community, the UN decided to suppress it, not just in the interests of the recently established Rwandan government but also to avoid further discredit to itself. The US and perhaps other member states concurred in this decision, largely to avoid weakening the new Rwandan government."[33] Lionel Rosenblatt, president of Refugees International, described the response of the international community to the refugee crisis in eastern Zaire as "a sad evasion of responsibility", adding that "it was a demonstrably false remark by the US Ambassador to Rwanda that the numbers of refugees in Zaire were 'in the tens to twenties of thousands rather than in vast numbers' that prompted me to respond heatedly and to demand that the Ambassador be recalled."[34] Because of what they perceive as an intolerable double standard in failing to identify Tutsi elements as the authors of crimes against humanity, many Hutu seriously question the meaning of some of the post-genocide initiatives to lay the groundwork for "a fresh start".

Post-genocide reconstruction strategies

Two radically different reconstruction strategies have been adopted in each state. After a decade of civil strife, Burundi has institutionalized a power-sharing formula based on the explicit recognition of ethnicity. In Rwanda, by contrast, ethnic differences have been legislated out of existence; Tutsi hegemony is mediated through a single-party system backed by a formidable coercive arsenal; despite gestures towards national reconciliation the goals of ethnic and political equality are as distant as they have ever been since the advent of independence.

Burundi: Reconciliation through power-sharing

This is not the place for a detailed analysis of the complex negotiations that have accompanied Burundi's tortuous trajectory from anarchy to a fragile peace. Suffice it to note that the present consociational model has its origins in Protocol II of the Burundi Peace and Reconciliation Accords of 28 August 2000. Its key provisions included a sharing of power in the future national assembly and government on the basis of 60 per cent for Hutu and 40 per cent for Tutsi, a senate with an equal proportion of Hutu and Tutsi, and the same proportion in the defence and security forces. At the communal level a slightly more generous quota was reserved for the Hutu majority: 67 per cent against 33 per cent for the Tutsi minority. The aim, in short, was to increase the representation of Tutsi candidates far beyond population figures, and thus give the minority a substantial stake in the new political system.

The model enshrined at Arusha was implemented with remarkable success during the local and legislative elections held respectively in June and July 2005.[35] The only significant difference concerns the substitution of ethno-political representation for straight ethnic quotas, meaning that Tutsi candidates belonging to a predominantly Hutu party could qualify as representatives of the Tutsi minority, and so also could Hutu elected on a predominantly Tutsi party. The net result has been to de-polarize the political arena to an even greater degree than had been previously contemplated. Thus of the 64 seats out of 118 in the National Assembly held by the Hutu-led *Conseil national pour la défense de la démocratie–Forces pour la défense de la démocratie*, 43 are Hutu and 21 Tutsi. Not only are there several parties competing for the vote of the same ethnic community, but it is not unusual for Hutu and Tutsi to belong to the same party. This is in striking contrast with the bipolar pattern that presided over the 1993 elections, where Hutu and Tutsi candidates confronted each other along party lines, the first overwhelmingly affiliated to the

Front pour la démocratie au Burundi, the second to the *Union pour le progrès national*. Another critical difference is that by 2005 the Burundi armed forces had undergone a sea change, in terms of their ethnic profile, degree of professionalization and discipline.

There can be little doubt that Burundi has gone further than any other African state in implementing power-sharing. Equally obvious is that although the elections must be seen as a technical success, in terms of successfully translating a complex consociational formula into a plural polity, there is no guarantee that it will be matched by a lasting political success. One of the most serious threats to peace is the radical, Hutu-dominated *Front national de libération*, which to this day has rejected all offers of a cease-fire. Furthermore, fairness of ethnic representation has yet to translate into a meaningful redistribution of economic wealth. The material needs of the hundreds of thousands of displaced peasants living in abject poverty remain unmet. And while thousands of political prisoners have been freed since the accession to power of President Pierre Nkurunziza, popular expectations that Ndadaye's assassins will be brought to justice and punished have been largely ignored.

"Dealing with the past", writes Filip Reyntens, "will be a delicate exercise. While setting up both a mixed Truth Commission and a Special Chamber within the domestic court system was recommended by the UN Security Council, the regime will probably seek to find a balance between accountability and stability. Of course impunity must be actively tackled, but those having committed heinous crimes belong to many of the parties involved in the current political dispensation. Therefore it will be important to avoid the impression of bias and revenge."[36] The likelihood that coming to terms with the country's genocidal past could re-awaken ethnic enmities is not to be discounted. All the more so given the potential support that Tutsi extremists in Burundi might well expect from their kinsmen in Rwanda. Ironically, in the years following independence the Rwanda model was seen by many Hutu in Burundi as the republican ideal to be emulated. Rwanda is still a powerful source of inspiration – but only for those unrepentant Tutsi who fear the "tyranny" majority.

Rwanda: Reconciliation through ethnic amnesia

Power-sharing in post-genocide Rwanda is ruled out by the logic of official memory: Ethnic identities have ceased to exist. The public ban on all references to ethnicity means that there are no longer Hutu or Tutsi in Kagame's Rwanda, only Banyarwanda (Rwandans). In justification of this drastic reconfiguration of social identities Rwandan officials invoke the exigencies of nation-building; the first priority in meeting this goal is to do away with "divisionism". The logic of the argument is straightforward: "If awareness of ethnic differences can be learned, so too can the idea that ethnicity does not exist."[37] This is why the crime of "divisionism" has been added to the penal code. Besides providing the government with a convenient weapon to ban almost any type of organized opposition, it offers a unique opportunity to suppress the public expression of ethnic memories.

By effectively controlling pockets of Hutu insurgency at home and in eastern Congo Rwanda has achieved a considerable degree of internal security for which there is as yet no equivalent in Burundi. Power-sharing is not nearly as much of an imperative as it is in Burundi, even though a number of "cosmetic" Hutu hold positions in the government. Although reconciliation is the subtext that runs through several of the political, judicial and constitutional reforms adopted in recent time, these have yet to be translated into minimal standards of social and political equality.

How to institutionalize multiparty democracy while at the same time averting the tyranny of the Hutu majority is the central dilemma faced by President Paul Kagame. The key lies in creating a Potemkin-like façade of free and fair elections while giving the ruling RPF the instruments of control designed to promote "consensual democracy". The latter presupposes the birth of a new mentality, where competence and "wisdom" will eclipse ethnic identities. This is the task assigned to the National Unity and Reconciliation Commission through the "solidarity camps" (ingando) set up for ideological training sessions. Equally crucial is the "politics and mass mobilization" campaign organized by RPF cadres throughout the country with a view to "mobilize, recruit and spread the RPF philosophy".[38] The cell and sector elections of March 1999, followed in March 2001 by district elections, bore testimony to the success of both strategies: though intended to be non-partisan elections the vast majority of the candidates elected to office were RPF sympathizers. Much of the credit for this predictable outcome also goes to the government-appointed National Electoral Commission (NEC), whose president and executive secretary were well-known RPF politicians. Careful screening of the candidates by the NEC made the victory of grass-roots "consensual democracy" a foregone conclusion.

Local elections are the basic instrument of decentralization policies. The aim is two-fold: to bring the rural sectors firmly under the control of the RPF, and "to break the administrative machinery that had facilitated the genocide and still inhibits the change in Rwanda's political culture ... to bury the prestige and authority of the former Commune leaders, the bourgmestres, who bore much of the responsibility for implementing the genocide, and to set up a new political culture, based on participation, collective decision-making and accountability."[39]

One of the most significant and controversial aspects of such policies refers to the so-called *gacaca* courts. Based upon a misconstruction of traditional local dispute resolution mechanisms, each of the 11,000 courts (one for each voting district) consists of nineteen "persons of integrity" elected to adjudicate cases of murder, rape and theft during the genocide. The principal merit of this local justice system is to offer a remedy to the appalling slowness and inefficiency of the ordinary justice system, which in fact amounted to a denial of justice. As of 2001 some 120,000 persons suspected of participating in the genocide languished in overcrowded jails (of whom at least a third were incarcerated for arbitrary reasons, many denounced as genocidaires by Tutsi returnees eager to lay their hands on their houses and belongings). Although it is too early to pass definitive judgment on the performance of the gacaca courts, preliminary evidence is anything but encouraging. Samantha Power compares the proceedings to "a public confessional process that recalls both the Salem witch trials and a Mississippi Christian revival".[40] After observing firsthand the gacaca proceedings, Scott Strauss noted that the strain put on the legal system had required something radical: Five years had seen only around 5,500 of the more than 105,000 prisoners tried. The trials themselves were often "long, sterile and vulnerable to corruption. Defendants had little legal representation; witnesses were intimidated; and penalties were arbitrarily assigned." There was no guarantee that gacaca would work, but its most promising aspect, he wrote was that it "opens a small, but real democratic space that creates the possibility for unforeseen, non-hegemonic discussions, whether on the genocide itself or on currently taboo topics, such as alleged government massacres or Hutu and Tutsi identities."[41]

Hardly more promising has been the judicial experiment conducted under the auspices of the Arusha-based International Criminal Tribunal for Rwanda (ICTR) since none of the crimes committed by the RPF are deemed justiciable. On the more positive side, among the 61 Hutu in custody, some apparently played a key role in organizing the genocide, notably Colonel Théoneste Bagosora, Ferdinand Nahimana and Joseph Nzirorera. Nonetheless, the ICTR's reputation has been severely tarnished by the many scandals that have been brought to light since its creation in 1995, and by the inordinately slow and costly handling of cases. Only nine verdicts have been issued in seven years, at a cost of some US$90 million a year. Perhaps the most telling criticism of the ICTR is the one voiced by Gérard Gahima, Rwanda's attorney general: "The tribunal was not set up for the people of Rwanda; it was set up to ease the world's guilty consciences, and in everything the court does, this shows."[42]

For all the flaws and shortcomings of the domestic and international justice systems, and in contrast with Burundi, the regime has consistently shown its determination to seek appropriate punishment for those Hutu guilty of committing genocide. And yet impunity remains the rule for crimes committed by the RPF within and outside Rwanda. Of all the obstacles in the way of national reconciliation, the application of double standards in meting out punishment for crimes of genocide is not the least problematic.

Inequality goes beyond the realm of judicial performance. It is most painfully obvious in the economic and social marginalization of the rural masses, in the restratification of society into a relatively well-off urban class of predominantly Tutsi origins and an overwhelmingly Hutu rural proletariat, with all the discrimination that implies in terms of access to education, status and material benefits. The extent to which discrimination affects the rural sectors is nowhere more evident than in the consequences of the government's National Habitat Policy (NHP): The forceful displacement of hundreds of thousands of rural dwellers into government-created villages, called *imidugudu*, has been accompanied by extensive destruction of property, the frequent use of coercion and widespread social disruptions. Though the official goal is to promote peace and reconciliation, "villagization" is essentially designed to facilitate the control of the rural populations. As Human Rights Watch reported, the implementation of NHP has been the source of serious human rights violations.[43] In principle the policy applies to both Tutsi and Hutu, but the latter are the principal victims. They are the ones who bear the brunt of the "poverty, hunger, disease and despair" resulting from "the forced displacement from their homes, the waste of resources entailed by the destruction of their houses, the reduction of productivity which has resulted from living far from the fields, and the loss of land given over to *imidugudu*".[44]

But discrimination operates in more complex ways. It also penetrates the Tutsi minority through the virtual exclusion of Tutsi survivors, the so-called *rescapés*, from positions of power and influence. Post-genocide Rwanda is not just a Tutsi state; it is state largely controlled by Tutsi returnees, with the "Ugandans" holding the top jobs in the government, the economy and the army.

Inequality is indeed the hallmark of the emergent political system. So deeply entrenched is the ruling RPF in both the state and the civil society that none of its opponents have the slightest chance of effectively challenging its hegemony. In the words of a recent International Crisis Group report, "Over the last three years, police control over all forms of opposition, both within and outside the regime, has steadily increased. The press, associations and opposition parties have been silenced, destroyed or co-opted. Fearing for their lives, critical politicians, members of opposition parties, former supporters or founding members of the RPF have chosen to leave the country and join other exiled opponents."[45] Rwanda's reconstruction strategy is thus based on the all-pervasive control of public life by the party-dominant state, reinforced by the ever-present threat of force.

The tragic legacy of genocide has produced a "never again" obsession that gives moral justification to the limitations placed on public liberties. Whether the short-term benefits of authoritarian rule can provide a viable foundation for long-run stability is what remains to be seen.

Policy implications

There is no magic recipe for the reconstruction of civil societies ripped apart by mutual hatreds and conflicting memories. Learning to look at the "other" through the lens of mutual tolerance will not happen overnight. It is a long-term, adaptive process aiming at healing the traumas on both sides of the ethnic fault line. In his contribution to this volume, Scott Straus suggests that reconciliation may be "an unrealistic goal for post-genocide Rwanda"; "coexistence", he suggests, is a more appropriate concept, as it "avoids the imperative to forgive and as such is a more plausible goal". The key issue, he adds, "concerns trust and confidence". In societies still vulnerable to unpredictable outbursts of violence, and in close physical proximity to actual or suspected killers, how to restore trust is a singularly problematic enterprise.

"A key dilemma", as some have suggested, "is how to balance the need for accountability for the past against the need for reconciliation in the future".[46] Nowhere is the dilemma more acute than in the cases at hand. Post-conflict strategies based on the notion that "truth" once revealed – and the culprits once punished – will make for mutual trust are unlikely to succeed. Short of meaningful political reforms aiming at widening the scope of political participation at the grass-roots level, stimulating community interactions and encouraging an interethnic dialogue, "telling the truth" will not suffice. In part because there are different versions of the truth, in part because the truth continues to be manipulated by the state. In part also because truth and accountability should be treated as two sides of the same reconciliation process.

Efforts to break down the barrier of mutual distrust must be undertaken at different levels. At the highest level a sustained effort must be made by the international community to encourage public acknowledgement of the shared responsibility incurred by Hutu and Tutsi extremists for the multiple tragedies experienced by both states. The crimes committed by Hutu are no excuse for ignoring the crimes committed by Tutsi. This is true of both Rwanda in 1994, and Burundi in 1972, 1988 and 1993. Acknowledgement is inseparable from accountability. Only if murderers are held accountable and punished can impunity cease to be the rule.

The manipulation of public memory remains a major obstacle. The systematic exclusion of Hutu victims from the annual commemoration of the Rwanda genocide is a telling commentary on how public memory helps nurture ethnic enmities: not a word, not a single gesture to remind the people of Rwanda of the tens of thousands of Hutu killed during the genocide, some by the *interahamwe*, others by the RPF. Especially pointed are Claudine Vidal's remarks: "Since 1996 the commemorations of the genocide ... explicitly deny the status of victims to those Hutu who, even though they did not kill, were massacred so as to create a climate of terror.... How can one speak of reconciliation when the exposure of skeletons has as its only purpose to remind the Tutsi that their own people were killed by Hutu? This is tantamount to keeping the latter in a permanent position of culpability."[47] Much the same could be said of the attitude of some Tutsi elites in Burundi when they repeatedly draw attention to the genocide of Tutsi perpetrated by Hutu in 1993, but ignore the vastly more devastating scale of the 1972 genocide, or for that matter the bloody repression of Hutu that followed in the wake of Ndadaye's assassination.

Historians in both states can play a decisive role in altering the negative perceptions that Hutu and Tutsi have of each other. Not only in laying to rest the shibboleths of missionary historians, but in showing how these have been replaced by equally objectionable constructions at the hands of extremist ideologues and public officials. To lay bare the calculated amnesia, cover-ups, and evasions that stand in the way of public acknowledgement of the facts, to challenge the distortions of ethnic memories, to call into question the ethnicization of guilt and bring to light the full complexity of the historical forces and circumstances that lie in the background of these traumatic events – these are the immediate tasks facing historians. More often than not at their own peril.

At yet another level, that of the medico-anthropological approach explored by Roberto Beneduce in this volume, are important lessons to be learned from Eva Hoffman's plea for "recognition", that is "recognition of what actually happened – of the victims' experience and the perpetrators' responsibility, and ultimately the broader structures of cause and effect".[48] Commenting on the "current rhetoric", she writes: "Memory always stands for victimological memory, embraced by particular groups, and foregrounding the darkest episodes of various pasts.... The injunctions to remember, if reiterated too often, can become formulaic – an injunction not to think or grapple with the past." Instead she invites us to "look beyond the fixed moment of trauma to those longer historical patterns, to supplement partisan memory with a more complex and encompassing view of history".[49]

This is very much part of what Paul Ricoeur has in mind when he urges upon us the imperative of a "labour of memory" (*travail de mémoire*). The phrase, he tells us, harks back to Freud's concept of *Durcharbeiten* (which he translates as *translaboration*), which he used to call attention to the obstacles to the psychoanalytic cure by the obsessive, repetitive memory of traumatizing events.[50] In Ricoeur's argument it brings into focus the need for a "critical use of memory". Rather than a one-sided compulsive urge to rehash the sufferings endured by one group at the hands of another, or allowing them to slip into oblivion, working through memory is first and foremost an exercise in narrative history. It aims at "narrating differently the stories of the past, telling them from the point of view of the other – the other, my friend or my enemy".[51] As alternative perceptions are brought into view, past events take on a different meaning: "Past events cannot be erased: one cannot undo what has been done, nor prevent what has happened. On the other hand, the meaning of what happened, whether inflicted by us unto others, or by them upon us, is not fixed once and for all.... Thus what is changed about the past is its moral freight (*sa charge morale*), the weight of the debt it carries.... This is how the working of memory opens the way to forgiveness to the extent that it settles a debt by changing the very meaning of the past."[52] Ricoeur and Hoffman are both sceptical of injunctions to remember; both reject the notion of oblivion as a vector of forgiveness; and both are aware of the need to give a central place to the claims of a "critical memory", immune to appropriation and manipulation. All of the above should figure prominently in grass-roots agendas aimed as fostering trust, and hopefully forgiveness, among local communities.

Ernest Renan famously observed that "getting its history wrong is part of being a nation". But as the cases at hand demonstrate, it is also part of impeding the rebirth of a nation. From the cumulative effects of "thwarted memory", "manipulated memory" and "enforced memory"[53] have emerged radically different cognitive frames through which the "other" is perceived. Failure to take into account this officially sanctioned dissonance raises grave doubts about current efforts to strengthen capacities for peace. There is, however, more than a glimmer of hope in the fact that not all Tutsi and Hutu are willing to remain prisoners of their tragic past, and that many in both states refuse to surrender to prejudice, official denials and enforced memory – and are willing to take risks to stand on the side of truth and justice. On their shoulders rests the burden of charting a new course towards peaceful cohabitation.

Notes

1. Michael Bowen, Gary Freeman and Kay Miller, "No Samaritan: The US and Burundi", *Africa Report*, July–August 1973, p. 32, a shortened version of the report issued by the Carnegie Endowment for International Peace in the wake of the killings.

2. See the devastating testimony of Abdul Joshua Ruzibiza, a former officer in Kagame's Rwanda patriotic Front (RPF), *Rwanda: L'histoire secrète*, Paris: Editions du Panama, 2005. The consternation it has caused among official circles in Burundi is unsurprising in view of the author's detailed description of the participation of the RPF in the shooting down of President Habyalimana's plane.

3. Quoted in Stanley Cohen, *States of Denial: Knowing about Atrocities and Suffering*, Cambridge: Polity, 2001, p. 243.

4. Paul Ricoeur, *La mémoire, l'histoire, l'oubli*, Paris: Seuil, 2002.

5. Stanley Cohen, *States of Denial*, p. 138.

6. For a discussion of the distinction between factual and interpretive or moral truth that bears directly on the cases at hand, see Michael Ignatieff, *The Warrior's Honor: Ethnic War and the Modern Conscience*, New York: Metropolitan Books, 1997, p. 171.

7. The expression is borrowed from Aristide Zolberg, Astri Suhrke and Giorgio Aquayo, eds, *Escape from Violence: Conflict and the Refugee Crisis in the Developing World*, New York: Oxford University Press, 1989.

8. Professor Yochanan (Jean) Bwejeri, a Murundi, is one of the key promoters of the idea that Tutsi are the lineal descendants of early Jewish communities established in the Kushitic region of Africa; his Havila Institute, based in Brussels, is attracting the sympathies of a growing number of Tutsi abroad and in Burundi through the publication of its militant newsletter. For further details, see *Le Combattant, Bulletin de Liaison des Forces Armées Tutsi-Juifs de Kush*, no. 1, June 2003, Remera and Bujumbura.

9. Maurice Niwese, *Le peuple rwandais un pied dans la tombe: Récit d'un réfugié étudiant*, Paris: Harmattan, 2001.

10. For further elaboration, see René Lemarchand, *Rwanda and Burundi*, London: Pall Mall Press, 1970.

11. See Jean-Pierre Chrétien, *L'Afrique des Grands Lacs*, Paris: Grasset, 2000, esp. pp. 31–46, 245–252, 262–314.

12. Filip Reyntjens, *L'Afrique des Grands Lacs en Crise: Rwanda, Burundi, 1988–1994*, Paris: Karthala, 1994, pp. 265–275.

13. Liisa Malkki, *Purity and Exile: Violence, Memory and National Cosmogony among Hutu Refugees in Tanzania*, Chicago: University of Chicago Press, 1995.

14. Bertrand Russell called it "The most terrible and systematic human massacre we have had occasion to witness since the extermination of the Jews by the Nazi," cited in René Lemarchand, *Rwanda and Burundi*, p. 224. This quote has now become a standard reference in countless pro-RPF publications.

15. Helen Fein, "Genocide: A Sociological Perspective", *Sociology* 38, no. 1, p. 30.

16. See René Lemarchand, "Le génocide de 1972 au Burundi: Les silences de l'histoire", *Cahiers d'etudes Africaines* 167, no. 42/43, 2002, pp. 551–567.

17. This quote and the next are from the cable traffic to and from the US Embassy in Bujumbura during the genocide. We are grateful to Michael Hoyt, who served at the time in the US Embassy as Deputy Chief of Mission, for making available to us the almost complete set of cables sent by the embassy to the State Department from April to August 1972. These are available from the University of Florida library at http://www.uflib.ufl.edu/cm/africana/fulltext.htm.

18. Robert Melson, *Revolution and Genocide*, Chicago: University of Chicago Press, 1992.

19. Jacques Sémelin, *Purifier et Détruire: Usages politiques des massacres et génocides*, Paris: Seuil, 2005.
20. See Stephen Smith, "Révélations sur l'attentat qui a déclenché le génocide rwandais", *Le Monde*, 10 March 2004, pp. 1–3; for an English-language version, see Stephen Smith, "Rwandan president implicated in death of predecessor by French magistrate", *Guardian Weekly*, 25–31 March 2004, p. 31. See also Abdul Joshua Ruzibiza, *Rwanda: L'histoire secrète*.
21. In 1995 the military arm of the RPF became known as the Rwandan Patriotic Army (RPA); Rwandan Patriotic Front (RPF) now refers to the dominant, Tutsi-dominated party in Rwanda.
22. This is the figure cited to the authors by Professor Filip Reyntjens; many of those who survived the massacres would consider this estimate too conservative, some going as far as to suggest twice as many casualties.
23. Refugees International, *The Lost Refugees: Herded and Hunted in Eastern Zaire*, Washington, DC: RI, September 1997.
24. Ibid., pp. 74, 76.
25. Maurice Niwese, *Le peuple rwandais un pied dans la tombe*, p. 168.
26. Ibid.
27. Helen Fein, "Genocide by Attrition in the Sudan and Elsewhere", *Institute for the Study of Genocide Newsletter*, no. 29, Fall 2002, p. 7.
28. Rony Brauman, Stephen Smith, Claudine Vidal, "Rwanda: Politique de terreur, privilège d'impunité," *Esprit*, August–September 2000, p. 150.
29. Philip Gourevitch, *We wish to inform you that tomorrow we will be killed with our families: Stories from Rwanda*, New York: Farrar Straus and Giroux, 1998, p. 202.
30. Alison Des Forges, *Leave None to Tell the Story: Genocide in Rwanda*, New York, Paris and Washington: Human Rights Watch and Féderation Internationale des Ligues des Droits de l'Homme, 1999, pp. 726–734.
31. "Democratic Republic of the Congo: Interview with Mr. Herman Cohen", *Congopolis*, 15 October 2002, reproduced in *Le Phare* (Kinshasa), 17 October 2002.
32. See Maurice Niwese, *Le peuple rwandais un pied dans la tombe*, pp. 128–130; see also Refugees International, *The Lost Refugees*, 74 ff.
33. Alison Des Forges, *Leave None to Tell the Story*, p. 726.
34. Refugees International, *The Lost Refugees*, p. ii.
35. For an outstanding discussion of the 2005 elections, see Filip Reyntjens, "Briefing: Burundi: A Peaceful Transition After a Decade of War?" *African Affairs* (forthcoming).
36. Ibid.
37. Mark Lacey, "Rwanda: There is no ethnicity there", *International Herald Tribune*, 10 April 2004, p. 2.
38. International Crisis Group, "'Consensual Democracy' in Post Genocide Rwanda: Evaluating the March 2001 District Elections", Africa Report no. 34, Nairobi and Brussels: ICG, 9 October 2001, p. 7.
39. Ibid., p. 5.
40. Samantha Power, "Rwanda: The Two Faces of Justice", *New York Review of Books*, 16 January 2002, p. 48.
41. Scott Strauss, "Letter from Rwanda: *Gacaca* Begins", *Institute for the Study of Genocide Newsletter*, no. 29, Fall 2002, p. 9, available at http://www.isg-iags.org/oldsite/newsletters/29/strauss.html.
42. Quoted in Samantha Power, "Rwanda", p. 47.
43. "The government violated the rights of tens of thousands of its citizens by compelling them to reside other than where they choose (sic), by arbitrarily and unlawfully interfering with their homes, by obliging them to destroy or cede their property without due

process and without compensation, by punishing those who spoke out against this policy, and by failing to provide adequate remedy for those whose rights were violated." Human Rights Watch, *Uprooting the Rural Poor in Rwanda*, Washington, London and Brussels: HRW, 2001, p. 2.

44. Ibid., p. 91.
45. International Crisis Group, "Rwanda at the End of the Transition: A Necessary Political Liberalisation", Africa Report no. 53, Nairobi and Brussels: ICG, 13 November 2002, p. 1.
46. Simon Chesterman, Michael Ignatieff and Ramesh Thakur, "Making States Work: From State Failure to State-Building", New York: International Peace Academy, July 2004, p. 15.
47. Claudine Vidal, "Les commémorations du génocide au Rwanda", *Temps Modernes*, March–April–May 2001, p. 24.
48. Eva Hoffman, "The Balm of Recognition", in Nicholas Owen, ed., *Human Rights, Human Wrongs*, Oxford: Oxford University Press, 1999, p. 280.
49. Ibid., p. 302.
50. Paul Ricoeur, "Le pardon peut-il guérir?," *Esprit*, March–April 1995, p. 78.
51. Ibid., p. 79.
52. Ibid., p. 80.
53. Paul Ricoeur, *La mémoire, l'histoire, l'oubli*, p. 643.

8

Speaking from the shadows: Memory and mass violence in Bali

Leslie Dwyer and Degung Santikarma

No, we have not forgotten, and we have not let our children forget. Forgetting has not been our problem. The problem is how to live together with what we still remember.
– Balinese survivor of the anti-communist massacres of 1965/66

Any attempt at facilitating reconciliation in the wake of mass crimes must address the place of memory.[1] For it is memory that links past violence, betrayal and community fragmentation to the ongoing politics of the present, shaping the limits and possibilities of re-imagining social life. The relationship of memory to peace-building may, however, be far more complex than is often considered by policymakers and practitioners. Memory may offer a language of hope, a grounding for assertions of "never again", but memory may also provide the spark for continuing conflict. Memory can foster a sense of shared experience and community solidarity, and memory can feed feelings of persecution and revenge. Memory can provide the material through which social mechanisms – from ritual to myth to informal narrative to formal truth and reconciliation commissions – work to reconsider history and open discussion of the traumatic experiences of individuals and communities. And memory can be suppressed, channelled and transmuted into new forms of subjectivity that may both reproduce and recode relations of inequality, violence and terror.

Since 1999, we have been engaged in a collaborative ethnographic fieldwork project with survivors of Indonesia's 1965/66 state-sponsored

After mass crime: Rebuilding states and communities, Pouligny, Chesterman and Schnabel (eds), United Nations University Press, 2007, ISBN 978-92-808-1138-4

anti-communist violence. Between October 1965 and March 1966, approximately one million Indonesians were killed as alleged communists, some 70,000 others were imprisoned without trial, untold numbers of women were sexually assaulted and hundreds of thousands of family members of those killed or imprisoned were stamped with the label of "unclean environment" (*tidak bersih lingkungan*) and deprived of basic civil rights until the fall of President Suharto's 32-year military-backed dictatorship in 1998.[2] The island of Bali is known to have experienced some of the most intense violence, with some 80,000 to 100,000 suspected leftists (approximately 5 to 8 per cent of the island's population) killed by military and paramilitary forces.[3] For the past four decades – and especially under Suharto's "New Order" government – Balinese have struggled with a legacy of oppression and violence and with ambivalence about articulating memories of terror in a social, political and economic milieu in which state power, tourism capital and the embeddedness of violence in intimate social relations have constrained discursive possibilities. Despite a change in regime, and with it calls for a National Truth and Reconciliation Commission (Komisi Kebenaran dan Rekonsiliasi Nasional) to be formed in Indonesia,[4] these issues have not lost their poignancy for most Balinese survivors of the violence of 1965/66, whose subjectivities and social pathways have been shaped by the ongoing engagement of past and present at the same time as their voices have been marginalized from mainstream discussions of "transitional justice" or "post-conflict peace-building".

Our aim in this chapter is to provide insight into how Balinese have lived together in the aftermath of mass violence, analysing the place of memory in both continuing community tensions and attempts at national reconciliation. Focusing most closely on the experiences of residents of the village of Kesiman on the outskirts of Bali's capital city of Denpasar, whom we have engaged in discussion about their memories of 1965/66 and their negotiations of social life in the aftermath of this period during four years of anthropological fieldwork, we pay special attention to how memories of violence tend to be neither mimetic nor fixed, examining how the public narration of past atrocities has been blocked and channelled in particular directions.[5] We argue that memory in this context is an inherently political act, but one that escapes easy conscription by conceptual oppositions such as oppression versus resistance, silence versus speech, history versus memory, conflict versus reconciliation or a distant past and its "working through" or "letting go". Through this close focus on processes of recalling and distancing violence, a number of key questions emerge: How is past violence located in contemporary social practice? How are memories expressed or hidden in a social field dense with traces of betrayal and the fragmentation of intimate relations? And how might processes of rebuilding self and society take place outside of or in critical dialogue with formal peace-building mechanisms?

Like the other chapters in this volume, ours is a work of committed scholarship, grounded in an engagement with local struggles and dedicated to a transformation of the terms through which social justice might be conceived and promoted. In highlighting the specificity of relations among violence, memory and social suffering in Bali, our aim is not to undermine efforts to promote healing and reconciliation through a sweeping deconstructive emphasis on the exceptional complexities of local contexts. Rather, our goal is to put ethnography to practice in diagnosing what the anthropologist and physician Paul Farmer has called "pathologies of power",[6] those relations of injustice and inequality that become situated in bodies, minds and social lives, using these insights to reflect critically and comparatively on contemporary international discourses of "reconciliation", "peace-building" and "transitional justice". Sharing a concern with understanding local concepts and practices of reconciliation, we detail the particularities of the Bali case, but concur with Kimberly Theidon in this volume that reflexive nods to "cultural sensitivity" risk reducing situated experiences of violence to generic platitudes or mere variations on a universalized theme. We argue, together with the editors in the Introduction, that without a fundamental rethinking of the post-conflict intervention packages that tend overwhelmingly to fail to recognize the complex transformations that terror engenders in the aftermath of mass crime, projects to promote social recovery are far more likely to be not merely unhelpful but actively dangerous. It is, we believe, only through serious engagement with the uneven textures of memory and the social fabric in which it figures, and with a commitment to unravelling our assumptions about the patterns peace-building should take in light of such local realities, that positive change has the hope of being achieved. We conclude our chapter with some suggestions for those involved in peace-building efforts, in the hope of helping to close the gaps that currently exist between conflict analysis and the experiences of conflict, between transitional justice programs and the hopes and fears of those who still face injustice, and between discourses of reconciliation and the everyday struggles of those who live together in the midst of continuing suffering and suspicion that all too often passes for "peace".

History, memory and power

> "*Sane pejah tan kecacah antuk babad*" ("The stories of the defeated go unnoted by history")
> – Balinese saying

With the end of 32 years of dictatorship in 1998, many Indonesians began to publicly reconsider the official state history of 1965/66, which framed the destruction of the Indonesian Communist Party (PKI) and its alleged sympathizers as a necessary defence against threats to national order, development, modernity, democracy and civilization. Taking advantage of new civil freedoms in the post-Suharto era, Indonesian human rights workers, some of them supported by international initiatives for transitional justice or truth and reconciliation, began to gather data on the military's involvement in the killings and on the systematic persecution during Suharto's reign of those alleged to have communist ties.[7] A number of Indonesian historians, often acting in concert with victims' advocacy groups, began to reinterpret historical records to challenge the state's official account of what happened on 30 September 1965, when six Army generals and a lieutenant were killed and their bodies thrown down a well called the Crocodile Hole (Lubang Buaya) in Jakarta, sparking accusations of a communist-backed attempted coup against Indonesia's first president, Sukarno, and giving the "smiling general" Suharto a justification for leading a campaign to destroy Indonesian communism "down to its roots" (*sampai ke akar-akarnya*). In 2000, local non-governmental organizations pressed Indonesia's Parliament to authorize a National Truth and Reconciliation Commission (although to date such a body has yet to begin its work). And in cities, towns and villages across the archipelago, those who lived through violence began to speak – sometimes openly, sometimes haltingly, sometimes shuttling nervously between enthusiasm and dread – about their memories of terror, fear and survival.

Such public acts of re-remembering 1965/66 have, however, been met by ambivalent responses, making it painfully clear that a change of regime has not produced simple corresponding shifts at the levels of community, culture and subjectivity. Attempts in 2001 to exhume a mass grave of massacre victims in Wonosobo, Java, sparked a violent anti-communist backlash by extremist Muslim groups, and victims' rights activists have found themselves threatened and harassed by those claiming to be guarding the nation against a revival of communism.[8] Even Abdurrahman Wahid, president of Indonesia from October 1999 to July 2001, who issued a public apology in March 2000 for the role that members of his Nahdlatul Ulama Islamic organization played in carrying out the violence,[9] could not succeed in persuading the Indonesian legislature to repeal the 1966 law (TAP XXV/MPRS/1966) banning both the Indonesian Communist Party and "Marxist–Leninist Ideology", leaving many survivors uncertain about the very legality of speaking about their experiences of suffering.

It is not, however, only an anti-communist right wing in Indonesia that has questioned activist calls to "bring the past to light" in the service of national reconciliation. In our discussions with Balinese survivors of the violence, one of the most important insights they shared with us is that 1965/66 is not simply an event of the past against which one can take a distanced stance. It is not something that one intentionally chooses to either "remember" by way of a truth commission or a revamped national curriculum that aims to replace falsehoods with facts, or to "forget" by way of erasure from the mass media or official histories or through more personal attempts to deny or disregard. It is not, as some Western psychological models might encourage us to think, a traumatic experience located safely in individual or social history, recovery from which involves a "working through" or "letting go" of a destructive past, or the arrival at "closure" through an imposition of meaningful narrative on the chaos of pathologically insistent and fragmentary memory.[10] Rather, the events of 1965/66 have channelled and dammed possibilities for speech, social action and religious and cultural meaning, giving rise to new relations between language, experience, social space and political practice. Violence – real, remembered and potential – continues to reverberate through social networks, marking everyday life and moulding aspirations for the future. For Balinese survivors, "reconciliation" implies not simply a "coming together" of opposing sides of a conflict, but a far more weighted re-imagining of discourses of self, society, community and citizenship.

In part, the endurance of the events of 1965/66 and their continuing poignancy in the present have been effects of the New Order state's persistent attempts to control understandings of what it termed the *Peristiwa '65* or "1965 Incident", to contain a diverse range of terrifying experiences within temporal bounds ("The Incident") while at the same time expanding them into a flexible master symbol ("Communism") that authorized ongoing political oppression. The New Order state's strategies for discursive management included both the repressive imposition of silence upon survivors, and an enthusiastic program of commemoration and symbolic control of the history of the violence. The Suharto regime's official account of 1965/66 was deployed to advertise its claims to rule and to justify its harsh social and political policies as a paternalistic protection against an ever-present threat of communist disorder. Under Suharto, public debate of the events was banned, and alternative analyses of both the alleged coup and the violence that followed were censored. Borrowing from modern biomedical imagery, those accused of being "infected" by the dangerous virus of communism – those who had once been known as neighbours, relatives and friends – were stigmatized and socially alienated, painted in official portrayals as shadowy, sadistic figures laying in wait for a chance to contaminate the beloved nation, which needed to be protected by a vigilant military and a powerful system of state surveillance. (Theidon, in chapter 4, discusses the use of similar rhetoric by the Peruvian military.) For a new generation of Indonesians, the halting tales their parents might have told of their experiences – or the deep silences they may have effected to preserve their safety – were drowned out by the insistent rhetoric of the New Order, which staged regular "remembrances" of the alleged 30 September coup and the state's victory over communism, and which spread images of communist evil and bloodthirstiness through the school curriculum, public monuments such as the Crocodile Hole and the Museum Pengkhianatan PKI (Museum of the PKI Treachery) in Jakarta and propaganda pieces such as the state-produced film *Pengkhianat G/30/S (The 30 September Movement Traitors)*, which was screened on public television and in classrooms each 30 September until 1999. One Balinese university student whose grandfather had been killed in the violence, which took place 15 years before his birth, described to us how his understanding of his family history had been shaped by such state rhetoric: "Starting in elementary school I learned that communists were evil and violent, and I was confused about how my own family could have been among them. But when I asked my mother how Grandfather could have been such a bad person, she said nothing. Only later did I realize that her silence was meant to protect me."

The maintenance of these official narratives of communist evil and threat continued throughout Suharto's reign, despite the global thaw in Cold War rhetoric that marked the 1990s. Up until Suharto's fall – and even after – state officials regularly animated the spectre of communism as an instrument of social control, dismissing almost any sort of social or political protest as the work of "formless organizations" (*organisasi tanpa bentuk*) of communist sympathizers or as the result of provocation by "remnants" of the PKI. Warnings to remain on guard against communism were typically expressed in the command *awas bahaya laten PKI/komunisme* ("beware of the latent danger of the PKI/communism"), rendering "communism" less a matter of party affiliation or intellectual position than an invisible but inevitable aspect of virtually any challenge to Suharto or his military regime.[11] Labour protests, attempts at unionization or the formation of political parties, or the use of discourses of "human rights" to counter state control of civil society – all were linked in state rhetoric to the lurking threat of communism.

The importance placed on capitalist development by Suharto's state also shaped the context in which memories of violence could be articulated. Beginning in the 1970s, the New Order, with the assistance of the World Bank, embarked on an ambitious project to build on colonial-era stereotypes of Bali as an exotic, enchanted island paradise, as well as classic anthropological representations of Balinese values of social harmony and consensus, to make the island the nation's premiere "cultural tourism" destination. By the mid-1990s, over 1,000,000 foreign tourists were visiting Bali each year. This tourism industry – upon which some 80 per cent of Balinese depend, directly or indirectly, for their livelihoods – has simplified and commodified representations of a harmonious Bali, turning them into spectacular commercial displays used to advertise the island as an outpost of peaceful, pre-modern culture where life revolves around ancient, apolitical religious ritual and social relations are based on the avoidance of conflict.[12] Not only Bali but the Balinese themselves have been subjects of a representational regime that defines appropriate touristic subjectivity through government campaigns such as *Sapta Pesona*, "The Seven Seductions", which exhorted Balinese to be clean (*bersih*), friendly (*ramah*), orderly (*tertib*), beautiful (*indah*), safe (*aman*), preservationist (*lestari*) and memorable (*kenangan*) in order to maintain their ability to attract tourists. Tourism attempted to cover up violence with layers of such symbolism, at the same time as it often literally covered up traumatic history, as in the case of one five-star beachfront resort in Seminyak, South Bali whose lushly landscaped grounds are known by the local community (but not, of course, by the vast majority of its guests) to cover a mass grave containing bodies of victims of 1965/66.[13]

It is important to recognize, however, that tourism is not merely a discourse produced by Balinese for consumption by an outside audience. Tourism in Bali acts not only as an image-producing industry but, to borrow a concept from Jacques Lacan, as an imaginary, a symbolic order that initiates humans into subjectivity, language and social law. Government agencies charged with promoting tourism as the key to developing Bali have recognized the power of tourism to not only attract foreign exchange but to work as a call to self-control for Balinese, who are exhorted neither to challenge the status quo nor to call public attention to past or present violence within families or communities because a fickle tourist audience might be watching. The combined effects of such discourses have had serious effects on survivors of 1965/66 and their ability or desire to speak about their experiences, especially in public. Under Suharto, articulating memories that contradicted official narratives was a dangerous act that risked harsh response from the state. But even in the post-Suharto period, when a new openness finally seemed possible, survivors with an economic interest in maintaining tourism-industry images of a non-violent Bali have often been deeply ambivalent about voicing traumatic memories, recognizing that this is generally not the kind of "culture" tourists wish to consume. Indeed, one of the many bitter ironies of 1965/66 is that many survivors of the violence who were marked as being linked to communism and thus were barred from most employment were forced into the informal economic sector. Many survivors who began by selling trinkets to tourists on the beach in the early 1970s when mass

tourism was first developing have ended up becoming successful participants in the industry, giving them a serious economic incentive to censor
their own memories. Speaking about 1965/66 in ways that counter official
history has, in other words, been understood as not only politically dangerous but economically irrational.

Recognizing the powerful role of the state in managing Balinese relations with the past has important implications for understanding Balinese
ambivalence about projects that call upon survivors of mass crimes to
support reconciliation in the name of national unity. In post-Suharto Indonesia, democratic subjects, reconciled among themselves, with their
histories, and with the responsibilities of citizenship, have been identified
as the necessary building blocks for constructing a new nation. Yet translating "reconciliation" into practices of reshaping power and personhood
has been a complex and contested endeavour. There are no terms in the
Balinese language that correspond to the key notions of "forgiveness",
"amnesty" and "witnessing" embedded in many models of truth-telling
and reconciliation. This is an important matter, for it highlights not only
the cultural implications of disseminating concepts of reconciliation, but
the ways in which many Balinese have perceived the Indonesianized
term *rekonsiliasi* as part of a language emanating from the Indonesian
state, and beyond it, the West. Speaking of rekonsiliasi, then, is to insert
oneself in a discursive space occupied by an array of powerful linked
terms, including *reformasi* (political reform), *partisipasi* (participation)
and *demokrasi* (democracy). To engage with rekonsiliasi as it has been
articulated by political elites within the context of national unity has
been to position oneself within particular framings of citizenship about
which Balinese victims of state violence and the curtailment of civil rights
have frequently been highly suspicious. Many Balinese also recognize
that despite the resignation of Suharto, numerous structures and relations of power and inequality remain intact, including the national history
textbooks, which still fail to even acknowledge that the mass killings ever
occurred. Reconciliation in this context becomes a matter not just of
dealing with a past, but also of facing its continuing traces in the present.

The intimacy of terror

If we recognize that peace-building in the aftermath of state-sponsored
violence entails far more complex transformations than replacing official
histories with local memories, what, then, of the place of memory in
reconciliation at the community level? As important a role as the state
played in directing discourses of communist threat and anti-communist
violence, the continuing power of 1965/66 to shape Balinese social life

and subjectivity has also been an artefact of the context in which the killings and their aftermath were embedded in Bali. To recognize this is not to fall into the worn rut of attributing the intensity of the 1965/66 violence in Bali to an exotic "Balinese culture" or to a fundamentally irrational Balinese temperament inclined to periodic outbursts of wild psychosis or *amuk*[14] – the double that constantly haunts the image of a peaceful, harmonious Bali that has been promoted by the state and the tourism industry. It is rather to recognize the extent to which violence entangled itself in local communities and kin groups, as neighbours killed neighbours and relatives killed relatives, and the very assumptions and expectations brought to bear on social life shifted. It is in the spaces created by these events and their continual unfolding in and into the present – spaces in which state scripts are reproduced even as they are rewritten – that memory arises in complex engagement with official history.

During the violence, there were few Balinese social groupings, whether familial, religious or community-based, that were not fractured by deaths, disappearances and arrests or the threat of such occurrences. Although there were serious tensions in pre-1965 Bali between the organized political left and the organized political right, much of the bloodshed on the island followed lines of social conflict that were local, diverse and shifting, conflicts that cross-cut and shaped formal political allegiances even as they were manipulated by the state to give particular forms to the violence. (See Theidon in this volume, and Scott Straus, also in this volume, for discussion of similar community violence in Peru and Rwanda respectively.) These conflicts erupted over issues of caste, over access to and ownership of land, over economic inequalities, and over status and inheritance within extended families. The violence also worked to exploit and intensify existing inequalities between classes and between genders, underscoring the marginality of women and the poor.

Unlike in many other areas of Indonesia, where the violence of 1965/66 can be described as an intensification of long-standing tensions between communist and nationalist party members or between communists and orthodox Muslims, these conflicts that presaged the violence of 1965/66 in Bali did not always map clearly onto party divisions or result in the same outcomes. For instance, by the 1960s, caste was openly acknowledged in many areas of the island as a major site of social tension, and in Kesiman several local *banjar* (sub-village hamlet associations that organize local politics and ritual) formally split in the late 1950s into separate high caste (*triwangsa*) and commoner (*sudra*) banjar. However, membership in political parties did not always follow one's caste status and local political parties, including the Bali branch of the PKI, did not necessarily or consistently place caste on their political agendas. In some villages, including Kesiman, where the traditional aristocracy was powerful enough to have had privileged access to modern Dutch-sponsored education, it was they who formed the core of the local leftist organizations' memberships. In Kesiman, the principle interests of aristocratic leftists were not in opposing "feudalism", including caste privilege, or in reordering systems of land ownership dominated by the royal houses, but in promoting an oftentimes diffuse notion of a universal modernity, including expanding access to modern education, bringing Balinese Hinduism in line with what they saw as the "pure" Hinduism of India (implying, most controversially, the elimination or "rationalization" of certain Hindu–Balinese rituals) and making Bali no longer seem "backward" in the eyes of the world. In other villages – especially those where the left-sponsored land reforms that began in early 1961 threatened to put substantial dents in royal land holdings – it was more often commoners who supported the leftist groups as a means of challenging exploitative land tenure and sharecropping arrangements and the aristocracy who opposed them. And in still other villages, traditional patron-client ties between aristocrats and commoners included shared party affiliations. Likewise, when the violence erupted in Bali in late 1965, it exploited caste conflicts differently according to these local political configurations. In some villages it was mainly those of the Brahmana caste – leftists and non-leftists alike – who were killed, in others the aristocracy (*satria*), and in still others commoners. In other locations, caste seems to have had little to do with the patterns the violence took.

In some cases, it would indeed even be inaccurate to say that killings were motivated by political conflicts, at least in the limited manner in which we normally understand such phenomena. Most of the personal narratives that we have heard claim that while there were indeed many Balinese who were known to be and who identified themselves as communists (or as members of other leftist organizations, including the Barisan Tani Indonesia [Indonesian Peasants' Front], Gerwani [Gerakan Wanita Indonesia or Indonesian Women's Movement] or Partindo [Partai Indonesia or Indonesia Party]), a great many of those killed went to their deaths denying formal party affiliation. However, after 1965/66, the label "communist" – a label that blotted out all other formations of identity – was attached to victims and, by extension, to their family and friends and even casual acquaintances once they were dead, as an after-the-fact explanation of their fate and its legitimacy. Stories are told of people being killed over land claims, over inheritance, over long-remembered insults or sexual jealousy or, as in Kesiman where many worked as labourers on the Sukarno-sponsored Bali Beach Hotel project, over resentment at not being hired or incidents that occurred at work. But events or emotions other than political party allegiance which might have provoked people to kill were *post facto* subsumed by a grand state-sponsored narrative of party participation, these alternative narratives dismissed as the products of ignorance, sentimentality or subversive inclinations. The creation and, in the years following 1965/66, maintenance of such thinking was a form of symbolic violence with very real material consequences for family members of dead "communists", who saw their civil rights sharply curtailed. In this context, any real reconciliation would require not only social rapprochement but also a rethinking of the very terms that have been used to describe and explain what happened in 1965/66.

Balinese survivors also describe how, when it became clear that no one with even the loosest of ties to the PKI – such as once having lent one's truck to a known PKI member or once having attended a PKI-sponsored arts performance – would be spared, many who feared being condemned asked family members to kill them, preferring to die at the hands of someone they trusted would carry out the necessary rituals for the dead, rather than at the hands of the military or paramilitary gangs who "disappeared" alleged communists and dumped their bodies in the ocean or in secret mass graves. Others "turned themselves in" at their local banjar halls, where the ritual offerings that are normally made after death were prepared in advance and where banjar members would join together to kill them. Others committed suicide rather than be tortured or disappeared, or drank poison publicly as a way of "proving" they were not communists. There were also several cases in Kesiman where brothers killed sisters, brothers killed brothers or fathers killed children rather than see them sexually abused or tortured or killed by paramilitary gangs, drawing upon and transforming notions of ritual sacrifice through these acts. In our discussions with victims and killers alike, it has become clear that few people felt at the time that there were clear "sides" to take or free options for action or restraint. As the historian Geoffrey Robinson describes in his account of 1965/66 in Bali, the military made it clear through a concerted propaganda campaign that a refusal to actively participate in the project of "cleansing" communism from the national body politic would be taken as an admission of one's own guilt.[15] Even if there were few "real communists" in a particular village, there were severe pressures to create some by whatever social and symbolic elaboration necessary. The strain caused by these injunctions was severe, and indeed some of those who were victimized by seeing family members killed then participated in violent acts themselves. In these cases, categories of "perpetrators" and "victims" overlap and blur, rendering reconciliation less a matter of effecting social intercourse between those estranged by violence than with finding ways to come to terms with the challenge to basic notions of society and self that terror engendered.

These particular configurations of violence have helped to create the context in which memory might now be articulated. To the extent that narrating one's experiences involves positioning oneself as a subject of and in the past, it evokes far more ambivalence for those who can neither imagine themselves as having been unequivocally "victimized" nor "victimizing". The modern juridical language of perpetrators, victims and witnesses, which presumes certain consistent subject positions, or the neo-liberal appeal for truth-telling and national reconciliation, which holds as its premise a transparent notion of historical narrative and as its goal the recovery of national subjects who can be brought together into a shared symbolic community, often falls far short of being able to encompass memory, its articulation and the contemporary politics in which it is embedded. As one Balinese woman survivor of 1965, who lost a husband and a son in the violence, responded to news that "people in Jakarta" were proposing a National Truth and Reconciliation Commission: "Why should I tell them what happened to my family? You know and I know the truth: that nobody knows what really happened." Her concern with the audience of memory, with the uses to which memory might be put, and with the sense that knowledge of the past can be at once shared ("you know and I know the truth") and ineffable ("nobody knows what really happened") requires a model for making sense of multiple pasts that does not limit sense-making to the realm of public narrative.

The end of most of the physical violence by mid-1966[16] signalled not an end to survivors' suffering but the beginning of decades of oppression, as the New Order state elaborated the alleged communist coup attempt into a historical justification for its repressive practices of rule. In the aftermath of the bloodshed, terror settled closely into the space of the family, which became a crucial site for the transmission of fear and the new state ideologies that depended upon it for their maintenance. Not only were families broken apart by deaths and arrests, but also the trauma of these losses was compounded by social sanctions against public mourning for the dead, who were demonized by the New Order state as dangerous criminals who deserved their fate. Especially in those cases where the bodies of victims were never recovered and the cremation rituals that would ensure them a place in the pantheon of divine ancestors were never able to be performed, there remain, to this day, ragged gaps in kinship networks. Normally, Balinese in the Kesiman area are thought to reincarnate back into their extended families, usually within a generation or two of their deaths, and people commonly visit spirit mediums (*balian peluasan*) to determine who has reincarnated in a child. But since 1965, there have been less than a handful of those killed in the violence who have been said to have returned to their families through reincarnation. These painful lingering absences, and the worry that attempts to address them by seeking out victims' remains and holding proper cremations could provoke the state to punch new holes in the social fabric, encouraged Balinese survivors to enact state scripts of appropriate citizenship with often-exaggerated deference, leading survivors to bitterly cite Bali's "successes" at implementing a host of New Order campaigns, from family planning to child immunization to "love your village" development projects to casting votes for the ruling Golkar party.

Despite the common use of concepts like "collective memory" to refer to the recollections submerged in post-conflict social life, the Balinese families that emerged from the violence were not homogenous repositories of shared understandings of the past which can now, in the post-conflict era, be tapped for the truths they contain. Gender was among the most crucial differences that shaped survivors' experiences and the limits and possibilities for their enunciation.[17] In families where men had been imprisoned, killed or "disappeared", women were often forced to shoulder the burdens of caring for themselves and their children alone or in cooperation with other widows. While some women were lucky enough to be received back into their natal families after the loss of their husbands, many were shunned out of fear of the dangerous political visibility thought to accompany them. The hundreds of Balinese women who were jailed for alleged communist affiliations also faced, upon their release, frequent refusals by their husbands' families to allow them to reclaim their children, who are considered by Balinese customary law (*adat*) to belong to the patriline. Not only were former women political prisoners thought to be politically dangerous, they were believed, because of their presumed bitterness and emotional instability, to be more likely to engage in black magic and thus doubly menacing, even to their own children. Women's rights as widows to the lands and possessions of husbands killed or abducted were also easily cast aside by using the stamp of "communist".

Violence did not simply "unmake" families, however. Rather, it simultaneously ossified ties that had previously been fluid to form fixed units amenable to state surveillance, and strained emotional bonds by inserting suspicion and silence into everyday family life. Post-1965, fragmented Balinese families were perversely knit back together by the "clean environment" (*bersih lingkungan*) policy of the New Order government, which claimed that spouses, parents, siblings, children and even grandchildren of those marked as communists were "infected" by political "un-cleanliness" and thus to be barred from participation in the government bureaucracy or civil society organizations. Balinese families, newly corporatized by the use of traditionally flexible and contested kinship relations as tools of political identification,[18] became important sites for social surveillance. Older relatives whose memories of the violence were still strong monitored the younger generation for actions or utterances that could be interpreted by the state as "political", thus risking new repressions on the entire family. Just as survivors of the violence describe the military and paramilitaries' intrusions into the enclosed space of the family compound as a traumatic violation of normal tenets of sociality, this new insertion of the state into family practice and subjectivity is identified as one of the most disturbing aspects of New Order rule. "We still spoke to each other", says one woman, remembering her relations with the several dozen family members with whom she shared both a family compound and a designation as politically "unclean", "but we no longer spoke in the same way. We guarded our words, not knowing who was helping the state guard us."

Extended kinship networks often became fraught with tensions, as "clean" segments of families grew resentful of being linked to their "dirty" relatives, and as those who had been terrorized or had experienced the deaths of close family members suspected their more distant relatives of having offered the information that led to their victimization. Families became sites for the education in and preservation of what Veena Das, writing about the experiences of women following the partition of India and Pakistan, has called "poisonous knowledge", the practical understanding that normative notions of social relations are fictions that may fragment under the strain of betrayal and disempowerment.[19] These stresses were sometimes compounded by family members who manipulated their "unclean" relatives' tenuous positions to claim communally held land as their individual possessions. Taking advantage of victims' fears of the government apparatus, they were able to obtain for themselves the land ownership certificates the Indonesian state, at the urging of the World Bank, began in the 1970s to promote in the name of order and development.[20] While a few Balinese succeeded in moving elsewhere on the island, attempting to leave the stigma of the past and the tensions of the present behind, the vast majority remained in their original communities, where they came face to face with those who had terrorized them or those they had terrorized while attending village temple ceremonies, shopping in the market or walking their children to school. Patterns of everyday life, speech and social interaction shifted to accommodate memories of violence and fears of further reprisals, rendering the past constantly present in social interaction.

The violence also created new ways of speaking and of imagining language. Survivors of 1965/66 often describe it as the time when *ulian raos abuku matemahing pati* – when one could die just because of a word. Spoken words are known in Bali to evoke actions, like the holy mantras of priests or the stories of shadow puppeteers that resonate across the visible (*sekala*) and invisible (*niskala*) worlds, temporarily binding and directing energies, channelling the impersonal potency known as *sakti* that imbues the organic and inorganic universe.[21] The word of a curse, spoken by the powerful, can bring illness or even death, and words can invest the inanimate – a mask, a *barong*, a jar of holy water – with *taksu* or charisma. But in 1965/66, words became new kinds of triggers. Improperly articulated words – an insult never quite forgotten, low Balinese spoken to someone who thought they should have been addressed in high Balinese, flirting exchanges with someone else's wife – could return from the past to provoke horrifically exaggerated responses. One 15-year-old in our village who was said to have "talked too much" for some people's liking was corralled in a wicker cage used to transport pigs and then thrown into the river to drown. A man who saw his neighbour helping to burn down someone's house called out in protest and the next day was dead. And one word above all, the word "communist", held power to determine who lived and died, a power no one word had ever been known to possess before. Uttering the word "communist", speakers shifted social assumptions: No longer did the powerful alone utter words of power but the word itself, for those who dared to speak it in accusation, was imagined capable of saving one's own life and determining others' destinies. Heady, extraordinary, horrific: language became an unstable weapon in terror's fantastic arsenal, like a mythical *keris* dagger, blade loose in the hilt, that could slip and wound its bearer should the flow of battle turn backwards. For as the word "communist" was wielded, it came to mean far more than one who had pledged to party membership or even felt sympathy with the PKI's aims. As the ambitions of those who spoke it extended beyond the mandate of uprooting the PKI to staking social claims, exacting revenge or protecting one's self and family in a treacherously shifting landscape, "communist" transmuted from a symbol of political affiliation in the narrow sense to an indexical sign pointing to the instability of knowledge itself, to the impossibility of accurately reading another's signs in an opaque field of highly charged power relations. As one man who saw several of his family members killed expressed it: "Today you call me a communist, tomorrow someone calls you a communist. Anyone could be a communist as long as someone was willing to name them as one."

Not only were words imbued with dangerous new potential, they became disarticulated from the things they had been thought to represent: *sentimen*, an Indonesianized word from Sukarno's "neo-imperial" West, was popularized in 1965 by army propagandists to refer to local affective ties, with people urged to sever their emotional bonds in order to root out communist evil in their families and villages. A *periksa* or "inspection",[22] an Indonesian word reeking of state authority, of efficient, top-down bureaucracy, could enter the intimate space of one's family home, bringing the state and its subjects into a terrifying new embrace, as paramilitary gangs searched for evidence of women's communist sympathies in the form of hammer and sickle tattoos on the vagina or abdomen, "inspections" that often ended in rape or forced concubinage. *Jatah*, an Indonesian word meaning an allotment or quota, was understood prior to 1965 to refer to the rations of kerosene, rice and sugar given by the government to supplement civil servants' wages, or to the share of the rice earned by a banjar's harvesting society (*sekehe manyi*) that was distributed to each member. But as the killings got underway, a jatah became the number of men a paramilitary group aimed to execute in a particular night – a gift of the state to those who served it, the fruit of one's cooperative labours, became one's gift to the state's vision of a new order through violent dismemberment of the social body. Even words like brother or neighbour or friend turned slippery and treacherous, transformed into new hazards like informers, collaborators and provocateurs. And the emotions this speech engendered often grew so strong as to choke off streams of language and to channel meaning into silent forms.

Articulating memory

Although violence imbued language and social relationships with new ambivalence and uncertainty – ambiguities that continued to fester in the years that followed as state surveillance inserted itself into intimate areas of community and family life – this did not preclude processes of remembering, but rather tended to shift them into indirect registers. One means by which memory has commonly been articulated is in the form of circulating stories, grounded in Balinese Hindu notions of justice, which locate the family as the site of karmic retribution. In our village these include the story of the well-known killer who boasted of hacking his victims apart whose child was later born with stump-like legs and arms. Another tale often told is that of the man, a member of the anti-communist Indonesian Nationalist Party (Partai Nasionalis Indonesia, or PNI), who killed one of his two brothers, a member of the PKI, and later killed himself. Ten years after the events, the surviving brother's wife gave birth to a child who, a psychic informed her, was the reincarnation of the murdered PKI brother. The child, once it became public who he was, was shunned as a "PKI child" within his staunchly nationalist family (although he later grew up to be an activist working to collect data on the killings). There is the story of the nationalist paramilitary leader known to have raped dozens of women accused of having communist ties, and who was later unable to father a child. And there are dozens of other stories of killers who died young, fell ill or suffered various misfortunes of supernatural origin. Such local histories, spread through community networks by rumour and gossip, exist in stark counterpoint to official government narratives, reaching as they do for a realm of justice and historical diagnosis outside the control of the state apparatus. Yet they share the same premise: that the violent past is very much a present matter.

Memory also arises in debates over ritual practice, especially over the role of the body in cremation rites and the role of the state in organizing religious ritual. During 1965/66, the body became a site of terror, both as a target of violent acts and as a locus of unsettling absence. The "disappearing" of those accused of communism not only deprived families of a means of localizing mourning through the performance of death rituals, including communal washing of the body and cremation (*ngaben*) rites, it also led to deep uncertainties about the efficacy of the rituals that were forced to substitute effigies for actual bodies. Beginning in the 1970s, as the state assumed greater control over religious practice in Indonesia, the Parisadha Hindu Dharma Indonesia (PHDI), the official state-regulated organization that claims authority over Hinduism in Indonesia, began to sponsor *nyapuh* – "sweeping" or "cleansing" rituals that were said to act in lieu of cremation for those who remained un-cremated due to neglect, lack of financial resources or, implicitly, because the location of their bodies was unknown to their families.[23] PHDI officials insisted that it was the cremation ritual's purification of the "soul" (*atma*), not the presence of the material body of the deceased, that made a cremation effective at returning the dead to the realm of the divine ancestors. Yet family members of those killed in 1965/66 often refused to accept this new theological stance, relying on the continuing absence of their disappeared family members as reincarnated in their children to keep memory alive in contradiction of official erasures from national belonging and in opposition to official claims about ritual practice.

Other sites of memory include the return of the dead via supernatural channels to a social influence from which the state attempted to exclude them. Some – although by no means a majority – of the family members of those killed in 1965/66 maintain contact with their lost relatives, communicating through spirit mediums, hearing their whispers (*pawisik*) in dreams or speaking with the voices of those dead considered to have already become deified ancestors in trance (*kerauhan*). Ibu Ari, a woman who lost her husband and brother in the violence, described the first time she was visited by her brother after his death:

> We were so close, so very close. So close that when he died that afternoon, when he was killed, who knows where, nobody knew the place, that same night he came looking for me. He called out to me three times. I had already fallen asleep over there, next to that small coconut tree. Already he was looking for me. We were so close. He would tell me everything. If he spoke to our older brother once a day, he would speak to me ten times. He had left his watch behind. The day he died, his first son was just 42 days old, it was the day of his

dedinan ceremony. He said to me [about the child], "Later, when he's grown, don't forget about him. It doesn't matter if you have nothing to eat, you must give him the food from your own mouth, for this child who still lives." He told me to sell the watch to pay for the dedinan ceremony. Three times he came to me, coming back and forth, telling me, "Remember, remember, remember". I was so shocked. I didn't know that he was dead until the next day, when someone came to tell us he had been killed. They never told us where the place was where he had died, just that he was dead. He told me to remember.

As the years passed and the New Order continued its project of history-making, characterizing those who died in 1965/66 as communists who were willing to destroy family, religion and state in pursuit of their evil aims, Ibu Ari continued to be visited by her brother. Often he would just greet her and then depart, but sometimes he would give her instructions about family ritual matters, which she and her relatives followed without question. These instructions had little to do with the stance he had taken while he was alive in favour of simplifying and "rationalizing" religious ritual – a stance that was later glossed by the state as communist "atheism" – but instead directed Ibu Ari to make additions to the offerings she was preparing to make them more "complete". That her brother, who had exhibited little interest while he was alive in the women's work of offering-making, was now instructing her in ritual procedure was not odd to Ibu Ari; she was aware that once a spirit entered the realms of the dead he or she could change in character. Indeed in the early 1970s, when Ibu Ari was among a group of women visiting a psychic to inquire as to who had reincarnated in a child of the family, it was she who was addressed by the psychic with the voice of her uncle, a PKI member who before his death in 1965 had caused controversy in the family by arguing that his own father should be cremated simply. This uncle, Ibu Ari said, told her that he had changed, that he was now a woman, and exhorted her, like her brother had, to "remember".

Memories too painful or politically dangerous to be uttered may also take root in forms that avoid spoken language altogether. One such case was that of Gung Ngurah, whose family compound had been attacked and set on fire by paramilitaries from a neighbouring banjar, who later killed four of his relatives, including his father. Gung Ngurah's family, although of high caste, had not been wealthy, and had owned little of value except a modern-style cabinet in which his father had stored books. This cabinet, hacked and scarred by the blades of the paramilitaries, who had emptied it and burned its contents, remained in Gung Ngurah's front parlour, where any guest of the family could see it, for over 35 years after the violence, long after Gung Ngurah had become a relatively successful businessman able to afford the furnishings more typical of modern, middle-class Balinese. The battered cabinet was not only strikingly out of place in a room full of chrome, glass and plastic, it sat awkwardly at odds with Gung Ngurah's absolute refusal to say anything about 1965/66, even when other family members brought it up tentatively in conversation. The cabinet, positioned not in the private interior of the house but in the space open to social interaction, was certainly a statement of memory, a political statement not without its own dangers, but one that did not rely on words for its meaning. With this material icon, Gung Ngurah displayed the traces of an alternative history.

Yet it is important to recognize that memory, despite its power to avoid conscription into official histories that replace the subjectivities of survivors with caricatures of political agency, is far from always liberatory. Pak Nyoman, a member of the Barisan Tani Indonesia (BTI), or Indonesian Peasants' Front, who made his living farming corn and sweet potatoes on a small plot of family dry land, managed to escape from the nationalist paramilitary group that had rounded up other BTI members in his village for execution by the military. Hiding behind a stand of trees in the dark, Pak Nyoman watched as his fellow villagers were forced to dig four holes in his sweet potato field, each twenty-five meters long, five meters wide and two meters deep. He watched as over 200 of his BTI compatriots were herded at rifle point, arms tied behind their backs, toward the edge of the trenches. He heard the cracks of the soldiers' rifles and saw the bodies fall into the pits, and then he could witness no more. Pak Nyoman managed to escape to another part of the island, where he found work as a houseboy for an anti-communist family who did not know his history. But several years later he was fired after his employer discovered him reading a newspaper and, suspicious that a poor farmer should be literate, investigated his past and found out he had political ties. Pak Nyoman felt he had no choice but to return to his village and resume his occupation as a farmer on his family lands. He planted sweet potatoes as he had before, and his father had before him. To stop planting the field, he explained, would have been to acknowledge that he knew what had happened there, and to acknowledge his memories would have been to threaten the tenuous peace in his village that allowed him to live. And so he planted, precisely because he remembered. But when the sweet potatoes, fertilized by death, that his hoe uncovered were unnaturally large, some the size of human heads, he sent them by truck to a faraway market, where those who would consume them had no claim on his memories.

Speaking from the shadows

"I'm so sorry," I say to Gung Aji, who has spent the morning showing us where the bones of his brother lie under what it now a plaza of modern shops selling

T-shirts, cellular phones and beauty supplies. "I didn't mean to cause you pain by asking you to remember such terrible experiences." Gung Aji smiles. "Ah, it's not you who has made me remember. I will have these memories until I'm also dead. No, you don't need to feel sorry. It is these memories that make me know I'm still alive."[24]

To understand processes of remembering 1965/66 in Bali, it is important, we have argued, to attend to the multiple ways in which memory may be situated, hidden or expressed in engagement with everyday life and in contradiction to official historical narratives. This is not, however, to suggest that there has been a shared "collective memory" preserved by Balinese survivors of the violence in defiance of state attempts at erasure or commemoration, nor to conclude that "history" and "memory" can be simply opposed. The "collectivities" shaped out of violence – collectivities that were often exaggerations of Balinese social forms encouraged by state surveillance and the "clean environment" policy – were beset by lingering tension and suspicion, saturated with a sense of the ineffability of experience and the inadequacy of language, grown alien and treacherous, to act as a means of free and transparent social communication. Likewise, memory has not been preserved in some sterile space, uncontaminated by the power-saturated discourses that emerged in the aftermath of violence. Yet to recognize the differences through which memory is filtered and out of which it arises – including differences of gender, social location, caste, class or political position – is to refuse to reproduce the master symbol of "Communism" that has terrorized Balinese for so long.

In the political and cultural milieu of Bali in the years following 1965/66, a context that has been distinctly unsympathetic to memory, neither speaking nor keeping silent is an entirely comfortable position to occupy. Memory, in this context, often refuses appropriation into familiar genres of "truth-telling" or realist historical narrative that describe an original trauma long since past. Rather, it is an unavoidable aspect of everyday engagement with the world. Few Balinese can avoid encountering traces of 1965/66 in their families and their communities; these sites of ambivalent memory – knife scars, sweet potatoes, spirit mediums, birth divinations, death rituals, chance encounters in the market or the street – all become unruly ghosts of violence, scars on a social body that may scab but rarely heal, for to close off the wounds would be to foreclose the possibility of memory, and to stop remembering would mean to stop participating in the world that has made survival possible.

Indeed, one of the most challenging lessons we have learned from our work in Bali is that to engage with the place of memory in the aftermath of violence is never a simple matter, whether ethically, politically or theoretically. There is no stable analytic ground from which one might de-

vise universally applicable programs for addressing memory's place in violence. Rather, violence itself shades and shapes memory, the languages
in which it might be articulated, and the social spaces in which it becomes
meaningful, in complex local ways.

We would suggest, however, that the case of Bali does offer some important general lessons for the practice of peace-building. Memory, as we
have stressed, is never simply liberatory, existing in resistant opposition
to official history. Rather, history and memory interpenetrate, as discourses that speak not merely to a long-ago past but to broader relations
of power in the present. Thus projects to promote peace should not assume that the creation of social or political spaces or mechanisms for the
articulation of local memory would necessarily undermine oppression or
recuperate the voices of victims. While silence is arguably an untenable
ethical position, in Bali, to engage with memories of 1965/66 is not only
to expose the terrible history of a state's violence against its own people
and the West's complicity in erasing it, but to enter an often more painful
domain where families and communities remain fractured by memories
of suspicion, betrayal and the intimate reproduction of state power. Likewise, while many Balinese cite a strong desire to speak of the past, expressions of memory cannot always be counted on to pave a linear path
to individual or social healing. Remembering is rarely simply therapeutic
or painful, but is frequently far more ambiguous and ambivalent in its
emotive power and social effects. Programs to address the aftermath of
conflict must recognize such complexities, grounding their work, as much
as possible, in ethnographically informed awareness of not only local
histories but also contemporary conflicts. Thus truth commissions, fact-
finding projects, national or community forums or other programs for
making memories of atrocity and betrayal public cannot be assumed to
constitute a final stage of psychosocial repair, but must be followed by attention to the social and political tensions such endeavours may expose
or let loose.

A linked lesson has to do with the role of "culture" in peace-building.
All too often, transitional justice programs work with general templates
that are then "translated" into local contexts in the name of "cultural
sensitivity". An understanding of local contexts is undeniably crucial; in
the Bali case, it helps to explain why Balinese have expressed much
more enthusiasm about, for instance, ritual means of articulating memory
or the reforging of ritual networks broken by violence than they have
about the prospects for a formal truth commission. An openness to the
diverse forms remembering might take is thus key to planning appropriate and effective projects. However, as we – along with the other contributors to this volume – have cautioned, it is equally important not to ro-
manticize or essentialize culture. In the Balinese case, as in so many

others, struggles over who gets to define "culture" were among those that provoked conflict, and determined whose memories were heard in its aftermath. Peace-building projects need to be wary of resorting to "culture" or "traditional means of conflict resolution" as uncritical categories of experience or analysis, instead making room for the diverse, and politically complex, interpretations of the meaning and import of culture in the wake of mass crimes.

Notes

1. This chapter is a revised version of a paper first prepared by Leslie Dwyer for the International Symposium on Anthropology in Indonesia, Udayana University, Denpasar, Bali, Indonesia, July 2002. It is based on over four years of ongoing collaborative field research in Bali, funded by a MacArthur Foundation Research and Writing Fellowship and grants from the H. F. Guggenheim Foundation, the Haverford College Faculty Research Fund and the United States Institute of Peace. Material from this article was presented at the UCLA Center for Southeast Asian Studies and at Harvard University; we thank audiences at both institutions for valuable feedback. For comments on versions of this article, we thank Mary Zurbuchen, Hildred Geertz, Henk Schulte-Nordholt, Byron Good, Mary-Jo DelVecchio Good and John MacDougall. This article is dedicated to the memory of Gung Nini Raka, one of hundreds of thousands of Balinese survivors whose stories have yet to be told.
2. The exact number of Indonesians killed is unknown and will likely remain so, despite recent efforts at "fact-finding" by Indonesian victims' advocacy groups such as the Yayasan Penelitian Korban Pembantaian (Foundation for Research on the Victims of Massacre). Estimates have ranged from around 300,000 deaths to as many as three million, with a figure of one million frequently cited in academic and journalistic accounts of the violence. The politics of numbering the dead is, of course, far from straightforward, speaking both to the state's desire to block access to non-official historical research and to activists' desires to ground calls for attention to the violence in statistical claims of its significance. It is important to note, however, that while the extent of the suffering wrought by the violence of 1965/66 should be undeniable, survivors often locate its import not in its scope but its intimacy, not in its manageable facticity but in its destabilizing incomprehensibility, not in its right to a place in the annals of the twentieth century's greatest tragedies but in its continuing power to inflect possibilities for living in the present. Gyanendra Pandey discusses a comparable politics of enumerating the deaths that occurred during the partition of British India in 1947, suggesting that such "extravagant, expandable, unverifiable but credible" (p. 91) statistics function to obscure the social production of history and its qualities of rumour. See Gyanendra Pandey, *Remembering Partition*, Cambridge: Cambridge University Press, 2001.
3. Geoffrey Robinson's historical account *The Dark Side of Paradise: Political Violence in Bali*, Ithaca: Cornell University Press, 1995, based on research carried out while Suharto was still in power, gives an estimate of 80,000 deaths in Bali. Activists conducting fact-finding projects after Suharto stepped down from power have estimated the figure to be closer to 100,000.
4. See Agung Putri, "Evading the truth: Will a Truth and Reconciliation Commission ever be formed?" *Inside Indonesia* 73, January–March 2003, available at http://www.insideindonesia.org/edit73/putri%20%truth%commission.htm; Mary S. Zurbuchen,

"Looking back to move forward: A truth commission could bring healing for a tragic past", *Inside Indonesia* 65, January–March 2001, available at http://www.insideindonesia.org/edit65/mary.htm.

5. Our work as anthropologists has drawn upon a range of participant-observation methodologies. Santikarma was born and raised in Kesiman, and together we have conducted fieldwork focused on 1965/66 during a total of four years of residence between 1999 and 2005. In addition to carrying out semi-structured interviews with survivors of the violence, their children and their grandchildren, we have paid close attention to how the violence has been portrayed in national and local public culture, including official speeches, media reports and school curricula, and how memories have emerged, transformed and recombined in everyday social life, especially in local political negotiations and ritual practice. The ability to place the voices of one's interlocutors in a broader social and cultural field of meaning, power and context is, we would suggest, of crucial importance for those working in post-conflict settings marked by barriers and disincentives to speaking openly about the past. Anthropologists, historians and human rights activists are often faced with the challenge of working with methodologies that are better suited to discovering what people are willing to remember than how, what and why they forget. This makes it crucial, we suggest, to consider how a reliance on formal contexts of fact-finding and truth-telling may miss important aspects of the social life of memory, as well as to give deep consideration to the ethical and political implications of one's work (see chapter 1).

6. Paul Farmer, *Pathologies of Power: Health, Human Rights, and the New War on the Poor*, Berkeley: University of California Press, 2003.

7. For an overview of recent work on 1965/66 conducted by Indonesian academics and activists, see Mary Zurbuchen, "History, Memory and the '1965 Incident' in Indonesia", *Asian Survey* 42, no. 4, 2002, pp. 561–581.

8. For discussion of the Wonosobo incident, see Zurbuchen, "History, Memory and the '1965 Incident'" and Femi Adi, n.d., "Corat-coret Tentang Perkuburan Massal di Hutan dekat Wonosobo" (Notes on the Mass Grave in the Forest near Wonosobo) on the Web site of the Foundation for Research on the Victims of Massacre (YPKP), http://www.wirantaprawira.de/ypkp/news.htm. In May 2000, the late Ibu Sulami, a former vice secretary of the leftist Indonesian Women's Movement (Gerwani) and one of the founders of the YPKP, was threatened by members of a group calling itself the "Anti-Communist Command". In September 2000, her house, which served as an office for the YPKP, was burned down (see http://www.wirantaprawira.de/ypkp/sulami.htm).

9. On Nahdlatul Ulama's role in 1965/66, see Robert Hefner, *Civil Islam: Muslims and Democratization in Indonesia*, Princeton: Princeton University Press, 2001.

10. We recognize, of course, that psychological approaches to engaging with the aftermath of mass crimes vary widely, ranging from traditional individual therapy based on biomedical or Western psychiatric models, to community-based or "culturally sensitive" models, including those that reposition the therapeutic process within discourses of witnessing and working against human rights abuses. We would caution against the inscription of oversimplistic dichotomies between Western "individualism" and non-Western "community", or between biomedicine/psychiatry and local healing, with the latter seen as the only appropriate response to suffering. We have, however, been concerned about the ways in which the Indonesian state's attempts to suppress memories of 1965/66 that contradict official narratives have resonated closely with a "pop psychology" prevalent in Indonesian public culture and sometimes present in international humanitarian work that locates memory as a problematic barrier to individual and national "recovery". For example, in the aftermath of the 2002 terrorists bombings of a crowded Bali nightclub, a US-based international aid organization sponsored the placement of a series of public

service newspaper announcements encouraging Balinese to seek treatment for post-traumatic stress disorder, using a headline reading "Ingin Melupakan?" or "Do You Want to Forget?" Those still suffering from the effects of the 1965/66 violence were not included in this program. For a more detailed discussion of the politics of framing suffering in the language of "trauma" or "post-traumatic stress disorder" in Bali, see Leslie Dwyer and Degung Santikarma, "Post-Traumatic Politics: Violence, Memory and Biomedical Discourse in Bali", in R. Lemelson and L. Kirmayer, eds, *Trauma, Culture and the Brain*, Cambridge University Press, forthcoming.

11. Honna details how Indonesian military ideology framed and reframed the notion of "communism" from 1966 to 1998 to address changing "threats" to its power, ranging from pro-democracy activism to globalization in Jun Honna, "Military Ideology in Response to Democratic Pressures During the Late Soeharto Era: Political and Institutional Contexts", in B. Anderson, ed., *Violence and the State in Suharto's Indonesia*, Ithaca: Cornell Southeast Asia Program Publications, 2001. Heryanto discusses the deployment of and resistances to the term "communist" during the New Order in Ariel Heryanto, "Where Communism Never Dies: Violence, Trauma and Narration in the Last Cold War Capitalist Authoritarian State", *International Journal of Cultural Studies* 2, no. 2, 1999, pp. 147–177.

12. For a discussion of how tourism and state developmentalism have shaped discourses of "Balinese culture", see Degung Santikarma, "The Power of 'Balinese Culture'", in U. Ramsayer, ed., *Bali: Living in Two Worlds*, Basel: Museum der Kulturen and Verlag Schwabe, 2001.

13. Much of the work of the Bali branch of the national Foundation for Research on the Victims of Massacre (YPKP) (a very small, poorly funded organization compared to its Java-based colleagues) has consisted of trying to identify mass graves from 1965/66. Hopes for exhuming the bodies they contain, as was done in Wonosobo, Java, have been slim, however. Such land is considered by Balinese to be *tenget* – spiritually "hot" or "contaminated", and thus unfit for Balinese to inhabit or cultivate. Much of this land was therefore sold to non-Balinese or, in South Bali, used to build tourism facilities, meaning that any attempt to find what lies beneath the ground would most likely face serious opposition from the owners of what now lies above the ground. As one activist reminded us: "Tourism is big business, big money. If you take on tourism, the next thing you know you're a communist, and the corrupt *aparat* ["security apparatus", military and police] make sure that you're buried as well."

14. Good and DelVecchio Good discuss the colonial history of *amuk*, described as a culture-bound syndrome unique to Malays, and how the term was later used by the New Order government to characterize political protest as pathology in Byron Good and Mary-Jo DelVecchio Good, "'Why Do the Masses So Easily Run Amuk?' Madness and Violence in Indonesian Politics", *Latitudes*, no. 5 (June 2001), p. 12.

15. See Geoffrey Robinson, *The Dark Side of Paradise*.

16. In Kesiman, there have continued to be sporadic incidences of violence that residents attribute to the tensions that remain in the wake of 1965/66.

17. For discussion of the gender politics of 1965/66, see Leslie Dwyer, "The Intimacy of Terror: Gender and the Violence of 1965–66 in Bali", *Intersections: Gender, History and Culture in the Asian Context* 10, 2004, available at http://wwwsshe.murdoch.edu.au/intersections/issue10/dwyer.html; Saskia Wieringa, *Sexual Politics in Indonesia*, New York: Palgrave Macmillan, 2002. Other works that address women's experiences of 1965/66 through testimonial genres include Annie Pohlman, "A Fragment of a Story: Gerwani and Tapol Experiences", *Intersections: Gender, History and Culture in the Asian Context* 10, 2004, available at http://wwwsshe.murdoch.edu/intersections/issue10/pohlman.html; Carmel Budiarjo, *Surviving Indonesia's Gulag: A Western Woman Tells*

Her Story, London: Cassell Academic, 2000; and Ibu Marni, "I am a leaf in a storm: A woman's political autobiography," *Inside Indonesia* 26, March 1991. Important Indonesian-language discussions of the gender dimensions of 1965/66 include Budiawan, "Merintis gerakan rekonsiliasi akar rumput berperspectif jender", *Kompas*, 1 March 2004; Ruth Indiah Rahayu, "Dampak peristiwa 1965: Hancurnya perempuan kita!" Sekitar.com Internet journal, 2004; Sulami, *Perempuan, Kebenaran dan Penjara*, Jakarta: Cipta Lestari, 1999; Sulami, *Merentang Perempuan*, Jakarta: Cipta Lestari, 2001; and sections of John Roosa, Ayu Ratih and Hilmar Farid, eds, *Tahun yang Tak Pernah Berakhir: Memahami Pengalaman Korban 65, Esai-Esai Sejarah Lisan*, Jakarta: ELSAM, 2004.

18. Hildred and Clifford Geertz's classic work *Kinship in Bali*, Chicago: University of Chicago Press, 1975, notes the contested, flexible nature of traditional Balinese kinship relations.

19. See Veena Das, "The Act of Witnessing: Violence, Poisonous Knowledge, and Subjectivity," in V. Das, A. Kleinman, M. Ramphele and P. Reynolds, eds, *Violence and Subjectivity*, Berkeley: University of California Press, 2000.

20. The politics of land tenure and use in Bali and their relationship to the violence of 1965/66 and the contested figure of "communism" are far too complex to be addressed here. For more detailed discussion of the politics of land in Bali, see Anton Lucas and Carol Warren, "The state, the people, and their mediators: The struggle over agrarian law reform in post-New Order Indonesia", *Indonesia* 76, 2003, pp. 87–126; Mary Zurbuchen and Degung Santikarma, "Bali after the bombing: Land, livelihoods, and legacies of violence", paper presented at the Yale University Agrarian Studies Colloquium Series, February 2004; and Graeme MacRae, "The value of land in Bali: Land tenure, land reform and commodification", in Thomas A. Reuter, ed., *Inequality, Crisis and Social Change in Indonesia: The Muted Worlds of Bali*, London: Routledge Curzon, 2002.

21. For discussion of Balinese concepts of *sakti* see Hildred Geertz, *Images of Power: Balinese Paintings Made for Margaret Mead and Gregory Bateson*, Honolulu: University of Hawaii Press, 1994.

22. Indonesia scholars reading our work have pointed out that the Indonesian noun for inspection should be *pemeriksaan*, not *periksa*. This is true; however, Balinese do not always speak Indonesian as they "should". Grammatically proper or not, Balinese identify *periksa* – both the word and the events – as emanating from the central Indonesian state.

23. These *nyapuh* were especially widespread before large-scale state-sponsored ceremonies, such as the Eka Dasa Rudra of 1979. The ritual claims and counter-claims made during the New Order by various factions within and without the PHDI over the issue of cremation are complex indeed and cannot be fully addressed here. The nyapuh were, as many survivors of 1965 recognized, part of an Indonesia-wide campaign of depoliticization of village life that sought to remove potential sites of local contestation by placing them under state control. For more analysis of discourses of cremation, Hindu "identity" and modernist reform, see Linda Connor, "Contesting and Transforming the Work for the Dead in Bali: The Case of *Ngaben Ngirit*", in *Being Modern in Bali: Image and Change*, New Haven: Yale Southeast Asia Studies Monographs no. 43, 1996.

24. Field notes from a discussion between Leslie Dwyer and a Balinese survivor of violence, August 2004.

9

Shaping political identity through historical discourse: The memory of Soviet mass crimes

Thomas Sherlock[1]

Written from the perspective of a political scientist, this chapter examines the importance of historical discourse in developing new political norms and values in the Soviet Union and in post-Soviet Russia. A polity's identity and self-understandings are influenced in significant ways by representations of the past, and the prospective choices of a political community – socio-political, inter-communal and inter-state – are bounded by official and private narratives. Directly relevant to Russia's developmental path is how it evaluates – or fails to evaluate – the abuses of the Soviet period, particularly the mass crimes committed under Stalin. The chapter advances this argument by examining historical discourse during Soviet *perestroika* and in post-Soviet Russia. Particular attention is devoted to history textbooks for secondary school (high school).

The totality of the mass crimes of the Stalin era is numbing. Alexander Yakovlev, the former Soviet Politburo member who has dedicated himself to uncovering the full scope of the "repressions" of the Soviet period, estimates that at least 20 to 25 million people were killed for political motives or died in prisons or camps during the entire Soviet period.[2] Most of these unnatural deaths occurred under Josef Stalin from the 1930s until his death in March 1953.

Despite the extraordinary dimensions of this tragedy, the Stalinist period is "cold" history for the vast majority of the Russian people. The memories and problems it has bequeathed to Russian society are very different from more recent cases of mass killings that are discussed in this volume, including those of Cambodia, Guatemala, Peru, Rwanda,

After mass crime: Rebuilding states and communities, Pouligny, Chesterman and Schnabel (eds), United Nations University Press, 2007, ISBN 978-92-808-1138-4

Burundi and Bali. In these latter cases, great numbers of perpetrators and victims are still alive and politically active, leaving society with fresh physical and psychological scars as well as significant and immediate political challenges. Here the problem is often re-building society anew through strategies that promote simple coexistence or perhaps reconciliation.

Similar conditions were most evident in the Soviet Union in 1956 as Nikita Khrushchev prepared to discuss tentatively the crimes of his predecessor, crimes in which he had participated. According to Khrushchev, both he and his colleagues remained "scared, really scared. We were afraid the thaw might unleash a flood, which we wouldn't be able to control and which could drown us."[3] Now fifty years later, temporal distance and the arrival of newly socialized generations have altered the relevance of these events for Russia's political elite and for Russian society. Long past are the emotional face-to-face encounters and communal attempts to confront the consequences of mass crimes that are described by several authors in this volume, particularly Kimberly Theidon.

Nevertheless, distant Soviet crimes still have the potential to shape the character of the Russian polity in positive ways if they are not marginalized in collective memory and if the interpretive and explanatory frames of remembrance help society erect safeguards against future abuses. None of this has yet been accomplished in the post-Soviet period. Although the passage of time has weakened Russia's collective memory of the mass crimes of Stalinism, an equally important reason for not properly remembering the past has been the failure over the past 50 years of Soviet, and now Russian, authorities to foster in a sustained way the public acknowledgement of Stalinist mass crimes or the commemoration of the victims of Stalinism. The "trans-generational transmission process" that Béatrice Pouligny, Bernard Doray and Jean-Clément Martin discuss in chapter 1 as the foundation for dignified remembrance, but also for societal reflection, has been supported only episodically by official discourse in Russia.

This political failure to confront the Soviet past in post-Soviet Russia is due most recently to the efforts of President Vladimir Putin to abandon the tentative and half-hearted attempts of Boris Yeltsin, his predecessor, to help Russian society understand the causes for the vast human toll of Stalinism. Putin favours an uplifting and patriotic narrative that supports the strengthening of the Russian state and the promotion of economic modernization. These discursive preferences make it difficult for Russian society to draw vital lessons from the past, define a clear democratic path of development and enforce clear and inviolable limits to state behaviour.

The behaviour of the Russian leadership has led Western observers to assume that the Russian state has completely avoided the Stalinist past. Anne Applebaum in her important book, *Gulag: A History*, concludes that in post-Soviet Russia "former communists have a clear interest in concealing the past: it tarnishes them, undermines them ... even when they had nothing to do with past crimes.... This matters: the failure to acknowledge or repent or discuss the history of the communist past weighs like a stone on many of the nations of post-communist Europe.... This past weighs on Russia most heavily of all."[4]

Applebaum rightly observes that the examination of the mass crimes of the Stalinist past can provide important support for democratization in Russia. However, she is wrong to see only neglect of the past by the Russian state. By not looking beyond the public behaviour of political leaders, she misses the examination and criticism of the Stalinist period in other arenas, particularly Russian history textbooks. For the first decade after the collapse of the Soviet Union, Russia's secondary school teachers, using textbooks written by critics of Stalinism, helped their students wrestle with their own past and draw meaningful conclusions about how Russian society might best govern itself.

Although liberals in the Yeltsin administration supported this process of reform in the school curriculum, Putin halted it after his election as President in 2000, criticizing the publication of liberal textbooks and more broadly undermining the attempts of Russian civil society to remember the painful past. Yet much of Russian society – including many self-described liberals – has collaborated with the state to promote forgetfulness. These pressures from "above" and from "below" to close off discussion of the past have hobbled Russia's ability to pursue the ultimate objective of history, which Pouligny, Doray and Martin define as the ability to "give meaning to past events ... with the hope of preventing or limiting the chances that tragedies will recur".[5]

This chapter, which explores Russia's failure to learn from the past, contains the following elements. The treatment of Stalinist mass crimes in history textbooks – and the fate of those textbooks – receives particular attention. The chapter begins with the delegitimation of orthodox Soviet narratives during Gorbachev's perestroika. This profound blow to the authority of the Communist Party cleared the way for more truthful accounts of Stalinist atrocities and fatally undermined the legitimacy of the Soviet system. The chapter then turns to the post-Soviet period and examines the unwillingness of the leadership of the newborn Russian state to confront Stalinist mass crimes – or the Soviet period as a whole – in any meaningful way. Despite this official silence, liberal scholars, teachers and government officials supported critical historical accounts, particularly in post-Soviet textbooks, which used the example of Stalinist repressions to draw powerful moral and political lessons for contemporary Russian society. The chapter then discusses the attack of the Putin administration on this emergent open discourse, using the case study of Chechnya to illustrate the retreat of the Russian polity from honest representations of the Stalinist past. The chapter concludes with an evaluation of the forces now arrayed against liberal historical discourse. Perceptions "on the ground" are significant in this regard. Putin's manipulation of the past has been supported or ignored by much of Russian society, including many liberals who are aware of the horrors of Stalinism, but who value the Stalin period as a source of national inspiration and cohesion. The growing collusion between state and society to weaken the memory of Stalinism may soon leave the Russian polity unable to guard against similar catastrophes in the future.

Orthodox and revisionist history during the Soviet period

When Mikhail Gorbachev was elected General Secretary in the spring of 1985, the honest study of Soviet political history was all but frozen. As the cornerstone of the regime's legitimacy, Soviet history seemed immutable. The official reconstruction of the past was in essence an elaborate mythology serving the party-state, and those who questioned its truths risked severe sanctions. Although all political systems rely on historical myths to generate support, the reliance on myths in the Marxist–Leninist system is extreme. Basing its rule on a purportedly infallible interpretation of Marxist–Leninist scriptures, the Communist Party purveys pseudo-scientific historical myths that support this claim.

Western scholars initially and logically assumed that Mikhail Gorbachev would follow his predecessors in his treatment of Soviet history given the objective requirement of shielding Soviet hegemonic myths from damaging historical revelations. Against these expectations, the Soviet past was progressively reopened by Gorbachev and regime reformers. Increasingly aware that economic reform was blocked by the weakened powers of his office and by the resistance of entrenched interest groups, Gorbachev began to view historical *glasnost* as a means to justify his program and delegitimate elements of the Stalinist model of development. The expectation of the General Secretary was that both history and Leninist mythology could ensure the dethronement of Stalinist orthodoxy without endangering the system's legitimacy. Glasnost in history was also intended to legitimate a new model of socialism that embodied neglected "Leninist" strands of Soviet ideology.

Gorbachev also came to believe that continued silence on what he called the "crucial" question of Soviet history – how the massive crimes of the Stalin era could occur in a socialist system – would tarnish his reformist credentials and continue to undermine the authority of the Party both abroad and at home. By condemning Stalinism, Gorbachev and the reformers demonstrated their sensitivity to the role that moral responsibility on the part of leadership can play in establishing authority and mobilizing support for reform.[6] And as he reached down into society to expand his political base, Gorbachev clearly expected political dividends from opening the past. On more than one occasion he reminded his audience that a party that finds the courage to "state its responsibility for everything that happened and for everything that did not happen [in the past]" deserved to be considered legitimate.[7]

History and the collapse of the Soviet Union

Perestroika followed a transitional pattern from non-democratic rule in which reformers within the regime mobilize previously excluded societal forces in order to broaden their support in struggles with regime hardliners. This calculated risk by reformers unleashes counter-discourses that challenge the structure of official political communication. In such transitions, anti-regime and anti-state discourse eventually shatters prevailing perceptions of the social and political order while generating new, or resurrecting submerged, collective identities. Previously isolated individuals now identify themselves as groups and mobilize against the regime.

Despite Gorbachev's efforts at controlled liberalization through glasnost and *demokratizatsiia*, these policies gradually escaped the leadership's control, frustrating the goals they were intended to serve. Instead of forging a strong coalition that favoured change within the one-party system, liberalization and then democratization polarized Soviet society. The Russian intellectuals and non-Russian nationalists who emerged from this process armed themselves with their own versions of history, which were turned not only against Communist conservatives, but against Gorbachev's program for system renewal. Calibrated historical criticism in the service of reform was transformed into an increasingly vituperative and one-sided debate about the legitimacy of the Soviet one-party system and its founding myth, the October Revolution of 1917.[8]

The public delegitimation of Soviet myths shocked Soviet society with a flood of negative revelations about the past, particularly the brutalities committed by Stalin. When Lenin was eventually subjected to the same withering scrutiny, the entire official Soviet narrative was called into question, forcing political leaders and academic authorities on the defensive. Emblematic of the crumbling ideology of the Soviet system was the Kremlin's decision in 1988 to cancel secondary school exams and discard existing history textbooks as useless.

Radical discourse weakened the ability of the Communist Party to defend its core myths by spreading confusion throughout its ranks. Those who failed to defect to the radicals were often left disoriented and disillusioned – poor material for political combat.[9] In this sense, radical discourse achieved the central goal of political argumentation – to successfully attack the social status, the public prestige and the self-confidence of one's opponent.[10] Acknowledging the political impact of the delegitimation of the Soviet grand narrative, L. I. Antonovich, the prorector of the Academy of Social Sciences, complained that efforts to connect the Party's "shameful" past with its present activities had "inculcated a sense of guilt in Communists" which had "paralysed" them.[11]

The testimony of Antonovich points to the role that official historical narratives play in the elite dimension of political legitimation. A function of core myths is to unify the governing elite and strengthen its will to rule. Both Karl Marx and Max Weber recognized that the will to power was crucial to elite cohesion and that the strength of this attribute depends on the efforts of the elite to justify to itself its privileged access to power and advantage.[12] Thus Weber observed that the holder of political power "is seldom satisfied with the fact of being fortunate. Beyond this, he needs to know that he has a *right* to his good fortune.... Good fortune thus wants to be 'legitimate' fortune."[13]

Myths – if they are believed – are crucial political assets because they enable the ruling stratum to justify to itself and to others its possession of power and privilege. Fundamental challenges to such myths are dangerous to a settled polity because they undermine the belief of elites in their right to rule. In the Soviet case, such challenges to core myths were particularly damaging because many of the harshest critics of Soviet history come from *within* the ruling elite, holding positions of high responsibility within the Party bureaucracy or political leadership.[14]

The case of Alexander Yakovlev is revealing. An architect of perestroika, Yakovlev was Gorbachev's closest political ally on the Soviet Politburo. By early 1990 the revelations of the Soviet past had led him to doubt the morality of violent revolution and its capacity to create a just and democratic society. Supervising the Politburo commission responsible for the rehabilitation of the millions who were executed or imprisoned under Stalin but were not exonerated during the rehabilitations under Khrushchev, Yakovlev found the work "spiritually exhausting", all the more so because "people I imagined to be heroes are turning out to be ... 'butchers'".[15]

This struggle over the Soviet past eventually destroyed the normative support of the Soviet state by forging new political identities among Russians and non-Russians alike. The institutional elites (armed forces, security forces, party *apparatchiki*) whose power was threatened by the denigration of core Soviet myths finally withdrew their support from Gorbachev and attempted to turn back the clock in the desperate and ill-planned putsch attempt of August 1991. The putsch failed in large part because the exposure of the past had not only threatened their power. It had also stripped these elites of cohesion and the will to rule.

Politics and history under Yeltsin

With the collapse of the Soviet Union, the new Russian Republic faced the problem of developing a meta-narrative that would define its emerging political identity. This essential task was never accomplished in official discourse and ritual. Instead, the regime of Boris Yeltsin pursued a half-hearted association with tsarist historical images while engaging in episodic criticism of the Soviet past. Yeltsin adopted the tsarist two-headed eagle as Russia's national emblem, declared that his personal model was Peter the Great, and attended the burial of the remains of the tsar Nicholas Romanov and his family. Many cities, streets and institutions were renamed or had their old tsarist names restored, and the new government made significant efforts to embrace the Orthodox Church. The regime also attempted to strengthen its nationalist credentials by paying tribute to the heroic victories of the Red Army, particularly those of Marshal Zhukov and the Soviet forces in the Great Patriotic War (World War II). A number of Soviet monuments were pulled down and the Communist Party itself was placed on trial (but to little political effect).

These bridges to the tsarist and heroic Soviet past were flimsy and were never incorporated into a larger, coherent frame that might have focused the attention and energy of Russia's society on the project of crafting a pluralist and civic national identity. Similarly, the new state failed to commemorate the victims of the Soviet regime in any significant way or to engage in effective acts of reconciliation. Monuments supported by civic groups that were intended to foster remembrance of Communist repression were generally denied official recognition or inclusion into official ceremonies. For many Russians, historical justice was denied when the regime failed to hold trials of leading Soviet-era communists, enact a lustration law or establish a truth and reconciliation commission. Although the Kremlin transformed the anniversary of the October Revolution into a national day of remembrance and reconciliation, it failed to commemorate the date in any meaningful way. A recent poll found that

35 per cent of the respondents still thought the day commemorated the Bolshevik Revolution while 43 per cent of the respondents were unable to answer the question.[16]

Yeltsin's extreme, if occasional, politicization of the past was evident during the political crisis of October 1993, which lead to the disbandment of the Russian parliament, and during the presidential campaign of 1996. At both times, the administration and its supporters relentlessly compared the Soviet regime with Nazism to discredit Russian Communists and their opposition to the post-Soviet order. These efforts to mobilize the past, however reminiscent of the Soviet approach to "history", were relatively infrequent, punctuating long periods of silence or indolent engagement on historical issues by the regime.

Yeltsin's erratic and autocratic political personality damaged the prospects for consistent reform, especially in the context of Russia's weak civil and political society. Perhaps most important, the new government failed to institutionalize political linkages with society, particularly through a political party. Had he done so, Yeltsin and his advisors would have had more incentives to frame their program in unified, ideological terms, linking a new historical narrative to questions of state, democracy and economy. That the reformers never accomplished this task allowed their conservative and reactionary opponents to define such issues as the boundaries, goals and character of the Russian political community. Nationalist arguments based on chauvinist historical myths became increasingly common in the marketplace of ideas, particularly in the pulp media and segments of the press.

What explains the Yeltsin regime's ambivalent and neglectful approach to the past? Apart from Yeltsin's poor leadership, and judging by the experience of other transitional cases, including post-Franco Spain, official neglect was due to the fact that Yeltsin and the reformers, having cast aside the (Soviet) sacralization of the past as the basis for regime legitimacy, found less political need for "history" as they shifted their legitimating claims from the past to the present (elections, economic reforms).[17]

Other factors reinforced the regime's approach to the past, particularly the Soviet period. Facing deep divisions in elite and mass society over the legitimacy of the new regime and its reforms and over the geographic boundaries of the new state, the government perceived less and less value in returning to the past. As market reforms and privatization began to exact a heavy political, social and economic toll, a growing segment of Russian society came to regret the fall of the Soviet Union and to view negative assessments of the Soviet past as irresponsible and unpatriotic masochism. Amid such attitudes, the leaders of the Russian government chose to tread lightly on historical controversies.

The ideological content of history textbooks in post-Soviet Russia

Although Yeltsin preferred to avoid the contested terrain of the Soviet past, the official legitimation of his regime rested not only on elections but on an ideology of liberal democracy and anti-communism, if only haphazardly formulated, articulated and practiced. In the absence of a coherent and consistent official narrative, post-Soviet history textbooks have provided the normative and empirical foundation for this fragmented ideology. Liberalism, joined to moderate or civic nationalism, forms the core perspective of these textbooks. The authors are a diverse group by occupation, including historians, political scientists and pedagogical specialists. Some authors are secondary school teachers.

Russian history textbooks under Yeltsin were written in an environment of significant cultural freedom due to the administrative chaos attending the collapse of the Soviet Union and to the liberal ideology of Yeltsin and his supporters.[18] The new regime abolished the Soviet system of tight state controls over the production of history textbooks (the state's selection of authors, the close review of their work and so forth), enabling the emergence of a competitive textbook market that fostered intellectual pluralism. Unlike the Soviet monopolization of the publishing industry, dozens of private and hybrid companies now publish history textbooks. Four of these firms have dominated the textbook market: Prosveshchenie (the reformed state company), Drofa, Mnemozina and Russkoe slovo.

As the writing and distribution of new history textbooks migrated to Russian civil society, the Russian state, through the Ministry of Education, still approved all textbooks for classroom use, and Russian schools could not purchase a textbook with public funds if it has been denied official sanction. Despite periodic allegations of corruption, the process of textbook approval was professionalized to a significant degree during the Yeltsin years and most of the history textbooks on twentieth century Russian history that Russian publishers issued during this period received at least provisional authorization from the Russian government.

Why is history education important to Russia's political development? The collapse of the Soviet Union starkly demonstrated the dangers of preventing the free discussion of the past. By contrast, civic intelligence in established democratic polities is shaped in important ways by knowledge of the past. According to the National Center for History in the Schools (United States),

Without history, a society shares no common memory of where it has been, what its core values are, or what decisions of the past account for present circumstances. Without history, we cannot undertake any sensible inquiry into the political, social, or moral issues in society. And without historical knowledge and inquiry, we cannot achieve the informed, discriminating citizenship essential to effective participation in the democratic processes.[19]

This approach to history is found in a number of Russian textbooks published during the Yeltsin era. These textbooks emphasize the tragedies and complexities of tsarist and Soviet history. Equally important, they often call on the student to explore historical problems and raise new questions, without fear of "incorrect answers". Students are explicitly encouraged to engage the textbook and the teacher in debate, working out "their own viewpoints".[20] Unfortunately, many Russian teachers, particularly those who received their professional education in the Soviet period, require retraining in order to conduct such complex dialogues with their students. Given the limited resources of the Russian government both at the national and local level, the retraining of teachers has advanced slowly. Joint efforts undertaken between Russian teachers and foreign non-governmental organizations such as Euroclio (Netherlands) provide some relief, but the problem remains a significant obstacle to effective history education.

Although the ability of the teacher to explain objectively competing narratives in the classroom is an important attribute of civic intelligence, the textbook and its historical perspective inevitably commands considerable authority in most secondary school classrooms, including those in Russia. What kind of history is remembered by society in its textbooks – which narratives of the past are privileged, and which are not – is therefore important to societal self-understanding.

Simple and complex accounts of the Soviet Past

To what extent do Russian textbooks construct a narrative that fosters critical thinking and democratic values? In analysing Russian textbooks, it is useful to characterize their narratives as either *simple* or *complex*. A simple account employs straightforward and uncomplicated emplotment to support an explicit, overarching message for the reader. This type of structure recalls the flat and unproblematic discourse of Soviet-era textbooks, which portrayed the Communist Party as the embodiment of historical wisdom, thereby justifying one-party rule. Any facts or assessments that might have damaged the integrity of this claim were excluded or substantially distorted. Post-Soviet textbooks with a similar structure reverse the polarity of the Soviet narrative and present the Soviet period as completely negative instead of entirely positive. The internal unity of this kind of narrative is maintained by the inclusion of facts and events that lend themselves to moral judgment, such as mass crimes and other gross violations of human rights. Simple narratives often employ the totalitarian model of politics to guide the reader at the conceptual level.

Unlike simple narratives, complex narratives usually avoid explicit moral judgments or unambiguous evaluations of the Soviet period. Complex narratives usually point to both positive and negative elements in specific historical developments or events, and the reader must be sensitive to the author's assignment of normative weights to such elements.

Textbooks with simple narratives appeared soon after the collapse of the Soviet Union as Yeltsin and his supporters sought to establish the legitimacy of their leadership and program on the basis of Russian nationalism and anti-Communism. A notable example is the first edition of V. P. Ostrovskii's text, which was published in a print-run of 3 million copies in 1992. The textbook carried forward into the post-Soviet period the condemnation of the Soviet past that began and quickly escalated during perestroika, undermining the ideological supports of the Soviet system. Ostrovskii's original text was one of the foundational scripts that helped define the ideology and nascent identity of the new Russian state through a process of "negative legitimation".[21]

In the introduction to a revised version (2001) of this textbook, Ostrovskii and A. I. Utkin, his co-author, approach the question of Russian identity by expressing the hope that their textbook will foster patriotism, which is the "most important condition" for a stable, strong state. But it is not the "state sponsored, hysterical patriotism ... based on contempt and envy" of the Soviet period that the authors value, but patriotism based on "order, freedom, tradition and openness to the world". Arguing that the Soviet period was a "catastrophe", they warn that "who forgets the past will be condemned to live through it again". Ostrovskii and Utkin hope that their "truthful examination" of the past will help Russia "find the right path".[22]

Textbooks with simple narratives approach events with emotional, moral judgments. Ostrovskii and Utkin trace the "catastrophe" of the Soviet period to the Bolsheviks' quest for total power, which engendered brutal attacks on political pluralism, cultural and religious freedoms and economic markets. Discussing the cruelty of the terror tactics used by both sides in the Russian Civil War (1918–1921), Ostrovskii and Utkin argue that the Red Terror was worse than that of the White counter-revolutionaries because it was designed not only to destroy the enemies of the state, but to discipline the working class by eliminating through coercion the right to strike or "even choose your place of work".[23]

The Communist program of forced drafted industrialization in the late 1920s further extended the loss of individual freedom because its enormous demands on society could only be achieved through "total control of the body and mind" of the Soviet citizen. This requirement dramatically increased the importance of the repressive and ideological institutions. The "new Soviet man" became a "cog-man" in the machine of the state, freely manipulated by the political leadership.[24]

Soviet-era narratives had heralded Stalinist industrialization as a heroic achievement that ushered in the Socialist epoch and also armed the Soviet Union for its titanic struggle with Nazi Germany. This account of Stalinist industrialization had been a source of pride and patriotism for generations of Soviet children who had little or no understanding of the social costs of the enterprise. In their counter-narrative, Ostrovskii and Utkin upend this earlier, heroic account. They do so by placing the event in a context of state-sponsored cruelty and suffering. The text emphasizes that Soviet industrialization was financed by inhumane exactions from the Russian peasantry made possible by the violent collectivization of agriculture from 1929–1932. The amount of grain extracted from the peasantry to earn foreign exchange was so excessive that it caused the great famine of 1932/33, a calamity that carried away millions of lives even though the grain bins of the state were full. The narrative attempts to further delegitimate Stalinist industrialization as a Soviet achievement by castigating as "lies" Soviet-era claims that the targets of the Five Year Plans were fulfilled. The entire industrialization program is said to have depended not on the much-praised development of Soviet technology, but on massive imports from the West, which supplied up to two-thirds of the machinery that equipped new Soviet factories built from 1929–1939.[25] In yet another blow against the Soviet heroic narrative, the authors return to the criminal and immoral nature of the Soviet industrialization. In order to secure necessary manpower, the state transformed the concentration camp system established under Lenin into a vast system of forced labour that unjustly condemned millions of Soviet citizens to inhumane work condition on projects of "national economic importance".

Simple narratives, like that of Ostrovskii and Utkin, condemn the entire Soviet period as one of human suffering and injustice caused by the Communist state. Ostrovksii and Utkin intensify the feeling of national loss by extending a positive evaluation to the late tsarist period, particularly the policies of Petr Stolypin. Other textbooks emphasize the lost opportunity of the pre-revolutionary period by arguing that Russian civil society – despite the hostility of the tsarist state – was developing at a rapid pace as a shelter for human freedom and dignity.

The integrity of the anti-Soviet leitmotif of Russian textbooks is challenged by a number of historical realities, including the fact that in the Great Patriotic War (1941–1945) millions of Russians went into battle against the German invaders with shouts of "For the Motherland! For Stalin!" In order to maintain thematic continuity but also pay tribute to the heroism and sacrifice of the Russian people, Ostrovskii and Utkin isolate the Soviet government from the achievements of the armed forces and the general population. For example, the reader is told that the Soviet leaders displayed only contempt for Soviet prisoners of war and their tragic circumstances, claiming that "everyone who falls prisoner is a traitor."[26] Those prisoners who survived their ordeal in Nazi prison camps were often sent to the penal colonies of the Soviet gulag.

Like simple narratives, Russian textbooks with complex narratives address the mass crimes of the Soviet period. However, the complex narrative is not committed to a single-minded condemnation of the Soviet era. Compared to simple narratives, complex narratives devote less attention to Soviet violations of political and civil rights, and unlike simple accounts might place Soviet-era crimes within a larger frame that is either neutral or positive. This reduced emphasis on Soviet repressions is due in part to the structure of the narrative, which examines socio-economic, technological and cultural developments that are not easily placed in a negative context or subjected to moral judgments, such as the expansion of public education under Stalin and the achievement of the first manned space flight under Khrushchev.

In their popular and well-regarded textbook, A. Danilov and L. Kosulina construct a complex narrative that discusses the seizure of power by the Bolsheviks and the establishment of a "single-party dictatorship". Attention is devoted to the brutal, mass nature of the Red Terror; Bolshevik attacks against the Orthodox Church and the intelligentsia who did not support the revolution; and the Bolshevik disbandment of the democratically elected Constituent Assembly. This material is presented without emotion or judgment, departing from the explicitly didactic and moral approach of a simple narrative. For example, the simple narrative of Igor Dolutskii quotes Lenin's approval of revolutionary violence "unconstrained by law" in its examination of the fate of the Russian Constituent Assembly in 1918. Dolutskii asks the student to "ponder the dangers" that Lenin's ideas held for Russia.[27] By contrast, Danilov and Kosulina offer a more subtle, incomplete judgment, writing that the Bolsheviks' elimination of the Constituent Assembly led many moderate socialists to consider violence as the only way to dislodge the Bolsheviks from power.

Danilov and Kosulina also offer a dispassionate assessment of Stalinism as they summarize its "contradictory" nature. On the one hand, they acknowledge that important strides were made by the Soviet state in eliminating unemployment and illiteracy, and in providing the population with social supports including access to free education and health care. Soviet scientists achieved global prestige and the highest international honours. Most important, the Stalinist system mobilized national resources to construct an industrial base that enabled the country to defeat the German war machine.[28] On the other hand, the authors point to the horrific losses in human life and freedom in all areas of society that were made possible by Stalin's complete control of the political system.

The most important recent textbook to employ a complex narrative is *Istoriia otechestva. XX – nachalo XXI veka* by N. Zagladin, S. I. Kozlenko, S. T. Minakov and Iu. A. Petrov, published in 2003 by the independent publishing house Russkoe slovo.[29] Addressing the central question of the Stalin era, the authors maintain that the Stalinist system "allowed for the concentration of national resources to resolve enormous and unprecedented problems". However, they find that "the cost of creating this centralized system of control ... was unimaginably high. The cost was the suffering and death of millions of our countrymen."[30]

Despite this assessment, Zagladin's text devotes more attention than other complex narratives to historical facts and events – before, during, and after the Stalin era – that are described as Soviet achievements. Contributions in science, sports, the arts and literature are discussed but emphasis is placed on socio-economic modernization. Evaluating the Soviet model of development, the text reminds the reader that Russia emerged from the economic destruction and horrendous human losses of two world wars to rebuild its economy and emerge as one of two superpowers on the world stage. In many sectors of scientific and technological development the Soviet Union "outstripped its rivals" including the United States.

As it discusses these and other positive elements, including Soviet initiatives under Gorbachev to end the Cold War, the textbook departs from other complex narratives in its evaluative tone, encouraging the reader to adopt a favourable assessment of these events. The text also proclaims that Russia has succeeded at a task which "no other country in history has ever confronted" – to create simultaneously a market economy and a democratic political system.

In their conclusion, the authors observe that the Soviet model of development, whose achievements were purchased at high cost in destroyed lives and lost freedoms, has been replaced by a new program of modernization based on the development of a market democracy and integration into the world economy. Russia's authority and influence are said to remain significant in international affairs; Russia remains one of the "centres of stability in the contemporary world", providing initiatives to solve global problems that affect the interests of all humanity.[31]

Although this account seeks to stimulate Russian pride through moderate Russian nationalism, it does not pass over in silence the crimes of the Stalin era. Furthermore, the textbook concludes with a strong expression of Russian nationalism that is civic and democratic in form. Nevertheless, given the enormity of the Soviet abuse of power and its legacy in shaping Russia's contemporary political institutions and political culture, the reader might logically expect Zagladin and his co-authors to devote more attention to the problems of Russian democratization, suggesting how the lessons of the Soviet period might help Russia grapple with those difficulties. Instead, the textbook implies that the problems of post-Soviet democratization were confined to the Yeltsin period and have now been solved in the Putin era. Of course, this elision may simply reflect the understandable reluctance of the authors to question Putin's efforts to circumscribe political pluralism. However, the very structure of the textbook – shaped by the concept of modernization – significantly limits the discussion of the intrinsic value of democracy. Unifying but also constraining the text, the concept of modernization places the Russian state at the centre of the narrative, not the issue of mass crimes or the problematic of the democratization.

Official discourse in the Putin era

The reassessment of the Soviet period in more positive terms in Zagladin's textbook reflects important political and cultural changes in Russia. The text's emphasis on Russian modernization points to the central preoccupation of Putin, who succeeded Yeltsin as president of Russia in 2000. Continuing Russia's centuries-old conceptualization of political and socio-economic development, Putin's view of modernization is dominated by the idea of a strong state that mobilizes society to achieve its goals. Gradually assuming more specific form over the period 2001–2004, Putin's program now threatens the significant freedom that characterized the production of Russian textbooks since the collapse of the Soviet Union.

In order to better understand this threat, it is useful to compare Putin's hortative rhetoric to that of Stalin. In 1931 Stalin sought to mobilize the Party and the nation for his forced-draft economic program by stressing the need to defend the Russian homeland against foreign threats:

> "We have a fatherland and shall defend its independence. Do you want our fatherland to be beaten and lose its independence? If not, then you must abolish its backwardness.... We are fifty or a hundred years behind the advanced countries. We must make good this lag in ten years. Either we accomplish this or we will be crushed."[32]

On 16 May 2003 Putin delivered his annual address to the Russian Federal Assembly. According to Putin, "Russia must concentrate all its energy in ensuring that Russia will take its recognized place among the ranks of the truly strong, economically advanced and influential nations.... Not only will people feel proud of such a country ... they will remember and respect our great history." In order to achieve this objective, "we must consolidate, we must mobilize our intellectual forces and unite the efforts of the state authorities, civil society and all the people of this land".[33] Putin told the audience that Russia's modernization must not be delayed:

> [History demonstrates that] when Russia is weak ... it threatens the collapse of the country.... We [now] face serious threats.... We are surrounded by countries with highly developed economies. We need to face the fact that these countries push Russia out of promising world markets whenever they have the chance. And their obvious economic advantages serve as fuel for their growing geopolitical ambitions.... It is my conviction that without consolidation at a minimum around basic national values and objectives, we will not withstand these threats.[34]

Reminding the gathering that Russia had always surmounted serious challenges to its existence in the past, Putin stated that the historical task of maintaining the immense Russian state and preserving Russia's international position was "not just an immense labor, it is also a task that has cost our people untold victims and sacrifice".

There is little evidence to suggest that Putin wants to return to extreme, Soviet methods of controlling society or that he rejects Russia's gradual integration into the global economy. However, Putin's refusal to condemn the character of Soviet modernization, and his apparent willingness to trace the human losses under Stalinism to the requirements of state survival, mark an important shift in official discourse that further reconstructs and simplifies the past through deliberate forgetfulness.

Putin's treatment of the Soviet past in other respects is also cause for concern. At a cabinet meeting in August 2001, Putin's prime minister (Mikhail Kasianov) reviewed the content of several history textbooks. Kasianov found their negative assessments of tsarist and Soviet history – and their criticism of post-Soviet reform – to be unwarranted and "astonishing".[35] He then announced a competition for new textbooks on Russian national history. The Zagladin text was later named the first of three winners in this competition.

Shortly afterward, in November 2003, the Russian Ministry of Education withdrew its official approval from Igor Dolutskii's textbook on twentieth century Russian history. Published in multiple editions over the past decade, the textbook portrays the Soviet state as a brutal, totalitarian institution. Dolutskii's dark account also bridges the post-Soviet divide, and in its last section the author asks the reader to evaluate the statements of Russian liberals who criticize Putin for introducing a "police state", an "authoritarian dictatorship" and a "regime of personal power".[36]

Dolutskii's provocative assessment of contemporary politics (absent from the previous edition of the textbook and unusual for Russian history textbooks as a whole) was not the only reason for the government's actions against Dolutskii. President Putin met with historians two days after the Ministry removed Dolutskii's textbook from its list of recommended history books. According to Putin, it was now time to "help raise young people in the spirit of pride for their fatherland and its history".[37] The harsh assessments of the Soviet period in many Yeltsin-era textbooks were understandable given the earlier need "to destroy the old [Soviet] system". But that task was now accomplished, and it was time to "clear out the scum from textbooks".[38]

The attack on Dolutskii put the academic and educational establishment on notice that history education was an important tool for the mobilization of support for state-led modernization. This incident followed other efforts by the government to remove, albeit gradually, the negative valuation of the communist period from the public sphere, replacing it with symbols and narratives celebrating the Russian state as the institution that unifies the tsarist, communist and post-communist periods. Thus, the old Soviet anthem is now played in halls emblazoned with the imperial double-headed eagle.

Soviet crimes against Chechnya and the problem of self-censorship

The obstacles in Russia to understanding and learning from the past are in full display in the Russian–Chechen crisis. At no point in the post-Soviet period has Russian policy been guided by an understanding that the Chechen people suffered greater political, physical, cultural and economic repression under the tsars and Communists than perhaps any other ethnic or religious group in the Russian empire or the Soviet Union. This legacy of almost two centuries of historical grievances against Russia largely accounts for Chechen secessionism in the 1990s and for the ferocity of Chechen resistance to Russian attempts to quell the Chechen rebellion.

It is not surprising that the most unstable region in Russia is the North Caucasus, which was the bloodiest outpost of tsarist expansion in the nineteenth century. Over a period of four decades (1816–1856), tsarist forces battled fierce resistance from mountain nationalities, particularly the Chechens. In this prolonged and brutal struggle, civilian casualties were high, and forced, mass deportations from the Caucasus to the interior of Russia were common. Hundreds of thousands of members of the autochthonous communities fled to Turkey and other regional states.

This pattern of extreme violence by the Russian-dominated state toward the Chechen nation recurred in early 1944, when the Chechen nation, now part of the Soviet Union, was accused by Stalin's regime of mass collaboration with the Nazi invaders. The Chechen nation was deported en masse to Siberia, Kazakhstan and Kyrgyzstan. The collective memories of these calamitous events have shaped Chechen identity and the Chechen "othering" of the Russian state and the Russian people. These memories are the fuel that fires the Chechen bid for independence from Russia, which has produced two sanguinary wars: 1994–1996 and 1999 to the present.

Why do contemporary Russian history texts examine more openly and honestly the Stalinist crimes committed against other non-Russian nationalities, such as the Balts and Ukrainians, but often remain silent on the brutalization of Chechens? The same fear that drove many Soviet historians to deny the forced incorporation of the Baltic states in 1940 now guides many Russian textbook authors in their treatment of Chechen history – that the open and honest discussion of past crimes will not lead to peaceful coexistence or perhaps reconciliation but to the further unravelling of the new Russian state.[39] In the case of Chechnya, the Stalinist past is still "hot": it is immediately relevant to the present, making its discussion potentially dangerous. In this sense, the fears of many Russian intellectuals are similar to those of the Russian leadership and political elite.

Russian textbooks also often avoid, minimize or mischaracterize the Chechen problem because the Russian state itself influences how history textbooks address the conflict in Chechnya. A comparison of Kremlin policy towards the Russian media in the two Chechen wars illustrates this point. In the first war, the Russian media exposed the brutality of the Russian army in Chechnya, generating sympathy and interest in the Chechen problem throughout Russian society.

Having "learned" from the past, the Russian government imposed strict controls over the media in the second war, punishing journalists and excluding observers who are critical of the Kremlin. Mindful of the potential costs of behaviour deemed oppositional by the Kremlin, most scholars and writers are unwilling to launch a frontal assault on Russian policies in Chechnya in their textbooks. Instead, they reluctantly accept the Kremlin's representations of the origins and course of the conflict.

Self-censorship on the issue of Chechnya is also common in textbooks. A good example is a new book on twentieth century Russian history by prominent liberal academics published in 2004. Written under the supervision of Academician Alexander Chubarian of the Institute of General History, the textbook condemns the mass crimes of the Stalin period at length and points to the necessity of democratic controls over the Russian state.[40] On Chechen history, the textbook tells the reader that on a single day – 23 February 1944 – hundreds of thousands of Chechens and Ingush were rounded up by Soviet army and police detachments and deported to Siberia. Stalin then abolished the Chechen–Ingush autonomous republic to "destroy among the indigenous peoples all memory of their homeland".[41]

However, when Chubarian's narrative reaches the late Soviet period it fails to explain Chechen support for secession in 1991 in terms of the long history of Russian and Soviet brutalization of Chechens. Although the text accurately describes the rule of Dzhokhar Dudaev (the secessionist leader) as dictatorial, it incorrectly traces the cause for the Russian invasion of Chechnya in 1994 to the emergence of Chechnya as a base of international Islamic terrorism during the period 1991–1993. Although this explanation for the invasion of Chechnya dovetails with Kremlin representations, it is a distortion of actual events. Chechnya became a centre of terrorist activities only after the radicalization (and fracturing) of Chechen society under the blows of the Russian Army. This avoidance as well as distortion of historical causation is discomfiting evidence that self-censorship constrains discourse on the issue of Chechnya.

Societal assessments: The West, the Chechen deportations and the image of Stalin

The failure of Russia to examine fully its painful history has left the Russian polity ambivalent about the value of democracy as a system of government. According to one scholar, the problem of self-definition remains the "single greatest challenge" facing Russian society.[42] Opinion and attitude surveys provide evidence of the problem. Fifteen years after the collapse of the Soviet Union, many Russians want to restore Russia as a Great Power and are relatively disinterested in the means used to regain that status. When asked in late 2003 how they wanted Russia to be perceived by other nations, 48 per cent of survey respondents said "mighty, unbeatable, indestructible, a great world power". Only 3 per cent wanted Russia to be viewed as "peace-loving and friendly", and only 1 per cent as "law-abiding and democratic". Another poll found that 56 per cent of the respondents "practically never" viewed themselves as "European" or "western".[43]

Opinion polls also reveal significant anti-Western sentiment in Russia. One survey found that 41.1 per cent of the respondents believed that the West was attempting to turn Russia into a third-world country, while 37.5 per cent of the respondents stated that Western nations were intent on breaking up and destroying Russia completely.[44] In other polls, 72 per cent of the respondents described themselves as "hostile toward the United States" and 69 per cent believed that the West desired the collapse of the Russian economy.[45]

It is somewhat unclear as to whether these anti-Western and anti-American sentiments are durable and deep-seated.[46] Other surveys find Russians less hostile towards the West.[47] Nevertheless, anti-Western sentiments of any breadth and intensity weaken support for political and cultural pluralism in Russia. Russian Nationalists and Communists view negative attitudes towards the West as vital political capital, encouraging them to intensify chauvinist discourse. Most important, such attitudes help discredit Western liberal democracy as a viable model for Russian development.

Opinion polls in contemporary Russia also reveal that the Soviet period, and particularly the Stalin era, is remembered by a majority of Russians as a time when Russia commanded international prestige and power. This orientation significantly weakens the ability of Russians to make sound moral judgements about the past or contemporary political life. One recent public opinion survey found that 48 per cent of all respondents believed that Stalin's mass deportation of the Chechen nation was "completely justified" or "mostly justified". Unfortunately, 52 per cent of the respondents aged 18–24 – the age group that is often the bearer of liberal values – supported such views.[48]

Due at least in part to this failure to see the deportations of Chechens as crimes against humanity, barely 16 per cent of Russians today profess concern over current human rights violations against Chechens by Russian security forces. Equally troubling is the fact that only about 12 per cent of Russians see themselves as strong supporters of civil liberties in general.[49]

The steady rehabilitation of the image of Stalin among Russians since the collapse of the Soviet Union graphically reflects the uncertain moral categories of the Russian polity. Marking the 50th anniversary in 2003 of the death of Stalin, the All-Russia Center for the Study of Public Opinion (VTsIOM) found that 53 per cent of respondents approved of Stalin overall while only 33 per cent disapproved (14 per cent declined to state a position). Twenty per cent of those polled agreed with the statement that Stalin "was a wise leader who led the USSR to power and prosper-ity", while the same number felt that only a "tough leader" could rule the country given the domestic and external challenges facing the Soviet state in the 1930s and 1940s. Only 27 per cent believed that Stalin was "a cruel, inhuman tyrant responsible for the deaths of millions".[50]

Similarly, opinion surveys conducted in 2003 and 2004 found that less than half of Russia's young people (aged 16–29) would definitely not vote for Stalin if he were running for president. In another poll, conducted in 2005 that focused exclusively on Russia's youth, over half (51 per cent) of the respondents (aged 16–29) felt that Stalin was a wise leader. 56 per cent of those polled also believed that Stalin did more good than harm.[51] Support for democracy and human rights in Russia cannot easily coexist with such views. Nor surprisingly, the same survey found that only 37 per cent of Russia's young people identified themselves as unambiguous supporters of democracy as a system of government.[52]

As we have seen, the Kremlin under Putin bears much of the responsibility for this state of affairs due to its silence on Stalin's crimes, and due to its attacks on intellectual and political pluralism. Given Putin's preference for historical narratives that generate patriotic sentiment and support for his leadership, will the Russian government impose a single hegemonic narrative on history textbooks and other media of historical knowledge? A few factors work to restrain the Russian state from imposing complete controls on historical discourse. The evidence suggests that the Kremlin does not want an open conflict between itself and those members of Russian society who view the Soviet system as the antithesis of modern democracy. Furthermore, the process of textbook production has moved steadily outside the direct control of the government and into areas of civil society, particularly the independent publishing industry, making it more difficult for the state to impose its will without negative publicity. Similarly, the Kremlin is constrained somewhat by its claim that it supports democracy. By intensifying its attacks on intellectual pluralism, the Kremlin will likely mobilize public criticism from liberals at home and, perhaps most important, from democratic governments and groups from abroad.

These constraints on the Russian state are exceedingly fragile, and have not prevented the Kremlin from constricting the marketplace of ideas in other arenas, including television and radio, in which the government has shut down or taken over a number of companies whose independence was deemed intolerable by the Kremlin. Among many other examples is the case of Iuri Levada, the respected sociologist and former head of VTsIOM, the polling agency. Levada was forced out of the company in late 2003 when the government appointed a new board of directors without his approval. Levada claimed that the Kremlin moved against him for collecting politically sensitive polling data on the war in Chechnya.

Other factors work against the survival of even weakened pluralism in historical discourse. Those members of Russian society who advocate the condemnation of the Soviet period or who simply support intellectual pluralism lack the political strength to challenge the government. Having lost all of their seats in the Russian legislature due to weak electoral support in the December 2003 elections to the State Duma, Russia's two liberal democratic parties and like-minded civic groups are poorly equipped to challenge the policies of the state.

Equally important is the fact that Russian liberalism is divided over how to evaluate the Soviet period, particularly the Stalin era. Many liberals now want history textbooks to foster pride and patriotism, helping to create citizens who will work for a stable and prosperous Russia instead of emigrating. Russian liberals increasingly associate harsh criticism of the Soviet era with the disorder and license of the Yeltsin period, and now desire a more "balanced" view of the past to accompany and support the greater political and socio-economic stability that has emerged under Putin.[53] This perspective, of course, is not universally held among liberal intellectuals, many of whom remember the cultural freedom of the Yeltsin period with a sense of loss.

Despite the divisions within their ranks on the issue of history, most Russian liberals – and many other Russians of different political orientations – would likely approve of textbooks that condemn Stalinist crimes and examine the lessons they hold for the present, but that also salvage from this same past some sense of pride and achievement. Such sentiments help explain the popularity of Zagladin's textbook, which attempts to weave achievements and crimes into a single narrative. However, in the absence of any significant counterweights to the power of the Russian state, it is also likely that the political pressures for a return to a simple, heroic narrative of the Soviet past will continue to grow. Unwilling to rely on civil society and political pluralism as central supports for Russian modernization, Putin has instead turned to the army and security forces – state institutions with a vested interest in vigilance against domestic and external enemies, real or imagined. As in the Imperial and Soviet past, the official discourse of these institutions is strongly nationalistic and statist, and their preferred historical images are not only heroic, but often chauvinistic.

Within the elite dimension of political legitimation, Putin and these "power ministries" favour a narrative that justifies, through the celebration of the Russian state, their power to other Russian elites and to the Russian public. Perhaps most important, this statist narrative enables the ruling stratum to justify to itself its possession of power and prestige.

Thus, the political imperative to accumulate symbolic capital provides a powerful motive for these elites to impose their interpretation of the past on Russian society.

In lieu of a conclusion

What can Western democracies do to offset these negative trends and reduce the normative and ideological distance between Western liberal democracies and Russia? Putin's conceptualization of Russian modernization is shaped in large measure by a view of the external world – and particularly the global economy – that is at best ambivalent and suspicious. But he is also apparently convinced that Russia's membership in key Western institutions, and its integration into the world economy, are necessary for Russian modernization. By offering substantial assistance to Russia to reach both of these objectives, while consistently pressing the Kremlin to adhere to democratic principles, the West may create viable linkages that undermine the mobilizational ethos of the Russian state and also help restore the cultural space that had nurtured pluralism in historical discourse during the first post-Soviet decade. Given the importance of Russia's cooperation with the West on a host of security issues, including non-proliferation, as well as Western reliance on Russian oil and gas, the task of promoting democracy would be a risky but nevertheless necessary endeavour. In an environment of more direct and consistent exposure to Western norms and values, Russia's national identity could over time incorporate an authentic and stable commitment to cultural and political pluralism.

One hopes that the intellectual ferment and enlightened educational practices of the initial post-Soviet period described in this chapter have left a positive imprint on Russian society that would support Western efforts and slow Russia's descent into national forgetfulness. However, if Russia continues on its present course, it seems likely that it will suffer increasingly from self-inflicted amnesia. If so, the Russian state may move closer to the behaviour of its Soviet predecessor, exacting a heavy toll on Russian society. If this loss of memory comes to pass, it will signal the end of a remarkable if brief period in which Russia finally remembered and confronted its Soviet past, primarily in its history textbooks.

Notes

1. This chapter does not necessarily reflect the views of the United States Department of Defense, the United States Army or the United States Military Academy.

2. Alexander Yakovlev, *A Century of Violence in Soviet Russia*, New Haven: Yale University Press, 2002, p. 234.

3. Nikita Khrushchev, *Khrushchev Remembers: The Last Testament*, Boston: Little, Brown, 1974, p. 79. Given the high number of persons who remained falsely imprisoned as late as 1956, it was understandable that Khrushchev expected an outpouring of social unrest after camp inmates were released. An additional fear was that a sharp confrontation would occur not only between state and society but within society itself. Khrushchev assumed that the former inmates would return to confront those who had denounced them or profited from their imprisonment, or both. Although the party was flooded with petitions for rehabilitation after the camps were emptied, it would appear that Khrushchev's fears were exaggerated. While it is uncertain how many former inmates were willing to confront the government, many, if not most, were simply too old or broken to engage in social protest. For an artistic treatment of the issue, see Vasilii Grossman, *Vse techet* (Forever Flowing), published in *Oktiabr'*, no. 6, 1989, pp. 30–108.

4. Anne Applebaum, *Gulag: A History*, New York: Doubleday, 2003, pp. 571–572.

5. Béatrice Pouligny, Bernard Doray and Jean-Clément Martin, "Methodological and ethical problems: A trans-disciplinary approach", this volume.

6. The historian Vladimir Naumov, a section chief at the CPSU Central Committee's Institute of Marxism–Leninism, noted in late 1987 that "the establishment of historical truth and historical glasnost has not only scientific but also moral aspects.... Historical glasnost is proof of our consistency in the implementation of restructuring." *Nedelia*, no. 52, 1987, p. 14.

7. *Pravda*, 17 November 1989, p. 1.

8. In early 1991, less than six years after Gorbachev took office, a Soviet historian complained that during this period "our passion for perestroika had moved far 'to the left,' toward rejecting October altogether.... Nowadays the triumph of the October Revolution is often boiled down to a seizure of power by a gang of Bolshevik fanatics who forced a murderous utopia upon the people." Vladimir Buldakov, "An Essential Postscript", *Soviet Studies in History*, Spring 1991, p. 56. See also his study of the October Revolution, "U istokov sovetskoi istorii: Put' k Oktiabriu", *Voprosy istorii*, no. 10, 1989, pp. 63–82.

9. A. I. Iakovlev, *Optimizatsiia ideologicheskoi raboty*, Moscow: Izdatel'stvo politicheskoi literatury, 1990, pp. 46 ff.

10. Karl Mannheim, *Ideology and Utopia: An Introduction to the Sociology of Knowledge*, London: Routledge and Kegan Paul, 1936.

11. *Rabochaia tribuna*, 6 May 1990, pp. 1–2.

12. On this point, see Karl Marx and Friedrich Engels, *The German Ideology*, London: Lawrence and Wishart, 1979, part 1.

13. Rodney Barker, *Political Legitimacy and the State*, Oxford: Clarendon, 1990, p. 59.

14. This relationship also helps to explain why heterodox discourse spread so rapidly and was not suppressed. As Samuel Huntington points out, opposition (whether to specific policies, to the political structure, or to the socio-economic system) articulated through a one-party system can be much more sweeping in its criticism than opposition voiced outside the system. Samuel Huntington, "Social and Institutional Dynamics of One-Party System", in Samuel Huntington and Clement Moore, eds, *The Dynamics of Established One-Party Systems*, New York: Basic Books, 1970, pp. 3–47, at p. 44.

15. Alexandr Iakovlev, "Only Moral Democracy Can Overcome Our Tragic Past", *Moscow News*, no. 1, 7 January 1990, pp. 6–7. Although Yakovlev continued to respect Lenin for his intellect and pragmatism, he faulted the leader for attempting to create a "commodity-free utopia" and relying on violence to resolve political problems.

16. On the question of the failure to address the past, see Alexei Miller, "Russian Strategies in Dealing with the Communist Past, 1985–1990", unpublished paper.

17. On this point as it applies to Spain, see Carolyn P. Boyd, *Historia Patria: Politics, History, and National Identity in Spain, 1875–1975*, Princeton: Princeton University Press, 1997.

18. Nevertheless, the Ministry of Education did intervene to shape the agenda for teaching history. In 1993 the ministry's list of sample examination topics included "The Formation of the Totalitarian System in Our Country and the Establishment of the Regime of Personal Power". Teachers and scholars were told that they must adopt this formulation for instruction in the classroom. Although the concept of totalitarianism had entered mainstream discourse "from below" during the political upheaval and intellectual ferment of the late perestroika period, the Ministry of Education now moved to ensure its continued use through institutionalization. R. W. Davies, *Soviet History in the Yeltsin Era*, New York: St. Martin's Press, 1997, p. 121.

19. For the NCHS and its standards for US history education, see http://www.sscnet.ucla.edu/nchs/standards.

20. See the foreword in L. N. Zharova and I. A. Mishina, *Istoria otechestva, 1900–1940*, Moscow: Prosveshchenie, 1992; and the forward in V. Ostrovskii, et al., *Istoriia otechestva: 1939–1941*, Moscow: Prosveshchenie, 1992.

21. V. P. Ostrovskii (head of authors' collective), *Istoriia otechestva*, Moscow: Prosveshchenie, 1992. The term "negative legitimation" is borrowed from Agnes Heller, "Phases of Legitimation in Soviet-type Societies", in T. H. Rigby and Ferenc Feher, eds, *Political Legitimation in Communist States*, New York: St. Martin's Press, 1982, pp. 45–63, at p. 62.

22. V. P. Ostrovskii and A. I. Utkin, *Istoriia Rossii. XX vek*, Moscow: Drofa, 2001, p. 4.

23. Ibid., p. 162.

24. Ibid., p. 191.

25. Ibid., p. 197.

26. Ibid., p. 316.

27. I. I. Dolutskii, *Otechestvennaia istoriia XX vek, Part I*, Moscow: Mnemozina, 2001, p. 152.

28. A. A. Danilov and L. G. Kosulina, *Istorii Rossii XX vek*, Moscow: Prosveshchenie, 2002, p. 239.

29. N. V. Zagladin, S. I. Kozlenko, S. T. Minakov and Iu. A. Petrov, *Istoriia otechestva XX-nachalo XXI veka*, Moscow: Russkoe slovo, 2003.

30. Ibid., p. 192.

31. Ibid., pp. 469–471.

32. Theodore Von Laue, *Why Lenin? Why Stalin?* New York: Harper and Row, 1936, p. 196.

33. Annual Address to the Federal Assembly, 16 May 2003, at President of Russia Official Web Portal, http://www.kremlin.ru.

34. Ibid.

35. "The Government Tries to Gain Control over History Schoolbooks", *Izvestia*, 31 August 2001 (from WPS Monitoring Agency).

36. The offending quotes appear on p. 254 of I. I. Dolutskii, *Otechestvennaia istoriia XX vek, Part II*. The quotes were removed for the textbook's 2003 printing.

37. Putin's address to historians at the Russian National Library, 27 November 2003, at http://www.kremlin.ru/eng/text/speeches/2003/11/271829_56332.shtml/.

38. ITAR-TASS, 27 November 2003, for more of Putin's comments to the historians.

39. See A. A. Danilov, and L. G. Kosulina, *Istoriia gosudarstva i narodov Rossii XX vek*, Moscow: Drofa, 2002, pp. 425, 439.

40. See Alexandr Chubarian, ed., *Otechestvennaia istoriia, XX-nachala XXI veka*, Moscow: Prosveshchenie, 2004.

41. Ibid., p. 150.

42. Gail Lapidus, "Transforming Russia: American Policy in the 1990s", in Robert J. Lieber, *Eagle Rules? Foreign Policy and American Primacy in the Twenty-First Century*, Upper Saddle River, N.J.: Prentice Hall, 2002, p. 108.

43. Richard Pipes, "Flight from Freedom", *Foreign Affairs*, May/June 2004, pp. 14–15.

44. Report on ROMIR poll, Reuters, 23 November 1999, published in *Johnson's Russia List*, 23 November 1999.

45. As cited in Vladimir Shlapentokh, "Aftermath of the Balkan War, the Rise of Anti-Americanism, and the End of Democracy in Russia", *The World and I*, October 1999, pp. 311–320.

46. See Eric Shiraev and Vladislav Zubok, *Anti-Americanism in Russia from Stalin to Putin*, New York: Palgrave, 2000; and Sarah Mendelson and Theodore Gerber, "Young, Educated, Urban, and Anti-American: Recent Survey Data", at http://csis.org/ruseura/ponars/policymemos.

47. See Timothy J. Colton and Michael McFaul, "America's Real Russian Allies", *Foreign Affairs* 80, no. 6, November/December 2001, pp. 46–58.

48. For the poll, see the article "Umer sam", by Alexei Levinson, a sociologist at VTsIOM, the well-known Russian public opinion firm, in *Neprikosnovennyi zapas*, no. 28, 2003.

49. Theodore Gerber and Sarah Mendelson, "The Disconnect in How Russians Think about Human Rights and Chechnya", Program on New Approaches to Russian Security Policy Memo no. 244, Washington, D.C.: Center for Strategic and International Studies, 2002, p. 6.

50. Quoted in RFE/RL Newsline, accessed at http://www.hri.org/news/balkans/rferl/2003/03-03-05.rferl.html#05.

51. Sarah Medelson and Theodore P. Gerber, "Failing the Stalin Test", *Foreign Affairs* 85, no. 1 (January–February 2006), pp. 2–8.

52. Sarah Mendelson and Theodore P. Gerber, "Soviet Nostalgia: An Impediment to Russian Democratization", *Washington Quarterly* 29, no. 1 (Winter 2005/06), pp. 83–96.

53. The observations contained in this paragraph are based on field research conducted in Russia in 2002, 2003 and 2004, which included dozens of interviews with self-described democrats.

Part IV

Insiders and outsiders

10

External contributions to post-mass-crime rehabilitation

Louis Kriesberg

In this chapter, I examine important ways in which external actors affect people in localities, regions and countries where mass crimes were committed, as those people try to recover from their dreadful experiences. External actors include innumerable persons and groups, including national governments and international non-governmental as well as governmental organizations, which intervene in ways that affect overcoming the legacy of mass crimes.

Many developments in this increasingly globalized world enhance the effects of external actors in mitigating, but also sometimes exacerbating, the occurrences of mass crimes and the subsequent traumas. The global developments include growing economic integration and interdependence; speedier, broader and more intensive information transmission; the expanding number and influence of international governmental and non-governmental organizations; and also increasingly shared values and norms. Consequently, the occurrence of mass crimes and their consequences are less and less isolated from involvement by external actors. Furthermore, the perpetrators and the survivors of mass crimes are aware of this possible engagement and they seek it out or fend it off, directly by appeals or indirectly by modifying their own conduct.

External actors, it should be kept in mind, have their own interests, values and perspectives, about which they themselves differ greatly. Therefore, the engagement of some external actors is likely to be consistent with those of some local groups, but many external actors may engage in ways that are not consistent with many other local groups. For ex-

After mass crime: Rebuilding states and communities, Pouligny, Chesterman and Schnabel (eds), United Nations University Press, 2007, ISBN 978-92-808-1138-4

ample, some external actors generally support external tribunals to pass judgment on those who may have committed gross human rights abuses. This may reflect a reasonable interest in deterring other such actions elsewhere in the world, but may be seen by some local actors as hampering efforts to minimize further bloodshed and efforts to restore economic activities, at least for an initial period of time.

The earlier chapters, which describe the great impact of direct involvement in mass crimes and the variability of that experience, suggest that external actors do not fully understand what has happened to the people in a locality, region or country where mass crimes occurred. The difficulty in grasping what happened affects the way external actors conduct themselves in trying to help people overcome the consequences of what they experienced.

Important external actors possessing values and norms at variance with those of particular local actors are likely to urge mass-crime-recovery policies that are not appreciated by major local groups. This is manifest in policies and actions regarding gender roles, with Western groups favouring more equality between men and women and greater protection of human rights for women, while many local men view such policies as misguided interference. Leaders of the external actors have their own constituencies to which they must give attention. Furthermore, occurrences of mass crime impact the many diverse external actors, in varying ways; this is notably the case for non-governmental organizations (NGOs) based in diaspora communities that help sustain policies opposing local accommodation.

Of course, external actors also provide many resources that make important contributions to recovery by the people who have been victimized. They may facilitate or mediate mutual understandings and respect, which in time become institutionalized. They may condition their continuing support upon fair and just treatment of formerly subordinated groups, basing their policies on widely shared standards regarding human rights.[1] They may monitor the way agreements reached about dealing with the aftermath of mass crimes are implemented and impose sanctions in accord with a group's compliance.

Authors all have personal ties with the issues they examine; those ties affect their interests and interpretation of the issues, as suggested in chapter 1. My lifetime experiences, my training and my studies of conflicts shape my approach to the matters discussed in this chapter. I grew up in Chicago, Illinois, in the 1930s, the son of immigrants from what was Tsarist Russia. I heard many stories of the anti-Semitic pogroms in Russia from my parents and relatives and I lived as a Jew in a non-Jewish neighbourhood, experiencing the anti-Semitism of that time and place. I became fascinated by the wars of the 1930s and the threats of horrendous future wars abroad, I collected pictures of the Japanese invading China and of the Spanish Civil War and I listened with apprehension to Adolf Hitler's speeches.

My response was not so much anger and the desire to retaliate, but to figure out what was going on and how to stop the horrors I knew of and prevent those I feared would soon occur. I went to college and graduate school wanting to learn what might be done; I discovered sociology and thought it would provide the most fundamental understanding of wars and mass violence, and thus how they could be controlled. At the same time, I also simply enjoyed the sociological perspective and found the academic life congenial.

I analysed aspects of international cooperation while also doing more conventional sociology. But in the early 1970s, I began to focus all my work on threats of war and how to counter them. In particular, I studied US–Soviet and Israeli–Palestinian relations, drawing from the literature in peace studies as well as in international relations. I also began to teach and do research in the emerging new field of problem-solving conflict resolution. All this, mixed with my decades of experience travelling to many parts of the world and living in Mexico, Germany, Israel and France, sensitizing me to the ongoing nature of large-scale conflicts as well as their changing trajectories. My present work is a response to the current world from the perspective of my past experience. In the last few years, I have been analysing the transformation of intractable conflicts and the role of reconciliation in such transformations.

This chapter builds on my past endeavours, but is focused on external organizational responses to mass crimes and how the responses sometimes contribute to the transformation of the destructive conflicts of which large-scale violence is a part. It is based on a wide range of personal accounts, secondary reports and interviews with persons who worked in governmental and non-governmental organizations engaged in peace-building, and with many people in countries where mass crimes had been committed.

The occurrence of mass crimes and their aftermath are examined here in the larger context of the conflicts in which they are embedded. Mass crimes are episodes, large and gruesome as they may be, within the course of conflicts that preceded the mass violence and that continue in some fashion afterward. Each outbreak of gross human rights violations examined in earlier chapters had a history of prior confrontations between members of the groups perpetrating and suffering grave injuries. The rehabilitation, which did and did not occur after those prior episodes, affected the outbreaks examined in this book.

Mass crimes also frequently have repercussions that spread out, resulting in additional destructive conflicts and new mass atrocities. The mass crimes committed by Nazi Germany and its allied forces against various peoples of Europe contributed to subsequent forced expulsions, profound hatreds and new atrocities in Yugoslavia, Czechoslovakia, the Middle East and the Soviet Union. The genocide in Rwanda reverberated throughout Central Africa and contributed to new wars and atrocities there. External actors clearly have a stake in the aftermath of mass crimes.

Particular conflicts, however, even those marked by the commission of mass crimes, become transformed and sometimes come to an end. The transformation and ending may be imposed, in varying degrees, by one party to the conflict or by external intervention. The endings vary in the degree to which they are mutually agreed upon and explicitly formulated. Even formal agreements to end or control violent conflicts often fail to be implemented and are soon followed by renewed destructive fighting. Other settlements, however, help transform violent conflicts and subsequently the relations between former adversaries improve.

The endurance of any settlement depends not only on the content of that settlement, but also on the nature of the conflict, the characteristics of the opposing sides, the nature of their relations and the way the agreement was achieved. In addition – and of special interest here – the durability of the settlement depends on the engagement of persons and groups who are outsiders to the settlement.[2] Those external actors include multinational corporations, trans-national churches and other religious associations, exile and diaspora organizations, international governmental organizations (IGOs) such as the United Nations and international non-governmental organizations (INGOs) such as Human Rights Watch.

External actors are particularly important in this increasingly integrated world. Indeed, globalization diminishes the very distinction between internal and external actors, factors and processes. For example, a multinational petroleum corporation has close ties with governments, local businesses and trade unions in many countries; consequently, the decisions made by such groups in one country impact many groups in other countries. Members of diaspora groups are another example. They often remain in close relations with compatriots in their native lands, sending remittances back to relatives, receiving information about the cultural and political life in their country of origin and engaging in political activities by providing funds or even weapons to political organizations in their homeland.

I focus here on ways IGOs and INGOs affect particular social processes that are often crucial for rehabilitation after the commission of mass crimes and for the attainment of a durable peaceful accommodation. Mass crimes have profound impacts at the individual, community, national and regional levels. At the individual level, the responses vary in emotions, cognitions and behaviour, including grief, depression, anxiety, apathy, anger and hate, but also resolve and engagement in recovery. At the community level, the deaths and injuries, physical disruption of services and communications, and other severe damages resulting from mass crimes can exacerbate inter-organizational differences and social cleavages across ethnic, religious and economic lines. But experiences also can increase the need for cooperation within a community and among communities. At the national level, leaders and institutions may become illegitimate and ineffective. New leaders and new solutions to the problems arising from the mass crimes may arise, but they may not be appropriate for the problems at hand.

The processes examined in this chapter pertain especially to reconciliation, which is briefly discussed later in this chapter. Durable and constructive agreements and other instruments of accommodation often contribute to and are based upon some degree of reconciliation. Reconciliation, as understood by members of the parties that had been involved in mass crimes or other destructive conflicts, however, may not figure significantly in reaching a stable, mutually acceptable accommodation. For example, in post-Franco Spain, the horrors of the Civil War and its aftermath have not been dealt with by explicit acts of reconciliation; indeed until recently they have been generally treated with widespread silence.[3] Nevertheless, analytically, the silence may provide a kind of minimal security and even regard, which are components of reconciliation as understood here.

To discuss the complex ways people do and do not accomplish post-mass-crime rehabilitation, the major components will be analysed separately here, before considering their interconnections. First, I examine the qualities that characterize a destructive conflict and the changes in those qualities that constitute the conflict's transformation into a more tractable or even constructive conflict. Second, I analyse the major dimensions of reconciliation, regarded broadly, and discuss the many groups between whom reconciliation occurs in varying degrees. Third, I examine the numerous IGOs and INGOs that may speed the degree to which a conflict is transformed constructively, recognizing as well that some may sustain and intensify the destructiveness of a conflict. In the final section of this chapter, I bring together the previous discussions and examine how various IGOs and INGOs affect major dimensions of reconciliation so as to foster equitable and stable accommodations, even after mass crimes have been committed.

Characteristics of destructive and constructive conflicts

Four components, or characteristics, of the adversaries and their relationship combine to constitute any social conflict.[4] First, at least one antagonist has a collective identity distinct from another group or people, and actions related to such views tend to result in members of each side regarding themselves to be in a contentious "us" against "them" relationship. Second, members of at least one side regard themselves as aggrieved, suffering threats or injustices. Third, members of at least one side formulate goals that include seeking a change in the other side that would reduce their grievance. Finally, members of an adversary side believe that they are able to take actions towards the other side that will change it so as to advance them toward their goals.

These components vary in ways that make for relatively more destructive or more constructive conflicts, as shown in table 10.1. Thus, some kinds of collective identities and conceptions of the adversaries contribute to a conflict's destructiveness and to the commission of mass atrocities, while other kinds foster constructively waged conflicts. For example, national identities vary in several relevant ways. They may be formulated in terms that make it hard for others to share an identity, defining membership in terms of ascribed qualities (those determined at birth) rather than achieved qualities (those acquired by later actions). Nationalism defined by ascribed qualities is one of the features of ethno-

Table 10.1 Conflict Components and Conflict Destructiveness

Components	More Destructive	More Constructive
Identity	Exclusive of other	Inclusive of other
	Ethno-nationalism	Civic nationalism
	Ascribed qualities	Achieved qualities
	Defining self by opposing other	Defining self independently of other
Grievance	Believe existence is threatened	Believe existence is not threatened
	Feel humiliated by others	Issues appear negotiable
Goals	Regarded as in zero-sum conflict	Regarded as in mixed-sum conflict
	Seek destruction of other	Other side's goal given legitimacy
	Seek revenge	
Methods	Believe violence only recourse	Believe non-coercive means possible
	Indiscriminate violence allowed	Use of violence greatly limited

nationalism, while civic nationalism is inclusive, allowing others to share it by participating in the country's life as a citizen who supports it.[5]

Furthermore, identities may be formulated in terms that rank the collective self as superior and another people as inferior, even sub-human. As discussed in the chapters by Scott Straus and by René Lemarchand and Maurice Niwese in this volume, prior to the genocide in Rwanda, some Hutu leaders mobilized people to commit the mass killings by characterizing the Tutsis as sub-human. It is possible, however, for other groups to be viewed as different without denigrating comparisons; after all, the tourist industry is so large partly because people enjoy seeing others who act differently than they do. There is evidence that people can be patriotic in the sense of celebrating their own qualities, without being nationalist in the sense of seeing others as inferior to them.[6] The tendency to denigrate the other rather than appreciate the differences that are believed to exist contributes to conflicts becoming destructive and results in mass crimes.

The nature of grievances also varies in ways that affect the destructiveness of conflicts. Thus, the members of a collectivity may fear that their individual or collective survival is endangered by another collectivity; or, they may believe themselves to be relatively disadvantaged, but not existentially threatened. In the former cases, conflicts are more likely to become destructive than in the latter. The analysis by Natalija Bašić demonstrates how combat solders on each side of the wars in the Balkans could believe that they were defending themselves against threats to their existential interests.

Goals also vary greatly in relevant ways. The goals may be premised on the belief that their attainment must come at the expense of the other side; or, the goals may be based on the expectation that significant mutual gains are possible. The former beliefs give the conflict a zero-sum character, and are conducive to a relatively destructive conflict, compared to the latter beliefs that give the conflict a mixed-sum character. For example, more security for one's own group may seem to require less security by the enemy; but alternatively, the situation may be configured so that one's own security can be attained only by the enemy also feeling safe.

Finally, the methods that are chosen to wage a conflict clearly affect the trajectory of a conflict, particularly since they tend to be reciprocated by the other side. For example, as seen in several chapters, targeted people often use the violence directed at them to justify their own more violent responses. Gross human rights violations can engender fear, anger, hate and other feelings and acts that contribute to destructive conflict escalation and prolongation.

Clearly, the qualities of these four components affect each other. Some kinds of identities, grievances, goals and conflict methods tend to reinforce each other in contributing to a conflict's destructiveness or to its constructiveness. These conflict qualities tend to change and become less conducive to destructiveness as a conflict de-escalates. As an accommodation between the adversaries is reached, further changes in these conflict qualities need to occur to help consolidate the accommodation.

This discussion should make clear how the commission of mass crimes tends to prolong and even escalate the destructiveness of a conflict. When a group has suffered mass crimes, the identity of survivors and others sharing that group membership may be affected in ways that increase the likelihood of future mass crimes. They tend to see themselves as beleaguered, vulnerable and isolated. The perpetrators' identity also may be affected in ways that perpetuate destructive conflicts; they may tend to justify their actions by thinking of themselves as being under attack.

Members of each side are likely to feel aggrieved, as they may fear the consequences of the crimes. As members of each side try to protect themselves from the threats, they may act in ways that confirm the other side's belief that they are being threatened; this epitomizes the security dilemma.

Experience with mass crimes may even make such acts more likely again because the barriers against them have been lowered, and the desire for retaliation helps justify gross human rights violations. Thus, the riots and massacres in Rwanda and neighbouring Burundi formed an escalating series of killings leading to the mass killing and consequent wars, as examined by René Lemarchand and Maurice Niwese in chapter 7.

Since this book is focused on the aftermath of mass crimes, attention to their termination is needed. Some end by expulsion or by imposition and the continued repression of the targets of the mass crimes, which may continue for a very long time. Such cases are discussed in the chapters in this book examining Bali and post-Soviet Russia. Many other cases can be cited, including the Ottoman treatment of Armenians, Chile under Pinochet and Spain under Franco. In such circumstances, past crimes are denied; people who might protest them are silenced and suffer not only the losses, but also feelings of guilt and fear, which are hidden. Rehabilitation then has those burdens to overcome as well.

Many conflicts that include mass crimes, however, are ended by agreements often marking important transitions in a conflict. They vary in comprehensiveness, specificity and explicitness. They may be reached through negotiations, with a great deal or very little engagement by outside actors. Whether the agreements help foster and solidify a constructive peace process or fail to do so and are followed by destructive breakdowns depends in part on how the agreement helps to transform the conflict components previously discussed. The agreement may settle some grievances and provide legitimate ways to manage future contentions, providing a basis for further progress. Various elements of reconciliation can contribute significantly to the transformation of a destructive conflict, particularly one with a legacy of oppression, atrocities and mass crimes.

Dimensions of "reconciliation"

Reconciliation is a complex multidimensional phenomenon, encompassing processes as well as particular aspects of the relationship between two or more persons or collectivities. As is evident in many chapters in this book, reconciling parties in large-scale conflicts is done by many diverse persons and groups. Particular individuals, who see each other as members of large collectivities with a history of antagonistic and destructive relations, may engage in conversations about that past, carry out cooperative work, or even form intimate friendly or marital relations. Often public attention is focused on official representatives of two previously antagonistic communities who engage in reconciliatory actions. These actions may range from carefully choreographed mutually arranged events to relatively spontaneous gestures by a leading figure from one party. Even when the reconciliatory steps are impelled by political and economic calculations, the steps may contribute to progress along the road toward rehabilitating relations after awful atrocities have occurred.[7]

Particular groups within one or more adversary may also take reconciliatory actions. The groups may include members of legislatures, audiences for films or readers of books about grievous past events, or participants in public commemoration events. Finally, reconciliation may be embodied in institutionalized conduct that contradicts past oppression and hostility. This includes promotion of social integration across lines of past divisions and laws against discrimination or disrespectful language. For example, in the village of Carhuahuran, Ayacucho, Peru, a law was passed against gossip (*Ley Contra Chismes*), banning spreading stories about a villager's past involvement with the Shining Path.

Noting the variety of persons and groups possibly engaged in reconciliation also indicates that some people may be acting in a reconciliatory manner in some capacities and situations, but not in others. Thus, while leaders, small groups or even general practice demonstrate steps of reconciliation, many other people on one or both sides of a destructive conflict may remain un-reconciled to its transformation. Some of the unreconciled may passively resist the new relationship while others may even seek to subvert it. Still others may reject the new accommodation and try to continue the fight and restore a previous relationship. Such groups, acting as spoilers, often undermine the implementation of agreements to settle a conflict.[8]

Furthermore, the boundaries of any system that adversaries make up are to a greater or lesser extent porous to outsiders. In communal conflicts, people who share communal identities with one or more sides often live outside the system, sometimes across borders dividing the land on which a people live. Some of them also live in distant countries, as members of diaspora groups. Frequently, members of such diaspora communities form organizations that support the struggle of their religious, ethnic or linguistic compatriots, sometimes even after the contenders in the primary locus of the conflict have reached an accord.

Before examining IGOs and INGOs and their impacts on rehabilitation after mass crimes, it is necessary to discuss four major dimensions of reconciliation.[9] The dimensions are shared truths, justice, regard and security. Different analysts have emphasized one or two of these dimensions and variously defined them. My use of the term reconciliation incorporates all of them and each dimension is regarded as broad and to occur in varying degree.

First, many partisans of a conflict, as well as analysts, regard truth as an important dimension of reconciliation since members of antagonistic sides tend to deny what members of the other side experience and believe to be true. At a minimal level, persons on each side may openly recognize that they have different views of reality. They may even acknowledge the possible validity of elements of what members of the other community believe. At a fuller level, members of the different communities develop a shared and therefore more comprehensive truth. Official investigations, judicial proceedings and literary and mass media reporting are ways for perpetrators and those complicit with them to acknowledge abuses that had been hidden or denied. In the larger global context, additional resources are available to seek and sustain truths that might otherwise be denied. Then, in some future time, matters that might have been hidden are brought into the light.

The second major dimension of reconciliation is justice, in its manifold meanings. Many persons who have suffered oppression and atrocities in the course of a destructive struggle seek redress for what they endured. Redress may take the form of tangible restitution or compensation for what was lost; it may also be in the form of punishment for those who committed injustices and it may be exhibited in policies that offer protection against future discrimination or harm.[10]

The third important dimension in reconciliation incorporates expressions of regard by members of each community towards the other. This includes according respect to the people in the community that has suffered mass crimes, by members of the community to which the perpetrators belonged. It also includes expressions, by those who have suffered harms, which acknowledge the humanity of those who inflicted the injuries. At a minimal level, this entails recognizing the humanity of the others and their human rights. At its most extreme, the acknowledgment may convey mercy and forgiveness, which is stressed by some advocates of reconciliation. It is given support by widespread religious beliefs regarding the value of every human being before God.[11] Frequently, recognition of the other side's humanity entails only expressing the thought that many members of the adversary community did not personally and directly carry out harmful actions and that the next generation is not responsible for the acts of past generations. Sometimes, members of previously hostile sides simply carry on social interactions without explicit acknowledgements of the past hurts. In so doing, a minimal level of regard may be evident.

Certainly, regard is not likely to be given by persons who have suffered mass crimes to everyone who belongs to the collectivity from which variously responsible perpetrators have come. The great range of responsibilities that people had and the various responses those who were injured have towards them is made evident at the interpersonal micro-level analyses provided in many chapters in this book.

Security is the fourth dimension of reconciliation, in the sense of personal or collective safety and well-being. Security exists as the adversaries have reason to believe they can look forward to living together without one side threatening the other, perhaps even in harmony and unity. This may be in the context either of high levels of integration or in the context of separation and little interaction. However the sense of security is supported, believing that it exists in good measure contributes to and is sustained by trust. Ethical dilemmas involving security arise when those who have committed criminal acts, or more likely ordered them, are given amnesty. That runs counter to the injured parties' insistence upon obtaining justice and truth, and it hampers according them decent regard.

Clearly, all these dimensions of reconciliation cannot be fully realized at the same time. Indeed, they are often contradictory at a given time.[12] Thus, forgiveness and justice often cannot be satisfied at the same time, although they may occur sequentially. Nevertheless, if expressed by different members of the previously antagonistic sides, some degree of forgiveness and justice may be compatible even simultaneously.

Significantly, these dimensions are interdependent in many ways. Thus, if many members of one community acknowledge that their acts have injured another community, forgiveness or at least acceptance of their humanity is easier to be felt and openly expressed by the injured party.

Members of a group who feel safe are more likely to acknowledge truths of past misdeeds. The complex, multi-levelled workings of the South African Truth and Reconciliation Commission illustrate the interdependence and the dilemmas such interdependence creates.

A high level of reconciliation is not a one-sided matter. Some members of one side may seek justice from another one that is viewed as responsible for the injustice; but members of that other side may deny responsibility and then there is no reconciliation movement, as is shown by Kimberley Theidon about Peru in chapter 4. Expressions of regret may be recognized by members of the injured party and not deemed fully adequate by some of them. Often both sides have suffered injuries at the hand of the other, although not in equal measure. Reconciliation actions by members of one party often are ineffective because they fail to reflect the appropriate symmetries and asymmetries.

The degree of asymmetry between the parties who had been involved in mass crimes is a major aspect of every dimension of reconciliation. A high degree of reconciliation usually entails significant complementary reciprocation. If members of one side assert truths that are ignored or denigrated by the other, their assertion is hardly a mark of reconciliation; the truths need to be shared or at least acknowledged to indicate some degree of reconciliation on that dimension. Expressions of regret and apology and acts of contrition must be recognized and in a sense accepted by the other side if reconciliation is to progress. Security for one side can hardly be called reconciliation when it means insecurity for the other side, even if the relationship remains stable. Similarly, terms that only one side deems just and the other regards as unjust do not indicate a significant level of reconciliation on that dimension.[13]

Varieties of IGOs and INGOs

This chapter is focused on international governmental and trans-national non-governmental organizations, but national governments and national non-governmental organizations also take actions that affect the people in other countries after experiencing mass crimes. For example, Augusto Pinochet, who ruled Chile for 17 years after the 1973 military coup he led, oversaw a harsh repression. In 1998, he was arrested in Britain at the request of Spanish courts on murder charges. Although he was allowed to return to Chile on the grounds of his poor health, court proceedings on various charges followed in Chile.

Enemies and former enemies relate to each other in a context that includes many international governmental and non-governmental organizations, which readily penetrate the boundaries of the adversaries, affecting each of them and their relations with each other. The organizations include businesses buying and selling products and services; public and private investors; and organizations transmitting news and producing entertainments. They also include religious and academic institutions, many of whose members set forth truths and norms to guide conduct. Here, I focus on the organizations that have relatively direct impact on the work of building peace after mass crimes have been perpetrated.

International governmental organizations vary greatly in their geographic and functional scope. Almost all the governments of the world are members of the United Nations and it has a wide scope of functions, but it has little supranational authority. Under some circumstances it has been able to act collectively and impose cessations of violence, acting under Chapter VII of the Charter. The UN undertakes many important activities to prevent wars, to end them if begun, to help those suffering the consequences of the wars and to build enduring peace. They are carried out by the various organs of the UN, including the United Nations High Commissioner for Refugees and by the associated specialized organizations such as UNESCO.

Of the 245 international intergovernmental organizations active in 2004, 177 were regionally oriented.[14] Regional IGOs are particularly important in Europe; those relevant to post-conflict peace-building include the Organization for Security and Co-operation in Europe (OSCE), the European Union, and NATO. Non-governmental international organizations are much more numerous and diverse than IGOs. In 2004, there were 7,261 such organizations. They tend to be based in the developed world and many operate globally. These trans-national organizations have grown in number and size as a result of the ever-greater integration of the world. The processes of globalization further enhance the effects of these organizations at the same time as their growth reflects and fosters increasing globalization.[15] Many INGOs are engaged in peace-building activities related to humanitarian relief, aid to refugees, economic development, protection of human rights and supporting non-violent conflict resolution methods.

In reality, IGOs and INGOs are not fully independent of each other. The UN has complex formal and informal ways of relating to INGOs.[16] INGOs provide information as well as propose options for IGO actions, sometimes lobbying for particular policies. Increasingly, IGOs contract INGOs to provide particular services in post-conflict situations, and therefore provide significant support for some INGO operations.

Finally, it is important to recognize that neither IGOs nor INGOs represent a unified "international community". Their member governments or national non-governmental associations differ immensely in power and influence, and in values and interests. Since the Cold War ended and the

Soviet Union dissolved, the United States' global dominance grew and that increased its influence in various IGOs. However, in the years of President George W. Bush's administration, this power has been used to bypass the UN and other major IGOs.

Non-state actors, including INGOs, can provide vehicles for action that complement or counter governmental actions. They can operate transnationally to influence national governments and thereby affect international norms and organizations, for example in leading the movement to ban landmines. Even INGOs, however, often are led by persons and groups from the United States and other developed Western countries, albeit representing diverse views in these pluralistic countries.[17] This is evident in the importance of the women's movement in the West and the consequent attention given to mass crimes committed against women, as in the criminalization and punishment of mass rapes.[18]

The impact of IGOs

This discussion of the effects of IGO activities upon reconciliation and rehabilitation after mass crimes is organized in terms of the IGO activities' impacts on the four dimensions of reconciliation and their contribution to changing the basic components of conflicts. See table 10.2.

Shared truths

IGOs can foster the development of shared truths among adversaries about their history and relationship in several ways. One important way is through public trials of individuals accused of committing specific criminal acts in the course of a war or state repression, which serve as an increasingly significant way in which some IGOs cast light on particularly awful events. For example, in 1993 the UN Security Council established the International Criminal Tribunal for the former Yugoslavia (ICTY).[19] Although the ICTY is located in the Hague, Netherlands, its proceedings receive attention in Serbia, Croatia, Bosnia and elsewhere in the former Yugoslavia.

The UN General Assembly convened the United Nations Diplomatic Conference of Plenipotentiaries on the Establishment of an International Criminal Court (ICC), and in 1998 it finalized a draft statute.[20] Some governments have not joined the ICC, including the United States, China, India, Pakistan, Iraq, Israel and Turkey; however, 137 nations do support it. The ICC formally opened in March 2003, in the Hague.[21] As discussed in Thomas Sherlock's chapter in this book, about remembering Soviet mass crimes, revealing truths about past relations can reduce the sense

Table 10.2 International Governmental Organizations' Activities Fostering Reconciliation and Conflict Transformation

Reconciliation Actions	Impacts on Conflict Conditions				
	Identities	Grievances	Goals	Methods	
Truths Trials Inquiries Curricular material	Revise history and self-concept	Lower injury Raise for others	More shared More complementary	Less purely coercive	
Justice Trials Restitution Set standards	More inclusive	Lower injury Raise for others Provide redress	More delimited claims Less revengeful	Judicial and political alternatives	
Regard Set standards Group dialogue Recognition	Includes sense of responsibility	Mitigate past grievance Reduce humiliation	More shared Accord other legitimacy	Consider others' humanity	
Security Peacekeeping Protecting rights Monitor standards Demobilization Police training	More overarching	Reduce fear Reduce security dilemma	More mutual	De-legitimize violence Rely more on political set procedures Less threatening	

of grievance among those who suffered from the actions of an adversary party but they may also be used to mobilize struggles to redress a raised sense of grievance. Furthermore, if the revelations are regarded as one-sided, which may be the case with trials conducted by members of one side against the other, new grievances are likely to be created. Other methods may be more productive of mutually shared truths. These could be the product of joint groups or commissions issuing reports or mutually accepted history texts, as fostered by UNESCO. History textbooks are often contested because they do influence self-identities as well as conceptions of adversaries.

IGOs may undertake fact-finding missions or support other inquiries that report on past human-rights violations or other atrocities. For example, the Commission for the Historical Clarification of Human Rights Violations and Acts of Violence That Have Caused Suffering to the Guatemalan Population, sponsored by the UN, issued its final report in 1999. It found that in the early 1980s the armed forces committed genocide and racism in a ruthless campaign against guerrillas.[22] However, external intervention was not adequate to provide enough security and safety for people to speak openly about their past experiences. This is also evident in chapter 8, on Bali after the bloody repression there in 1965/66.

Justice

Of course, trials represent a primary vehicle to achieve various components of justice, particularly after the commission of mass crimes. For example, the International Criminal Tribunal for Rwanda (ICTR), established in 1995 and convened in Arusha, Tanzania, is "trying the masterminds behind the genocide" of 800,000 Rwandan Tutsis and moderate Hutus.[23] In addition, lower-level suspects are being tried within Rwanda in local communities in a process called *gacaca*. As Scott Straus observes in chapter 5, the traditional gacaca process was used to settle community disputes and now allows survivors to confront those accused of murder, rape and theft. This process can deal more speedily with many more cases than the ICTR and, due to the engagement of the people in the local community where the alleged perpetrators committed atrocities, it can help restore some measure of mutual regard.

IGOs play a significant role in advancing justice by setting standards about what constitutes justice. A transformational step in this regard was the 1948 proclamation by the UN General Assembly of the Universal Declaration of Human Rights. This has been followed by numerous UN declarations and covenants, notably the International Covenant on Economic, Social and Cultural Rights and the International Covenant on Civil and Political Rights, both of which entered into force in 1976. Several regional intergovernmental organizations have also adopted human rights declarations.

Regard

The various human rights declarations contribute to people acknowledging the rights of others, as well as asserting their own. Such acknowledgment is a way of respecting others. To some degree, then, such declarations and the standards they proclaim help create an atmosphere of mutual tolerance, which contributes to self-identities and conceptions of others that are less likely to contribute to destructive conflicts. That also lessens the likelihood of resorting to methods of struggle that violate human rights.[24]

The OSCE includes important structures to help prevent, limit and end destructive conflicts and practices, including the High Commissioner on National Minorities and the Office for Democratic Institutions and Human Rights. The OSCE's activities include consultations, mediation, monitoring and missions in specific countries such as Croatia, Georgia, Moldova, Tajikistan and the Ukraine.

Trials and truth commissions can also contribute to regard between communities that committed and suffered mass crimes. They can enable people in each community to differentiate among individuals and groups within the communal category that committed particular crimes. They can reveal that some members of the community from which offenders came actually resisted the commission of the crimes. Such differentiation helps to change the image that members of one community have about the other, and even their self-images. The official and non-official international support and celebration of the South African Truth and Reconciliation Commission and the transforming negotiations and agreements that ended apartheid contributed to the pride and hope that the peoples of South Africa had as they undertook their recovery from the crimes of apartheid.

Security

IGOs are particularly important in providing safety for persons or groups that are at risk even after a ceasefire or peace agreement has been reached. For example, a major activity of the UN is providing for the introduction of peacekeeping and then peacemaking missions. Such activities help reduce grievances that would otherwise arise as one or more groups live in fear of harassment and attacks from the other. As each group feels threatened and prepares to defend itself, the other side feels more threatened, resulting in a security dilemma. For example, peacekeeping interventions in parts of the former Yugoslavia such as Kosovo, Bosnia and Macedonia helped sustain agreements by helping to ensure their implementation. The work to protect human rights also helps to provide security. For example, the UN Verification Mission in Guatemala (MINUGUA) helped deter human rights abuses against opposition political groups during the peace implementation period of the 1990s. Such external interventions enhance the safety needed to sustain political institutions within a country, which then provide non-destructive ways of conducting internal conflicts.

In rare cases, external actors take responsibility for overseeing the implementation of agreements to establish a new political order. For example, in 1991, the Cambodian factions and 19 states signed what is commonly referred to as the "Paris Agreement", the Agreements on a Comprehensive Political Settlement of the Cambodian Conflict. It established the UN Transitional Authority in Cambodia to ensure the Agreements' implementation.[25] However, as Maurice Eisenbruch points out in chapter 3, unless the people staffing such externally based agencies are attuned to the local culture and work closely with local leaders, their efforts may be ineffective.

Care for refugees from territories where inhabitants face life-threatening conditions due to violent conflicts is an important service provided by the UN High Commissioner for Refugees (UNHCR). That care often makes the survival of the refugees possible and also helps prevent the persistence of the original conflict or the outbreak of new ones. There are also times, however, when refugee camps become havens for fighters who recruit new members to their fighting units and renew their struggle. This was the sequence to a significant degree for the refugee camps dominated by Hutu fighters who had been defeated by Tutsi forces, who had intervened in Rwanda to stop the killing of Tutsis and moderate Hutus, as discussed in chapter 7 by Lemarchand and Niwese.

The handling of Palestinian refugees illustrates some of the complexities of internationally provided care for refugees.[26] The United Nations Relief and Works Agency for Palestine Refugees in the Near East (UNRWA) was created in 1949 to aid the 726,000 Palestinians who fled or were driven from their homes as a result of the war to establish Israel. UNRWA defines them and their descendents (3.8 million currently) to be refugees and aids them in camps in the West Bank, the Gaza Strip, Lebanon, Syria and Jordan. UNHCR, which was established in 1951 and which provides assistance to all other refugees, defines refugees differently and follows different policies. By UNHCR definitions, the number of Palestinian refugees would be fewer than one million. UNHCR status would provide for rights presently denied to Palestinian refugees. As it is,

living with limited rights and imbued with the unimplemented wish to return to their homes in Israel, their right to return was one of the issues
that was a great obstacle to reaching a final status agreement between
the Israeli government and the Palestinian Authority in the negotiations
of 2000/01. UNRWA was not charged with seeking a durable solution to
the refugee problem: repatriation, local integration or third-country resettlement; but rather only to provide interim assistance, which helps perpetuate the refugee situation.[27]

General impact

Since these various components of reconciliation are interrelated and affect each other, IGO activities that contribute to supporting one of them
will also often help others as well. This is obviously the case for the contributions made by providing funds and staff training for reconstructing a
society scarred by mass crimes. Such assistance can help rebuild the society's physical and social infrastructure. However, given the complexity of
reconciliation and issues about harmonizing progress among the various
dimensions of reconciliation and also given the variety of missions and
interests among IGOs and INGOs, attention to coordinating the activities of various intervening organizations is needed.

The impact of INGOs

As shown in table 10.3, INGOs can affect each dimension of reconciliation in ways that transform a conflict away from destructiveness and contribute to rehabilitation after mass crimes.

Shared truths

Human rights advocacy groups such as Amnesty International and
Human Rights Watch contribute a great deal to raising awareness and acceptance of basic human rights and conduct activities that reveal their violations. Their work gives victims allies and resources in telling their
truths with some degree of protection. Diaspora groups often are active
in telling the story of their people to the world at large. They express
truths that others take up and convey to those who would deny them, as
has been the case for the Armenian diaspora groups' accounts of the
massacres of Armenians by Ottoman authorities at the time of World
War I.

Table 10.3 International Non-governmental Organizations' Activities Fostering Reconciliation and Conflict Transformation

Reconciliation Actions	Impacts on Conflict Conditions			
	Identities	Grievances	Goals	Methods
Truths				
Investigations Cultural media Curricular material	Revise history and self-concept	Lower injury Raise for others	More shared More complementary	Less purely coercive
Justice				
Consultation Restitution Future equity End oppression	More inclusive	Lower injury Raise for others Provide redress	More delimited claims Less revengeful	Judicial and political alternatives
Regard				
Official apology Group dialogue Recognition Therapy	Includes sense of responsibility More self-esteem	Mitigate past grievance Reduce humiliation	More shared Accord other legitimacy	Consider others' humanity
Security				
Accompaniment Autonomy Consultation Monitor	More overarching	Reduce fear Reduce security dilemma	More mutual Internally diverse procedures	De-legitimize violence Rely more on political procedures

Justice

Trans-national religious and ethnic organizations often provide assistance to people of the same religion or ethnicity who have suffered hardships in a particular country. Such humanitarian or other assistance provides the survivors with some restitution and compensation for their suffering, and so reduces their sense of injustice. Assistance includes aid in resettlement of refugees in other countries where compatriots have settled.

Diaspora groups, however, also often engage in activities to sustain struggles of resistance and liberation for their compatriots in the homeland. They sometimes uphold more extreme positions than many of their compatriots, rejecting terms of agreement that may even have been accepted, albeit reluctantly, by most of their compatriots. They may resort to violence and even terrorism to rally attention to their cause and ignite a wider fight. This may be seen in the activities of organizations whose members or whose forebearers came from Palestine, Northern Ireland, Cuba or Sri Lanka.

Regard

A great many trans-national non-governmental organizations now work to foster coexistence, reconciliation, mutual tolerance and mutual respect. They provide training in skills contributing to such relations through workshops, dialogue circles and other structured experiences.[28] INGOs such as International Alert and Search for Common Ground, among other activities, foster cooperative economic and social projects by members of adversarial groups. Associations with members from different ethnic, religious or other communal groups help prevent intercommunal conflicts from erupting into riots, as evidenced in research on Hindu–Muslim relations in India.[29]

Many religious and humanist advocacy groups directly advocate the celebration of human diversity. Significantly, too, however, some transnational religious and ethnic groups proclaim their superiority and denigrate other religions and ethnicities. Trans-national networks opposing immigration and rights for immigrants in various countries wax and wane in strength; they counter efforts at building enduring, mutually acceptable accommodations.

Security

Many INGOs provide services that supplement IGO activities that help protect and care for endangered minorities, returning refugees and other vulnerable groups. For example, peace accords for Guatemala included provisions for the return and resettlement of Guatemalan refugees. Between 1993 and 1999, persons associated with INGOs accompanied the returning refugees, ensuring some protection for them.[30]

Organizations such as Amnesty International and Human Rights Watch also conduct activities that help protect persons whose rights have been or may be infringed upon. The Carter Center and other INGOs help monitor elections and many non-governmental organizations help provide food and medical relief.

These protective actions tend to sustain political institutions that offer alternatives to violent struggle and hence provide more constructive ways to engage in the inevitable societal conflicts. Relieving some of the suffering from the mass crimes' consequences can alleviate the resentments and grievances that might otherwise help revive a destructive conflict.

General contributions

Many INGO activities contribute to promoting more than one of these components of reconciliation. The high interest in peace-building by strengthening political institutions and civil society results in projects that foster various combinations of increased security, mutual regard, truth and justice. One such way is by helping local organizations to analyse the circumstances they confront, assess the impacts of their projects and devise useful adaptations. See, for example, the work on peace and conflict impact assessment.[31]

Conclusions and implications

This chapter has focused on external actors intervening in conflicts in which mass crimes have been committed. They can contribute significantly to overcoming the terrible legacies of mass crimes and reaching an enduring and equitable accommodation between communities that include members who have committed and/or have suffered such crimes. Nevertheless, as indicated throughout this volume, it is the members of the antagonistic communities, or, better said, those with the capability of acting in their names that must articulate the nature of that accommodation. If there is an explicit agreement, it needs to be implemented by the parties to the agreement; if conditions change, the parties should change the agreement by new negotiations and mutual affirmations.

Reaching stable and mutually acceptable accommodations between antagonistic collectivities, however, is particularly difficult after mass violence. Even if one party is able to impose its terms and the other is forced to accept them, when circumstances change the defeated group may rise up and try to overturn the terms of the imposed accommodation. Or, if the suppression is extreme and over time is widely and increasingly regarded as unjustifiable, mutually acceptable accommodations might not be reached until a new relationship is forged between the parties. Furthermore, different groups within each side usually are at different places on the road to conflict transformation. No collectivity is monolithic and settlement of a conflict is likely to favour some groups within each side while disadvantaging others.

Reconciliation often contributes to conflict transformation and recovery from criminal atrocities. Some efforts to bring about reconciliation, however, can also hamper the movement towards a fair and enduring accommodation. After all, advancing one aspect of reconciliation may undermine attaining another at a particular time. Furthermore, advancements for one group in a complex set of social relationships may be accompanied by setbacks for another. Leaders of opposing sides often forge settlements that provide safeguards for each other; but consequently, the rank and file supporters on each side may feel that they have been denied justice.

External actors sometimes can help to overcome or at least reduce these difficulties. Although reconciliation actions may be more effective if conducted by the opponents themselves, rather than by outsiders, the antagonists are often unable to overcome the challenges in undertaking them. It then falls on the external groups to help initiate the necessary tasks – for example, to document what had happened – to bring individuals to trial and to ensure safety for vulnerable persons and groups, such as occurred to some degree in Guatemala.

External actors, however, do not always mitigate a conflict's destructiveness. Indeed, they may prolong and intensify it. This usually happens as national governments or even IGOs join a fight to defeat one side in the conflict; but even attempts to pacify a situation may result in intense destructive escalation. Much more needs to be known about the impact of interventions by IGOs and INGOs, particularly since those interventions will probably continue to increase in this ever more integrated world. Furthermore, globalization is likely to benefit and harm subgroups on each side differentially, and thus generate new conflicts.

Admittedly, reconciliation can never be complete after mass crimes have been committed, at least for the generations that directly experienced them. Many people live on with little experience of reconciliation. Some will feel continuing pain, anguish, fear and hatred. Many others will appear to set aside what had happened and appear to have forgotten terrible occurrences; at least they do not discuss them. Some may seem to be numbed by the past, or possess what has been called collective autism.[32] Various forms of post-traumatic stress impact interpersonal relations, even affecting the children of those who suffered the traumas. Nevertheless, there are many actions people can undertake that will mitigate the inevitable difficulties that challenge any accommodation reached after mass crimes have ended.

This analysis has policy implications. Rehabilitating inter- or intra-societal relations after mass crimes have been perpetrated is immensely complex. INGOs and IGOs have particular capabilities, interests and ways of intervening in a conflict and in peace-building. They can contribute much, but too often they fail to make effective use of their resources. Four policy guidelines, suggested by the preceding analyses, can help maximize the potential helpful contributions of IGOs and INGOs.

First, great attention needs to be given to the local conditions of each specific case. IGOs and INGOs risk choosing policies that derive from their previous experiences somewhere else in the world and ones they feel comfortable in implementing. Those policies often are not the most suitable for a given time and place. For example, economic development projects that may have been effective in stable societies with legitimate institutions may not work in countries that are in considerable disorder and whose institutions are weak.[33]

Policies to promote rehabilitation and to create equitable and stable relations between former enemies need to be constructed so as to fit each unique post-mass-crime situation. A fundamental way to accomplish that is to work closely with local persons and organizations in analysing what the current situation looks like to people from diverse vantage points. Working with local persons, however, risks collaborating with dominant groups that are oppressive or exploitive of subordinate groups. External interveners may usefully be guided by international human rights standards as they try to balance a wide variety of considerations. The ethical issues discussed at the outset of this book cannot be avoided.

Local persons should be engaged in planning and executing policies as much as possible, helping to generate a vested interest in the conflict's transformation and the building of peace. Persons and groups that are inclined to foster rehabilitation and conflict transformation should be recruited, but they should be drawn from a wide range of communities. Even some members of groups whose leaders may be "spoilers" can be usefully incorporated in peace-building projects. Large-scale engagement by outside personnel in the tasks of reconstruction can generate animosity because they tend to be relatively well-paid and prompt increased local prices. Involving local people can provide employment and training; it also contributes to effective implementation and the legitimacy of the effort.

Second, rehabilitation takes a long time. Recognizing and planning for that can help prepare constituents and supporters for the necessary long-term policies. This is important for governments, whose leaders will not sustain the needed effort if they do not believe they have an important stake in transforming the conflict and achieving a durable peace. Some INGOs, for example many faith-based ones, can sustain lengthy commitments to particular localities as part of their ongoing mission.

Recognizing that years of sustained effort are generally needed to build the conditions for an enduring peace can help the peace-building process. It may be a reminder that some conditions that cannot be achieved immediately can still be attained in the future. For example, in many cases justice in the sense of bringing perpetrators of mass crimes to trial does not seem possible if a negotiated end of a destructive conflict is to be achieved. Yet, in some of those cases major alleged perpetrators have been put on trial years later.

Differences in the sequences of various aspects of reconciliation for different segments of each side in a conflict are inevitable. But reconciliation might not be attained for generations, if ever. What happens depends not only on the strategies various parties adopt, but also on many other factors, such as changing economic conditions, shifting political relations, normative changes and relative demographic trends.

Third, given the uniqueness of every situation, the people fashioning and implementing policies must think freshly, while drawing on relevant experience and knowledge.[34] The general guidelines already noted can contribute to creative thinking and help construct an effective strategy for the unique situation at hand. The analysis in this chapter presents an approach that can help fashion appropriate strategies. The approach presumes that rehabilitation is part of a conflict's transformation away from destructiveness. Former enemies create new ways of contending with each other such that mutual benefits become increasingly possible. That kind of transformation means altering the basic elements of a conflict so that they are less conducive to waging the conflict destructively. Keeping in mind the significance of affecting identities, grievances, goals and means of struggle focuses the attention of interveners on the fundamental purpose of their peace-building efforts. That helps break away from the tendency to start with a set of policies as tools, choosing one that feels right because it is available and familiar. Rather, thinking about the basic goals that are being sought can help develop new ways to attain them. Furthermore, in this chapter I have examined how reconciliation contributes to conflict transformation, discussing how reconciliation actions may affect the components of conflict so that the legacies of mass crimes are overcome. More assessments of what has worked well and what has not are needed and the knowledge gained should be incorporated in educating policy makers as well as the people working in the field.

Fourth, the special capabilities of IGOs and INGOs relevant to overcoming the legacies of mass crimes should be recognized and utilized. They can contribute many kinds of social and material resources that are sorely needed in the aftermath of mass crimes. They can provide refuge and assistance to those bereft of home and safety. They can contribute credible security in some degree to those in fear.

Caught in their own tragedies, persons who have experienced the consequences of mass crimes are sensitive to the reasons why overcoming their awful consequences is difficult. Members of IGOs and INGOs often have had experience with previous conflicts that can provide them with a useful professional distance for handling subsequent ones. Outsiders with other experiences and cognizant of how other people have made progress in overcoming tragic legacies can give hope to people who feel hopeless.

As relative outsiders, they can make suggestions that members of antagonistic sides can hear and consider seriously. They can make commitments to help ensure that agreements between opposing sides will be implemented. However, if past suggestions by a particular organization come to be seen as unfair or the commitments fail to be honoured, the credibility of that organization and others like it will be destroyed or seriously damaged. The responsibilities of IGOs and INGOs are great and in some ways inescapable. They need to be undertaken with care, so that the interventions do not do more harm than good.[35] That is possible.

Notes

1. This is evident in the use of possible membership in the European Union as an inducement to countries that wished to join to ensure equal rights for all its citizens. The mediation efforts of the Organization for Security and Co-operation in Europe, particularly in the Baltic countries after their independence from the Soviet Union, has drawn on human rights standards to establish institutions and rules that would avoid punitive policies in light of the suffering these countries experienced during Soviet Russian rule. Patrice C. McMahon, *Taming Ethnic Hatred: Ethnic Cooperation and Transnational Networks in Eastern Europe*, Syracuse, NY: Syracuse University Press, forthcoming; and Eileen F. Babbitt, *Principled Peace: Conflict Resolution and Human Rights in Intra-State Conflicts*, Ann Arbor, Mich.: University of Michigan Press, forthcoming.
2. Fen Osler Hampson, *Nurturing Peace: Why Peace Settlements Succeed or Fail*, Washington, D.C.: US Institute of Peace Press, 1996; Stephen John Stedman, Donald Rothchild and Elizabeth M. Cousens, eds, *Ending Civil Wars: The Implementation of Peace Agreements*, Boulder, Colo. and London: Lynne Rienner, 2002.
3. Colim Toibin, "Return to Catalonia", *New York Review of Books*, 7 October 2004, pp. 36–39.
4. Louis Kriesberg, *Constructive Conflicts: From Escalation to Resolution*, 3rd ed., Lanham, Md.: Rowman & Littlefield, 2006.
5. Anthony Smith, *National Identity*, Reno, Nev.: University of Nevada Press, 1991.
6. Daniel Druckman, "Social Psychological Aspects of Nationalism", in John L. Comaroff

and Paul C. Stern, eds, *Perspectives on Nationalism and War*, Luxembourg: Gordon and Breach, 1995, pp. 55–59. Also see Anthony Smith, *National Identity*.

7. Yehudith Auerbach, "The Role of Forgiveness in Reconciliation", in Yaacov Bar-Siman-Tov, ed., *From Conflict Resolution to Reconciliation*, Oxford: Oxford University Press, 2003, pp. 149–175.

8. John Stephen Stedman, "Spoiler Problems in Peace Processes", *International Security* 22, no. 2, Fall 1997, pp. 5–53.

9. John Paul Lederach, *Building Peace: Sustainable Reconciliation in Divided Societies*, Washington, D.C.: United States Institute of Peace Press, 1998; Louis Kriesberg, "Paths to Varieties of Inter-Communal Reconciliation", in Ho-Won Jeong, ed., *Conflict Resolution: Dynamics, Process and Structure*, Fitchburg, Md.: Dartmouth, 1999, pp. 105–129; and Louis Kriesberg, *Constructive Conflicts: From Escalation to Resolution*, 3rd ed., Lanham, Md.: Rowman & Littlefield, 2006.

10. Neil J. Kritz, ed., *Transitional Justice*, Washington, D.C.: United States Institute of Peace Press, 1995.

11. Michael Henderson, *The Forgiveness Factor*, London: Grosvenor Books, 1996; Yaacov Bar-Siman-Tov, ed., *From Conflict Resolution to Reconciliation*.

12. Martha Minow, *Between Vengeance and Forgiveness*, Boston: Beacon Press, 1998.

13. Timothy W. Ryback, "Dateline Sudetenland: Hostages to History", *Foreign Policy*, no. 105, 1996/97, pp. 162–178.

14. Of course there are many more intergovernmental organizations, many of them based in one country and operating internationally; the number of other intergovernmental organizations that are presently active is 1,743. Similarly, the number of non-governmental organizations cited in the text is for non-governmental organizations that are international in composition and operations; the number of other international non-governmental organizations is much greater, totalling 13,590. See Union of International Associations, *Yearbook of International Organizations* vol. 1B, Munich: K. G. Saur, 2004, p. 2914, appendix 3, table 1.

15. Pamela Aall, "What Do NGOs Bring to Peacemaking?" in Chester A. Crocker, Fen Osler Hampson and Pamela Aall, eds, *Turbulent Peace: The Challenges of Managing International Conflict*, Washington, D.C.: United States Institute of Peace Press. 2001, pp. 365–383; Larry Dunn and Louis Kriesberg, "Mediating Intermediaries: Expanding Roles of Transnational Organizations", in Jacob Bercovitch, ed., *Studies in International Mediation: Essays in Honour of Jeffrey Z. Rubin*, London and New York: Palgrave Macmillan, 2002, pp. 194–212; and Louis Kriesberg, "Social Movements and Global Solidarity", in Charles Chatfield, Jackie Smith and Ron Pagnucco, eds, *Transnational Social Movements and Global Solidarity*, Syracuse: Syracuse University Press, 1997, pp. 3–18.

16. Carolyn M. Stephenson, "NGOs and the Principal Organs of the United Nations", in Paul Taylor and A. J. R. Groom, eds, *The United Nations at the Millennium*, London and New York: Continuum, 2000, pp. 271–295.

17. Anna C. Snyder, *Setting the Agenda for Global Peace*, Aldershot: Ashgate, 2003.

18. Beverly Allen, *Rape Warfare: The Hidden Genocide in Bosnia-Herzegovina and Croatia*, Minneapolis: University of Minnesota Press, 1996.

19. See http://www.un.org/icty/.

20. See http://www.un.org/law/icc/.

21. Christopher Marquis, "U.N. Begins Choosing The Judges For New Court", *New York Times*, 6 February 2003, p. A9.

22. William Stanley and David Holiday, "Broad Participation, Diffuse Responsibility: Peace Implementation in Guatemala", in Stephen John Stedman, Donald Rothchild and Elizabeth M. Cousens, eds, *Ending Civil Wars*, Boulder, Colo. and London: Lynne Rienner, 2002, pp. 421–462.

23. Samantha Power, "Rwanda: The Two Faces of Justice", *New York Review of Books*, 16 January 2003, pp. 47–50.

24. For information about the activities of organizations relating to the UN, see "A New Database on the United Nations Human Rights Treaty System", available at http://www.bayefsky.com.

25. Sorpong Peou, "Implementing Cambodia's Peace Agreement", in John Stephen Stedman, Donald Rothchild and Elizabeth M. Cousens, eds, *Ending Civil Wars*, Boulder, Colo. and London: Lynne Rienner, 2002, pp. 499–530.

26. Eric Schechter, "Redefining the Refugees", *The Jerusalem Report* 12, no. 20, 28 January 2002, pp. 22–27.

27. Donna E. Arzt, *Refugees Into Citizens: Palestinians and the End of the Arab–Israeli Conflict*, New York: Council on Foreign Relations, 1997, pp. 102–103.

28. Yeshua Moser-Puangsuwan and Thomas Weber, eds, *Nonviolent Intervention Across Borders*, Honolulu: Spark M. Matsunaga Institute of Peace, University of Hawaii, 2000.

29. Ashutosh Varshney, *Ethnic Conflict and Civic Life: Hindu and Muslims in India*, New Haven, Conn.: Yale University Press, 2002.

30. For an examination of one such INGO, the Guatemalan Network Coordinating Committee, see Beth Abbott, "Project Accompaniment: A Canadian Response", in Yeshua Moser-Puangsuwan and Thomas Weber, eds, *Nonviolent Intervention Across Borders*, Honolulu: Spark M. Matsunaga Institute of Peace, University of Hawaii, 2000, pp. 163–174.

31. Manuela Leonhardt, Patricia Ardon, Njeri Karuru and Andrew Sheriff, *Peace & Conflict Impact Assessment (PCIA) and NGO Peacebuilding*, London, Nairobi, Guatemala: International Alert, The Centre for Conflict Research (CCR), and Instituto de Ensenanza para el Desarrollo Sostenible (IEPADES), 2002.

32. Chris Hedges, *War Is a Force That Gives Us Meaning*, New York: Public Affairs, 2002.

33. Susan L. Woodward, "Economic Priorities for Successful Peace Implementation", in John Stephen Stedman, Donald Rothchild and Elizabeth M. Cousens, eds, *Ending Civil Wars*, Boulder, Colo. and London: Lynne Rienner, 2002, pp. 183–214; and Roland Paris, *War's End: Building Peace After Civil Conflict*, New York: Cambridge University Press, 2004.

34. Chester A. Crocker, Fen Osler Hampson and Pamela Aall, eds, *Herding Cats: Multiparty Mediation in a Complex World*, Washington, D.C.: United States Institute of Peace Press, 1999.

35. A highly influential book in this regard is Mary Anderson, *Do No Harm: How Aid Can Support Peace – or War*, Boulder, Colo.: Lynne Rienner, 1999.

11

Re-imagining peace after mass crime: A dialogical exchange between insider and outsider knowledge

Roberta Culbertson and Béatrice Pouligny

The aim of this concluding chapter is to offer an integrative analysis, intending to tie the different chapters together and summarize the main theoretical principles that have been articulated in the course of this volume. It is not meant to reflect all the nuances and interests of the contributors, but rather to reflect an overall perspective within which ground-level empirical analysis and abstract theoretical reflection can be pursued and some comparative opportunities assured. Indeed, one important first lesson that can be drawn from the different analyses in this volume is the necessity of keeping a close connection between theoretical discussion and fieldwork. We also pull out common themes and general lessons that can be drawn from the more contextually based analyses found here. In so doing, we suggest broad principles that might guide those who wish to help in the processes of "building peace" after mass crime, and that might serve as a point of departure for any fieldwork on the subject.

A core idea can summarize our overall approach: Peace must be re-imagined, even re-invented, after mass crime. The idea of "re-imagining peace" contains three main elements. First, there is the imagination itself. All actions and responses begin as thoughts, individual mental analyses of perceived conditions. All thoughts are framed according to the individual's mental preconditions – cognitive learning, subconscious structures of meaning and embodied, deeply encoded non-verbal and relatively automatic responses to stimuli. These in turn are socially and culturally mediated and determined. One thinks only within the frame of whatever cognitive tools and emotional experiences have formed in him in the

After mass crime: Rebuilding states and communities, Pouligny, Chesterman and Schnabel (eds), United Nations University Press, 2007, ISBN 978-92-808-1138-4

course of his development. Imagination works within this dialectic between experience and socially mediated meaning, adapting the one to the other so as to produce some sense of "fit". It is here, in the interstices between thought and shared meaning that all experiences of massacre and all hopes of peace are born. Second, building on this imaginal element, the idea of re-imagining peace requires that collective and individual imaginations find ways to create a relatively small set of shared meanings and patterns of thought that will create a perception of safety, in which more complex forms of shared meanings and mutuality might grow. Peace as a social condition is sustainable only if people can imagine that those with whom they interact are safe and legitimate. The imagination must be able to use the conceptual social "glues" of trust, hope, identity and community to identify and respond to those it encounters. Finally, massacres are what happens when the opposite occurs: when the imagination takes other concepts as descriptive of social situations and begins to expand its meaning-making in the direction of suspicion, revenge and hatred.

As we use the term, *imagination* is ultimately a matter of individual thought, but there is also social or cultural imagination – the syncretic and synergistic adaptation of stock symbols and social structures to changing circumstances that happens when people share experiences and attempt to make sense of them in shared venues, from newspapers to public squares to history. What is produced in these social settings – the product of multiple imaginations working to make sense of circumstances with the available cognitive and symbolic tools – we call *imaginaries*.

The project begins with the recognition that it is extremely difficult to turn the imagination from the effects of massacre to the imaginal tasks of rebuilding. Even silence and denial of massacres are in fact effects of their power and terror, and of the ways in which these foreclosures of discussion limit or direct the imagination in the direction of self-protection, denial and revenge. And yet until the imagination is turned toward the task of rebuilding and the impossible considered – justice, reconciliation, truth-telling, compassion, confession, happiness – efforts at rebuilding will founder. Outsider efforts (from civil society specialists to engineers and economists) will encounter seemingly inexplicable road blocks in projects to re-establish markets, civil society and workable post-massacre identities unless these fluid and yet constrained dimensions of individual, social and cultural realities are taken into account. Outsiders can support insiders' efforts in that direction if they understand both local roots of past conflicts and local resources for rebuilding – including those of local and cultural symbologies and imaginaries. A dialogical exchange between insiders and outsiders – and between different groups of insiders and different groups of outsiders – in which some effort is made to identify the constraints and categories within which any imagining must work is imperative if those who were part of bloodshed and those who come from elsewhere to help rebuild are to create together the space for re-imagining peace.

Here our analysis focuses on three important components of this approach. First, we stress the need for understanding the nature of the transformations enforced by war and mass violence. This means both that there cannot be a mere return to the past and that the past should not be romanticized. Second, we insist on the importance of moving between different levels of organization on the ground, and understanding the multiple connections and disconnections between micro and macro dimensions of violence and post-violence. Third, we focus on some key elements regarding the work of reintegration in survivor communities. This is not to say that we do not have a commitment to or interest in the higher levels of social organization, including the state. But what we hope to offer is a perspective that is more "lococentric" than that shaped by institutional categories or academic fields, so as to add this perspective to the work of others.

Understanding transformation in post-mass-crime situations

Wars and massacres are destructive, but in the hands of time and culture they are also transformative. This is a first important characteristic underlined by all the contributions. Memory, psychology, outside influences, politics and belief all play a role in the reconstruction and transformation of a social and ideational world as survivors reconstruct meaning that will allow them to continue, using whatever cultural materials are at hand. Kimberly Theidon's work on post-massacre rebuilding in Peru, for instance, shows how evangelical Christian perspectives have been adopted by indigenous communities as explanatory of their own experiences, lending meaning to the intense emotions and grief that surround the experience of massacre, and – through the concept of repentance – re-incorporating combatants. These Christian perspectives are not seen as separate from or replacing other, more "traditional" perspectives, but rather as of a piece with them as they are incorporated into a syncretic whole.[1] Similarly, chapters on African situations, Cambodia and Bali (Indonesia) underline the dialectic of tradition and innovation at play in the aftermath of mass crime.

Indeed, it is often suggested that local groups return to traditional means of solving conflict and resolving grief after massacres. The contributors in this book agree with this perspective in principle, and some of them very strongly advocate it, but also recognize that innovation is part of every culture's reality, and that borrowing and grafting ideas from the outside and reshaping old concepts to new experiences are also important local strategies.[2] We understand that it is quite possible that there will be no such thing as a simple "return to traditions" in a community: such traditions or those who carried them may no longer exist, or may have been compromised by their wartime uses and activities. What are labelled "returns to tradition" may in fact be inventions, recalled or resurrected ideas layered on and informed by new information. They should be understood as such and not romanticized. It is important to be clear. Peace-building is first and foremost a matter of mobilizing cultural endeavours to incorporate rather than deny the massacre experience, while also regenerating local cultural mores that eschew violence as a means of social action. In these efforts, the contextualizing benefits of history and political analysis, support of the "re-invention" of community and peace and the usefulness of culturally acceptable "cures" to counter the wounds of violence are all useful strategies.[3] These will be addressed in turn.

Contextualizing violence and post-violence

When political actors seek to use populations rather than armies to attain their goals, the resultant large-scale movements of people re-configure the boundaries of ethnic identity and social life. Interethnic social networks are soon torn asunder and acts of terror grow. The limits of individual understanding and cultural explanation are soon passed, and what is happening becomes unfathomable. Uncertainty goes beyond ordinary limits and precipitates general violence. The devices of violence and massacre, the mutilation of bodies and torture, become a strategy aimed at creating "a macabre form of certainty", in times of a high level of uncertainty.[4] In the words of Roberto Beneduce, in chapter 2, the devastation of bodies paradoxically becomes a device for creating certainty in the face of the assumed power of the "other", a brutal technique for redefining "them" against "us".[5]

In such contexts, "war or generalized violence represent practices of existence". These practices could also be considered strategies of formation and assertion of individual and collective identity – diffused and profoundly internalized relational models. This perspective helps avoid a risk: the assumption that the breakdown of social order, mass atrocities and the ghastly violence that distinguishes them constitute an "anomaly", an exception, a circumscribed time of chaos which can be ended through the (re)installation of state structures. Instead, they often come to constitute another kind of order, however brutal, macabre or *dis*orderly it may appear. All the contributions in this volume show how far this reality may impact – and sometimes obstruct – the reconstruction of everyday life in communities that have lived through a long siege of violence. Nor are the acts so performed easily seen for what they were in the light of a more peace-based morality or social structure; it is easier to retain the perspective that promoted or allowed them: The other is still other, the dangerous are still dangerous, the untrusted remain untrusted.[6]

How can a state be (re)built when such conditions continue to prevail? Analysis of the genealogy and the reproduction of violence call for a methodological approach that is able to systematically combine social and political analysis, local history and a global perspective.[7] In the absence of this interweaving, interpretations remain fragmented, leaving key aspects in the shadows. Contributions to this volume more specifically show how much historical discourses may support or oppose any effort at building peace and achieving some kind of reconciliation. Peace-building is a highly politicized process in which conflicting visions of the past and future interfere with multiple discourses and interactions between insiders and outsiders, as underlined in Louis Kriesberg's chapter. As clearly illustrated by the most micro-focused chapters of this volume, one important dimension of community healing is establishing within the community a context for what happened, making it not necessarily morally defensible, but at the very least understood. The questions that emerge immediately and remain – "How could this happen?" and "Why is it happening?" – must be answered in the most objective manner possible. This is a job that involves creating and supporting the development of local histories and local historians, and also the presence of outside actors who are legitimate and offer insight into how history can best be researched and performed in ways that allow for credibility. It is often suggested that history is itself political, and that historians, as creatures of power structures, create histories that support those structures. The truth is always more complex and nuanced than can be addressed in related histories, which take narrative form and offer explanations – often very simplistic ones – for what happened, when explanations may in fact be nearly impossible. It is easy to hijack history to serve hegemonic interests, as Thomas Sherlock's chapter shows. Yet history itself as a global discipline is aware of these difficulties, and is developing methods to improve its accuracy – to create if not objectivity then at least intersubjectivity in which different perspectives are allowed to carry weight.[8] Whether this is done in specific cases is of course dependent upon those circumstances, but some means of reaching fuller accountings of events from all sides is certainly part of postmodern historiography. This means that the issue of how history should be practiced and who should do so is a central question for regions emerging from periods of massacre, and that the means for answering that question are at hand. The details of history, the careful mining of all resources – from letters to computer files to court records to artefacts and newspapers – provide a focus for questions and both open the imagination to possibilities and deny it the freedom to lie against the facts. One should never forget how key is this dialogical exchange in the rebuilding process: It is important to always take into consideration what people think and believe about their own past, present and future; but they also often require outsider resources and information to support the writing of stories from a perspective wide enough to counter calls for simple vengeance.

Such histories, if they are to be effective in reducing the likelihood of renewed enmity, must be careful and exact, and even avoid condemnatory or biased language, however difficult it may be to do so. For instance, an overarching, moralizing and binary view that involves merely the struggle between "good" and "evil" may lead to an impasse in reasoning, as argued by Bernard Doray, Jean-Clément Martin and Béatrice Pouligny. Ideas of "irrationality", disorder or evil obscure not only the organization, rational means, reasoned arguments and deliberate methods employed in massacres and which are always at work in these kinds of practices, but also overshadow the banality of the actors, who are, after all, ordinary humans. Instead of resorting to such all-encompassing notions, one should be attentive to the oft-present mechanisms (political, social and psychological) that allow analogous events to emerge under different circumstances. It is important to organize local events in their regional, national and international contexts; to elaborate the ideological, technical, cultural and other means by which the massacre was perpetrated; and to understand to local satisfaction to what degree matters were local and to what degree they were products of outside developments. Such work can be extremely sensitive politically and there may be no way to resolve certain economic and social issues that thereby come to the fore. But this does not negate the importance of such work or suggest that there is no point in doing it. People, even the most powerless, cannot escape a circumstance in a reasoned and perhaps useful way until they are sure of its dimensions and their options.

Even when they are not explicitly set as "therapeutic" objectives, it is certain that the compilations of testimony that re-establish the truth of great massacres and acts of multiple, organized cruelties have a powerful effect on survivors. Although in the short run survivors invested in a view of themselves as victims or perpetrators can feel dispossessed by or lost in the process of grounding their intimate experiences in a wider framework, they can in the longer run benefit from the recognition of their own story as the local consequence of wider forces. The process can result in major liberation from personal trauma and re-symbolization (reinserting subjects back into their culture and the history of their community) on both sides. In this sense, the description of these events, if indeed there is an attempt to seek the most exact and precise account, cannot claim to be neutral or non-judgmental, especially when it ultimately becomes a question of selecting the form in which this individual and collective story is to be made public. It also cannot be unfairly biased. All sides of the story must be told in as unflinching a way as possible, with the recognition of culpability on all sides widening as the tolerance for truth – however it may run counter to myth or belief – increases. Perhaps what definitively defines mass crimes is the ubiquity of immediate instances of culpability on all sides. All mass violence is made up of single acts. In the most intimate sites of any instance of mass violence – the street, the household, the public square, the prison cell – individuals make choices and take action, and remain haunted by them. Victims may turn in their neighbours and so become indirect perpetrators. Many witness atrocities without defending the victims or even speaking out. Many perpetrators at the last moment turn away and cannot fire. Others do in the moment what they regret in the aftermath and try to lay blame on the victims to assuage their own guilt. All of these subtleties must come out in the stories of mass crime if those involved are to see themselves as human actors rather than monsters and saints.

Cultural trauma

This is not to say that events of massacre and post-massacre can simply be reduced to a collection of individual tragedies, because no massacre is simply that.[9] The authors here stress that it is the culture itself, the possibility of social life, that is under attack in massacres, a dimension that is worsened by the gravity of symbolic attacks generally committed at the same time as massacres. In the narratives of victims and survivors the religious, cultural and symbolic dimensions of the violence form an integral part of the violation of their rights and of their emotional experiences. In the existing literature, there is of course a host of models stressing other dynamics – political, economic and social; here we suggest that cultural trauma – or cultural destruction – be added to these. Trauma is a social as well as a personal reality, and it is framed and carried out by collective action. It is this cultural trauma – the capture and distortion of cultural symbols, the twisting of history and symbolic categories, the redefinition of ethnicity – that must also be countered if cultural symbols are not to retain their valence as tools of war. Ancient or contemporary symbols, practices, naming devices and myths must be reclaimed and reconstructed after mass crimes, taking full account of what was done to these symbols by conscious effort during the period of violence. This is another form of contextualization.

At the same time, however, it must be said that cultural trauma may hold the most promising opportunities for cultural reconfiguration and re-imagining, for the materials of culture are at base imaginative materials – they are the tools of thought. Cultural trauma, when recognized, may point to directions for peace-building. Jeffrey C. Alexander suggests that cultural trauma, and an understanding of trauma at a collective level, may precipitate action: "Social groups, national societies, and sometimes even entire civilizations not only cognitively identify the existence and source of human suffering but 'take on board' some significant responsibility for it. Insofar as they identify the cause of trauma, and thereby assume such moral responsibility, members of collectivities define their solidary relationships in ways that, in principle, allow them to share the sufferings of others."[10]

Re-imagining peace

Bringing the above together – the transformative power of mass crimes, the importance of context to an understanding of it, the importance of understanding in peace-building and the degree to which cultural trauma is both an intended and a hidden consequence of mass violence – an outline arises of a general set of issues that confront the post-war or post-mass-crime environment and those who would change it.

The tenacity of violence-based organization

The first issue to be encountered and addressed in a post-war or post-mass-crime environment is the simple fact that not all communities formed or re-formed in the aftermath of war give up war's organizing principles. In fact, the process of reconfiguring forms of social interaction may fall well behind the conclusion of peace agreements and even the arrival of peacekeeping forces, new economic incentives and new market opportunities. Nor do the efforts of outside organizations, from non-governmental organizations to national or international tribunals, as Kriesberg analyses them, necessarily succeed in replacing war-based imaginaries and the social patterns they create with notions of trust and forgiveness. A significant degree of individual and communal self-reflection and self-discipline are in order in any rebuilding process, and they must be engaged in the face of great resistance.[11]

The imaginaries of war – those socially and culturally framed categories that hold the experiences of war and with which the imagination works to make sense of what happens on the battlefield or the field of massacre – do not by their nature support this sort of self-reflective analysis; they are largely instrumental or ideological in focus and do not offer structures or clues to the development of the more subtle and nuanced social interactions of peacetime. At the same time, the imaginaries of outsiders – the conceptual tools that relief agencies and their employees bring to bear on the post-war situation – are relevant to entirely different contexts, and are often too distant to seem applicable. Both sides must work overtime to make experience fit the mould of conceptual constructions that are a function of peace. The aftermath of war draws first from the logic of war: vengeance, punishment and reparations. In so doing it retains a strong link to war and its methods and experiences. Thus the vast literature on justice, retribution, human rights and reconciliation begins not from the perspective of communal life but from its rupture, and attempts to initiate "repair". To some degree, this makes repair the handmaiden of wounding, and as such limits what can be explored in the way of post-massacre community.

Community and the "repair" perspective

However wars may be occasioned by international dynamics and national power struggles, they work themselves out on the ground in communities – in habitations of some two or three thousand or several thousand, or even only a few hundred, who have some sense of shared identity, history and destiny. When the wars that ensue drive such communities into smaller communities constructed upon "ethnic" or other lines, it is community that is the rallying cry – and the victim. In the name of group identity communities are often torn apart, and massacres serve to concretize in blood and death divisions between former neighbours. In the aftermath, the imaginal reconstruction of communities takes a variety of forms, and makes use of cultural categories to address vexing but immediate existential issues such as the nature and locus of good and evil, the limits of responsibility and loyalty, the reality of betrayal and the power of the absurd or incomprehensible, all so much in evidence in the countries dealt with in this volume.

Recognizing the ways in which communities are often sundered by war, and by massacres in particular, however, the different contributors to this volume also recognize that people continually re-form and seek to re-establish themselves in communities following conflict, albeit likely along shifting lines of affiliation, and often with a great deal of difficulty. As Karl Jaspers puts it, "Everyone tends to interpret great losses and trials as a sacrifice. But the possible interpretations of this sacrifice are so abysmally different that, at first, they divide people."[12] Community bonds are a critical source of individual healing and purpose, and establish the basic social bedrock of markets, production and civic life, and thus must be reconstituted in some form. In ways very complementary to the work done by the Human Rights Center at the University of California, Berkeley, the analyses gathered in this volume suggest a kind of syncretic model to accommodate and systematize the host of elements involved in this process, moving between different levels of organization on the ground, particularly from the individual to the social, with reference to the cultural frames that unite these two.

Community will be attempted after war, or may be imposed through processes of reconciliation. It may keep the lines set by massacres and war or outside pressures may require it to do so, as in the Balkans.[13] In other contexts, outside pressures may push for reintegration. Various contributions to this book confirm the suggestion by other authors that efforts by outside forces to impose change on ethnic struggles may be less than successful if certain conditions continue to persist, including the marginalization of actors on one side or another of the ethnic divide.[14] But whatever is done, on the ground, locally, on the streets and in the apartment blocks and villages that recently ran with blood and sang with bullets, some form of regularized social interaction will begin to emerge, whether imposed or not. This is community not as a utopian or communitarian goal, but community in reality; social groups engaging in some sort of social life that is or can be shaped by three dialectics touched on at the beginning of this volume: that of insider–outsider; that of emotion–rationality; and that of tradition–innovation.[15]

Among other terms broadly used for this process in the literature is "social repair", suggesting the need to rebuild social ties broken in the course of conflict. But with or without the notion of "repair", which suggests some kind of outside intervention, the reality of life is that humans must act in social contexts and to do so must share some degree of meaning. Thus, after conflict efforts will always be made to normalize social and cultural conditions in order to make life manageable.[16] Much of the existing literature addressing the issues of reconstituting community after violence focuses on the matter of justice following mass violence as the *sine qua non* of "repair". Yet such repair may be as divisive as it is uniting. Other mechanisms of community, and indigenous means of finding justice, are as critical as justice itself. The contributors to this volume add to the repair perspectives ways to deal with less accessible local imaginaries and assumptions about community and cohesion and to recognize how these might have been altered by the process of massacre itself.

Cultural resources for re-imagining peace

Now we are able to describe more fully just how the contributors to this volume expand on the field of post-massacre recovery to include changes in the ways surviving societies and individuals might conceive of or imagine peace, when they have been caught in an imaginary of war. They have several sources of conceptual materials and other fuel for the imagination that come from their own indigenous systems of belief and categorization, from new global perspectives and from new syncretic versions of the two.

Indigenous imaginaries

These are issues with which all human cultures have dealt since the beginning, and in every community there are many cultural resources at hand that describe this necessary balance between accounting and bloodletting, punishment and reinstatement – and how to reach it. Because the process is undoubtedly the most difficult in the human repertoire, its description is located in cultures' most hallowed and respected languages: religious, poetic and legal. In short, traditional religious perspectives, healing traditions and philosophies, narrative styles from heroic to lyric poetry, song, dance and other performance, all encapsulate and recapitulate what is crucial to cultural and social survival as opposed to mere human survival. They can be brought to bear as communities seek to re-establish imaginaries of peace and community over war. But because many of these cultural resources may have also been tainted in the process of war, they too must be subjected to scrutiny by communities seeking to re-assert a reality that is not war-based. Here, certain "outsider" perspectives, from the neurobiology of fear to the various formal means of achieving justice, can be of use, when they are offered in formats and contexts that meet local needs.

Global contributions

The field of trauma studies is growing, but it remains relatively new and its findings often do not enter the plans of national and international groups engaged in reconstruction after massacres. To the degree it enters the discussion and is included in programming, it is usually at the level of individual sufferers, and does not address how personal anguish becomes public reality. Yet it appears from research that the ways in which traumatic events shape human psyches and social systems play a major role in the shaping of subsequent social structures and cultural categories. All cultures reflect an iterative process of coming to grips with various periods of violence, but the process is always hampered by the very effects of trauma themselves. In contemporary reconstruction efforts, as in other times, the precise ways in which the experience of violence skews and complicates perceptions, interactions and reconstruction in their own right has not been addressed enough. This is the focus of various contributions in this book, which explore and articulate with the communities suffering them the effects of violence on psyche, society and cultural assumptions. As stressed by the authors, this requires operating at the nexus between what is now being learned in scientific circles about the nature of perception, embodiment and violence, and what has been known in every culture for millennia about the importance and use of non-violent cultural tools.

It appears that even cross-culturally, traumatic memory differs from cognitive, spoken memory by being highly embodied, unarticulated in words, intrusive and state-dependent.[17] Traumatically produced mental structures and their resultant social and cultural counterparts after violent trauma are rooted in the body's adaptive fight-or-flight response and its related memory states, which manifest as unspoken and unarticulated anxiety, confusion and perceived threat, often coupled with a high degree of silence about traumatic events themselves, or an overemphasis on control and power in a world *a priori* defined as dangerous.[18] Traumatic memory leads to worldviews and phenomenologies that are likewise different from those that draw on cognitive sources like law, literature and myth for their root structures, and thus presents a problematic that must be resolved culturally rather than being structured by culture.[19]

In addition to the particular psychological structures that shape the perceived aftermath of massacres there are also the more easily discerned social ones: the destruction of families through the death of family members and betrayal; the long-term destabilization of marriage patterns and support networks; the interruption of the flow of goods and services; and the distrust and discrediting of civil authorities. These create their own crises of socio-political thought and patterns of accommodation that tend to perpetuate certain massacre-based behaviours, such as a general fear of authority figures, the constant splitting of small groups unable to handle internal conflict or increased reliance on rumour over direct communication.

Connecting inner and outer perspectives

These individual psychological and phenomenological changes and social instabilities as they are understood from an "outsider's" perspective can be incorporated culturally in resurrected or new overarching myths, interpretations and explanations that serve as templates for the absorption of new information by individuals and groups. These often incoherent and contradictory cultural frames are necessarily created and cobbled together from past understandings and symbols in the aftermath of violence. They reflect the pain and loss of the massacre and its social consequences, but also the embodied effects that are not articulated. These instead surface as desires for revenge, deep guilt, feelings of entitlement and abiding restlessness, and so prove extremely difficult to discern or challenge.[20] But their contradictions are not lost on the people who hold them, who remain in a state of constant dissonance between beliefs and actualities, between some beliefs and others and between groups in which different beliefs are held sacrosanct.

Here is where external perspectives that show the intercultural, violence-engendered bases of what appear to be essential realities can be brought to bear on the details of local knowledge in ways that release members from the conceptual prisons of war's making. The authors in this volume articulate the benefits of such an approach in a variety of cases and circumstances. They also make the case that this process is extremely embedded in the community itself, and in its means of expression and symbology. It cannot be imposed from the outside. At the same time, without some outside tools and options local communities may remain trapped in the power of war-based structures of thought, with little to move them to another perspective. Even their own literatures may continue to be subverted by war-based experiences.

Conclusion

In order to work in communities at a level that is appropriate, the matter of insider and outsider knowledge must become a dialogical exchange in the hands of the local community, as outsiders' and insiders' conceptual categories are put in service to the imagination that seeks to re-imagine peace. Outsiders can serve in the role of idea givers, researchers and facilitators, as well as advocates. Insiders can examine traditional resources and perhaps rehabilitate those that have been sullied by appropriation or misuse. They can conduct deep and detailed historical analyses of what happened and even of widely accepted "truths". They may develop new, locally valid approaches to post-massacre issues and carry them out with outsider resources. This might entail using outside funding to establish a database of survivor accounts, for example. In all circumstances, emotion and reason must be carefully explored and clarified by all parties, as the matter of working with the aftermath of violence is overwhelmingly emotional and requires reason. At the same time, too much reason stifles the realities of the pain of massacres, and so both elements must be kept in balance, often consciously, by all sides involved. Finally, the benefits of both tradition and innovation must be weighed, in order that the communities might draw on the widest range of possibilities as they reconstruct their individual, social and cultural lives. In other words, concepts and frames within which local events are interpreted and local action developed should quite naturally combine the insider/outsider perspective, the emotional and rational, and the traditional and innovative. Different resources can be developed to that end; they would support one another and, taken as a whole, suggest a means by which a community can return from the brink of disaster, from massacre to peace, by learning what it needs to know about what happened, establishing justice and accountability and engaging in necessary cures to remove the taint of the experience. With this accomplished or ongoing, they can then also draw on cultural materials that promote codes of conduct and behaviours and create imaginaries that will sustain peace and make for a more solid context that will not be so easily shaken by disruptive imaginaries, or even by economic downturns or outside pressures.

Of course, cultural resources, particularly those of symbolization, memorials and history, are often co-opted by dominant forces in a community along political and gender lines. At the same time, however, the "invisible", including women, are often re-creating their own coping strategies and cultural products and projects in the more hidden sectors of cultural life.[21] These often incorporate the artistic dimensions of everyday life, including artisanship, work songs, prayers and narratives. They include rituals from birthing to burial. In these realms, the culture is both re-instituted along non-violent lines, and women and other disenfranchised and disempowered proceed to take back a degree of subjectivity and self-empowerment.[22]

Research-action efforts should focus on three areas in which a community must work if it is to not re-enter a cycle of violence, if it is to "re-invent" cultural processes of non-violence. These must recognize the overarching power of violent experience, its emotional and psychological dimensions and, most important, the macabre phenomenology it imposes on all who live in its midst. The three areas in which the effects of violence can and must be ameliorated include accountability, justice and a re-imagining of the quotidian. In three realms of a community's life in particular, the quotidian must come to hold sway again. First, the realm of everyday life must come to contain elements that encourage and valourize the quotidian, the dull, the average, the mundane and the quiet. Second, local moral and ethical codes must come to include non-violent behaviours as preferable to violent ones, replacing, for example, the call for vengeance with a call for redress, and the call for redress finally and in time with a call for community. This is already a large part of much social activity after war but it is not addressed in these terms, which suggests the need for a meta-level of cultural awareness and commitment. Finally, the local metaphysical structures must open sufficiently to allow for the phenomenology of violence, and must offer explanations for the most extreme experiences and their fallout, but without enforcing Manichean or other demonizing perspectives that threaten some group or another with scapegoating and sacrifice.

In short, a community's worldview must become articulate about the nature of violence, its effects, its demands and its perspective, and must make conscious choices to both incorporate the reality that violence teaches and eschew its destructive capacities. If it does not do so, a culture will find itself inevitably drawn back to violence and its blandishments.[23] In this process, it can make use of the discoveries of other cultures, that have themselves experienced violence, and of global efforts to comprehend how best to move from the structures and perceptions of mass crime and mass violence to those of the mundane and peaceful. Yet it can only effectively do so by combining the inner and outer perspectives into a new synthesis that is local by nature.

The authors and editors of this volume hope that, overall, the work here contributes to the exploration of a dimension of post-violence recovery that is less studied than others, by offering ways to think of how people must re-imagine their ways to peace as much as they must repair their economies and infrastructures. The authors here demonstrate various ways in which such re-imaginings occur, and are stymied. We hope that the attention paid here to the subtle, to the un-discussed and unobserved, to the ways that imagination is both expanded and limited by the framing power of concepts and history, will give ideas for further development of this critical dimension of re-imagining peace.

Notes

1. See chapter 4.
2. For another example of field work that makes this point, see M. Brinton Lykes, Martin Terre Blanche and Brandon Hamber, "Narrating survival and change in Guatemala and South Africa: The politics of representation and a liberatory community psychology", *American Journal of Community Psychology*, no. 31, March 2003, pp. 79–90.
3. Such "cures" include social and cultural strategies for managing the effects of mass violence, including the taking on of responsibility by relevant parties and recognition of the cognitive, physical and metaphysical changes brought about by the violence.
4. Arjun Appadurai, "The past as scarce resource", *Man* 16, no. 2, 1981, pp. 201–219.
5. See also Christopher Taylor, *Sacrifice as terror: The Rwandan genocide of 1994*, Oxford and New York: Berg, 1999.
6. See Anatoly Isaenko and Peter Petschauer, "The Long Arm of the Dead: Traumas and Conflicts in the Caucasus", *Mind and Human Interaction* 6, no. 3, August 1995, pp. 103–115.

7. See Paul Antze and Michael Lambek, eds, *Tense past: Cultural essays in trauma and memory*, London: Routledge and Kegan, 1996. See also Eric Stover and Harvey Weinstein, eds, *My neighbor, my enemy: Justice and community in the aftermath of mass atrocity*, London: Cambridge University Press, 2004.

8. See also Bernard Doray, Jean-Clément Martin and Béatrice Pouligny's reflections on that particular aspect in chapter 1.

9. See M. Lumsden, "Three zones of social reconstruction in war-traumatized societies", in Ho Wo Jeong ed., *Conflict resolution: Dynamics, process and structure*, Brookfield, Vt.: Ashgate, 1999, pp. 131–151.

10. Jeffrey C. Alexander, *The meanings of social life: A cultural sociology*, New York: Oxford University Press, 2003, p. 85. See especially chapter 3, "Cultural trauma and collective identity", pp. 85–108.

11. Stover and Weinstein, *My neighbor, my enemy*.

12. Jaspers quoted in Laurel Fletcher and Harvey Weinstein, "Violence and social repair: Rethinking the contribution of justice to reconciliation", *Human Rights Quarterly* 24, no. 3, 2002, pp. 573–639.

13. Sanin Mirvic, "Bosnian History and the Issue of Survival", presented at the Virginia Foundation for the Humanities conference "Re-Imagining Peace after Massacres", Charlottesville, Va.: November 2004.

14. See Holly Hughson, *You, me, and never the twain shall meet: Perceptions of education, history, justice and ethnicity in Kosovo*, Denmark: ADRA, with assistance from the Human Rights Center, University of California, Berkeley, 2004.

15. See Introduction.

16. For this idea in its clearest theoretical form see Clifford Geertz, *The interpretation of cultures*, New York: Basic Books Classics, 1977.

17. Bruce D. Perry, "Memories of fear: How the brain stores and retrieves physiologic states, feelings, behaviors and thoughts from traumatic events", in J. Goodwin and R. Attias, eds, *Splintered reflections: Images of the body in trauma*, New York: Basic Books, 1999. Also see the Child Trauma Academy, http://www.ChildTrauma.org.

18. Much significant work on this subject is now in hand. Among the new directions the research is taking is exploration of the particular mental states that trauma survivors seem to inhabit and their origins and dimensions: Many traumatized individuals alternate between re-experiencing their trauma and being detached from, or even relatively unaware of the trauma and its effects (see in particular R. S. Nijenhuis Ellert and O. Van der Hart, *Forgetting and Reexperiencing Trauma: From Anesthesia to Pain*, New York: Basic Books, 1999; and the publications of the American Psychological Association). This alternating pattern has been noted for more than a century by students of psychotraumatology, who have observed that it can ensue after different degrees and kinds of traumatization. Being detached from trauma does not itself exclude being joyful, ashamed, sexually aroused or curious – it may co-exist with relatively normal degrees of affect at least some of the time. At the same time, re-experiencing trauma, perhaps in the face of certain "triggers" that replicate some element of the original event, can encompass states such as fleeing, freezing, psychosomatic pain or physical as well as emotional numbness. For historical studies, see Pierre Janet, *L'automatisme psychologique: Essai de psychologie expérimentale sur les formes inférieures de l'activité humaine*, Paris: Alcan, 1889; Pierre Janet, "L'amnésie et la dissociation des souvenirs par l'émotion", *Journal de psychologie normale et pathologique* 1, 1904, pp. 417–453; Abram Kardiner, *The traumatic neuroses of war*, New York: Hoeber, 1941; and M. J. Horowitz, *Stress Response Syndromes*, New York: Aronson, 1976. See also "Trauma-related structural dissociation of the personality", Trauma Information Pages, January 2004, available at http://www.trauma-pages.com/nijenhuis-2004.htm.

19. This said, of course, one must understand that, entering the process at another point, one might find that the experience of violence is resolved culturally by promoting more violence, as in revenge, and so that culture can also structure violence.

20. This pattern relates to what Maurice Eisenbruch calls "cultural bereavement" (see chapter 3), a term he uses to incorporate culturally informed ways of dealing with grief and the other effects of trauma.

21. For an introduction to the subject, see James Scott, *Domination and the arts of resistance: Hidden transcripts*, New Haven: Yale University Press, 1992.

22. Kimberley Theidon, "How we learned to kill our brother: Memory, morality, and reconciliation in Peru", paper presented at the Center for African Studies conference "Memory and history: Remembering, forgetting and forgiving in the life of the nation and the community", University of Cape Town, South Africa, September 2002.

23. Chris Hedges, *War is a force that gives us meaning*, New York: Anchor Books, 2003.

Selected bibliography

A more full bibliography is maintained by the Center for International Studies and Research. It is available online at http://www.ceri-sciencespo.com/themes/re-imaginingpeace/va/resources/bibliography.htm.

Socio-politics and history of mass crime

Books

Alvarez, Alex, *Governments, Citizens and Genocide: A Comparative and Interdisciplinary Approach*, Bloomington: Indiana University Press, 2001.

Andreopoulos, George J., ed., *Genocide: Conceptual and Historical Dimensions*, Philadelphia: University of Pennsylvania Press, 1994.

Apter, David E., *The Legitimization of Violence*, Geneva: United Nations Research Institute for Social Development and Basingstoke: MacMillan, 1997.

Bell-Fialoff, Andrew, *Ethnic Cleansing*, New York: St. Martin's Press, 1996.

Benot, Yves, *Massacres coloniaux: 1944–1950: La 4ème République et la mise au pas des colonies françaises*, Paris: Découverte, 2001.

Breitman, Richard, *The Architect of Genocide: Himmler and the Final Solution*, New York: Alfred Knopf, 1991.

Brossat, Alain, *L'épreuve du désastre: Le 20e siècle et les camps*, Paris: Albin Michel, 1996.

Browning, Christopher R., *Des hommes ordinaires: Le 101ème bataillon de réserve de la police allemande et la solution finale en Pologne*, Paris: Belles Lettres, 1994.

Browning, Christopher R., *The Path to Genocide: Essays on Launching the Final Solution*, Cambridge and New York: Cambridge University Press, 1992.

Chalk, Frank and K. Jonassohn, *The History and Sociology of Genocide*, London and New Haven, Conn.: Yale University Press, 1990.

Charny, Israel W., ed., *Toward the Understanding and Prevention of Genocide: Proceedings of the International Conference on the Holocaust and Genocide*, Boulder, Colo. and London: Westview Press, 1984.

Charny, Israel W. (in collaboration with Chanan Rapaport), *How Can We Commit The Unthinkable? Genocide, the Human Cancer*, Boulder, Colo.: Westview Press, 1982.

Chobardjian, Levon and Georges Chirinian, *Studies in Comparative Genocide*, New York: St Martin's Press, 1999.

Clastres, Pierre, *De l'ethnocide: Recherches d'anthropologie politique*, Paris: Seuil, 1980.

Conquest, Robert, *La grande terreur: Les purges staliniennes des années 30*, 2 ed., Paris: Robert Laffont, 1995.

Corbin, Alain, *Le village des cannibales*, Paris: Aubier, 1990.

Crouzet, Denis, *La nuit de la Saint-Barthélemy: Un rêve perdu de la renaissance*, Paris: Fayard, 1994.

Delanoé, Nelcya, *L'entaille rouge: Des terres indiennes à la démocratie américaine*, Paris: Albin Michel, 1996.

Fein, Helen, *Genocide: A Sociological Perspective*, London: Sage Publications, 1990.

Fein, Helen, ed., *Genocide Watch*, New Haven, Conn.: Yale University Press, 1992.

Friedrich, David O., ed., *State Crime*, Ashgate: Dartmouth Company, 1998.

Furet, François and Ernest Nolte, *Fascisme et communisme*, Paris: Commentaires/ Plon, 1998.

Giddens, Anthony, *The Nation State and Violence*, Cambridge: Polity, 1985.

Goldstone, Richard J., *For Humanity: Reflections of a War Crimes Investigator*, New Haven, Conn.: Yale University Press, 2000.

Hannyoer, Jean, *Guerres civiles: Economies de la violence, dimensions de la civilité*, Paris: Karthala, 1999.

Heidenreich, John G., *How to Prevent Genocide: A Guide for Policymakers, Scholars, and the Concerned Citizen*, Westport, Conn.: Praeger, 2001.

Hinton, Alexander Laban, ed., *Annihilating Difference: The Anthropology of Genocide*, Berkeley: University of California Press, 2002.

Holsti, Kalevi, *The State, War and the State of War*, Cambridge: Cambridge University Press, 1996.

Horowitz, Donald, *Deadly Ethnic Riots*, Berkeley: University of California Press, 2000.

Horowitz, Irving Louis, *Taking Lives: Genocide and State Power*, New Brunswick, N.J.: Transaction, 1997.

Human Rights Watch, *Sierra Leone – Sowing Terror: Atrocities against Civilians in Sierra Leone*, New York/Washington/London/Brussels, July 1998.

Jaulin, Robert, *La paix blanche: Introduction à l'ethnocide*, Paris: Seuil, 1970.

Keegan, John, *Anatomie de la bataille: Azincourt 1415, Waterloo 1815, La Somme 1916*, Paris: Laffont, 1993.

Kressel, Neil J., *Mass Hate: The Global Rise of Genocide and Terror*, New York: Plenum Press, 1996.

Kuper, Leo, *Genocide: Its Political Use in the 20th Century*, London and New Haven, Conn.: Yale University Press, 1981.

Kuper, Leo, *The Prevention of Genocide*, New Haven, Conn.: Yale University Press, 1985.

Las Casas, Bartholomé, ed., *La destruction des Indes*, Paris: Michel Chandeigne, 1995.

Levvene Marc and P. Robert, eds, *The Massacre in History*, Oxford and New York: Berghan Books, 1999.

Marienstras, Elise, *Wounded-Knee: L'Amérique fin de siècle*, Brussels: Complexes, 1996.

Martin, Jean-Clément, *La France et la Vendée*, Paris: Seuil, 1987.

Midlarsky, Manus, *Genocides and Mass-Murders in the 20th Century*, Cambridge: Cambridge University Press, forthcoming.

Montesquieu, Charles de Secondat, *De l'esprit des lois*, Livre V, Paris: Garnier, 1973.

Naimark, Norman, *Fires of Hatred: Ethnic Cleansing in Twentieth-Century Europe*, Cambridge, Mass.: Harvard University Press, 2001.

Nordstrom, Carolyn, *A Different Kind of War Story*, Philadelphia: University of Pennsylvania Press, 1997.

Plumelle-Uribe, Rosa Amelia, *La férocité blanche: Des non Blancs aux non Aryens: Génocides occultés de 1492 à nos jours*, Paris: Albin Michel, 2001.

Poliakov, Léon, *La causalité diabolique*, Paris: Calmann-Lévy, 1980.

Prinsloo, Rachel, ed., *Identity? Theory, Politics, History*, Pretoria: Human Sciences Research Council, 1999.

Radford, Jill and Russel Diana, eds, *Femicide: The Politics of Woman Killing*, Buckingham: Open University Press, 1992.

Richard, Guy, *L'Histoire inhumaine: Massacres et génocides des origines à nos jours*, Paris: Armand Colin, 1992.

Rummel, Rudolf J., *Death by Government*, New Brunswick, N.J. and London: Transaction Publishers, 1994.

Rummel, Rudolf J., *Lethal Politics: Soviet Genocide and Mass Murder since 1917*, New Brunswick, N.J.: Transaction Publishers, 1990.

Simpson, Christopher, *The Splendid Blond Beast: Money, Law and Genocide in the Twentieth Century*, New York: Grove Press, 1993.

Smith, Robert W., ed., *Genocide: Essays Toward Understanding, Early Warning and Prevention*, Association of Genocide Scholars, 1999.

Sofsky, Wolfgang, *Die Ordnung des Terrors: Das Konzentrationslager*, Frankfurt: S. Fischer Verlag, 1993.

Sofsky, Wolfgang, *Traktat über die Gewalt*, Frankfurt: S. Fischer Verlag, 1996.

Staub, Ervin, *The Roots of Evil: The Origins of Genocide and Other Group Violence*, Cambridge: Cambridge University Press, 1998.

Summers, Craig and Eric Markusen, eds, *Collective Violence: Harmful Behavior in Groups and Governments*, Lanham, Md.: Rowman and Littlefield, 1999.

Ternon, Yves, *Du négationnisme: Mémoire et tabou*, Paris: Desclée de Brouwer, 1999.

Ternon, Yves, *L'Etat criminel: Les génocides au XXème siècle*, Paris: Seuil, 1995.

Ternon, Yves, *L'innocence des victimes au siècle des génocides*, Paris: Desclée de Brouwer, 2001.

Todoro, Tzvetan, *Face à l'extrême*, Paris: Seuil, 1990.

Totten, Samuel, William S. Parsons and Israel W. Charny, *Century of Genocide: Eyewitness Accounts and Critical Views*, New York: Garland, 1997.

Uekert, Brenda K., *Rivers of Blood: A Comparative Study of Government Massacres*, Westport, Conn.: Praeger, 1995.

Walzer, Michael, *Guerres justes et injustes*, Paris: Belin, 1999.

Werner, Eric, *De l'extermination*, Lausanne: Thael, 1993.

Articles and chapters in books

Appadurai, Arjun, "Dead Certainty: Ethnic Violence in the Era of Globalization", *Public Culture* 10, no. 2, 1998, pp. 225–247.

Beres, Louis René, "Genocide, State and Self", *Denver Journal of International Law and Policy* 18, no. 2, 1989, pp. 37–57.

Bhabha, Homi K., "DissemiNation", in: Homi K. Bhabha, ed., *Nation and Narration*, London: Routledge, 1990, pp. 291–323.

Bloch, Maurice, "Internal and External Memory: Different Ways of Being in History", in Paul Antze and Michael Lambek, eds, *Tense Past: Cultural Essays in Trauma and Memory*, London: Routledge & Kegan, 1996, pp. 215–234.

Boucherau, Philippe, "Discours sur la violence (sauvage, guerrière, génocidaire)", *L'Intranquille* 2/3, 1994, pp. 7–78.

Braud, Philippe, "Violences physiques, violences symboliques: Éléments de problématisation", in Jean Hanoyer, ed., *Guerres civiles, dimensions de la violence, économies de la civilité*, Paris: Karthala, 1999.

Charny, Israel W., "Toward a Generic Definition of Genocide", in George J. Andreopoulos, ed., *Genocide: Conceptual and Historical Dimensions*, Philadelphia: University of Pennsylvania Press, 1994, pp. 64–94.

Dedering, Tilman, "A Certain Rigorous Treatment of All Parts of the Nation: The Annihilation of the Herero in German South-west Africa in 1904", in Mark Leven and Penny Roberts, eds, *The Massacre in History*, New York: Bargain Books, 1999, pp. 205–222.

De Figueiredo Jr., R. J. P. and B. R. Weigast, "The Rationality of Fear: Political Opportunism and Ethnic Conflict", in B. F. Walter and J. Snyder, eds, *Civil Wars, Insecurity and Intervention*, New York: Columbia University Press, 1999, pp. 261–301.

Druckman, Daniel, "Social Psychological Aspects of Nationalism", in John L. Comaroff and Paul C. Stern, eds, *Perspectives on Nationalism and War*, Luxembourg: Gordon and Breach, 1995, pp. 56–59.

Fein, Helen, "Ethnic Cleansing and Genocide: Definitional Evasion, Fog, Morass or Opportunity?", conference presentation, Association of Genocide Scholars Conference, Minneapolis, June 10–12, 2001.

Fein, Helen, "Genocide: A Sociological Perspective", *Current Sociology* 38, no. 1, 1990, pp. 1–126.

Freeman, Michael, "The Theory and Prevention of Genocide", *Holocaust and Genocide Studies* 6, no. 2, 1991, pp. 185–199.

Green, Linda, "Fear as a Way of Life", in Alexander L. Hinton, ed., *Genocide: An Anthropological Reader*, Malden, Mass.: Blackwell, 2002, pp. 307–334.

Gurr, Ted, "People against States: Ethnopolitical Conflict and the Changing World System", *International Studies Quarterly* 38, no. 3, 1994, pp. 344–378.

Harff, Barbara and Ted Robert Gurr, "Genocide and Politicide in Global Perspective: The Historical Record and Future Risks", in Stan Windass, ed., *Just War and Genocide: A Symposium*, London: Macmillan and Foundation for International Security, 2001.

Harff, Barbara and Ted Robert Gurr, "Toward Empirical Theory of Genocides and Politicides: Identification and Measurement of Cases since 1945", *International Studies Quarterly*, no. 32, 1988, pp. 369–381.

Huttenbach, Henry R., "From the Editor", *Journal of Genocide Research* 3, no. 1, 2001, pp. 7–9.

Huttenbach, Henry R., "Locating the Holocaust under the Genocide Spectrum: Towards a Methodology of Definition and Categorization", *Holocaust and Genocide Studies* 3, no. 3, 1988, pp. 289–303.

Kalyvas, Stathis, "Aspects méthodologiques de la recherche sur les massacres: Le cas de la guerre civile grecque", *Revue Internationale de Politique Comparée* 8, no. 1, 2001, pp. 23–42.

Kalyvas, Stathis, "'New' and 'Old' Civil Wars: A Valid Distinction?", *World Politics* 54, no. 1, 2001, pp. 99–118.

Kalyvas, Stathis, "The Ontology of 'Political Violence': Action and Identity in Civil Wars", *Perspectives on Politics* 1, no. 3, pp. 475–494.

Kalyvas, Stathis, "Warfare in Civil Wars", in Isabelle Duyvesteyn and Jan Angstrom, eds, *Rethinking the Nature of War*, Abingdon: Frank Cass, 2005, pp. 88–108.

Kiernan, Ben, "Sur la notion de génocide", *Débat*, no. 104, 1999, pp. 179–192.

Leven, Mark, "Why is the 20th Century the Century of Genocide?", *Journal of World History* 11, no. 2, 2000, pp. 305–336.

Makino, Uwe, "Final Solution, Crimes against Mankind: On the Genesis and Criticisms of the Concept of Genocide", *Journal of Genocide* 3, no. 1 pp. 49–73.

Mann, Michael, "The Dark Side of Democracy: The Modern Tradition of Ethnic and Political Cleansing", *New Left Review*, no. 235, 1999, pp. 18–46.

Mann, Michael, "Democracy and Ethnic War", *Hagar* 1, no. 2, 2000, pp. 115–133.

Marchal, Roland, "Atomisation des fins et radicalisme des moyens: De quelques conflits africains", *Critique Internationale*, no. 6, Winter 2000, pp. 159–175.

Melson, Robert, "Problèmes soulevés par la comparaison entre le génocide arménien et l'holocauste", in Comité de Défense de la Cause Arménienne, *L'Actualité du génocide arménien*, Créteil: EDIPOL, 1999, pp. 373–385.

Nordstorm, Carolyn, and JoAnn Martin, "The Culture of Conflict: Field Reality and Theory", in Carolyn Nordstorm and JoAnn Martin, eds, *The Paths to Domination, Resistance, and Terror*, Berkeley: University of California Press, 1992, pp. 3–17.

Rummel, Rudolph J., "Democracy, Power, Genocide, and Mass Murder", *Journal of Conflict Resolution* 39, no. 1, 1995, pp. 3–26.

Semelin, Jacques, "Du massacre au processus génocidaire", *Revue Internationale des Sciences Sociales*, no. 174, December 2002, pp. 483–492.

Semelin, Jacques, ed., dossier [special issue] "Rationalités de la violence extrême", *Critique Internationale*, no. 6, Winter 2000.

Semelin, Jacques, "Toward a vocabulary of massacre and genocide", *Journal of Genocide Research* 5, no. 2, 2003, pp. 193–210.

Solchany, Jean, "De la régression analytique à la célébration médiatique: Le phénomène Goldhagen", *Revue d'histoire moderne et contemporaine* 44, no. 3, July–September 1997, pp. 514–523.

Stoett, Peter John, "This Age of Genocide: Conceptual and Institutional Implications", *International Journal (Toronto)* 50, no. 3, 1995, pp. 594–618.

Tilly, Charles, "La guerre et la construction de l'État en tant que crime organisé", *Politix* 13, no. 49, 2000, pp. 97–122.

Trinh, Sylvaine, "Aum Shinrikyö: Secte et violence", in Michel Wieviorka, ed., *Un nouveau paradigme de la violence? Cultures et conflits*, L'Harmattan, no. 29–30, 1998, pp. 229–290.

Valention, Benjamin, "Final Solutions: The Causes of Mass Killings and Genocide", *Security Studies* 9, no. 3, 2000, pp. 1–59.

Veinstein, Gilles, "Trois questions sur un massacre", *L'Histoire*, no. 187, April 1995, pp. 40–41.

Wilkinson, S. I., "Froids calculs et foules déchaînées: Les émeutes intercommunautaires en Inde", *Critique Internationale*, no. 6, Winter 2000, pp. 125–142.

Zins, Max-Jean, "Les massacres entre hindous et musulmans dans le contexte de la partition de l'Inde", Conference on the political use of massacre, CERI Paris, October 2000.

Journals and special editions of journals

Critique internationale, "Les rationalités de la violence extrême", no. 6, January 2000.

Dimensions: A Journal of Holocaust Studies, New York: Anti-Defamation League of B'nai B'rith, since 1987.

Holocaust and Genocide Studies, Oxford: Oxford University Press, since 1986.

Journal of genocide research, Abingdon: Carfax, since 1999.

Revue Internationale de Politique Comparée, "L'utilisation politique des massacres", vol. 8, no. 1, De Boeck-Université, Spring 2001.

Revue Internationale des Sciences Sociales, "Violences extrêmes", no. 174, December 2002.

Ethics and philosophy

Books

Arendt, Hannah, *Eichmann à Jérusalem: Rapport sur la banalité du mal*, Paris: Gallimard, 1996.

Arendt, Hannah, *La condition de l'homme moderne*, Paris: Calmann-Lévy, 1994.

Arendt, Hannah, *Le système totalitaire*, Paris: Seuil, 1972.

Bensoussan, Georges, *Idéologie du rejet*, Paris: Manya, 1993.

Bloch, Marc, *Réflexions d'un historien sur les fausses nouvelles de la guerre* (Extracts from *Ecrits de guerre 1914–1918*), Paris: Allia, 1999.

Chomsky, Noam, *Bains de sang*, Paris: Seghers-Laffont, 1975.

Coquio, Catherine, ed., *Parler des camps, penser les génocides*, Paris: Albin Michel, 1999.

Das, Veena et al., eds, *Violence and Subjectivity*, Berkeley: University of California Press, 2000.

Delacampagne, Christian, *De l'indifférence: Essai sur la banalisation du mal*, Paris: Odile Jacob, 1998.

Faye, Jean-Pierre, *Langages totalitaires*, Paris: Hermann, 1972.

Horkheimer, Max and Theodor Adorno, *La dialectique de la raison*, Paris: Gallimard, 1990.

Levi, Primo, *Les naufragés et les rescapés*, Paris: Gallimard, 1989.

Articles and chapters in books

Aron, Raymond, "Comment l'historien écrit l'épistémologie: À propos du livre de Paul Veyne", *Annales, Economie, Société, Civilisation*, no. 6, November/December 1971, pp. 1319–1354.

Chazel, François, "Sur quelles bases établir des relations stables entre historiens et sociologues?", in Yves Beauvois and Cécile Blondel, eds, *Qu'est-ce qu'on ne sait pas en histoire?*, Villeneuve-d'Ascq: Presses universitaires du Septentrion, 1998, p. 117–129.

Coquio, Catherine, "L'extrême, le génocide et l'expérience concentrationnaire: Productivité et aporie de trois concepts", *Critiques*, no. 60, May 1997.

Hassner, Pierre, "Par-delà la guerre et la paix: Violence et intervention après la guerre froide", *Etudes* 385, no. 3, September 1996, pp. 149–158.

Laleye, Issiaka-Prosper, "Génocide et ethnocide: Comment meurent les cultures; Interrogations philosophico-anthropologiques sur le concept de génocide culturel", in Katia Boustany and Daniel Dormoy, eds, *Génocide: Réseau Vitoria*, Brussels: Bruylant/Éditions de l'Université de Bruxelles, 1999, pp. 265–293.

Laure, J. H., "Ethical Considerations in Choosing Intervention Roles", *Peace and Change* 8, no. 2/3, 1982, pp. 29–42.

Pouligny, Béatrice, "An Ethic of responsibility in practice"/"Une éthique de responsabilité en pratique", *International Social Science Journal*, special issue on Extreme Violence, vol. 54, no. 174, December 2002, pp. 529–538.

Representations and imaginaries (sociology and anthropology)

Books

Althabe, G., *Oppression et libération dans l'imaginaire*, Paris: Découverte, 1982.

Amèrie, Jean, *Par-delà le crime et le châtiment: Essai pour surmonter l'insurmontable*, Paris: Actes Sud, 1995.

Antze, Paul and Michael Lambek, *Tense Past: Cultural Essays in Trauma and Memory*, London: Routledge, 1996.

Balandier, Georges, *Sens et puissance: Les dynamiques sociales*, Paris: PUF, 1971.

Bayart, Jean-François, *L'illusion identitaire*, Paris: Fayard, 1996.

Broosk, Peter, *Troubling Confessions: Speaking Guilt in Law and Literature*, Chicago: University of Chicago Press, 2000.

Chesterman, Simon, ed., *Civilians in War*, Project of the International Peace Academy, Boulder, Colo., and London: Lynne Rienner Publishers, 2001.

Comaroff, Jean and John, eds, *Modernity and Its Malcontents: Ritual and Power in Postcolonial Africa*, Chicago: Chicago University Press, 1993.

Douglas, Mary, *De la souillure: Essai sur les notions de pollution et de tabou*, Paris: Découverte, 2001.

Geschiere, Peter, *Sorcellerie et politique en Afrique: La viande des autres*, Paris: Karthala, 1995.

Girard, René, *Le bouc émissaire*, Paris: Grasset, 1982.

Girard, René, *La violence et le sacré*, Paris: Grasset, 1972.

Govier, Trudy, *Social Trust and Human Communities*, Montreal: McGill-Queens University Press, 1997.

Gross, Jan T., *Neighbors*, Princeton, N.J.: Princeton University Press, 2001.

Hinton, Alexander L., ed., *Annihilating Difference: The Anthropology of Genocide*, Berkeley and Los Angeles: University of California Press, 2002.

Hinton, Alexander L., ed., *Genocide: An Anthropological Reader*, Malden, Mass.: Blackwell, 2002.

Hobsbawm, Eric and Terence Ranger, eds, *The Invention of Tradition*, Cambridge: Cambridge University Press, 1983.

Malkki, Liisa, *Purity and Exile: Violence, Memory, and National Cosmology among Hutu Refugees in Tanzania*, Chicago: University of Chicago Press, 1995.

Martin, Denis-Constant, *Cartes d'identité: Comment dit-on "nous" en politique?*, Paris: Presses de la FNSP, 1994.

Merleau-Ponty, Maurice, *Le visible et l'invisible*, Paris: Gallimard, 1964.

Vidal, Claudine, *Sociologie des passions*, Paris: Karthala, 1993.

Articles and chapters in books

Appadurai, Arjun, "The Past as Scarce Resource", *Man* 16, no. 2, 1981, pp. 201–219.

Comaroff, Jean, "Healing and Cultural Transformation: The Tswana of Southern Africa", *Social Science and Medicine* 15, no. 3, 1981, pp. 367–368.

Fein, H., "Genocide: A Sociological Perspective", *Current Sociology* 38, no. 1, 1990, pp. 1–126.

Geertz, Clifford, "The politics of meanings", *The interpretation of cultures*, New York: Basic Books, 1973.

Malki, Liisa H., "Speechless Emissaries: Refugees, Humanitarianism, and Dehistoricization", in Alexander L. Hinton, ed., *Genocide: An Anthropological Reader*, Malden, Mass.: Blackwell, 2002, pp. 344–367.

Martin, Denis-Constant, "Identity, culture, pride and conflict", in S. Bekker, and R. Prinsloo, eds, *Identity? Theory, Politics, History*, Pretoria: Human Sciences Research Council, 1999, p. 197.

Martin, Denis-Constant, "La découverture des cultures politiques: Esquisse d'une approche comparatiste à partir des expériences africaines", *Les Cahiers du CERI No. 2*, 1992.

Martin, Denis-Constant and Benetta Jules-Rosette, "Cultures populaires, identités et politique", *Les Cahiers du CERI No. 17*, 1997.

Mor, Naomi, "Holocaust Messages from the Past", *Contemporary Family Therapy* 12, no. 5, 1990, p. 371–379.

Schwebel, Milton "Looking Forward, Looking Backward: Prevention of Violent Conflict", *Peace and Conflict* 5, no. 4, 1999, pp. 297–371.

Strauss, Scott, "Contested Meanings and Conflicting Imperatives: A Conceptual Analysis of Genocide", *Journal of Genocide Research* 3, no. 3, pp. 349–375.

Taussig, Michael, "History as Sorcery", *Representations*, no. 7, Summer 1984, pp. 87–109.

Totten, Samuel, William S. Parsons and Robert K. Hitchcock, "Confronting Genocide and Ethnocide of Indigenous People: An Interdisciplinary Approach to Definition, Intervention, Prevention, and Advocacy", in Alexander L. Hinton, ed., *Annihilating Difference: The Anthropology of Genocide*, Berkeley and Los Angeles: University of California Press, 2002, pp. 54–94.

Memories, reconciliation and transitional justice

Books

Abu-Nimer, Mohammed, ed., *Reconciliation, Justice and Coexistence: Theory and Practice*, New York: Lexington, 2001.

Amos, D. B. and L. Weissber, eds, *Cultural Memory and the Construction of Identity*, Detroit: Wayne State University Press, 1999.

Bacot, Jean-Pierre and Christian Coq, *Travail de mémoire, 1914–1998: Une nécessité dans un siècle de violence*, Paris: Autrement, 1999.

Ball, Howard, *Prosecuting War Crimes and Genocide: The Twentieth-Century Experience*, Lawrence: University Press of Kansas, 1999.

Barkan, Elazar, *The Guilt of Nations: Restitution and Negotiating Historical Injustices*, Baltimore, Md.: Johns Hopkins University Press, 2001.

Bar-On, Dan, ed., *Bridging the Gap: Storytelling as a Way to Work Through Political and Collective Hostilities*, Hamburg: Korber-Stiftung, 2000.

Barsalou, Judy, *Trauma and Transitional Justice in Divided Societies*, Special Report 135, Washington, D.C.: United States Institute for Peace, 2005.

Bar-Simon-Tov, Yaacov, ed., *From Conflict Resolution to Reconciliation*, Oxford: Oxford University Press, 2003.

Bass, Gary Jonathan, *Stay the Hand of Vengeance: The Politics of War Crimes Tribunals*, Princeton, N.J.: Princeton University Press, 2000.

Baxter, Victoria, *Empirical Research Methodologies of Transitional Justice Mechanism*, Stellenbosch: Association for the Advancement of Science and CSVR, 2002.

Best, Geoffrey, *Nuremburg and After: The Continuing History of War Crimes Against Humanity*, Reading: University of Reading, 1984.

Biggar, Nigel, ed., *Burying the Past: Making Peace and Doing Justice after Civil Conflict*, Washington, D.C.: Georgetown University Press, 2001.

Bloomfeld, David, Teresa Barnes and Luc Huyse, *Reconciliation after Violent Conflict: A Handbook*, Stockholm: International Institute for Democracy and Electoral Assistance, 2003.

Boustany, Katia and Daniel Dormy, eds, *Génocide: Réseau Vitoria*, Brussels: Bruylant/Éditions de l'Université de Bruxelles, 1999.

Bronkhort, Daan, *Truth and Reconciliation: Obstacles and Opportunities for Human Rights*, Amsterdam: Amnesty International – Dutch Section, 1995.

Centre de Droit International de l'Institut de sociologie de l'université libre de Bruxelles, *Le Procès de Nuremberg: Conséquences et actualisation*, Brussels: Bruylant, 1988.

Chayes, Antonia and Martha Minow, eds, *Imagine Coexistence: Restoring Humanity after Violent Ethnic Conflict*, San Francisco: Jossey-Bass, 2003.

Connerton, Paul, *How Societies Remember*, Cambridge: Cambridge University Press, 1989.

Cragg, Wesley, *The Practice of Punishment: Towards a Theory of Restorative Justice*, London: Routledge, 1992.

De Greiff, P. and C. Croning, eds, *Global justice and transnational politics: Essays on the moral and political challenges of globalization*, Cambridge, Mass.: MIT Press, 2002.

De Gruchy, John W., *Reconciliation: Restoring Justice*, Minneapolis: Fortress Press, 2002.

Falk, Richard A. et al., eds, *Crimes of War: A Legal, Political-Documentary, and Psychological Inquiry into the Responsibility of Leaders, Citizens, and Soldiers for Criminal Acts in Wars*, New York: Random House, 1971.

Fatic, Aleksander, *Reconciliation via the War Crimes Tribunal?* Aldershot: Ashgate, 2000.

Fentress, James and Chris Wickham, *Social Memory*, Oxford: Blackwell, 1992.

Forges, Jean-François, *1914–1998: Le travail de mémoire*, Paris: ESF, 1998.

Glendon, M. A., *Rights Talk: The Impoverishment of Political Discourse*, New York: Free Press, 1991.

Godwin Phelps, Teresa, *Shattered Voices: Language, Violence and the Work of Truth Commissions*, Philadelphia: University of Pennsylvania Press, 2004.

Goldstone, Richard J., *For Humanity: Reflections of a War Crimes Investigator*, New Haven, Conn.: Yale University Press, 2000.

Green, Robin, *A Step Too Far: Explorations into Reconcilliation*, London: Darton, Longman & Todd, 1990.

Grosser, Alfred, *Le crime et la mémoire*, Paris: Flammarion, 1989.

Hacking, Ian, *L'âme réécrite: Étude sur la personnalité multiple et les sciences de la mémoire*, Le Plessis-Robinson: Les empêcheurs de penser en ronde, 1998.

Halbwachs, Maurice, *La mémoire collective*, Paris: Albin Michel, 1997.

Hayner, Priscilla B., *Unspeakable Truths: Facing the Challenge of Truth Commissions*, New York: Routledge, 2000.

Helmick, Raymond G. and Rodney L. Petersen, eds, *Forgiveness and Reconciliation: Religion, Public Policy and Conflict Transformation*, Radnor, Penn.: Templeton Foundation Press, 2001.

Henderson, Michael, *The Forgiveness Factor*, London: Grosvenor Books, 1996.

Henkin, Alice H., ed., *Honoring Human Rights Under International Mandates: Lessons from Bosnia, Kosovo and East Timor; Recommendations to the United Nations*, Washington, D.C.: Aspen Institute, 2003.

Honeyman, C., *Gacaca Jurisdictions: Transitional Justice in Rwanda*, Boston: Harvard University Press, 2002.

Human Rights Center (University of California) and Centre for Human Rights (University of Sarajevo), *Justice, Accountability and Social Reconstruction: An Interview Study of Bosnian Judges and Prosecutors*, May 2002, available at http://www.law.berkeley.edu/clinics/ihrlc/pdf/JUDICIAL_REPORT_ENGLISH.pdf, reviewed 13 June 2006.

Human Rights Center (University of California) and International Center for Transitional Justice, *Iraqi Voices: Attitudes Toward Transitional Justice and Social Reconstruction*, May 2004, available at http://www.hrcberkeley.org/download/Iraqi_voices.pdf, reviewed 13 June 2006.

Humphrey, M., *The Politics of Atrocity and Reconciliation: From Terror to Trauma*, London: Routledge, 2002.

Ignatieff, Michael, *Warriors' Honour: Ethnic War and the Modern Conscience*, New York: Metropolitan Books, 1998.

Jacoby, Susan, *Wild Justice: The Evolution of Revenge*, New York: Harper and Row, 1988.

Jonassohn, Kurt and Karin Solveig Björnson, *Genocide and Gross Human Rights Violations in Comparative Perspective*, New Brunswick, N.J.: Transaction, 1998.

Kritz, Neil J., ed., *Transitional Justice*, Washington, D.C.: United States Institute of Peace Press, 1995.

Larrabee, F. Stephen, *The Politics of Reconciliation*, New York: Columbia University Press, 1978.

Lederach, John Paul, *The Journey Toward Reconciliation*, Scottdale, Penn. and Waterloo, Ont.: Herald Press, 1999.

Lederach, John Paul, *The Moral Imagination: The Art and Soul of Building Peace*, Oxford and New York: Oxford University Press, 2005.

Lefranc, Sandrine, *Politiques du pardon: Amnistie et transitions démocratiques: Une approche comparative*, Paris: Presses universitaires de France, 2002.

Mani, Rama, *Beyond Retribution: Seeking Justice in the Shadows of War*, Malden, Mass.: Blackwell, 2002.

Maynard, Kimberley A., *Healing Communities in Conflict*, New York: Columbia University Press, 1999.

McAdams, James, ed., *Transitional Justice and the Rule of Law in New Democracies*, Notre Dame, Ind.: University of Notre Dame Press, 1997.

Minow, Martha, *Between Vengeance and Forgiveness: Facing History After Genocide and Mass Violence*, Boston: Beacon Press, 1998.

Minow, M. and N. Rosenblum, *Breaking the Cycles of Hatred: Memory, Law, and Repair*, Princeton, N.J.: Princeton University Press, 2003.

Mokhiber, C., *Local Perspectives: Foreign Aid to the Justice Sector*, Geneva: International Council on Human Rights Policy, 2000.

Newman, Edward and Albrecht Schnabel, eds, *Recovering from Civil Conflict: Reconciliation, Peace, and Development*, Portland, Ore., and London: Frank Cass Publishers, 2002.

Off, Carol, *The Lion, the Fox, and the Eagle: A Story of Generals and Justice in Rwanda and Yugoslavia*, Toronto: Random House Canada, 2000.

Osiel, Mark, *Mass Atrocity, Collective Memory and the Law*, New Brunswick, N.J.: Transaction, 1997.

Pennebacker, J. W., D. Paez and B. Rime, eds, *Collective Memory of Political Events: Social Psychological Perspectives*, Mahwah, N.J.: Lawrence Erlbaum Associates, 1997.

Porter, Jack N., ed., *Genocide and Human Rights: A Global Anthology*, Washington, D.C.: University Press of America, 1982.

Prager, Carole A. L. and Trudy Govier, eds, *Dilemmas of Reconciliation: Cases and Concepts*, Waterloo, Ont.: Wilfrid Laurier University Press, 2003.

Ratner, Steven R., and Jason S. Abrams, *Accountability for Human Rights Atrocities in International Law: Beyond the Nuremberg Legacy*, Oxford: Clarendon Press, 1997.

Redekop, Vern Neufeld, *From Violence to Blessing: How an Understanding of Deep-rooted Conflict Can Open Paths of Reconciliation*, Ottawa: Novalis, 2002.

Ricoeur, Paul, *La mémoire, l'histoire, l'oubli*, Paris: Seuil, 2000.

Ricoeur, Paul, *Soi-même comme un autre*, Paris: Seuil, 1990.

Ricoeur, Paul, *Temps et récit, Tome III: Le temps raconté*, Paris: Seuil, 1985.

Rigby, Andrew, *Justice and Reconciliation: After the Violence*, Boulder, Colo.: Lynne Rienner Publishers, 2001.

Ross, B. M., *Remembering the Personal Past*, Oxford: Oxford University Press, 1991.

Rotberg, Robert and Dennis Thompson, eds, *Truth Versus Justice: The Morality of Truth Commissions*, Princeton: Princeton University Press, 2000.

Rothstein, Robert L., *After the Peace: Resistance and Reconciliation*, Boulder, Colo.: Lynne Rienner Publishers, 1999.

Schabas, William A., *Genocide in International Law: The Crimes of Crimes*, Cambridge and New York: Cambridge University Press, 2000.

Schreiter, Robert J., *The Ministry of Reconciliation: Spirituality and Strategies*, Maryknoll, N.Y.: Orbis Books, 1998.

Steiner, Henry, ed., *Truth Commissions: A Comparative Assessment: World Peace Foundation Reports*, Cambridge: Cambridge University Press, 1997.

Stover, Eric, *The Witnesses: War Crimes and the Promise of Justice in The Hague*, Philadelphia: University of Pennsylvania Press, 2005.

Stover, E. and H. M. Weinstein, eds, *My Neighbor, My Enemy: Justice and Community in the Aftermath of Mass Atrocity*, Cambridge and New York: Cambridge University Press, 2004.

Tavuchis, Nicholas, *Mea Culpa: A Sociology of Apology and Reconciliation*, Stanford, Calif.: Stanford University Press, 1991.

Teitel, Ruti G., *Transitional Justice*, Oxford: Oxford University Press, 2000.

Thakur, Ramesh and Peter Macontent, eds, *From Sovereign Impunity to International Accountability: The Search for Justice in a World of States*, Tokyo: United Nations University Press, 2004.

Toprey, John, ed., *Politics and the Past: On Repairing Historical Injustices*. Lanham, Md.: Rowman & Littlefield, 2003.

Tutu, Desmond, *No Future Without Forgiveness*, New York: Doubleday, 1999.

Volf, Miroslav, *Exclusion and Embrace: A Theological Exploration of Identity, Otherness, and Reconciliation*, Nashville, Tenn.: Abingdon Press, 1996.

Weschler, Lawrence, *A Miracle, a Universe: Settling Accounts with Torturers*, New York: Pantheon, 1990.

Articles and chapters in books

Assefa, Hizkias, "The Meaning of Reconciliation", in *People Building Peace*, Utrecht: European Platform for Conflict Prevention and Transformation, available at http://www.gppac.net/documents/pbp/part1/2_reconc.htm, reviewed 13 June 2006.

Assefa, Hizkias, "Reconciliation", in Luc Reychler and Thania Paffenholz, eds, *Peacebuilding: A Field Guide*, Boulder, Colo. and London: Lynne Reiner Publishers, 2001, pp. 336–342.

Balint, Jennifer, "Law's Constitutive Possibilities: Reconstruction and Reconciliation in the Wake of Genocide and State Crime", in Emilios Christodoulidis and Scott Veitch, eds, *Lethe's Law: Justice Law and Ethics in Reconciliation*, Oxford: Hart Publishing, 2001, pp. 129–149.

Bassiouni, M. Cherif and Madeline H. Morris, eds, "Accountability for International Crimes and Serious Violations of Fundamental Human Rights", *Law and Contemporary Problems*, special edition, vol. 59, no. 4, Fall 1996.

Bloch, Maurice, "Internal and External Memory: Different Ways of Being in History", in Paul Antze and Michael Lambek, eds, *Tense Past: Cultural Essays in Trauma and Memory*, London: Routledge and Kegan, 1996, pp. 215–234.

Bodei, Remo, "Farewell to the Past: Historical Memory, Oblivion and Collective Identity", *Philosophy and Social Criticism* 18, no. 3/4, 1993, pp. 251–265.

Borneman, John, "Reconcilation after Ethnic Cleansing: Listening, Retribution, Affiliation", *Public Culture* 14, no. 2, Spring 2002, pp. 281–302.

Brodeur, H.-P., "Justice des droits de l'homme ou justice des vainqueurs?", *Le Monde des Débats*, July–August, 1999.

Cabera, L., "Efectos de la impunidad en el sentido de justicia", *Psicología Política*, no. 23, November 2001, pp. 37–58.

Chapman, Audrey R. and Patrick Ball, "The Truth of Truth Commissions: Comparative Lessons from Haiti, South Africa, and Guatemala", *Human Rights Quarterly* 23, no. 1, 2001, pp. 1–43.

Chesterman, Simon, "Human rights as subjectivity: The age of rights and the politics of culture", *Millenium* 27, no. 1, 1998, pp. 97–118.

Colletta, N. J., M. Kostner and I. Wiederhofer, "Case Studies in War-to-Peace Transition", World Bank Discussion Paper no. 331, Washington, D.C.: World Bank, 1996.

Crang, Mike, "Spacing Time, Telling and Narrating the Past", *Time & Society* 3, no. 1, 1994, pp. 29–45.

Crocker, David, "Punishment, Reconciliation, and Democratic Deliberation", *Buffalo Criminal Law Review* 6, no. 4, 2002, pp. 509–549.

Crocker, David, "Reckoning with Past Wrongs: A Normative Framework", *Ethics and International Affairs* 13, 1999, pp. 43–64.

Darbon, Dominique, "La Truth and Reconciliation Commission: Le miracle sudafricain en question", *Revue francaise de science politique* 48, no. 6, December 1998, pp. 707–724.

Dardian, Vahakn N., "Genocide as a Problem of National and International Law: The World War I Armenian Case and its Contemporary Legal Ramifications", *Yale Journal of International Law* 14, no. 2, 1989, pp. 221–334.

Digeser, Peter, "Forgiveness, the Unforgivable and International Relations", *International Relations*, December 2004, pp. 79–98.

Dwyer, Susan, "Reconciliation for Realists", *Ethics and International Affairs* 13, 1999, pp. 81–98.

Fletcher, L. and H. M. Weinstein, "Violence and Social Repair: Rethinking the Contribution of Justice to Reconciliation", *Human Rights Quarterly* 24, no. 3, 2002, pp. 573–639.

Garapon, Antoine, "De Nuremberg au TPI: Naissance d'une justice universelle?", *Critique Internationale*, no. 5, Fall 1999, pp. 167–180.

Gardner Feldman, Lily, "The Principle and Practice of 'Reconciliation' in German Foreign Policy: Relations with France, Israel, Poland and the Czech Republic", *International Affairs* 75, no. 2, 1999, pp. 333–356.

Govier, Trudy and Wilhelm Verwoerd, "Trust and the Problem of National Reconciliation", *Philosophy of the Social Sciences* 32, no. 2, 2002, pp. 178–205.

Grunebaum-Ralph, Heidi, "Saying the Unspeakable: Language and Identity after Auschwitz as a Narrative Model for Articulating Memory in South Africa", *Current Writing* 8, no. 2, pp. 13–22.

Hacking, Ian, "Memory Sciences, Memory Politics", in Paul Antze and Michael Lambek, *Tense Past: Cultural Essays in Trauma and Memory*, London: Routledge & Kegan, 1996, pp. 67–88.

Hammer, John, "Identity, Process, and Reinterpretation: The Past Made Present and the Present Made Past", *Anthropos* 89, no. 1/3, 1994, pp. 181–190.

Hassner, Pierre, "Mémoire, justice et réconciliation", *Critique Internationale*, no. 5, Fall 1999, pp. 121–180.

Hoepken, Wolfgang, "War, Memory and Education in a Fragmented Society: The Case of Yugoslavia", *East European Politics and Societies* 13, no. 1, 1999, pp. 190–227.

Humphrey, M., "From Victim to Victimhood: Truth Commissions and Trials as Rituals of Political Transition and Individual Healing", *Australian Journal of Anthropology* 14, no. 2, 2003, pp. 171–187.

Irani, George, "Rituals of Reconciliation: Arabic-Islamic Perspectives", *Mind and Human Interaction: Windows between History, Culture, Politics, and Psychoanalysis* 11, no. 4, 2000, pp. 226–245.

Lanzmann, Claude, "Les non lieux de la mémoire", *Nouvelle Revue de Psychanalyse*, no. 33, 1986, p. 11–24.

Lavabre, Marie-Claire, "Usages et mésusages de la notion de mémoire", *Critique Internationale*, no. 7, April 2000, pp. 48–57.

Lemkin, Raphael, "Le génocide", *Revue internationale de droit pénal*, no. 17, 1946, p. 371–386.

Lerche III, Charles O., "Truth Commissions and National Reconciliation: Some Reflections on Theory and Practice", *Peace and Conflict Studies* 7, no. 1, May 2000, pp. 1–20.

Malkki, Liisa, "Dystopia and Subjectivity in the Social Imagination of the Future", presentation given at the CERI colloquium "La guerre entre le local et le global: Sociétés, etats, systèmes", Paris, 29–30 May 2000.

Marchal, Roland, "Justice et Réconciliation: Ambiguïtés et impensés; Introduction au thème Justice Internationale et Réconciliation Nationale – Ambiguïtés et débats", *Politique Africaine*, no. 92, 2003, pp. 5–17.

Marks, Stephen, "Forgetting the Policies and Practices of the Past: Impunity in Cambodia", *Fletcher Forum of World Affairs* 18, no. 2, 1994, pp. 17–43.

Oomen, Barbara, "Donor-Driven Justice and Its Discontents: The Case of Rwanda", *Development & Change* 36, no. 5, 2005, pp. 1–24.

Opotow, Susan, "Reconciliation in Times of Impunity: Challenges for Social Justice", *Social Justice Research* 14, no. 2, June 2001, pp. 149–170.

Pankhurst, Donna, "Issues of Justice and Reconciliation in Complex Political Emergencies: Conceptualising Reconciliation, Justice and Peace", *Third World Quarterly* 20, no. 1, 1999, pp. 239–256.

Pham, P. N. et al., "Trauma and PTSD Symptoms in Rwanda: Implications for Attitudes Toward Justice and Reconciliation", *Journal of the American Medical Association* 292, no. 5, 2004, pp. 602–612.

Pouligny, Béatrice, "Building Peace in Situations of Post-Mass Crime", *International Peacekeeping* 9, no. 2, Summer 2002, pp. 201–220.

Sewel, James P., "Justice and Truth in Transition", *Global Governance* 8, no. 1, 2002, pp. 199–234.

Staub, Ervin, "Preventing violence and generating humane values: Healing and reconciliation in Rwanda", *International Review of the Red Cross*, no. 852, 2003, pp. 791–806.

Steinberg, Maxime, "Le génocide: Histoire d'un imbroglio juridique", in Katia Boutsany and Daniel Dormoy, eds, *Génocide: Réseau Vitoria*, Brussels: Bruylant/University of Brussels Press, 1999, pp. 161–177.

Uvin, Peter, "The Gacaca Tribunals in Rwanda", in D. Bloomfield, T. Barnes and L. Hyuse, eds, *Reconciliation after Violent Conflict: A Handbook*, Stockholm: International Institute for Democracy and Electoral Assistance, 2003, pp. 116–129.

Uvin, Peter and C. Mironko, "Western and Local Approaches to Justice in Rwanda", *Global Governance* 9, no. 2, 2003, pp. 219–231.

Verhoeven, Joe, "Le crime de génocide: Originalité et ambiguïté", *Revue belge de droit international* 24, no. 1, 1991, pp. 5–26.

Zalaquett, Jose, "Moral Reconstruction in the Wake of Human Rights Violations", in J. Moore, ed., *Hard Choices: Moral Dilemmas in Humanitarian Intervention*, Boston: Rowman and Littlefield, 1998, 211–228.

Trauma and mental health

Books

Adorno, Theodor W. et al., *The Authoritarian Personality*, New York: Harper, 1950.

Altounian, Janine, *La survivance: Traduire le trauma collectif*, Paris: Dunod, 2000.

Basoglu, Metin, ed., *Torture and Its Consequences: Current Treatment Approaches*, Cambridge: Cambridge University Press, 1995.

Bracken, Patrick J. and Petty Cecila, eds, *Rethinking the Trauma of War*, New York: Free Associations Books, 1998.

Cohen, Stanley, *States of Denial: Knowing about Atrocities and Suffering*, Cambridge: Polity, 2001.

Crocq, L., *Les traumatismes psychiques de guerre*, Paris: Odile Jacob, 1999.

Das, Veena et al., eds, *Remaking a World: Violence, Social Suffering, and Recovery*, Berkeley: University of California Press, 2001.

De Jong, J., ed., *Trauma, War and Violence: Public Mental Health in Socio-Cultural Context*, New York: Kluwer Academic/Plenum Publishers, 2002.

Hilbeg, Raul, *Exécuteurs, Victimes, Témoins: La catastrophe juive 1943–1945*, Paris: Galimard, 1994.

Irani, George, Vamik D. Volkan and Judy Carter, eds, *Perspectives from the Front Lines: A workbook of ethnopolitical conflict?* New York: Prentice-Hall, forthcoming.

Kaës, René, *Violence d'Etat et Psychanalyse*, Paris: Dunod, 1989.

Kleber, Rolph, Charles Figley and Berthold Gersons, *Beyond Trauma: Cultural and Societal Dynamics*, New York: Plenum Press, 1995.

Metraux, Jean-Claude, *Deuils collectives et creation sociale*, Paris: Dispute, 2004.

Nowrojjee, Binaifer, *Shattered Lives: Sexual Violence during the Rwandan Genocide and Its Aftermath*, New York: Human Rights Watch, 1996.

Schacter, Daniel L., *Searching for Memory: The Brain, the Mind, and the Past*, New York, 1996.

Sereny, Guita, *Au fond des ténèbres: Un examen de conscience*, Paris: Denoël, 1974.

Sironi, Françoise, *Bourreaux et victimes: Psychologie de la torture*, Paris: Odile Jacob, 1999.

Summerfield, Derek, *The Impact of War and Atrocity on Civilian Populations: Basic Principles for NGO Interventions and a Critique of Psychosocial Trauma Projects*, London: RRN-ODI, 1996.

Volkan, Vamik D., *Blind Trust: Large Groups and Their Leaders in Times of Crises and Terror*, Charlottesville, Va.: Pitchstone Publishing, 2004.

Von Franz, Marie-Louise, *L'Interprétation des contes de fées*, Paris: Fontaine de Pierre, 1980.

Von Franz, Marie-Louise and Emma Jung, *La Légende du Graal*, Paris: Albin Michel, 1988.

Young, Allan, *The Harmony of Illusions: Inventing Post Traumatic Stress Disorder*, Princeton, N.J.: Princeton University Press, 1995.

Articles and chapters in books

Argenti-Pillen, Alexandra, "The Discourse on Trauma in Non-Western Cultural Contexts: Contributions of an Ethnographic Method", in Arieh Shalev, Rachel Yehuda and Alexander C. MacFarlane, eds, *International Handbook of Human Response to Truama*, Amsterdam: Kluwer Academic, 2000, pp. 87–102.

Baumeister, R., A. Stillwell and T. Heatherton, "Guilt: An Interpersonal Approach", *Psychological Bulletin* 115, no. 2, 1994, pp. 23–36.

Baumeister, Roy F., Arlene Stillwell and Sara R. Wotman, "Victim and Perpetrator Accounts of Interpersonal Conflict: Autobiographical Narratives About Anger", *Journal of Personality and Social Psychology* 59, no. 5, 1990, pp. 994–1005.

Beneduce, Roberto, *WHO Mission to Albania on Mental Health of Refugees from Kosovo*, Report for WHO Copenhagen, 1999, pp. 1–28 (unpublished).

Brinkman, Inge, "Ways of death: Accounts of terror from Angolan refugees in Namibia", *Africa* 70, no. 1, 2000, pp. 1–24.

Eisenbruch, Maurice, "From Post-Traumatic Stress Disorder to Cultural Bereavement: Diagnosis of Southeast Asian Refugees", *Social Science & Medicine* 33, no. 6, 1991, pp. 673–680.

Eisenbruch, Maurice, "Mental Health and the Cambodian Traditional Healer for Refugees Who Are Resettled, Were Repatriated or Internally Displaced, and for Those Who Stayed at Home", *Collegium Antropologicum* 18, no. 2, 1994, pp. 219–230.

Eisenbruch, Maurice, "The Ritual Space of Patients and Traditional Healers in Cambodia", *BEFEO* 79, no. 2, 1992, pp. 283–316.

Eisenbruch, Maurice, "Toward a culturally sensitive DSM: Cultural bereavement in Cambodian refugees and the traditional healer as taxonomist", *Journal of Nervous and Mental Disease* 180, no. 1, 1992, pp. 8–10.

Haney, C., Curtis Banks and Philip Zimbardo, "Interpersonal Dynamics in a Simulated Prison", *International Journal of Criminology and Penology* 11, no. 1, 1983, pp. 69–97.

Honwana, Alcinda, "Healing for Peace: Traditional Healers and Post-War Reconstruction in Southern Mozambique", in R. Porter and J. Hinnels, eds, *Religion, Health and Suffering*, London: Kegan Paul, 1997.

Mudimbe, Valentin Y., "Where Is the Real Thing? Psychoanalysis and African Mythical Narrative", *Cahiers d'Études Africaines* 27, no. 107/108, 1987, pp. 311–327.

Roseman, S. and I. Handelsman, "The Collective Past, Group Psychology and Personal Narrative: Shaping Jewish Identity by Memoirs of the Holocaust", *American Journal of Psychoanalysis* 50, no. 2, 1990, p. 151–170.

Sironi, Françoise, "L'universalité est-elle une torture?", *Nouvelle Revue d'Ethnopsychiatrie*, no. 34, 1997, pp. 43–58.

Stagnaro, J.-C., "Les masques de Thanatos: Effets cliniques et psychosociaux à court et long terme du terrorisme d'Etat en Argentine", *L'information psychiatrique* 76, no. 3, 2000, pp. 259–263.

Summerfield, Derek, "Effects of war: Moral knowledge, revenge, reconciliation, and medicalised concepts of 'recovery'", *British Medical Journal* 325, no. 7372, 2002, pp. 1105–1107.

Summerfield, Derek, "The invention of post-traumatic stress disorder and the social usefulness of a psychiatric category", *British Medical Journal* 322, no. 7228, 2001, pp. 95–98.

Summerfield, Derek, "The Social Experience of War and Some Issues for the Humanitarian Field", in Patrick Bracken and Celia Petty, eds, *Rethinking the Trauma of War*, London: Free Association Books, 1998, pp. 9–37.

Summerfield, Derek, "War and mental health: A brief overview", *British Medical Journal* 321, no. 7255, 2000, pp. 232–235.

Vikman, Elisabeth, "Sexual Violence in Warfare", *Anthropology and Medicine* 12, no. 1, 2005, pp. 21–46.

Wessels, Michael, "Culture, Power, and Community: Intercultural Approaches to Psychosocial Assistance and Healing", in K. Nader, N. Dubrow and B. Stamm, eds, *Honoring Differences: Culture Issues in the Treatment of Trauma and Loss*, Philadelphia: Taylor & Francis, 1999, pp. 267–282.

West, Harry G., "Creative Destruction and Sorcery of Construction: Power, Hope and Suspicion in Post-War Mozambique", *Cahiers d'études africaines* 37, no. 147, 1997, pp. 675–698.

Zwi, Anthony and Antonio Ugalde, "Towards an epidemiology of political violence in the third world", *Social Science & Medicine* 28, no. 7, 1989, pp. 633–642.

The role of the "international community"

Books

Cahill, Kevin, ed., *A Framework for Survival: Health, Human Rights, and Humanitarian Assistance in Conflicts and Disasters*, New York: Basic Books, 1993.

Chaumont, Jean-Michel, *La concurrence des victimes: Génocide, identité, reconnaissance*, Paris: Découverte, 1997.

Chesterman, Simon, *Just War or Just Peace? Humanitarian Intervention and International Law*, Oxford: Oxford University Press, 2001.

Destexhe, Alain, *L'Humanitaire Impossible, ou Deux Siecles d'Ambiguïté*, Paris: Colin, 1993.

Heidenrich, John G., *How to Prevent Genocide: A Guide for Policymakers, Scholars, and the Concerned Citizen*, Westport, Conn.: Praeger, 2001.

Kumar, Krishna, ed., *Rebuilding Societies After War: Critical Roles for International Assistance*, Boulder, Colo.: Lynne Rienner, 1997.

Médecins Sans Frontières, *Life, Death and Aid*, New York: Routledge, 1994.

Mercier, Michele, *Crimes without Punishment: Humanitarian Action in Former Yugoslavia*, London: Pluto Press, 1994.

Minear, Larry and Thomas Weiss, *Mercy under Fire: War and the Global Humanitarian Community*, Boulder, Colo.: Westview Press, 1995.

O'Halloran, Patrick J., *Humanitarian Intervention and the Genocide in Rwanda*, London: Research Institute for the Study of Conflict and Terrorism, 1995.

Articles and chapters in books

Abbott, Beth, "Project Accompaniment: A Canadian Response", in Yeshua Moser-Puangsuwan and Thomas Weber, eds, *Nonviolent Intervention across Borders*, Honolulu: Spark M. Matsunaga Institute of Peace, University of Hawaii, 2000, pp. 163–174.

Boisson de Chazournes, Laurence, "Les ordonnances en indication de mesures conservatoires dans l'affaire relative à l'application de la Convention pour la prévention et la répression du crime de génocide", *Annuaire français de droit international* 39, 1993, pp. 514–539.

Brauman, Rony, Stephen Smith and Claudine Vidal, "Politique de terreur et privilège d'impunité au Rwanda", *Esprit*, no. 266/267, 2000, pp. 147–161.

DeMars, William, "Mercy without Illusion: Humanitarian Action in Conflict", *Mershon International Studies Review*, supplement to *International Studies Quaterly* 40, no. 1, 1996, pp. 81–89.

Farouk, Mawlawi, "New Conflicts, New Challenges: The Evolving Role of Non-Governmental Actors", *Journal of International Affairs* 46, no. 2, 1993, pp. 391–413.

Hassner, Pierre, "Les impuissances de la communauté internationale", in Véronique Nahoum-Grappe, ed., *Vukovar-Sarajevo: La guerre en ex-Yougoslavie*, Paris: Esprit, 1993, pp. 86–118.

Pouligny, Béatrice, "La 'communauté internationale' face aux crimes de masse: Les limites d'une 'communauté d'humanité'", *Revue Internationale de Politique Comparée* 8, no. 1, Spring 2001, pp. 93–108.

Power, Samantha, "Bystanders to Genocide", *Atlantic Monthly* 288, no. 2, September 2001, pp. 84–108.

Index